First International Workshop on Designing Meaning Representations 2019

Florence, Italy
1 August 2019

ISBN: 978-1-5108-9104-3

ACL 2019

The First International Workshop on Designing Meaning Representations

Proceedings of the Workshop

August 1, 2019
Florence, Italy

Preface

There are many pressing questions that need to be answered in the field of designing and parsing meaning representations. First and foremost, does the field have an existential crisis in the face of the powerful combination of distributed representations and deep neural networks that recently led to many advances in the field or Natural Language Processing? In other words, will the distributed representations displace the "traditional" symbolic meaning representations that have been in development for many decades? If the answer is no, what are the areas where the symbolic meaning representation is most needed and has an advantage over distributed representations? There are currently also different schools of thoughts on how meaning should be represented. Can a consensus be forged on the key elements of meaning representation that are most needed given our current understanding of the needs in natural language applications? Regardless of the breadth of their use in natural language processing, how can meaning representations help us to advance theoretical linguistic research?

The workshop intends to bring together researchers who are producers and consumers of meaning representations and through their interaction gain a deeper understanding of the key elements of meaning representations that are the most valuable to the NLP community. The workshop also provides an opportunity for meaning representation researchers to critically examine existing meaning representations with the goal of using their findings to inform the design of next-generation meaning representations. A third goal of the workshop is to explore opportunities and identify challenges in the design and use of meaning representations in multilingual settings. A final goal of the workshop is to understand the relationship between distributed meaning representations trained on large data sets using neural network models and the symbolic meaning representations that are carefully designed and annotated by CL researchers and gain a deeper understanding of areas where each type of meaning representation is the most effective.

We received 27 valid submissions, and accepted 10 papers for oral presentations and 12 for poster presentations . The papers address topics ranging from meaning representation methodologies to issues in meaning representation parsing, to the adaptation of meaning representations to specific applications and domains, to cross-linguistic issues in meaning representation. We thank the authors and reviewers for their contributions. In addition to the regular program, we also have three invited speakers, Omri Abend, Alexander Koller, and Fei Liu, to speak on typologically informed meaning representation design, cross-framework meaning representation parsing, and the application of meaning representations to abstractive summarization. We look forward to a stimulating and exciting workshop in Florence.

Nianwen Xue, William Croft, Jan Hajič, Chu-Ren Huang, Stephan Oepen, Martha Palmer, James Pustejovsky

Organizers:

Nianwen Xue, Brandeis University
William Croft, University of New Mexico
Jan Hajič, Charles University
Chu-Ren Huang, The Hong Kong Polytechnic University
Stephan Oepen, University of Oslo
Martha Palmer, University of Colorado
James Pustejovsky, Brandeis University

Program Committee:

Abend, Omri, The Hebrew University of Jerusalem
Aroonmanakun, Wirote, Chulalongkorn University
Artzi, Yoav, Cornel University
Bender, Emily, University of Washington
Blache, Philippe, LPL/CNRS and Aix-Marseille University
Bos, Johan, University of Groningen
Butler, Alastair, Hirosaki University
Chersoni, Emmanuele, The Hong Kong Polytechnic University
Dalrymple, Mary, Oxford University
dePaiva, Valeira, Nuance Communications
Flanigan, Jeffrey. University of Mass, Amherst
Flickinger, Dan, Stanford University
Griffit, Kira, UPenn/LDC
Haug, Dag, University of Oslo
Hershcovich, Daniel The Hebrew University of Jerusalem
Kanzaki, Kyoko, Toyohashi University of Technology
Kennedy, Chris, The University of Chicago
Kim, Hansaem, Yonsei University
Lascarides, Alex, University of Edinburgh
Levin, Lori, CMU
Li, Bin, Nanjing Normal University,China
Lopez, Adam, University of Edinburgh
May,Jonathan, USC/ISI
Moeller, Sara, University of Colorado at Boulder
Nguyen, Thi Minh Huyen, VNU University of Science, Hanoi
Nivre, Joakim, Uppsala universitet
O'Gorman, Tim, University of Colorado
Øvrelid, Lilja, University of Oslo
Peng, Xiaochang, Facebook
Qu, Weiguang, Nanjin Normal University
Rutherford, Attapol, Chulalongkorn University
Schneider, Nathan, Georgetown University
Sun, Weiwei, Peking University
Tokunaga, Takeobu, Tokyo Institute of Technology
Uresova, Zdenka, Charles University
Voss, Clare, Army Research Lab

Wang, Chuan, Google
Webber, Bonnie, University of Edinburgh
Xu, Hongzhi, University of Pennsylvania
Zhang, Yuchen, Brandeis University

Invited Speakers:

Omri Abend, Hebrew University of Jerusalem
Alexander Koller, Saarland University
Fei Liu, University of Central Floria

Table of Contents

Cross-Linguistic Semantic Annotation: Reconciling the Language-Specific and the Universal
Jens E. L. Van Gysel, Meagan Vigus, Pavlina Kalm, Sook-kyung Lee, Michael Regan and William Croft 1

Thirty Musts for Meaning Banking
Lasha Abzianidze and Johan Bos 15

Modeling Quantification and Scope in Abstract Meaning Representations
James Pustejovsky, Ken Lai and Nianwen Xue 28

Parsing Meaning Representations: Is Easier Always Better?
Zi Lin and Nianwen Xue 34

GKR: Bridging the Gap between Symbolic/structural and Distributional Meaning Representations
Aikaterini-Lida Kalouli, Richard Crouch and Valeria dePaiva 44

Generating Discourse Inferences from Unscoped Episodic Logical Formulas
Gene Kim, Benjamin Kane, Viet Duong, Muskaan Mendiratta, Graeme McGuire, Sophie Sackstein, Georgiy Platonov and Lenhart Schubert 56

A Plea for Information Structure as a Part of Meaning Representation
Eva Hajicova 66

TCL - a Lexicon of Turkish Discourse Connectives
Deniz Zeyrek and Kezban Başıbüyük 73

Meta-Semantic Representation for Early Detection of Alzheimer's Disease
Jinho D. Choi, Mengmei Li, Felicia Goldstein and Ihab Hajjar 82

Ellipsis in Chinese AMR Corpus
Yihuan Liu, Bin Li, Peiyi Yan, Li Song and Weiguang Qu 92

Event Structure Representation: Between Verbs and Argument Structure Constructions
Pavlina Kalm, Michael Regan and William Croft 100

Distributional Semantics Meets Construction Grammar. towards a Unified Usage-Based Model of Grammar and Meaning
Giulia Rambelli, Emmanuele Chersoni, Philippe Blache, Chu-Ren Huang and Alessandro Lenci 110

Meaning Representation of Null Instantiated Semantic Roles in FrameNet
Miriam R L Petruck 121

Copula and Case-Stacking Annotations for Korean AMR
Hyonsu Choe, Jiyoon Han, Hyejin Park and Hansaem Kim 128

ClearTAC: Verb Tense, Aspect, and Form Classification Using Neural Nets
Skatje Myers and Martha Palmer 136

Preparing SNACS for Subjects and Objects
Adi Shalev, Jena D. Hwang, Nathan Schneider, Vivek Srikumar, Omri Abend and Ari Rappoport 141

A Case Study on Meaning Representation for Vietnamese
Ha Linh and Huyen Nguyen 148

VerbNet Representations: Subevent Semantics for Transfer Verbs
Susan Windisch Brown, Julia Bonn, James Gung, Annie Zaenen, James Pustejovsky and Martha
Palmer 154

Semantically Constrained Multilayer Annotation: The Case of Coreference
Jakob Prange, Nathan Schneider and Omri Abend 164

Towards Universal Semantic Representation
Huaiyu Zhu, Yunyao Li and Laura Chiticariu 177

A Dependency Structure Annotation for Modality
Meagan Vigus, Jens E. L. Van Gysel and William Croft 182

Augmenting Abstract Meaning Representation for Human-Robot Dialogue
Claire Bonial, Lucia Donatelli, Stephanie M. Lukin, Stephen Tratz, Ron Artstein, David Traum and
Clare Voss 199

Workshop Program

Thursday, August 1, 2019

08:50–10:30   **Session A: invited talk + oral presentations**

08:50–09:00   **Opening remarks, by Nianwen Xue, William Croft, Jan Hajic, Churen Huang, Stephan Oepen, Martha Palmer, James Pustejovsky**

09:00–09:40   **Invited talk: "The Case for Typologically informed meaning representations", by Omri Abend**

09:40–10:00   *Cross-Linguistic Semantic Annotation: Reconciling the Language-Specific and the Universal*
Jens E. L. Van Gysel, Meagan Vigus, Pavlina Kalm, Sook-kyung Lee, Michael Regan and William Croft

10:00–10:20   *Thirty Musts for Meaning Banking*
Lasha Abzianidze and Johan Bos

10:20–10:30   *Modeling Quantification and Scope in Abstract Meaning Representations*
James Pustejovsky, Ken Lai and Nianwen Xue

10:30–11:00   **Coffee break**

11:00–12:40   **Session B: invited talk + oral presentations**

11:00–11:40   **Invited Talk: "Compositional semantic parsing across graphbanks", by Alexander Koller**

11:40–12:00   *Parsing Meaning Representations: Is Easier Always Better?*
Zi Lin and Nianwen Xue

12:00–12:20   *GKR: Bridging the Gap between Symbolic/structural and Distributional Meaning Representations*
Aikaterini-Lida Kalouli, Richard Crouch and Valeria dePaiva

12:20–12:40   *Generating Discourse Inferences from Unscoped Episodic Logical Formulas*
Gene Kim, Benjamin Kane, Viet Duong, Muskaan Mendiratta, Graeme McGuire, Sophie Sackstein, Georgiy Platonov and Lenhart Schubert

12:40–14:10   Lunch

14:10–15:50   Session C: Invited talk and poster session

14:10–14:50   Invited talk: "Toward Deep Abstractive Summarization Using Meaning Representations", by Fei Liu

14:50–15:50   Poster session

A Plea for Information Structure as a Part of Meaning Representation
Eva Hajicova

TCL - a Lexicon of Turkish Discourse Connectives
Deniz Zeyrek and Kezban Başıbüyük

Meta-Semantic Representation for Early Detection of Alzheimer's Disease
Jinho D. Choi, Mengmei Li, Felicia Goldstein and Ihab Hajjar

Ellipsis in Chinese AMR Corpus
Yihuan Liu, Bin Li, Peiyi Yan, Li Song and Weiguang Qu

Event Structure Representation: Between Verbs and Argument Structure Constructions
Pavlina Kalm, Michael Regan and William Croft

Distributional Semantics Meets Construction Grammar. towards a Unified Usage-Based Model of Grammar and Meaning
Giulia Rambelli, Emmanuele Chersoni, Philippe Blache, Chu-Ren Huang and Alessandro Lenci

Meaning Representation of Null Instantiated Semantic Roles in FrameNet
Miriam R L Petruck

Copula and Case-Stacking Annotations for Korean AMR
Hyonsu Choe, Jiyoon Han, Hyejin Park and Hansaem Kim

ClearTAC: Verb Tense, Aspect, and Form Classification Using Neural Nets
Skatje Myers and Martha Palmer

Preparing SNACS for Subjects and Objects
Adi Shalev, Jena D. Hwang, Nathan Schneider, Vivek Srikumar, Omri Abend and Ari Rappoport

A Case Study on Meaning Representation for Vietnamese
Ha Linh and Huyen Nguyen

VerbNet Representations: Subevent Semantics for Transfer Verbs
Susan Windisch Brown, Julia Bonn, James Gung, Annie Zaenen, James Pustejovsky and Martha Palmer

Thursday, August 1, 2019 (continued)

15:50–16:20   **Coffee break**

16:20–18:00   **Session D: Oral presentations + panel discussion**

16:20–16:40   *Semantically Constrained Multilayer Annotation: The Case of Coreference*
Jakob Prange, Nathan Schneider and Omri Abend

16:40–16:50   *Towards Universal Semantic Representation*
Huaiyu Zhu, Yunyao Li and Laura Chiticariu

16:50–17:10   *A Dependency Structure Annotation for Modality*
Meagan Vigus, Jens E. L. Van Gysel and William Croft

17:10–17:20   *Augmenting Abstract Meaning Representation for Human-Robot Dialogue*
Claire Bonial, Lucia Donatelli, Stephanie M. Lukin, Stephen Tratz, Ron Artstein, David Traum and Clare Voss

17:20–18:00   **Panel Discussion on how to represent tense, aspect and modality. Panelists: Lucia Donatelli, Yunyao Li, Meagan Vigus, and others**

Cross-Lingual Semantic Annotation: Reconciling the Language-Specific and the Universal

Jens E. L. Van Gysel, Meagan Vigus, Pavlina Kalm,
Sook-kyung Lee, Michael Regan, William Croft
MSC 03 2130 Linguistics
1 University of New Mexico
Albuquerque NM 87131-0001, USA
`{jelvangysel,mvigus,pavlinap,sklee,reganman,wcroft}@unm.edu`

Abstract

Developers of cross-lingual semantic annotation schemes face a number of issues not encountered in monolingual annotation. This paper discusses four such issues, related to the establishment of annotation labels, and the treatment of languages with more fine-grained, more coarse-grained, and cross-cutting categories. We propose that a lattice-like architecture of the annotation categories can adequately handle all four issues, and at the same time remain both intuitive for annotators and faithful to typological insights. This position is supported by a brief annotation experiment.

1 Introduction

In recent years, the field of computational linguistics has become increasingly interested in annotation schemes with cross-lingual applicability (Ponti et al., 2018). For syntactic annotation, the Universal Dependencies scheme for grammatical relations between constituents (Nivre et al., 2016) is probably the best-known representative of this new tendency.

On the semantic side, various annotation schemes have been proposed for specific conceptual domains. The Abstract Meaning Representation project (Banarescu et al., 2013) aims to provide a language-neutral representation of argument structure, and was shown by Xue et al. (2014) to have potential in this direction. The Universal Conceptual Cognitive Annotation (Abend and Rappoport, 2013) has the same objective. Annotation schemes designed for cross-lingual application have also been proposed for such semantic domains as the meanings of discourse connectives (Zufferey and Degand, 2017), temporal information (Katz and Arosio, 2001; Pustejovsky et al., 2003), epistemicity (Lavid et al., 2016), modality in general (Nissim et al., 2013), and preposition-like senses (Saint-Dizier, 2006).

However, languages diverge widely in the semantic distinctions they conventionally express, and in the formal means they use to do so (Comrie, 1989; Croft, 2002). Therefore, devising a cross-lingual annotation scheme poses challenges that developers of language-specific schemes need not face. This paper discusses some crucial choices developers of cross-lingual semantic annotation schemes must make with regards to the granularity of linguistic categories. To a large extent, these apply to syntactic annotation as well. In particular, the following four issues need to be accounted for by any annotation scheme with cross-linguistic ambitions:

1. What are the values of the basic labels of the semantic annotation scheme, i.e. which distinctions are annotators expected to make?

2. How are languages with more coarse-grained semantic distinctions accommodated?

3. How are languages with more fine-grained semantic distinctions accommodated?

4. How are languages with distinctions that cross-cut the categories distinguished in the base level annotation scheme treated?

Section 2 of this paper discusses these issues in more detail, exemplifying each of them with data from a range of semantic domains and a range of languages, and section 3 provides a brief overview of how previous cross-lingual annotation schemes have treated them. In section 4, we survey a wider range of possible solutions for these challenges, each with their advantages and drawbacks, and make an argument in favour of establishing a lattice-like structure of hierarchically organized, typologically motivated categories. We also propose a set of guidelines for annotators on which levels of this lattice to use. Section 5 presents an exploratory cross-lingual annotation exercise using such an architecture.

1

Proceedings of the First International Workshop on Designing Meaning Representations, pages 1–14
Florence, Italy, August 1st, 2019 ©2019 Association for Computational Linguistics

2   Issues in Cross-Lingual Annotation

When devising an annotation scheme for a semantic domain, one must carve up this region
of conceptual space into discrete subregions.
For a monolingual scheme, one can straightforwardly base these annotation values on distinctions overtly made in the language. One is likely
to run into trouble, however, trying to apply such
monolingual categories to a wider sample of languages.

For example, Zufferey and Degand (2017) and
Zufferey et al. (2012) have shown that the English-
based feature set for the semantics of discourse
connectives used by the Penn Discourse Tree Bank
(Prasad et al., 2008) needed to be refined when
applying it to closely related languages such as
French, German, Dutch and Italian. Divergences
are expected to be even larger when applying a
monolingual scheme to genetically unrelated languages. This section discusses how one can devise a principled cross-linguistic set of labels, and
make allowances for languages that do not fit it.

2.1   Establishing the Categories

We propose two heuristics to help one decide on
a subdivision of a semantic domain with maximal
cross-linguistic applicability. Firstly, choosing semantic categories distinguished by the majority of
languages in the world naturally makes the labels
of the annotation scheme widely applicable.

For example, Boye (2012) finds that the typologically most common way in which languages
subdivide the conceptual domain of epistemic
strength, defined as "judgements about the factual status of a proposition" (Palmer, 2001), is a
three-way distinction between full support (certainty about the reality status of an event), partial
support (less than certain knowledge about the reality status of an event), and neutral support (non-
commitment as to the reality status of an event).[1]

Similarly, in the domain of entity quantification, a simple singular vs. non-singular distinction is highly common in the languages of the
world (Corbett, 2000). In a cross-lingual annotation scheme for these semantic domains, choosing [FULL, PARTIAL, NEUTRAL] and [SINGULAR,

NON-SINGULAR] as basic annotation categories
allows most languages to be felicitously analyzed.

A second, practical rather than theoretical, criterion for establishing the main annotation categories is the ease of making the semantic distinctions regardless of the language of annotation.
When developers assert that their chosen categories are cross-linguistically applicable, they implicitly argue that they are interpretable even for
speakers of languages which do not make them.
They also need to provide sufficiently clear guidelines for annotators of many if not all languages
to successfully implement them. In the temporal
domain, for instance, this would be an argument
for an annotation scheme to adopt distinctions between [PAST, PRESENT, FUTURE]. Such categories are both highly salient in our real-world experience, and can be defined in a non-ambiguous
way. Therefore, even though some languages
(such as Mandarin) lack grammaticalized means
to express these categories, one can reasonably assume that annotators will be able to annotate sentences for past, present, or future time reference
based on contextual information.

2.2   More Coarse-Grained Distinctions

Not all languages will make the semantic distinctions chosen by the developers as the base values
for a conceptual domain. One way in which languages can diverge from them is by lumping together distinctions, i.e. dividing up this region of
conceptual space in a more coarse-grained way.

In the domain of modality, for instance, Boye
(2012) finds languages that use more coarse-
grained distinctions than [FULL, PARTIAL, NEU-
TRAL]. Southern Nambiquara lumps together
partial and neutral support, making a two-way
distinction within verbal suffixes (Boye, 2012,
p. 99). This two-way distinction corresponds to
full ("Declarative") vs. non-full ("Dubitative")
epistemic strength. In the temporal domain, Hua
shows a Future vs. Non-Future distinction, lumping together past and present (Haiman, 1980), as
do many other languages. One may want the annotation scheme to allow for flexibility beyond the
use of the base categories to accommodate such
languages.

2.3   More Fine-Grained Distinctions

Languages can also subdivide conceptual space in
more specific ways than the chosen annotation categories. In the number domain, for instance, more

---

[1] In keeping with general typological practice, semantic
concepts are capitalized in the text when they are language-
specific, and are written with a lower-case first letter when
they have cross-linguistic reference. Labels for annotation
categories are represented in small caps.

fine-grained distinctions within the non-singular region of conceptual space can be made. Languages may distinguish sets of two entities from sets of more than two entities (Dual vs. Plural, Upper Sorbian); sets of two entities, sets of three entities and sets of more than three entities (Dual vs. Trial vs. Plural, Larike); or "small" sets of entities from "large" sets of entities (Paucal vs. Plural, Bayso, Corbett 2000, chapter 2). In the domain of modality, Limbu (Sino-Tibetan) subdivides the Partial category into Weak Partial and Strong Partial support (Boye, 2012).

These cases do not necessarily form problems for an annotation scheme. Since the more fine-grained categories discussed here are all neatly categorized as subdivisions of the chosen basic annotation categories, annotators are expected to be able to identify the correct category label without problems. Nevertheless, in order to preserve as much information as possible, it may be desirable to provide annotators with a way to use more fine-grained categories made in their language instead of (or in addition to) the pre-established category values.

2.4 Cross-Cutting Distinctions

The largest challenge to cross-lingual annotation schemes is posed by languages which divide semantic space in ways that cross-cut, or overlap with, the pre-established categories. This will inevitably be the case in semantic domains that form a continuum which has to be carved up into discrete values for the annotation labels. Examples of such categories can once again be found in the modality and number domains.

Boye (2012), based on data from Craig (1977), shows that Jacaltec distinguishes only Strong Support (*chubil*) and Weak Support (*tato*) in its complementizers. Strong Support corresponds to the cross-linguistic prototype of full support and strong partial support, while Weak Support corresponds to the cross-linguistic prototype of neutral support and weak partial support. In other words, these categories cross-cut the partial support category. For a sentence containing the Weak Support marker, an annotator who wishes to adhere to the proposed category labels must judge whether it falls under the NEUTRAL or PARTIAL category - a judgement they cannot make based on explicit evidence from the language.

Similarly, a small number of languages (e.g.

Ainu, Eastern Pomo) make a Few vs. Many distinction in the number domain rather than a Singular vs. Non-Singular one (Veselinova, 2013). They have one category that refers to single referents or small groups (typically up to a maximum of three for Ainu), and a different one to refer to groups greater than this number - dividing up the semantic space in a different, rather than more fine-grained or more coarse-grained, way than the categories found in the majority of languages. In such situations, it is difficult to guide annotators on what to do when they encounter such an overlapping category.

3 Related Work

Previous cross-lingual annotation schemes have not often explicitly addressed the issues laid out in section 2. One scheme accounting for at least two of these issues is Zufferey and Degand's (2017) multilingual adaptation of the PDTB guidelines for discourse connectives. Establishing a hierarchical set of annotation labels based on a small sample of genetically related languages allows them to deal with more fine-grained and more coarse-grained distinctions. Individual annotators are allowed to freely choose values from any level in the hierarchy. When a language divides the semantic domain up in a more fine-grained way, annotators can simply choose values from lower levels of the hierarchy, while for languages with more coarse-grained categories, annotators can choose categories higher up in the structure.

When a given markable is either ambiguous between two pre-established categories, or semantically intermediate between them, they allow annotators to annotate the markable with two tags. Implicitly, this seems meant to solve the problem of cross-cutting categories outlined in 2.4. It does not, however, capture the typological insight that many semantic domains are internally structured and can be captured in semantic maps (Haspelmath, 2003). We know, for example, that in the domain of modality, it should be exceedingly rare if not impossible for a language to show a semantic category subsuming full and neutral support, but not partial support. Therefore, allowing annotators to freely combine annotation labels seems to be too unconstrained of a mechanism to deal with cross-linguistic variation in category boundaries.

Other cross-lingual annotation schemes (e.g. UCCA, Abend and Rappoport 2013; SSA, Griffitt et al. 2018), aim to keep the scheme as intuitive as possible while maintaining cross-linguistic comparability. To this end, UCCA only provides highly schematic annotation categories on the order of [PARTICIPANT, TEMPORAL RELATION, EVENT]. These categories are so general that no language would have more coarse-grained categories. Because of their high level of abstraction, they are also so far apart in conceptual space that languages are unlikely to show overlapping categories. On the other hand, every language will have more fine-grained categories than provided in this scheme. These are not annotated in the base level UCCA, but left to additional annotation layers which researchers can develop for their own purposes.

Lavid et al. (2016) use a similar approach to Zufferey and Degand (2017). They provide a hierarchical structure with three levels of categories for annotating epistemicity, encouraging the use of the lowest levels. When in doubt between the lower-level categories, annotators can choose a higher-level category instead. Nissim et al.'s (2013) cross-lingual scheme for modality also allows annotators to choose coarse-grained categories if they are not confident judging an utterance as an instance of a lower-level category.

While this solution works for languages with coarse-grained categories, strict hierarchical architectures do not allow for easy annotation of overlapping categories. For example, while both these annotation schemes distinguish values for [CERTAINTY, PROBABILITY, POSSIBILITY], the immediately higher-level category is simply one of EPISTEMIC MODAL/FACTUALITY. There is no way to capture categories like those of Jacaltec where some cases of PROBABILITY group with CERTAINTY and others with POSSIBILITY.

4 Potential Solutions

We believe that the most promising architecture for a cross-lingual semantic annotation scheme is to structure the typologically motivated labels as a lattice with different levels, rather than a strict hierarchy. One level contains the categories originally chosen based on the criteria set out in 2.1. This level is designated as the "base level": annotators are encouraged to use categories from this level as the default. The higher and lower levels, respectively, contain equally typologically motivated coarser-grained and finer-grained categories,

which can be used when called for by certain applications or certain language-specific categorizations. Such lattices capture the idea that many semantic categories are structured as hierarchical scales, where the middle values can group together with either end, but the extremes of the scale are highly unlikely to be categorized together in any language. Illustrations are provided in figure 1 and figure 2, and in the supplementary materials.

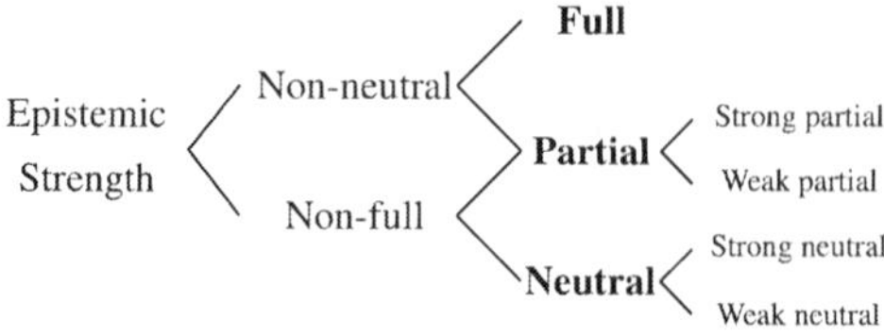

Figure 1: Annotation lattice for epistemic strength

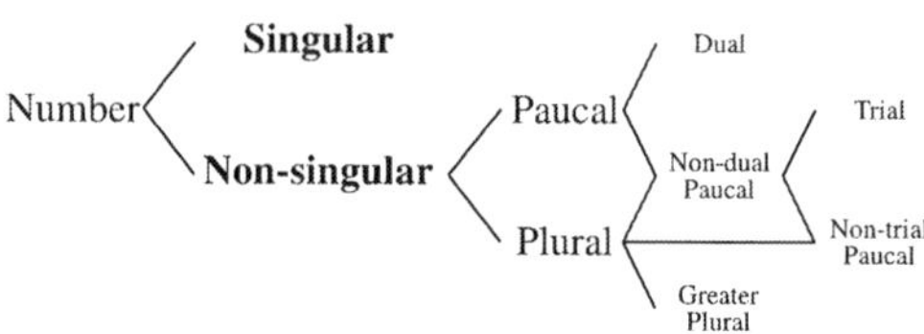

Figure 2: Annotation lattice for number

4.1 More Coarse-Grained Categories

If a language has more coarse-grained semantic categories in a certain domain than those provided in the base level of the lattice (in bold in figures 1-2), it might be difficult for annotators to judge which label to apply to a given use of such a category. For example, for any use of the Nambiquara Dubitative, one would have to judge whether it expresses NEUTRAL or PARTIAL support. This could lead to increased disagreements between annotators. On the one hand, one may still want to require annotators to adopt the base level categories. On the other hand, one might want to ease the annotation process for annotators of languages like Nambiquara.

The lattice architecture allows both goals to be met. As seen in figure 1, [FULL, PARTIAL] strength form an overlapping NON-NEUTRAL category; [PARTIAL, NEUTRAL] strength group together as NON-FULL. Following the aforementioned typological insight, no category groups together [FULL, NEUTRAL] to the exclusion of PARTIAL. Such a lattice avoids the drawback of a strict hierarchy in that it allows for flexibility in the treatment of the in-between category, which can group with either FULL or NEUTRAL support.

For each use of the Nambiquara Dubitative, then, annotators would be encouraged to judge whether in context it expresses PARTIAL or NEUTRAL support. If such a judgement is too hard to make, annotators may use higher-level values in the lattice, in this case NON-FULL.

4.2 More Fine-Grained Categories

Even though annotators of languages with more fine-grained distinctions than the main level of the lattice should be able to accurately use this level, they may, with an eye on certain downstream applications, want to preserve more specific information encoded in the language. In the Universal Dependencies scheme, annotators are able to add lower-level language-specific categories where needed (e.g. Pyysalo et al. 2015 for Finnish). In order to eliminate the potential proliferation of incommensurable language-specific categories that could result from this, we would encourage annotators to use the base level values as much as possible. In addition, we would provide a set of typologically-based fine-grained categories on a lower level of the lattice. In figure 1, this corresponds to the [STRONG PARTIAL, WEAK PARTIAL, STRONG NEUTRAL, WEAK NEUTRAL] labels, in figure 2 to the [PAUCAL, PLURAL] labels and all labels subsumed underneath them.

In example (1a) from Limbu (van Driem, 1987, p. 244), annotators could follow the distinctions the language makes by labeling the epistemic marker *li·ya* as WEAK PARTIAL. In (1b), they can label *laʔba* as STRONG PARTIAL. Similarly, annotators for a language with fine-grained number categories, such as Yimas, could use the lower-level categories in figure 2. The Yimas Dual, used for reference to exactly two entities, can be marked as DUAL. The Yimas Paucal (typically used for reference to sets containing three to seven entities, Foley, 1991, p. 111) can be marked as NON-DUAL PAUCAL.

(1) a. *ya·ʔl li·ya.*
     groan EPMOD
     'He's perhaps groaning.'

     b. *ya·ʔl laʔba.*
     groan EPMOD
     'He's probably groaning.'

In this way, the specific information expressed in these forms is preserved. At the same time,

comparability to other languages is safeguarded: because of the structure of the lattice, lower-level annotations can be traced back, e.g. to the NON-SINGULAR base level category for the DUAL label, and to the PARTIAL category for the STRONG PARTIAL label, and compared to instances of this category in other languages.

Annotators may, in addition, encounter typologically rare fine-grained categories that do not correspond to a pre-specified value in the lattice. They are encouraged in these cases to use base level categories from the lattice. If they feel very strongly that this is not sufficient for their purposes, they will be able to create a language-specific semantic label and specify its position in the lattice.

4.3 Cross-Cutting Categories

Languages with categories that cross-cut the distinctions in the lattice, such as the Jacaltec Strong Support vs. Weak Support system, are the hardest to deal with. The Few vs. Many verbal number system of Ainu, (typically called "Singular" and "Plural", Veselinova 2013), also shows this (2). *Ek* 'come' is used with a set of one to four participants, *arki* 'come' is used with more than four participants (Tamura 1988, p. 40) - cross-cutting the [SINGULAR, NON-SINGULAR] distinction.

(2) a. *tu   okkaypo ek.*
     two youth   come.SG
     'Two youths came.'

     b. *tupesaniw ka   arki   ruwe ne.*
     eight   even come.PL NMLZ COP
     'Eight people came.'

We present four options for the annotation of such cross-cutting categories, and argue that the fourth one strikes the best balance between ease of annotation and cross-lingual portability. Firstly, one could allow annotators to completely follow the distinctions their language makes. This would mean that Ainu annotators would establish a FEW category, subsuming the [SINGULAR, DUAL, TRIAL] categories in the lattice, and a MANY category, subsuming [NON-TRIAL PAUCAL, PLURAL]. Alternatively, these categories could be named SINGULAR and PLURAL, since they spread outwards from the cross-linguistic singular and plural prototypes. Along the same lines, Jacaltec annotators would establish a STRONG (or FULL) category for *chubil* and a WEAK (or NEUTRAL) category for *tato*.

This option gives maximal advantage to annotators, who can make use of the exact distinctions expressed in their language. They would not have to distinguish between the different uses of these forms.[2] It comes, however, with a great reduction in cross-linguistic comparability of the resulting annotations. Either the same semantic value will come to be annotated differently in different languages (partial epistemic support would be annotated as PARTIAL in most languages but as either FULL or NEUTRAL in Jacaltec), or the same annotation would mean different things in different languages (SINGULAR would mean "exactly one entity" in Yimas, but "one to three entities" in Ainu).

The second option is a weakened version of the first. Under this approach, the primary annotation of each form is the prototype of this category, but annotators are expected to add the accurate category of the more fine-grained level of the lattice as a secondary annotation.

The Ainu form *ek* would, then, be annotated as SINGULAR:SINGULAR when referring to the coming of one entity, and SINGULAR:NON-SINGULAR when referring to the coming of two or three entities. The first SINGULAR refers to the fact that the cross-linguistic singular category is the prototype of the semantic category expressed by Ainu *ek*. The second annotation expresses the actual semantic value of an utterance on the base level of the annotation lattice. As for modality, Jacaltec annotators would annotate strong partial and full support uses of *chubil* as FULL:STRONG PARTIAL and FULL:FULL respectively.

While this is probably fairly intuitive for annotators, the drawback is that labels such as STRONG PARTIAL no longer exclusively belong to one overarching category. In Jacaltec, it would belong under FULL, while in other languages it would fall under PARTIAL. As a result, annotators for languages with a canonical strong partial vs. weak partial distinction, as proper subcategories of the base level partial support category, would consistently have to employ a secondary annotation as well, specifying the overarching PARTIAL to make the value of this annotation clear. The necessity for two annotation labels to be selected for each

form makes this solution fairly cumbersome.

The third option favours cross-linguistic comparison, but is perhaps less intuitive for annotators. It calls for consistent use of the categories specified in the lattice. In such a system, strong partial uses of Jacaltec *chubil* would always be PARTIAL:STRONG PARTIAL. In other words, annotation is done purely on semantic grounds, disregarding language-specific forms. This means that the various uses of the same (polysemous) Jacaltec form will receive different annotations. Even though we believe annotators for all languages should be able to distinguish the base level values of the lattice based on semantic criteria, interpreting such differences which lack overt expression in a language may still be challenging.

Therefore, we believe that our fourth option holds the most promise. This solution allows annotators to use a value in the lattice two levels higher than the markable meaning. For example, for any use of Jacaltec *chubil*, annotators would be allowed to use the label NON-NEUTRAL. This higher-level label allows for the inference that this particular use is either genuinely "in between" the two relevant base level categories (e.g. overlapping the prototypes of partial support and full support), or ambiguous between those two categories. In this way, two levels of the lattice that are problematic from a Jacaltec point of view (FULL VS. PARTIAL on the base level and FULL VS. STRONG PARTIAL at the lower level) are avoided. Of course, as was the case for the treatment of more coarse-grained categories, annotators are still encouraged to specify lower-level values when they can be clearly judged from the context. Thus, strong partial uses of Jacaltec *chubil* could be labeled either NON-NEUTRAL:STRONG PARTIAL, or simply NON-NEUTRAL.

Few cross-lingual annotation schemes have adopted explicit guidelines for languages whose categories cross-cut the pre-established values. Our use of a typologically motivated lattice to organize semantic categories provides various ways to deal with this issue, and at the same time captures insights into regularities in the division of semantic space. We believe that the fourth approach outlined in this section has the best chances of finding wide acceptance. It allows annotators for specific languages to do justice to the semantic structure of the language by recognizing the fine-grained uses of language-specific categories. In

---

[2]It must be kept in mind, however, that many formal grammatical categories in languages are polysemous. In semantic annotation, annotators must be wary of labeling expressions in a deterministic way based on the most prototypical use of a grammatical marker. Instead, each utterance must be judged based on its meaning in context.

addition, the use of a secondary annotation with a label not one, but two levels higher in the lattice avoids the problem of which superordinate category an in-between usage should be categorized as, and also guarantees cross-lingual portability.

5 Cross-Lingual Annotation Pilot

In order to explore the practicality of a semantic annotation scheme using a lattice structure and the guidelines for label selection outlined above, a small cross-lingual annotation experiment was performed, and is discussed in this section.

5.1 Annotation Procedure and Materials

Thirty-six English sentences expressing spatial figure-ground relations were taken from the STREUSLE corpus (Schneider et al., 2016), and provided thirty-six PPs as annotation targets. These sentences came originally from travel blogs, and were chosen to express spatial scenarios ranging from surface support, to attachment, to containment (figure 3, see also Bowerman and Choi 2001). This continuum was chosen because it is similar to the modality continuum discussed above. While it is exceedingly rare for languages to have one category for only support and containment, the attachment category frequently groups with either containment or support (Bowerman and Choi, 2001). In addition, the existence of spatial situations in between these three base level categories (such as adhesion, for a band-aid on a body part) allows us to confront difficult cross-cutting categories with our lattice architecture.

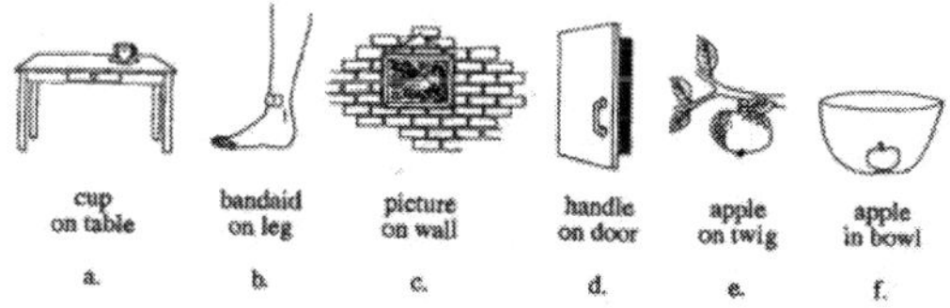

Figure 3: Support-Attachment-Containment continuum (Bowerman and Choi, 2001, p. 485)

Each sentence was translated into Dutch, Czech and Korean by a native speaker of each language (the first, third, and fourth authors of this paper, respectively), and annotated by the same native speaker. The English sentences were annotated by the second author, also a native speaker.

The lattice in figure 4 contains the annotation values, defined based on figure 3. The base level categories are [SUPPORT, ATTACHMENT,

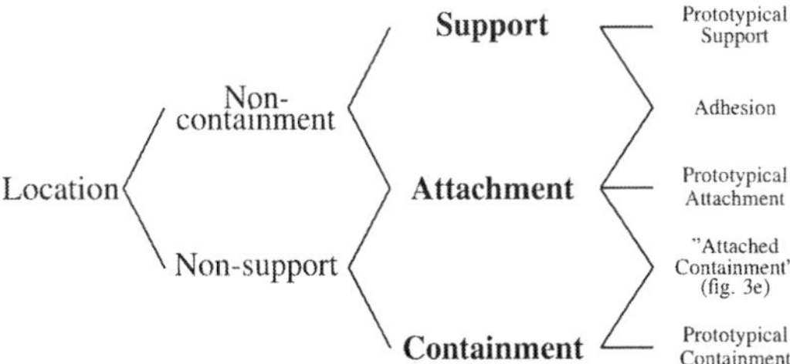

Figure 4: Annotation lattice for spatial relations

CONTAINMENT]. At the higher level, [NON-CONTAINMENT, NON-SUPPORT] group together [SUPPORT, ATTACHMENT] and [ATTACHMENT, CONTAINMENT], respectively. On the lowest level of the lattice, ADHESION cross-cuts the SUPPORT vs. ATTACHMENT distinction, while ATTACHED CONTAINMENT cross-cuts the ATTACHMENT vs. CONTAINMENT distinction.

Annotators were given the following guidelines:

1. Choose a label from the base level of the lattice based on the meaning of the sentence.

2. If the sentence is ambiguous between two base level values, choose the relevant overarching category.

3. If the sentence expresses a category that is in between two base level values, choose the relevant lower-level category when confident. Otherwise, choose the applicable coarse-grained category above the base level.

4. If the sentence expresses a more fine-grained distinction within one of the base level categories which is not given in the lattice, simply use the applicable base level value.

5.2 Evaluation Procedure

We are aware of few previous experiments annotating multilingual parallel corpora with one set of semantic categories. Closest to our pilot study is probably Zufferey and Degand (2017), who calculate agreement between annotations of a parallel corpus in English, French, German, Dutch, and Italian. Pairwise agreement between English and every other language is reported for each level of the hierarchy in which their categories are structured. The agreement values are given only in raw percentages.

We report pair-wise agreement between all pairs of languages in our pilot. We report both the exact correspondence of annotations between languages, and the compatibility of these annotations. The first set of values is conceptualized as a measure of the discrepancies between the semantic categories of individual languages. For example, an attachment scenario might be annotated as ATTACHMENT in Dutch (which has a preposition *aan* specialized for attachment), but as NON-CONTAINMENT in English, because of its more coarse-grained semantic structure. Under this first measure, these cases are counted as disagreements.

Under the second measure, they are seen as compatible. Since ATTACHMENT is a subcategory of NON-CONTAINMENT, the Dutch annotation can be traced back in the lattice to NON-CONTAINMENT, and the two languages have equivalent annotations on this level. The difference between the exact correspondence score for a language pair and its compatibility score measures the portability of the lattice architecture, and its ability to abstract away from language-specific subdivisions of semantic space.

Both the exact correspondence measure and the compatibility measure are reported as agreement proportions, and as Cohen's Kappa scores (Cohen, 1960). We believe that, even though we are calculating cross-lingual interannotator agreement rather than monolingual agreement between two annotators, the tasks performed by the annotators are still comparable. Since we use a parallel corpus and the same set of annotation values, Cohen's Kappa provides a meaningful measure of how much the proposed annotation system improves labeling over a chance distribution.

5.3 Annotation Results

Table 1 reports cross-lingual interannotator agreement for identity between the chosen labels. The raw proportions of agreement are high, ranging from 82% (Czech-English and Korean-English) to 93% (Czech-Dutch). The Cohen's Kappa scores are also acceptable (between 0.64 and 0.86).

As shown in table 2, pairwise compatibility proportions are on average 7% higher than the corresponding identity scores, and compatibility Kappa scores are on average 0.15 higher than the corresponding identity scores. All language pairs show agreement greater than 90%, and all but one show a Kappa value greater than 0.80.

The organization of annotation categories in a

	Czech	Dutch	English
Dutch	93% ($\kappa = 0.86$)		
English	82% ($\kappa = 0.64$)	86% ($\kappa = 0.74$)	
Korean	85% ($\kappa = 0.67$)	89% ($\kappa = 0.78$)	85% ($\kappa = 0.66$)

Table 1: Identity between cross-lingual annotations

	Czech	Dutch	English
Dutch	96% ($\kappa = 0.91$)		
English	93% ($\kappa = 0.86$)	94% ($\kappa = 0.90$)	
Korean	90% ($\kappa = 0.79$)	97% ($\kappa = 0.94$)	92% ($\kappa = 0.84$)

Table 2: Compatibility between cross-lingual annotations

lattice paired with clear guidelines as to which levels of the lattice to use in different situations therefore seems to be a promising way of guaranteeing both ease of annotation and cross-linguistic comparability. It seems fairly successful at abstracting away from language-specific differences in category boundaries, as evidenced by the improvement in the scores for compatibility of annotations as compared to those for exact identity.

A reviewer points out that it is hard to assess the improvement our annotation lattice offers over a flat annotation scheme where annotators are required to choose between [SUPPORT, ATTACHMENT, CONTAINMENT]. We agree that a comparison with such a control condition would be interesting. However, re-annotating this small corpus with such a flat annotation scheme would lead to skewed results, because the present annotators have built up familiarity with the sentences. Since time constraints prevent us from conducting a new annotation experiment in accordance with this suggestion, or from finding new annotators to provide the baseline annotation, we will simply keep it in mind for further work.

5.4 Error Analysis

The differences between the values in table 1 and table 2 stem from annotations which are compatible, but not identical between languages. These annotations reflect both the presence of more coarse-grained categories and cross-cutting categories. As for the former case, examples such as (3a) were annotated as SUPPORT in Czech and Dutch, but as NON-CONTAINMENT in English and (sometimes) Korean. The lattice thus allows annotators in languages with coarse-grained categories to suspend judgement on the base level annotation categories where necessary, while maintaining cross-linguistic comparability.

(3) a. ...*right **on the back of my car***.

     b. ...*had nail polish **on a couple of toes***.

The same can largely be said for cross-cutting categories. For the single example of surface adhesion in our corpus (3b), the English and Dutch annotators followed guideline 3, choosing the lower-level ADHESION category. The Czech and Korean annotators chose ATTACHMENT and SUPPORT, respectively, both of which are compatible with the Dutch and English choices. This yields compatible annotations in five of the six language pairs, indicating that a category lattice does fairly well in treating cross-cutting categories.

This sentence also illustrates again the problematic character of continuous semantic categories with values in between the base level annotation categories. The ADHESION category cross-cuts the SUPPORT vs. ATTACHMENT distinction, and annotators for different languages (and, conceivably, within one language) will sometimes make different judgements as to which of these two base level categories is appropriate. Choosing a category two levels higher in the lattice instead of just one, as proposed in this paper, would ideally prevent disagreements.

Disagreements also arose with the examples in 4, for which we offer two tentative explanations. Examples (4a-4b), on the one hand, seem likely to give rise to different conceptualizations on the part of annotators. One can interpret *the product* in (4a) to be strictly on top of the hair (leading to the SUPPORT annotations in Dutch and Korean), as clinging to every single hair (resulting in the English ATTACHMENT annotation), or as being contained within the space delimited by the totality of the hair (explaining the Czech CONTAINMENT annotation). Similar conceptualizations can be proposed for *on burger* in (4b): the meat can be seen as contained within the space delimited by the two halves of the bun, or as supported by the bottom half of the bun. Such alternative construals are likely to lead to a certain proportion of disagreements.

(4) a. ...*put product **on my hair**...*

     b. *No meat **on burger**...*

     c. ...*when I am **in the chair**...*

The disagreement in (4c) - CONTAINMENT in English vs. SUPPORT in Czech, Dutch, and Korean - is likely to stem from different language-specific conventionalized construals for specific figure-ground configurations. In Dutch, for example, the most natural translation of *in the chair* would be *op de stoel*, using the prototypical support preposition *op*. Using *in*, the containment preposition, is hardly possible. In other words, the relation between a sitter and a chair is always construed as a support relation rather than a containment relation. There does not seem to be a straightforward solution for such cases either. It remains to be seen, however, whether this source of disagreements is recurrent across semantic domains - it might well be more common in the domain of figure-ground relations than in other regions of conceptual space.

6 Conclusions

This paper proposes a lattice-like architecture of cross-lingual semantic annotation systems, with category labels organized in different levels and forming overlapping groupings. This allows us to be faithful to both individual languages and typological generalizations. An approach where cross-cutting categories either receive a low-level, highly specific label (when annotators are confident), or a high-level and uncontroversial label, presents a middle ground between maximizing ease of annotation and maximizing typological rigor. An exploratory cross-lingual annotation task on a small parallel corpus in four languages shows that such an approach has the potential to tackle the issues discussed.

Acknowledgements

This research was supported in part by grant 1764091 by the National Science Foundation to the last author.

References

Omri Abend and Ari Rappoport. 2013. Universal conceptual cognitive annotation (UCCA). In *Proceedings of the 51st Annual Meeting of the Association for Computational Linguistics (Volume 1: Long Papers)*, pages 228–238, Sofia, Bulgaria. Association for Computational Linguistics.

Laura Banarescu, Claire Bonial, Shu Cai, Madalina Georgescu, Kira Griffitt, Ulf Hermjakob, Kevin Knight, Philipp Koehn, Martha Palmer, and Nathan

Schneider. 2013. Abstract meaning representation for sembanking. In *Proceedings of the 7th Linguistic Annotation Workshop and Interoperability with Discourse*, pages 178–186, Sofia, Bulgaria. Association for Computational Linguistics.

Robert Botne. 2012. Remoteness distinctions. In Robert I. Binnick, editor, *The Oxford handbook of tense and aspect*, pages 536–562. Oxford University Press.

Melissa Bowerman and Soonja Choi. 2001. Shaping meanings for language: universal and language-specific in the acquisition of semantic categories. In *Language acquisition and conceptual development*, pages 475–511. Cambridge University Press.

Kasper Boye. 2012. *Epistemic meaning: A crosslinguistic and functional-cognitive study*, volume 43 of *Empirical Approaches to Language Typology*. De Gruyter Mouton, Berlin.

Joan L. Bybee, Revere Dale Perkins, and William Pagliuca. 1994. *The Evolution of Grammar: Tense, Aspect, and Modality in the Languages of the World*. University of Chicago Press Chicago.

Jacob Cohen. 1960. A coefficient of agreement for nominal scales. *Educational and psychological measurement*, 20(1):37–46.

Bernard Comrie. 1989. *Language universals and linguistic typology: Syntax and morphology*. University of Chicago press.

Greville G. Corbett. 2000. *Number*. Cambridge University Press.

Colette Grinevald Craig. 1977. *The structure of Jacaltec*. University of Texas Press.

William Croft. 2002. *Typology and universals*. Cambridge University Press.

William Croft. 2012. *Verbs: Aspect and Causal Structure*. Oxford University Press.

William Croft, Pavlína Pešková, and Michael Regan. 2017. Integrating decompositional event structures into storylines. In *Proceedings of the Events and Stories in the News Workshop*, pages 98–109, Vancouver, Canada. Association for Computational Linguistics.

Östen Dahl. 1981. On the definition of the telic-atelic (bounded–nonbounded) distinction in tense and aspect. *Syntax and Semantics*, 14:79–90.

Östen Dahl. 1983. Temporal distance: Remoteness distinctions in tense-aspect systems. *Linguistics*, 21(1):105–122.

Georg van Driem. 1987. *A Grammar of Limbu*. Mouton de Gruyter.

William A Foley. 1991. *The Yimas language of New Guinea*. Stanford University Press.

Kira Griffitt, Jennifer Tracey, Ann Bies, and Stephanie Strassel. 2018. Simple semantic annotation and situation frames: Two approaches to basic text understanding in LORELEI. In *Proceedings of the 11th Language Resources and Evaluation Conference*, pages 1672–1676, Miyazaki, Japan. European Language Resource Association.

John Haiman. 1980. *Hua, a Papuan language of the Eastern highlands of New Guinea*. John Benjamins Publishing.

Martin Haspelmath. 2003. The geometry of grammatical meaning: Semantic maps and cross-linguistic comparison. In *The new psychology of language*, pages 217–248. Psychology Press.

Graham Katz and Fabrizio Arosio. 2001. The annotation of temporal information in natural language sentences. In *Proceedings of the ACL 2001 Workshop on Temporal and Spatial Information Processing*. Association for Computational Linguistics.

Julia Lavid, Marta Carretero, and Juan Rafael Zamorano-Mansilla. 2016. Contrastive annotation of epistemicity in the multinot project: preliminary steps. In *Proceedings of the ISA-12, Twelfth Joint ACL-ISO Workshop on Interoperable Semantic Annotation, held in conjunction with Language Resources and Evaluation Conference*, pages 81–88.

Malvina Nissim, Paola Pietrandrea, Andrea Sanso, and Caterina Mauri. 2013. Cross-linguistic annotation of modality: a data-driven hierarchical model. In *Proceedings of the 9th Joint ISO - ACL SIGSEM Workshop on Interoperable Semantic Annotation*, pages 7–14, Potsdam, Germany. Association for Computational Linguistics.

Joakim Nivre, Marie-Catherine de Marneffe, Filip Ginter, Yoav Goldberg, Jan Hajic, Christopher D. Manning, Ryan McDonald, Slav Petrov, Sampo Pyysalo, Natalia Silveira, Reut Tsarfaty, and Daniel Zeman. 2016. Universal dependencies v1: A multilingual treebank collection. In *Proceedings of the Tenth International Conference on Language Resources and Evaluation (LREC 2016)*, pages 1659–1666, Portorož, Slovenia. European Language Resources Association (ELRA).

Frank Robert Palmer. 2001. *Mood and modality*. Cambridge University Press.

Edoardo Maria Ponti, Helen O'Horan, Yevgeni Berzak, Ivan Vulic, Roi Reichart, Thierry Poibeau, Ekaterina Shutova, and Anna Korhonen. 2018. Modeling language variation and universals: A survey on typological linguistics for natural language processing. *CoRR*, abs/1807.00914.

Rashmi Prasad, Nikhil Dinesh, Alan Lee, Eleni Miltsakaki, Livio Robaldo, Aravind Joshi, and Bonnie Webber. 2008. The penn discourse treebank 2.0. In *Proceedings of the Sixth International Conference on Language Resources and Evaluation (LREC'08)*, pages 2961–2968, Marrakech, Morocco. European Language Resources Association (ELRA).

James Pustejovsky, José M Castano, Robert Ingria, Roser Sauri, Robert J Gaizauskas, Andrea Setzer, Graham Katz, and Dragomir R Radev. 2003. Timeml: Robust specification of event and temporal expressions in text. *New directions in question answering*, 3:28–34.

Sampo Pyysalo, Jenna Kanerva, Anna Missilä, Veronika Laippala, and Filip Ginter. 2015. Universal dependencies for Finnish. In *Proceedings of the 20th Nordic Conference of Computational Linguistics (NODALIDA 2015)*, pages 163–172, Vilnius, Lithuania. Linköping University Electronic Press, Sweden.

Patrick Saint-Dizier. 2006. PrepNet: a multilingual lexical description of prepositions. In *Proceedings of the Fifth International Conference on Language Resources and Evaluation (LREC'06)*, pages 1021–1026, Genoa, Italy. European Language Resources Association (ELRA).

Nathan Schneider, Jena D. Hwang, Vivek Srikumar, Meredith Green, Abhijit Suresh, Kathryn Conger, Tim O'Gorman, and Martha Palmer. 2016. A corpus of preposition supersenses. In *Proceedings of the 10th Linguistic Annotation Workshop held in conjunction with ACL 2016 (LAW-X 2016)*, pages 99–109, Berlin, Germany. Association for Computational Linguistics.

Suzuko Tamura. 1988. *The Ainu Language*. Sanseido, Tokyo. Reprinted in 2000, translated from Japanese into English by Sanseido Co. Ltd.

Ljuba N. Veselinova. 2013. Verbal number and suppletion. In Matthew S. Dryer and Martin Haspelmath, editors, *The World Atlas of Language Structures Online*. Max Planck Institute for Evolutionary Anthropology, Leipzig.

Nianwen Xue, Ondrej Bojar, Jan Hajic, Martha Palmer, Zdenka Uresova, and Xiuhong Zhang. 2014. Not an interlingua, but close: Comparison of English AMRs to Chinese and Czech. In *Proceedings of the Ninth International Conference on Language Resources and Evaluation (LREC'14)*, pages 1765–1772, Reykjavik, Iceland. European Language Resources Association (ELRA).

Sandrine Zufferey and Liesbeth Degand. 2017. Annotating the meaning of discourse connectives in multilingual corpora. *Corpus Linguistics and Linguistic Theory*, 13(2):399–422.

Sandrine Zufferey, Liesbeth Degand, Andrei Popescu-Bellis, and Ted Sanders. 2012. Empirical validations of multilingual annotation schemes for discourse relations. In *Eighth Joint ISO-ACL/SIGSEM Workshop on Interoperable Semantic Annotation*, pages 77–84, Pisa, Italy. Association for Computational Linguistics.

Supplementary Materials

Proposed annotation lattice for epistemic strength

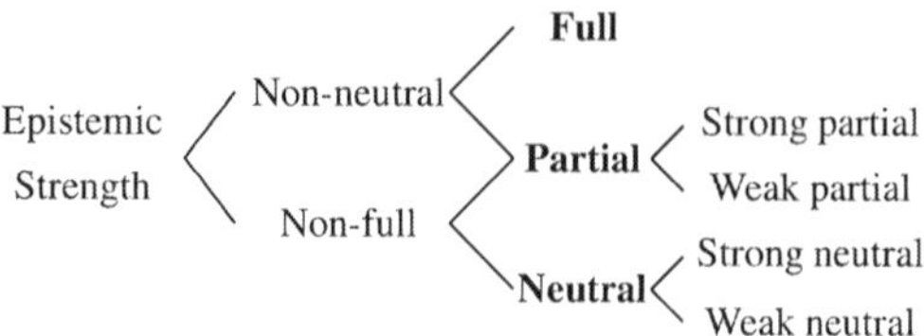

Proposed annotation lattice for number

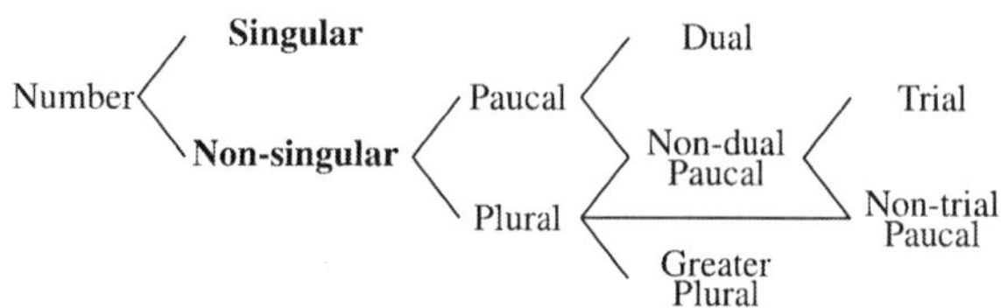

Proposed annotation lattice for spatial relations

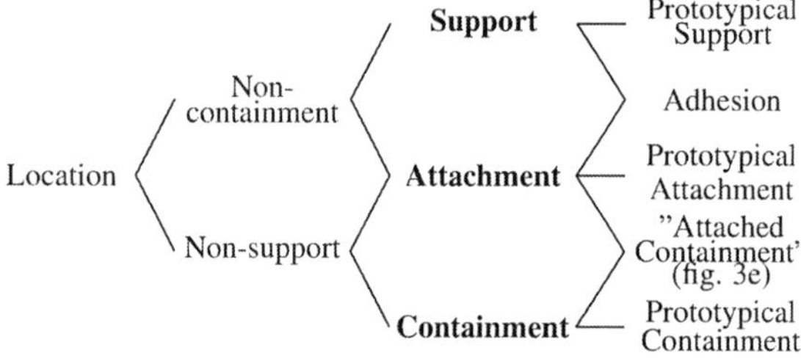

Proposed annotation lattice for aspect

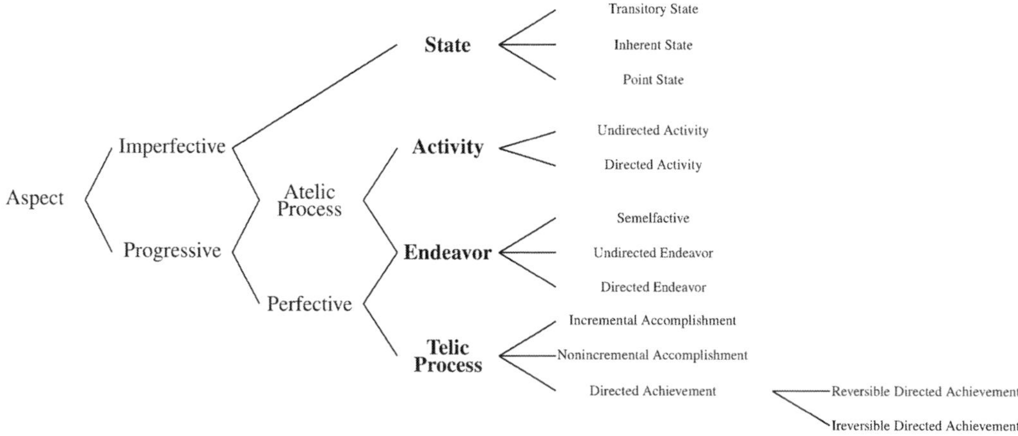

Proposed annotation lattice for time reference

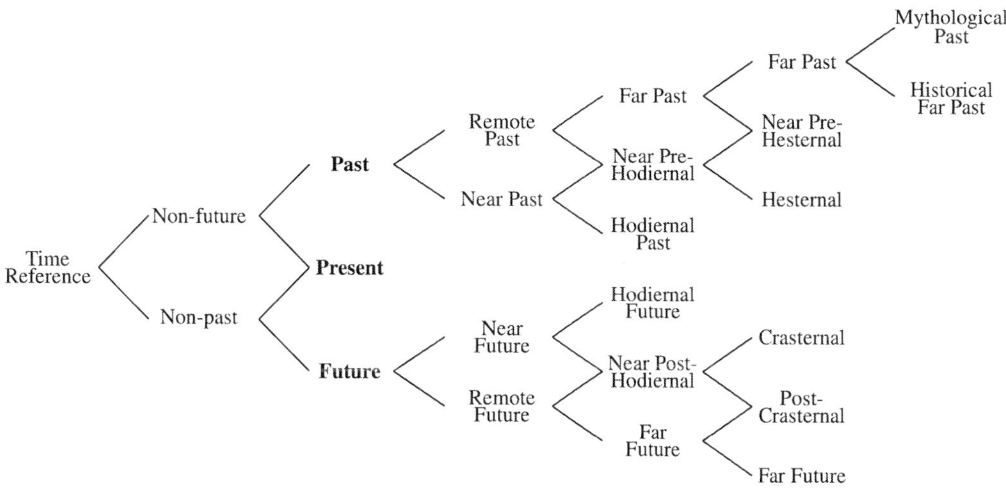

These lattices are based on Dahl (1983), Bybee et al. (1994) and Botne (2012) for time reference, Boye (2012) for epistemic strength, Corbett (2000) for number, and Bowerman and Choi (2001) for spatial relations. The aspect lattice is based on the fine-grained aspectual types defined in Croft (2012), with the addition of the category of endeavors (processes that terminate without reaching a natural endpoint or telos), described in Croft et al. (2017). Endeavors are sometimes grouped with telic processes, sometimes not (Dahl, 1981). Imperfectives group together unbounded processes and states, while progressives group together processes, unbounded or bounded (although they describe the state of being in the middle of the process).

References

Robert Botne. 2012. Remoteness distinctions. In Robert I. Binnick, editor, *The Oxford handbook of tense and aspect*, pages 536–562. Oxford University Press.

Melissa Bowerman and Soonja Choi. 2001. Shaping meanings for language: universal and language-specific in the acquisition of semantic categories. In *Language acquisition and conceptual development*, pages 475–511. Cambridge University Press.

Kasper Boye. 2012. *Epistemic meaning: A crosslinguistic and functional-cognitive study*, volume 43 of *Empirical Approaches to Language Typology*. De Gruyter Mouton, Berlin.

Joan L. Bybee, Revere Dale Perkins, and William Pagliuca. 1994. *The Evolution of Grammar: Tense, Aspect, and Modality in the Languages of the World*. University of Chicago Press Chicago.

Greville G. Corbett. 2000. *Number*. Cambridge University Press.

William Croft. 2012. *Verbs: Aspect and Causal Structure*. Oxford University Press.

William Croft, Pavlína Pešková, and Michael Regan. 2017. Integrating decompositional event structures into storylines. In *Proceedings of the Events and Stories in the News Workshop*, pages 98–109, Vancouver, Canada. Association for Computational Linguistics.

Östen Dahl. 1981. On the definition of the telic-atelic (bounded–nonbounded) distinction in tense and aspect. *Syntax and Semantics*, 14:79–90.

Östen Dahl. 1983. Temporal distance: Remoteness distinctions in tense-aspect systems. *Linguistics*, 21(1):105–122.

Thirty Musts for Meaning Banking

Johan Bos
Center for Language and Cognition
University of Groningen
`johan.bos@rug.nl`

Lasha Abzianidze
Center for Language and Cognition
University of Groningen
`l.abzianidze@rug.nl`

Abstract

Meaning banking—creating a semantically annotated corpus for the purpose of semantic parsing or generation—is a challenging task. It is quite simple to come up with a complex meaning representation, but it is hard to design a simple meaning representation that captures many nuances of meaning. This paper lists some lessons learned in nearly ten years of meaning annotation during the development of the Groningen Meaning Bank (Bos et al., 2017) and the Parallel Meaning Bank (Abzianidze et al., 2017). The paper's format is rather unconventional: there is no explicit related work, no methodology section, no results, and no discussion (and the current snippet is not an abstract but actually an introductory preface). Instead, its structure is inspired by work of Traum (2000) and Bender (2013). The list starts with a brief overview of the existing meaning banks (Section 1) and the rest of the items are roughly divided into three groups: corpus collection (Section 2 and 3, annotation methods (Section 4–11), and design of meaning representations (Section 12–30). We hope this overview will give inspiration and guidance in creating improved meaning banks in the future.

1 Look at other meaning banks

Other semantic annotation projects can be inspiring, help you to find solutions to hard annotation problems, or to find out where improvements to the state of the art are still needed (Abend and Rappoport, 2017). Good starting points are the English Resource Grammar (Flickinger, 2000, 2011), the Groningen Meaning Bank (GMB, Bos et al. 2017), the AMR Bank (Banarescu et al., 2013), the Parallel Meaning Bank (PMB, Abzianidze et al. 2017), Scope Control Theory (Butler and Yoshimoto, 2012), UCCA (Abend and Rappoport, 2013), Prague Semantic Dependencies

(Hajič et al., 2017) and the ULF Corpus based on Episodic Logic (Kim and Schubert, 2019). The largest differences between these approaches can be found in the expressive power of the meaning representations used. The simplest representations correspond to graphs (Banarescu et al., 2013; Abend and Rappoport, 2013); slightly more expressive ones correspond to first-order logic (Oepen et al., 2016; Bos et al., 2017; Abzianidze et al., 2017; Butler and Yoshimoto, 2012), whereas others go beyond this (Kim and Schubert, 2019). Generally, an increase of expressive power causes a decrease of efficient reasoning (Blackburn and Bos, 2005). Semantic formalisms based on graphs are attractive because of their simplicity, but will face issues when dealing with negation in inference tasks (Section 21). The choice might depend on the application (e.g., if you are not interested in detecting contradictions, coping with negation is less important), but arguably, an open-domain meaning bank ought to be independent of a specific application.

2 Select public domain corpora

Any text could be protected by copyright law and it is not always easy to find suitable corpora that are free from copyright issues. Indeed, the relationship between copyright of texts and their use in natural language processing is complex (Eckart de Castilho et al., 2018). Nonetheless, it pays off to make some effort by searching for corpora that are free or in the public domain (Ide et al., 2010). This makes it easier for other researchers to work with it, in particular those that are employed by institutes with lesser financial means. The GMB only includes corpora from the public domain (Basile et al., 2012b). Free parallel corpora are also available via OPUS (Skadiņš et al., 2014). Other researchers take advantage of vague legislation and

Proceedings of the First International Workshop on Designing Meaning Representations, pages 15–27
Florence, Italy, August 1st, 2019 ©2019 Association for Computational Linguistics

distribute corpora quoting the right of fair use (Postma et al., 2018). Recently, crowd sourcing platforms such as Figure Eight make datasets available, too ("Data For Everyone"), under appropriate licensing. While targeting the public domain corpora, one might need to bear in mind the coverage of the corpora depending on the objectives of semantic annotation.

3 Freeze the corpus before you start

Once you start your annotation efforts, it is a good idea to freeze the corpora that will comprise your meaning bank.[1] In the GMB project (Basile et al., 2012b), the developers were less strict in maintaining this principle. During the project they came across new corpora, but after adding them to the GMB they were forced to fix and validate annotations on many levels to get the newly added corpus up to date and in sync with the rest. This problems manifests itself especially for corpora that are constructed via a phenomenon-driven annotation approach (Section 24).

4 Work with raw texts in your corpus

Keep the original texts as foundation for annotation. Never ever carry out any semantic annotation on tokenised texts, but use stand-off annotation on character offsets (Section 5). Tokenisation can be done in many different ways, and the *atoms of meaning* certainly do not correspond directly to words. Most of the current conventions in tokenisation are based on what has been used in (English) syntax-oriented computational linguistics and can be misleading when other languages are taken into consideration (Section 29). Moreover, if you use an off-the-shelf tokeniser, you will find out soon that it makes mistakes—and correcting those would break any annotations done at the word token level. More likely, during your annotation project, you will find the need to change the tokenisation guidelines to deal properly with multi-word expressions (Section 22). In addition, punctuation and spacing carry information that could be useful for deep learning approaches, and their original appearance should therefore in one way or another should be preserved. An example: a "New York-based" company could be a new

company based in York, but the other interpretation is more likely. In an NLP-processing pipeline, it is too late for syntax to fix this in a compositional way—the tokenisation needs to be improved.

5 Use stand-off annotation

Stand-off annotation is a no-brainer as it offers a lot more flexibility. It enables keeping annotations separate from the original raw text, where ideally each annotation layer has its own file (Ide and Romary, 2006; Pustejovsky and Stubbs, 2012). It is best executed with respect to the character offsets of the raw texts in the corpus (Section 4). A JSON or XML-based annotation file can always be generated from this, should the demand be there. Stand-off annotation is in particular advantageous in a setting where several layers of annotation interact with each other (typically in a pipeline architecture). This was extremely helpful in the GMB (Bos et al., 2017) where the document segmentation (sentence and word boundaries) got improved several times during the project, without having any negative effect on annotation occurring later in the semantic processing pipeline (such as part-of-speech tagging and named entity recognition).

6 Consider manual annotation

Several meaning banks are created with the help of a grammar. The best example here is the sophisticated English Resource Grammar (Flickinger, 2000, 2011) used to produce the treebanks, Redwoods (Oepen et al., 2004) and DeepBank (Flickinger et al., 2012), annotated with English Resource Semantics (ERS) in a compositional way, by letting the annotator pick the correct or most plausible analysis. Similarly, the meaning representations in the GMB are system-produced and partially hand-corrected (Bos et al., 2017), using a CCG parser (Clark and Curran, 2004). Likewise, the meaning representations in the PMB are system-produced with the help of a CCG parser (Lewis and Steedman, 2014) and some of it is completely hand-corrected. In contrast, the meaning representations of the AMR Bank are completely manually manufactured—without the aid of a grammar—with the help of an annotation interface and an extensive manual (Banarescu et al., 2013). Bender et al. (2015) argue that grammar-based meaning banking requires less annotation guidelines, that it provides more consistent anal-

---

[1] Freezing the corpora already fixes certain data statements for your meaning bank, like curation rationale, language variety, and text characteristics. Communicating these data statements is important from an application point of view (Bender and Friedman, 2018).

yses, and that it is more scalable. The downside of grammar-based annotation is that several compound expressions are not always compositional (negative and modal concord, postnominal genitives ("of John's"), odd punctuation conventions, idioms), and that grammars with high recall and precision are costly to produce (the impressive English Resource Grammar took about several years to develop, but it is restricted to just one language).

7 Make a friendly annotation interface

Annotation can be fun (especially if gamification is applied, see Section 9), but it can also be tedious. A good interface helps the annotator to make high-quality annotations, to work efficiently, and to be able to focus on particular linguistic phenomena. An annotation interface should be web-based (i.e., any browser should support it), simple to use, and personalised.[2] The latter grants control over annotations of particular users. The "Explorer" (Basile et al., 2012a) introduced in the GMB and later further developed in the PMB, has various search abilities (searches for phrases, regular expressions, and annotation labels), a statistics page, a newsfeed, and a user-friendly way to classify annotations as "gold standard". The inclusion of a "sanity checker" helps to identify annotation mistakes, in particular if there are several annotation layers with dependencies. It is also a good idea to hook the annotation interface up with a professional issue reporting system.

8 Include an issue reporting system

Annotators will sooner or later raise issues, have questions about the annotation scheme, or find bugs in the processing pipeline. This is valuable information for the annotation project and should not get lost. The proper way to deal with this is to include a sophisticated bug reporting system in the annotation interface. For the GMB (Bos et al., 2017) and the PMB (Abzianidze et al., 2017), the Mantis Bug Tracker[3] was incorporated inside the Explorer (Basile et al., 2012a). Besides Mantis there are many other free and open source web-based bug tracking systems available. A bug tracker enables one to categorize issues, assign them to team members, have dedicated discussion thread for each issue, and keep track of all

---

improvements made in a certain time span (useful for the documentation in data releases).

9 Be careful with the crowd

Following the idea of Phrase Detectives (Chamberlain et al., 2008), in the GMB (Bos et al., 2017) a game with a purpose (GWAP) was introduced to annotate parts of speech, antecedents of pronouns, noun compound relations (Bos and Nissim, 2015), and word senses (Venhuizen et al., 2013). The quality of annotations harvested from gamification was generally high, but the amount of annotations relatively low—it would literally take years to annotate the entire GMB corpus. An additional problem with GWAPs is recruiting new players: most players play the game only once, and attempts to make the game addictive could be irresponsible (Andrade F.R.H., 2016). The alternative, engaging people by financially awarding them via crowdsourcing platforms such as Mechanical Turk or Figure Eight, solves the quantity problem (Pustejovsky and Stubbs, 2012), but introduces other issues including the question what a proper wage would be (Fort et al., 2011) and dealing with tricksters and cheaters (Buchholz and Latorre, 2011).

10 Profit from lexicalised grammars

A lexicalised grammar gives an advantage in annotating syntactic structure. In case of the compositional semantics, this also leads to automatic construction of the phrasal semantics. This is because, in a lexicalised grammar, most of the grammar work is done in the lexicon (there is only a dozen general grammar rules), and annotation is just a matter of giving the right information to a word (rather than selecting the correct interpretation from a possibly large set of parse trees). In the PMB a lexicalised grammar is used: Combinatory Categorial Grammar (CCG, Steedman 2001), and the core annotation layers for each word token are a CCG category, a semantic tag (Abzianidze and Bos, 2017), a lemma, and a word sense. Annotating thematic roles (Section 18) is also convenient in a lexicalised grammar environment (Bos et al., 2012). Finally, a lexicalised grammar coupled with compositional semantics facilitates annotation projection for meaning preserving translations and opens the door to multilingual meaning banking (Section 29). Projection of meaning representation from one sentence to another is reduced to word alignment and word-level annotation transfer. This type of projection is underlying the idea of moving from the monolingual GMB to the multilingual PMB.

11 Try to use language-neutral tools

Whenever possible, in machine-assisted annotation, get language technology components that are not tailored to specific languages, because this increases portability of meaning processing components to other languages (Section 29). The statistical tokeniser (for word and sentence segmentation) used in the PMB is Elephant (Evang et al., 2013). The current efforts in multi-lingual POS-tagging, semantic tagging (Abzianidze and Bos, 2017) and dependency parsing are promising (White et al., 2016). In the PMB a categorial grammar is used to cover four languages (English, Dutch, German, and Italian), using the same parser and grammar, but with language-specific statistical models trained for the EasyCCG parser (Lewis and Steedman, 2014). Related are grammatical frameworks designed for parallel grammar writing (Ranta, 2011; Bender et al., 2010).

12 Apply normalisation to symbols

Normalising the format of non-logical symbols (the predicates and individual constants, as opposed to logical symbols such as negation and conjunction) in meaning representations decreases the need for awkward background knowledge rules that would otherwise be needed to predict correct entailments. Normalisation (van der Goot, 2019) can be applied to date expressions (e.g., the 24th of February 2010 vs. 24-02-2010 or dozens of variations on these), time expressions (2pm, 14:00, two o'clock), and numerical expressions (twenty-four, 24, vierundzwanzig; three thousand, 3,000, 3000, 3 000). Compositional attempts to any of the above mentioned classes of expressions are highly ambitious and not recommended. Take, for instance, the Dutch clock time expression "twee voor half vier", which denotes 03:28 (or 15:28)—how would you derive this compositionally in a computational straightforward way? Other normalisations for consideration are expansion of abbreviations to their full forms, lowercasing proper names, units of measurement, and scores of sports games. To promote inter-operability between annotated corpora, it is a good idea to check whether any standards are proposed for normalisation (Pustejovsky and Stubbs,

2012).

13 Limit underspecification

Underspecification is a technique with the aim to free the semantic interpretation component from a disambiguation burden (Reyle, 1993; Bos, 1996; Copestake et al., 2005). In syntactic treebanks, however, the driving force has been to assign the most plausible parse tree to a sentence. This makes sense for the task of statistical (syntactic) parsing. The same applies to (statistical) semantic parsing: a corpus with the most likely interpretation for sentences is required. Moreover, it is not straightforward to draw correct inferences with underspecified meaning representations (Reyle, 1995). So it makes sense, at least from the perspective of semantic annotation, to produce the most plausible interpretation for a given sentence. Consider the following examples. A "sleeping bag" could be a bag that is asleep, but it is very unlikely (even in a Harry Potter setting), so should be annotated as a bag designed to be slept in. In the sentence "Tom kissed his mother", the possessive pronoun could refer to a third party, but by far the most likely interpretation is that Tom's mother is kissed by Tom, and that reading should be reflected in the annotation. Genuine scope ambiguities are relatively rare in ordinary text, and it is questionable whether the representational overhead of underspecified scope is worth the effort given the low frequency of the phenomenon. Nonetheless, resolving ambiguities is sometimes hard, in particular for sentences in isolation. What is plausible for one annotator is implausible for another. Finally, one needs to be careful, as annotation guidelines that give preference for one particular reading (based on statistical plausbility) have the danger of introducing or even amplifying bias.

14 Beware of annotation bias

Assigning the most likely interpretation to a sentence can also give an unfair balance to stereotypes. In the PMB, gender of personal proper names are annotated. In many cases this is a straightforward exercise. But there are sometimes cases where the gender of a person is not known. The disturbing distribution of male versus female pronouns (or titles) strongly suggests that a female is the least likely choice (Webster et al., 2018). But following this statistical suggestion only causes greater divide. The PMB annotation guidelines for choosing word senses (Secion 15) are such that when it is unclear what sense to pick, the higher sense (thus, the most frequent one), must be selected. This is bad, because systems for word sense disambiguation already show a tendency towards assigning the most frequent sense (Postma et al., 2016). More efforts are needed to reduce bias (Zhao et al., 2017).

15   Use existing resources for word senses

The predicate symbols that one finds in meaning representation are usually based on word lemmas. But words have no interpretation, and a link to concepts in an existing ontology (Lenat, 1995; Navigli and Ponzetto, 2012) is something that is needed to make the non-logical symbols in meaning representations interpretable. In the AMR Bank, verbs are disambiguated by OntoNotes senses (Banarescu et al., 2013). In the PMB, nouns, verbs, adjectives and adverbs are labelled with the senses of (English) WordNet (Fellbaum, 1998). Picking the right sense is sometimes hard for annotators, sometimes because there is too little context, but also because the definitions of fine-grained senses are sometimes hard to distinguish from each other (Lopez de Lacalle and Agirre, 2015). Annotation guidelines are needed for ambiguous cases where syntax doesn't help to disambiguate: "Swimming is great fun." (`swimming.n.01` or perhaps `swim.v.01`?), "Her words were emphasized." (`emphasized.a.01` or `emphasize.v.02`?). WordNet's coverage is impressive and substantial, but obviously not all words are listed (example: names of products used as nouns) and sometimes it is inconsistent (for instance, "apple juice" is in WordNet, but "cherry juice" is not). Many Word-Nets exists for languages other than English (Navigli and Ponzetto, 2012; Bond and Foster, 2013).

16   Apply symbol grounding

Symbol grounding helps to connect abstract representations of meaning with objects in the real world or to unambiguous descriptions of concepts or entities. This happens on the conceptual level with mapping words to WordNet synsets or to a well-defined inventory of relations. Princeton WordNet (Fellbaum, 1998) lists several instances of famous persons but obviously the list is incomplete. The AMR Bank includes links from named entities to wikipedia pages, but obviously not every named entity has a wikipedia entry. To our knowledge, no other meaning banks apply wikification. Other interesting applications for symbol grounding are GPS coordinates for toponyms (Leidner, 2008), visualisation of concepts or actions (Navigli and Ponzetto, 2012), or creating timelines (Bamman and Smith, 2014).

17   Adopt neo-Davidsonian events

It seems that in most (if not all) semantically annotated corpora a neo-Davidsonian event semantics is adopted. This means that every event introduces its own entity as a variable, and this variable can be used to connect the event to its thematic roles. In the original Davidsonian approach, an event variable was simply added to the predicate introduced by the verb (Davidson, 1967; Kamp and Reyle, 1993) as a way to add modifiers (e.g., moving from `eat(x,y)` to `eat(e,x,y)` for a transitive use of *to eat*). In most modern meaning representations thematic roles are introduced to reduce the number of arguments of verbal predicates to one, also known as the neo-Davidsonian tradition (Parsons, 1990) (e.g., moving from `eat(e,x,y)` to `eat(e) AGENT(e,x) PATIENT(e,y)`). A direct consequence of a neo-Davidsonion design is the need for an inventory of thematic roles. But there is also an alternative, which is given a fixed arity to event predicates, of which some of them may be unused (Hobbs, 1991) when the context does not provide this information (e.g., for the intransive usage of *to eat*, still maintain `eat(e,x,y)` where y is left unspecified).

18   Use existing role labelling inventories

A neo-Davidsonian approach presupposes a dictionary of thematic (or semantic) role names. There are three popular sets available: PropBank, VerbNet, and FrameNet. PropBank (Palmer et al., 2005) proposes a set of just six summarising roles: ARG0 (Agent), ARG1 (Patient), ARG2 (Instrument, Benefactive, Attribute), ARG3 (Starting Point), ARG4 (Ending Point), ARGM (Modifier). The interpretation of these roles are in many cases specific to the event in which they participate. The AMR Bank adopts these PropBank roles (Banarescu et al., 2013). VerbNet has a set of about 25 thematic roles independently defined from the verb classes (Kipper et al., 2008). A few examples are: Agent, Patient, Theme, Instrument, Experiencer, Stimulus, Attribute, Value, Location, Destination, Source, Result, and Material. The PMB adopts the thematic roles of VerbNet. FrameNet is organised quite differently. Its starting point is not rooted in linguistics, but rather in real-world situations, classified as frames (Baker et al., 1998). Frames have frame elements that can be realised by linguistic expressions, and they correspond to the PropBank and VerbNet roles. There are more than a thousand different frames, and each frame has its own specific role set (frame elements). For instance, the Buy-Commerce frame has roles Buyer, Goods, Seller, Money, and so on. There are also recent proposals for comprehensive inventories for roles introduced by prepositional and possessive constructions (Schneider et al., 2018). In the PMB, we employ a unified inventory of thematic roles (an extension of the VerbNet roles) that is applicable to verbs, adjectives, prepositions, possessives or noun modifiers.

19 Treat agent nouns differently

Agent and recipient nouns (nouns that denote persons performing or receiving some action, such as employee, victim, teacher, mother, cyclist, victim) are intrinsically relational (Booij, 1986). Modelling them like ordinary nouns, i.e., as one-place predicates, can give rise to contradictions for any individual that has been assigned more than one role, because while you want to be able to state that a violin player is not the same thing as a mother, a person could perfectly be a mother and a violin player at the same time. Moreover, a fast cyclist could be a slow driver. Incorrect modeling can furthermore lead to over-generation of some unmanifested relations (for instance, if Butch is Vincent's boss and Mia's husband, a too simple model would predict that Butch is also Vincent's husband and Mia's boss. In the AMR Bank (Banarescu et al., 2013) agent nouns are decomposed (e.g., an "investor" is a person that invests). In the PMB agent nouns introduce a mirror entity (e.g. an "investor" is a person with the role of investor).

20 Beware of geopolitical entities

Names used to refer to geopolitical entities (GPEs) are a real pain in the neck for semantic annotators. How many times did we change the annotation guidelines for these annoying names! The problem is that expressions like "New York", "Italy", or "Africa" can refer to locations, their govern-ments, sport squads that represent them, or the people that live there (and in some case to multiple aspects at the same time, as in "Italy produces better wine than France"). This instance of systematic polysemy manifests itself for all classes of GPE, including continents, countries, states, provinces, cities, and so on. Detailed instructions for annotating GPEs can be found in the ACE annotation guidelines (Doddington et al., 2004).

21 Give scope to negation

Sentence meaning is about assigning truth conditions to propositions (Section 23). Negation plays a crucial role here—in fact, the core of semantics is about negation, identifying whether a statement is true of false. Negation is a semantic phenomenon that requires scope, in other words, it cannot be modelled by simply applying it as a property of an entity. It should be clear—explicit or implicit—what the scope of any negation operator is, i.e. the parts of the meaning representation that are negated. The GMB, PMB and Deep-Bank (Flickinger et al., 2012) assign proper scope to negation (the latter with the help of underspecification). In AMR Bank negation is modelled with the help of a relation, and this doesn't always get the required interpretation (Bos, 2016). Negation can be tricky: negation affixes (Section 23) require special care, negative concord (Section 6) and neg raising (Liu et al., 2018) are challenges for compositional approaches to meaning construction.

22 Pay attention to compound words

In the GMB (Bos et al., 2017) we largely ignored multi-word expressions (MWEs), believing that compositionality would eventually do away with it. Except it doesn't. MWEs come in various forms, and require various treatments (Sag et al., 2002). Think about proper names (names of persons, companies, locations, events), titles and labels (of people, of books, chapters, of songs), compounds, phrasal verbs, particle verbs, fixed phrases, and idioms. Consider for instance "North and South Dakota", it is quite a challenge to derive the representation state(x) & name(x,'North-Dakota') in a compositional way. And many compounds are not compositional ("peanut butter" is not butter, and "athlete's foot" is not a body part but a nasty infection). It is hard to decide where to draw the line between a compositional and non-compositional approach to multiword expressions. Even though "red wine" is written in English with two words, in German it is written in one word ("rotwein"). WordNet (Fellbaum, 1998) lists many multi-word expressions and could be used as a resource to decide whether a compounds is analysed compositionally or not. In the PMB, titles of songs or other artistic works are treated as a single token (because they are proper names), which works fine for "Jingle Bells" but becomes a bit awkward and uncomfortable with longer titles such as Lennon and McCartney's "Lucy in the Sky with Diamonds", or Pink Floyds's "Several Species of Small Furry Animals Gathered Together in a Cave and Grooving With A Pict". It is quite unfair and unrealistic to expect the tokeniser to recognise this as a multi-word expression. The alternative, applying some reinterpretation after having first carried out a compositional analysis, puts a heavier burden on the syntax-semantics interface. The bottom line is that MWEs form a wild bunch of expressions for which a general modelling strategy covering all types does not seem to exist. There also seems to be a connection with quotation (Maier, 2014).

23 Use inference tests in design

The driving force to motivate how to shape or what to include in a meaning representation should be textual entailment or contradiction checks (this is a practice borrowed from formal semantics). For instance, when designing a meaning representation for adjectives, the meaning for "ten-year-old boy" should not imply that the boy in question is old. Likewise, the meaning representation for "unhappy" should not be the same as that for "not happy", because the meanings of these expressions are not equivalent (as "Bob is not happy" doesn't entail "Bob's unhappy"—Bob can be both not happy and not unhappy—even though the entailment holds in the reverse direction: if Bob is unhappy, he is not happy). Similarly, the meaning representation for "Bologna is the cultural capital of Italy" should not lead to the incorrect inference that "Bologna is the capital of Italy". In addition, or as alternative to inference checks, is applying the method of model-theoretic interpretation (Blackburn and Bos, 2005) when designing meaning representations. It should be clear what a representation actually means, in other words, under which conditions it is true or false. A formal way of defining this is via models of situation, and

a satisfaction definition that tells us, given a certain situation, whether a statement holds or doesn't. This method was introduced by the logician Tarski (Tarski and Vaught, 1956). It bears similarities with posing a query to a relational database. The method forces you to make a strict distinction between logical (negation, disjunction, equality) and non-logical symbols (the predicates and individual constants in your meaning representation).

24 Divide and conquer

Do not try to do model all semantic phenomena the first time around. There are just too many. Some good candidates to put on hold are plurals, tense, aspect, focus, presupposition (see Section 25), and generics (more in Section 27), because a proper treatment of these phenomena requires a lot more than a basic predicate-argument structure. A strict formalisation of plurals quickly leads to complicated representations (Kamp and Reyle, 1993), leading to compromising approximations in the AMR Bank (Banarescu et al., 2013) or PMB (Abzianidze et al., 2017). In the GMB (Bos et al., 2017) and the AMR Bank tense is simply ignored. Annotating aspect is complex—for instance, the use of the perfect differs enormously even between closely related languages such as English, Dutch, and Italian (van der Klis et al., 2017). These complications lead to a simple annotation model in the PMB where tense is reduced to a manageable set of three tenses: past, present and future. There are, therefore, a lot of interesting problems left for the second round of semantic annotation!

25 Put complex presuppositions on hold

Presuppositions are propositions that are taken for granted. Several natural language expressions introduce presuppositions. These expressions are called presuppositions triggers. (For instance, "Mary left, too." presupposes that someone else besides Mary left. Here "too" is the trigger of this presupposition.) There are many different kinds of triggers, and many do not contribute to the meaning of the sentence, but rather put constraints on the context. The question, then, is what to do with them in a meaning banking project. Some classes of presupposition triggers, referring expressions including proper names, possessive phrases, and definite descriptions, can be treated in a similar way as pronouns, as is done in the GMB and the PMB, following Bos (2003). Yet there are other classes of triggers that are notoriously hard to represent, because they require some "copying" of large pieces of meaning representation, interact with focus, and require non-trivial semantic composition methods. To these belong implicative verbs (manage), focusing adverbs (only, just), and repetition particles (again, still, yet, another). For instance, although in the PMB a sentence like "The crowd applauded again." is the presupposition trigger, "again" is semantically tagged as a repetition trigger, for now it doesn't perform any costly operations on the actual meaning representation. The first alternative, a meaning representation with two different applauding events that are temporally related, is complicated to construct. The second alternative, introducing "again" as a predicate, doesn't make sense semantically (what is the meaning of "again"?), or as an operator (again, how will it be defined logically?) isn't attractive either. There are, currently no good ways to deal with complex presupposition triggers, and more research is needed here turning formal ideas (Kamp and Rossdeutscher, 2009) into practical solutions.

26 Respect elliptical expressions

They are invisible, but omnipresent: elliptical expressions. Comparative ellipsis is present in many languages ("My hair is longer than Tom's"). In English, verb phrase ellipsis occurs ("Tom eats asparagus, but his brother doesn't."), which is well studied (Dalrymple et al., 1991), and annotated corpora exist as well (Bos and Spenader, 2011). Dutch and German exhibit a large variety of gapping cases ("Tom isst Spargel, aber sein Bruder nicht."). Italian is a language with pro-drop ("Ho fame", i.e., (I) am hungry). Ellipsis requires a dedicated component in a pipeline architecture. In the PMB the inclusion of an ellipsis layer has been postponed for the benefit of other components, features, and efforts. As a consequence, a growing number of documents cannot be added to the gold set because there isn't an adequate way of dealing with a missing pronoun, an odd comparison expression, or an elided verb phrase.

27 Think about generics

Generic statements and habituals are hard to model straightforwardly in first-order logic (Carlson, 1977). The sentence "a lion is strong" or "a dog has four legs" is not about a particular lion or dog, nor is it about all dogs or lions. The inventor of "the typewriter" was not the inventor of a particular typewriter, but of the typewriter concept in general. Such generic concepts are also known as *kinds* in the literature (Reiter and Frank, 2010). It is not impossible to approximate this in first-order logic, but it requires an ontological distinction between entities denoting individuals and entities denoting concepts (kinds). A further question is how tense should be annotated in habitual sentences, as in "Jane used to swim every day" (in some period in the past, Jane swam every day) or "Jane swims every day" (in the current period, Jane swims every day). To our knowledge, none of the existing meaning banks have a satisfactory treatment of generics, even though techniques have been proposed to detect generics (Reiter and Frank, 2010; Friedrich and Pinkal, 2015). Recent proposals try to change this situation (Donatelli et al., 2018).

28 Don't try to be clever

The English verb "to be" (and its counterpart in other Germanic languages) is a semantic nuisance. When used as an auxiliary verb—including predicative usages of adjectives—there isn't much to worry about it, as it only semantically contributes tense information. However, when used as a copula it can express identity, locative information, or predications involving nouns. From a logical perspective, it might seem attractive to use equality in these cases and interpret "to be" logically rather than lexically, (Blackburn and Bos, 2005), but this makes it impossible to include tense information, unless equality is (non-standardly) viewed as a three-place relation. There are various senses for "be" in WordNet, and it makes pragmatically sense to use these: "This is a good idea" (sense 1), "John is the teacher" (sense 2), "the book is on the table" (sense 3), and so on. A similar story can be told for "to have" in expressions like "Mary has a son", where the first attempt in the PMB was to analyse "to have" in such possessive constructions as logical, i.e. only introducing tense information, and coerce the relational noun "son" into a possessive interpretation. This was soon abandoned due to complications in composition.

29 Don't focus on just one language

Most meaning banks consider just one language, and usually this is English. This is understandable, as English is the current scientific language, but it is also risky, because when designing meaning representation decisions could be made that work for English but not for other languages. Phenomena such as definite descriptions, ellipsis, possessives, aspect, and gender, behave even in closely related languages quite differently from each other. Dealing with multiple languages is, without any doubt, harder, but if one takes several languages into account at the same time the result is more likely to be more language-neutral meaning representations. And that's what meanings should be, they are abstract objects, independent of the language used to expressed them. Of course, there are concepts that can be expressed in certain languages with a single word that other languages are not capable of, but the core of meaning representations should be agnostic to the source language. A good starting point is to work with typologically-related languages. An efficient annotation technique to cover multiple languages is *annotation projection* (Evang and Bos, 2016; Liu et al., 2018). This requires a parallel corpus and automatic word alignment, and existing semantic annotations for at least one language.

30 Measure meaning discrepancies

A large part of the users of semantically annotated corpora are from the semantic parsing area, and they need to be able to measure and quantify their output with respect to gold standard meanings. The currently accepted methods are based on precision and recall on the components of the meaning representation by converting them to triples or clauses (Allen et al., 2008; Dridan and Oepen, 2011; Cai and Knight, 2013; Van Noord et al., 2018; Kim and Schubert, 2019). In a parallel corpus setting, such evaluation measures can also be used to compare the meaning representation of a source text and its translation (Saphra and Lopez, 2015). This is done in the PMB, where a non-perfect meaning match between source and target helps the annotator to identify possible culprits. It is important to note that most of these matching techniques check for syntactic equivalence, and don't take semantic equivalence into account—the same meaning could be expressed by syntactically different representations. The approach by Van Noord et al. (2018) applies normalisation steps for word senses to make matching more semantic.

Acknowledgments

We would like to thank the two anonymous reviewers for their comments—they helped to improve this paper considerably. Reviewer 1 gave us valuable pointers to the literature that we missed, and spotted many unclear and ambiguous formulations. Reviewer 2 was disappointed by the first version of this paper— we hope s/he likes this improved version better. This work was funded by the NWO-VICI grant Lost in Translation Found in Meaning (288-89-003).

References

Omri Abend and Ari Rappoport. 2013. Universal conceptual cognitive annotation (ucca). In *Proceedings of the 51st Annual Meeting of the Association for Computational Linguistics (Volume 1: Long Papers)*, pages 228–238, Sofia, Bulgaria. Association for Computational Linguistics.

Omri Abend and Ari Rappoport. 2017. The state of the art in semantic representation. In *Proceedings of the 55th Annual Meeting of the Association for Computational Linguistics (Volume 1: Long Papers)*, pages 77–89, Vancouver, Canada. Association for Computational Linguistics.

Lasha Abzianidze, Johannes Bjerva, Kilian Evang, Hessel Haagsma, Rik van Noord, Pierre Ludmann, Duc-Duy Nguyen, and Johan Bos. 2017. The parallel meaning bank: Towards a multilingual corpus of translations annotated with compositional meaning representations. In *Proceedings of the 15th Conference of the European Chapter of the Association for Computational Linguistics*, pages 242–247, Valencia, Spain.

Lasha Abzianidze and Johan Bos. 2017. Towards universal semantic tagging. In *Proceedings of the 12th International Conference on Computational Semantics (IWCS 2017) – Short Papers*, pages 1–6, Montpellier, France.

James F. Allen, Mary Swift, and Will de Beaumont. 2008. Deep Semantic Analysis of Text. In Johan Bos and Rodolfo Delmonte, editors, *Semantics in Text Processing. STEP 2008 Conference Proceedings*, volume 1 of *Research in Computational Semantics*, pages 343–354. College Publications.

Isotani S. Andrade F.R.H., Mizoguchi R. 2016. The bright and dark sides of gamification. *Intelligent Tutoring Systems. ITS 2016. Lecture Notes in Computer Science*, 9684.

Collin F. Baker, Charles J. Fillmore, and John B. Lowe. 1998. The Berkeley FrameNet project. In *36th Annual Meeting of the Association for Computational Linguistics and 17th International Conference on*

Computational Linguistics. Proceedings of the Conference, pages 86–90, Université de Montréal, Montreal, Quebec, Canada.

David Bamman and Noah A. Smith. 2014. Unsupervised discovery of biographical structure from text. *Transactions of the Association for Computational Linguistics*, 2:363–376.

Laura Banarescu, Claire Bonial, Shu Cai, Madalina Georgescu, Kira Griffitt, Ulf Hermjakob, Kevin Knight, Philipp Koehn, Martha Palmer, and Nathan Schneider. 2013. Abstract Meaning Representation for Sembanking. In *Proceedings of the 7th Linguistic Annotation Workshop and Interoperability with Discourse*, pages 178–186, Sofia, Bulgaria.

Valerio Basile, Johan Bos, Kilian Evang, and Noortje Venhuizen. 2012a. A platform for collaborative semantic annotation. In *Proceedings of the Demonstrations at the 13th Conference of the European Chapter of the Association for Computational Linguistics (EACL)*, pages 92–96, Avignon, France.

Valerio Basile, Johan Bos, Kilian Evang, and Noortje Joost Venhuizen. 2012b. Developing a large semantically annotated corpus. In *Proceedings of the Eighth International Conference on Language Resources and Evaluation (LREC'12)*, Istanbul, Turkey. European Language Resources Association (ELRA).

Emily M. Bender. 2013. *Linguistic Fundamentals for Natural Language Processing: 100 Essentials from Morphology and Syntax*. Synthesis Lectures on Human Language Technologies. Morgan & Claypool Publishers.

Emily M. Bender, Scott Drellishak, Antske Fokkens, Laurie Poulson, and Safiyyah Saleem. 2010. Grammar customization. *Research on Language & Computation*, 8(1):23–72.

Emily M. Bender, Dan Flickinger, Stephan Oepen, Woodley Packard, and Ann Copestake. 2015. Layers of interpretation: On grammar and compositionality. In *Proceedings of the 11th International Conference on Computational Semantics*, pages 239–249, London, UK. Association for Computational Linguistics.

Emily M. Bender and Batya Friedman. 2018. Data statements for natural language processing: Toward mitigating system bias and enabling better science. *Transactions of the Association for Computational Linguistics*, 6:587–604.

Chris Biemann, Kalina Bontcheva, Richard Eckart de Castilho, Iryna Gurevych, and Seid Muhie Yimam. 2017. Collaborative web-based tools for multi-layer text annotation. In Nancy Ide and James Pustejovsky, editors, *The Handbook of Linguistic Annotation*, Text, Speech, and Technology book series, pages 229–256. Springer Netherlands.

P. Blackburn and J. Bos. 2005. *Representation and Inference for Natural Language. A First Course in Computational Semantics*. CSLI.

Francis Bond and Ryan Foster. 2013. Linking and extending an open multilingual Wordnet. In *Proceedings of the 51st Annual Meeting of the Association for Computational Linguistics (Volume 1: Long Papers)*, pages 1352–1362, Sofia, Bulgaria. Association for Computational Linguistics.

Geert Booij. 1986. Form and meaning in morphology; the case of dutch agent nouns. *Linguistics*, 24:503–518.

J. Bos. 2003. Implementing the Binding and Accommodation Theory for Anaphora Resolution and Presupposition Projection. *Computational Linguistics*, 29(2):179–210.

Johan Bos. 1996. Predicate Logic Unplugged. In *Proceedings of the Tenth Amsterdam Colloquium*, pages 133–143, ILLC/Dept. of Philosophy, University of Amsterdam.

Johan Bos. 2016. Expressive power of abstract meaning representations. *Computational Linguistics*, 42(3):527–535.

Johan Bos, Valerio Basile, Kilian Evang, Noortje Venhuizen, and Johannes Bjerva. 2017. The Groningen Meaning Bank. In Nancy Ide and James Pustejovsky, editors, *Handbook of Linguistic Annotation*, volume 2, pages 463–496. Springer.

Johan Bos, Kilian Evang, and Malvina Nissim. 2012. Annotating semantic roles in a lexicalised grammar environment. In *Proceedings of the Eighth Joint ACL-ISO Workshop on Interoperable Semantic Annotation (ISA-8)*, pages 9–12, Pisa, Italy.

Johan Bos and Malvina Nissim. 2015. Uncovering noun-noun compound relations by gamification. In *Proceedings of the 20th Nordic Conference of Computational Linguistics*.

Johan Bos and Jennifer Spenader. 2011. An annotated corpus for the analysis of vp ellipsis. *Language Resources and Evaluation*, 45(4):463–494.

Sabine Buchholz and Javier Latorre. 2011. Crowdsourcing preference tests, and how to detect cheating. In *INTERSPEECH-2011*, pages 3053–3056.

Alistair Butler and Kei Yoshimoto. 2012. Banking meaning representations from treebanks. *Linguistic Issues in Language Technology*, 7(6):1–22.

Shu Cai and Kevin Knight. 2013. Smatch: an evaluation metric for semantic feature structures. In *Proceedings of the 51st Annual Meeting of the Association for Computational Linguistics (Volume 2: Short Papers)*, pages 748–752, Sofia, Bulgaria. Association for Computational Linguistics.

Gregory Norman Carlson. 1977. *Reference to Kinds in English*. Ph.D. thesis, University of Massachusetts.

Richard Eckart de Castilho, Giulia Dore, Thomas Margoni, Penny Labropoulou, and Iryna Gurevych. 2018. A legal perspective on training models for natural language processing. In *Proceedings of the 11th Language Resources and Evaluation Conference*, Miyazaki, Japan. European Language Resource Association.

John Chamberlain, Massimo Poesio, and Udo Kruschwitz. 2008. Addressing the Resource Bottleneck to Create Large-Scale Annotated Texts. In Johan Bos and Rodolfo Delmonte, editors, *Semantics in Text Processing. STEP 2008 Conference Proceedings*, volume 1 of *Research in Computational Semantics*, pages 375–380. College Publications.

Stephen Clark and James R. Curran. 2004. Parsing the WSJ using CCG and Log-Linear Models. In *Proceedings of the 42nd Annual Meeting of the Association for Computational Linguistics (ACL '04)*, pages 104–111, Barcelona, Spain.

Ann Copestake, Dan Flickinger, Ivan Sag, and Carl Pollard. 2005. Minimal recursion semantics: An introduction. *Journal of Research on Language and Computation*, 3(2–3):281–332.

Mary Dalrymple, Stuart M. Shieber, and Fernando C.N. Pereira. 1991. Ellipsis and Higher-Order Unification. *Linguistics and Philosophy*, 14:399–452.

Donald Davidson. 1967. The logical form of action sentences. In Nicholas Rescher, editor, *The Logic of Decision and Action*, pages 81–95. University of Pittsburgh Press.

George Doddington, Alexis Mitchell, Mark Przybocki, Lance Ramshaw, Stephanie Strassel, and Ralph Weischedel. 2004. The automatic content extraction (ACE) program – tasks, data, and evaluation. In *Proceedings of the Fourth International Conference on Language Resources and Evaluation (LREC'04)*, Lisbon, Portugal. European Language Resources Association (ELRA).

Lucia Donatelli, Michael Regan, William Croft, and Nathan Schneider. 2018. Annotation of tense and aspect semantics for sentential AMR. In *Proceedings of the Joint Workshop on Linguistic Annotation, Multiword Expressions and Constructions (LAW-MWE-CxG-2018)*, pages 96–108, Santa Fe, New Mexico, USA. Association for Computational Linguistics.

Rebecca Dridan and Stephan Oepen. 2011. Parser evaluation using elementary dependency matching. In *Proceedings of the 12th International Conference on Parsing Technologies*, pages 225–230, Dublin, Ireland. Association for Computational Linguistics.

Kilian Evang, Valerio Basile, Grzegorz Chrupała, and Johan Bos. 2013. Elephant: Sequence labeling for word and sentence segmentation. In *Proceedings of the 2013 Conference on Empirical Methods in Natural Language Processing*, pages 1422–1426.

Kilian Evang and Johan Bos. 2016. Cross-lingual learning of an open-domain semantic parser. In *Proceedings of COLING 2016, the 26th International Conference on Computational Linguistics*, pages 579–588, Osaka, Japan.

Christiane Fellbaum, editor. 1998. *WordNet. An Electronic Lexical Database*. The MIT Press.

Dan Flickinger. 2000. On building a more efficient grammar by exploiting types. *Natural Language Engineering*, 6(1):15–28.

Dan Flickinger. 2011. Accuracy vs. robustness in grammar engineering. In Emily M. Bender and Jennifer E. Arnold, editors, *Language from a cognitive perspective: Grammar, usage, and processing*, pages 31–50. CSLI Publications.

Daniel Flickinger, Yi Zhang, and Valia Kordoni. 2012. Deepbank: A dynamically annotated treebank of the wall street journal. In *Proceedings of the Eleventh International Workshop on Treebanks and Linguistic Theories*, pages 85–96. Edições Colibri.

Karën Fort, Gilles Adda, and K. Bretonnel Cohen. 2011. Last words: Amazon mechanical turk: Gold mine or coal mine? *Computational Linguistics*, 37(2):413–420.

Annemarie Friedrich and Manfred Pinkal. 2015. Discourse-sensitive automatic identification of generic expressions. In *Proceedings of the 53rd Annual Meeting of the Association for Computational Linguistics and the 7th International Joint Conference on Natural Language Processing (Volume 1: Long Papers)*, pages 1272–1281, Beijing, China. Association for Computational Linguistics.

Jan Hajič, Eva Hajičová, Marie Mikulová, and Jiří Mírovský. 2017. *Prague Dependency Treebank*. Springer Verlag, Berlin, Germany.

Jerry R. Hobbs. 1991. SRI international's TACITUS system: MUC-3 test results and analysis. In *Proceedings of the 3rd Conference on Message Understanding, MUC 1991, San Diego, California, USA, May 21-23, 1991*, pages 105–107.

Nancy Ide, Christiane Fellbaum, Collin Baker, and Rebecca Passonneau. 2010. The manually annotated sub-corpus: a community resource for and by the people. In *Proceedings of the ACL 2010 Conference Short Papers*, pages 68–73, Stroudsburg, PA, USA.

Nancy Ide and Laurent Romary. 2006. Representing linguistic corpora and their annotations. In *Proceedings of the Fifth International Conference on Language Resources and Evaluation (LREC'06)*, Genoa, Italy. European Language Resources Association (ELRA).

Hans Kamp and Uwe Reyle. 1993. *From Discourse to Logic; An Introduction to Modeltheoretic Semantics of Natural Language, Formal Logic and DRT*. Kluwer, Dordrecht.

Hans Kamp and Antje Rossdeutscher. 2009. Drs construction and lexically driven inferences. *Theoretical Linguistics*, 20(2-3):165–236.

Gene Louis Kim and Lenhart Schubert. 2019. A type-coherent, expressive representation as an initial step to language understanding. *CoRR*.

Karin Kipper, Anna Korhonen, Neville Ryant, and Martha Palmer. 2008. A large-scale classification of English verbs. *Language Resources and Evaluation*, 42(1):21–40.

Martijn van der Klis, Bert Le Bruyn, and Henriëtte de Swart. 2017. Mapping the perfect via translation mining. In *Proceedings of the 15th Conference of the European Chapter of the Association for Computational Linguistics: Volume 2, Short Papers*, pages 497–502, Valencia, Spain. Association for Computational Linguistics.

Oier Lopez de Lacalle and Eneko Agirre. 2015. Crowdsourced word sense annotations and difficult words and examples. In *Proceedings of the 11th International Conference on Computational Semantics*, pages 94–100, London, UK. Association for Computational Linguistics.

Jochen L. Leidner. 2008. *Toponym Resolution in Text : Annotation, Evaluation and Applications of Spatial Grounding of Place Names*. Universal Press, Boca Raton, FL, USA.

Douglas Lenat. 1995. Cyc: A large-scale investment in knowledge infrastructure. *Communications of the ACM*, 38:33–38.

Mike Lewis and Mark Steedman. 2014. A* ccg parsing with a supertag-factored model. In *Proceedings of the 2014 Conference on Empirical Methods in Natural Language Processing (EMNLP)*, pages 990–1000, Doha, Qatar. Association for Computational Linguistics.

Qianchu Liu, Federico Fancellu, and Bonnie Webber. 2018. NegPar: A parallel corpus annotated for negation. In *Proceedings of the 11th Language Resources and Evaluation Conference*, Miyazaki, Japan. European Language Resource Association.

Emar Maier. 2014. Pure quotation. *Philosophy Compass*, 9(9):615–630.

Roberto Navigli and Simone Paolo Ponzetto. 2012. BabelNet: The automatic construction, evaluation and application of a wide-coverage multilingual semantic network. *Artificial Intelligence*, 193:217–250.

Stephan Oepen, Dan Flickinger, Kristina Toutanova, and Christopher D. Manning. 2004. Lingo redwoods. *Research on Language and Computation*, 2(4):575–596.

Stephan Oepen, Marco Kuhlmann, Yusuke Miyao, Daniel Zeman, Silvie Cinková, Dan Flickinger, Jan Hajič, Angelina Ivanova, and Zdeňka Urešová. 2016. Towards comparability of linguistic graph banks for semantic parsing. In *Proceedings of the 10th International Conference on Language Resources and Evaluation*, pages 3991–3995, Portorož, Slovenia.

Martha Palmer, Paul Kingsbury, and Daniel Gildea. 2005. The proposition bank: An annotated corpus of semantic roles. *Computational Linguistics*, 31(1):71–106.

Terence Parsons. 1990. *Events in the semantics of English: A study in subatomic semantics*. Cambridge, MA: The MIT Press.

M.C. Postma, F. Ilievski, and P.T.J.M. Vossen. 2018. Semeval-2018 task 5: Counting events and participants in the long tail. In *SemEval-2018 : International Workshop on Semantic Evaluation 2018*.

M.C. Postma, R. Izquierdo, E. Agirre, G. Rigau, and P.T.J.M. Vossen. 2016. Addressing the mfs bias in wsd systems. In *LREC 2016*, pages 1695–1700.

James Pustejovsky and Amber Stubbs. 2012. *Natural Language Annotation for Machine Learning - a Guide to Corpus-Building for Applications*. O'Reilly.

Aarne Ranta. 2011. *Grammatical Framework: Programming with Multilingual Grammars*. Center for the Study of Language and Information/SRI.

Nils Reiter and Anette Frank. 2010. Identifying generic noun phrases. In *Proceedings of the 48th Annual Meeting of the Association for Computational Linguistics*, pages 40–49, Uppsala, Sweden. Association for Computational Linguistics.

Uwe Reyle. 1993. Dealing with Ambiguities by Underspecification: Construction, Representation and Deduction. *Journal of Semantics*, 10:123–179.

Uwe Reyle. 1995. On Reasoning with Ambiguities. In *Proceedings of the 7th Conference of the European Chapter of the Association for Computational Linguistics*, pages 1–8, Dublin, Ireland.

Ivan A. Sag, Timothy Baldwin, Francis Bond, Ann Copestake, and Dan Flickinger. 2002. Multiword expressions: A pain in the neck for nlp. In *Computational Linguistics and Intelligent Text Processing*, pages 1–15, Berlin, Heidelberg. Springer Berlin Heidelberg.

Naomi Saphra and Adam Lopez. 2015. AMRICA: an AMR inspector for cross-language alignments. In *Proceedings of the 2015 Conference of the North American Chapter of the Association for Computational Linguistics: Demonstrations*, pages 36–40, Denver, Colorado. Association for Computational Linguistics.

Nathan Schneider, Jena D. Hwang, Vivek Srikumar, Jakob Prange, Austin Blodgett, Sarah R. Moeller, Aviram Stern, Adi Bitan, and Omri Abend. 2018. Comprehensive supersense disambiguation of English prepositions and possessives. In *Proceedings of the 56th Annual Meeting of the Association for Computational Linguistics*, Melbourne, Australia. Association for Computational Linguistics.

Raivis Skadiņš, Jörg Tiedemann, Roberts Rozis, and Daiga Deksne. 2014. Billions of parallel words for free: Building and using the eu bookshop corpus. In *Proceedings of the Ninth International Conference on Language Resources and Evaluation (LREC'14)*, pages 1850–1855, Reykjavik, Iceland. European Language Resources Association (ELRA).

Mark Steedman. 2001. *The Syntactic Process*. The MIT Press.

A. Tarski and R. Vaught. 1956. Arithmetical extensions of relational systems. *Compositio Mathematica*, 13:81–102.

David R. Traum. 2000. 20 questions for dialogue act taxonomies. *Journal of Semantics*, 17(1):7–30.

Rob Matthijs van der Goot. 2019. *Normalization and parsing algorithms for uncertain input*. Ph.D. thesis, University of Groningen.

Rik Van Noord, Lasha Abzianidze, Hessel Haagsma, and Johan Bos. 2018. Evaluating scoped meaning representations. In *Proceedings of the Eleventh International Conference on Language Resources and Evaluation (LREC 2018)*, pages 1685–1693, Miyazaki, Japan.

Noortje Venhuizen, Valerio Basile, Kilian Evang, and Johan Bos. 2013. Gamification for word sense labeling. In *Proceedings of the 10th International Conference on Computational Semantics (IWCS 2013) – Short Papers*, pages 397–403, Potsdam, Germany.

Kellie Webster, Marta Recasens, Vera Axelrod, and Jason Baldridge. 2018. Mind the gap: A balanced corpus of gendered ambiguous pronouns. *Transactions of the Association for Computational Linguistics*, 6:605–617.

Aaron Steven White, Drew Reisinger, Keisuke Sakaguchi, Tim Vieira, Sheng Zhang, Rachel Rudinger, Kyle Rawlins, and Benjamin Van Durme. 2016. Universal decompositional semantics on universal dependencies. In *Proceedings of the 2016 Conference on Empirical Methods in Natural Language Processing*, pages 1713–1723, Austin, Texas. Association for Computational Linguistics.

Jieyu Zhao, Tianlu Wang, Mark Yatskar, Vicente Ordonez, and Kai-Wei Chang. 2017. Men also like shopping: Reducing gender bias amplification using corpus-level constraints. In *EMNLP*.

Modeling Quantification and Scope in Abstract Meaning Representations

James Pustejovsky, Nianwen Xue, Kenneth Lai
Department of Computer Science
Brandeis University
Waltham, MA USA
{jamesp,xuen,klai12 }@brandeis.edu

Abstract

In this paper, we propose an extension to Abstract Meaning Representations (AMRs) to encode scope information of quantifiers and negation, in a way that overcomes the semantic gaps of the schema while maintaining its cognitive simplicity. Specifically, we address three phenomena not previously part of the AMR specification: quantification, negation (generally), and modality. The resulting representation, which we call "Uniform Meaning Representation" (UMR), adopts the predicative core of AMR and embeds it under a "scope" graph when appropriate. UMR representations differ from other treatments of quantification and modal scope phenomena in two ways: (a) they are more transparent; and (b) they specify default scope when possible.

1 Abstract Meaning Representations

Abstract Meaning Representations (AMRs) have recently become popular as a strategy for encoding a kind of canonical meaning for natural language sentences (Banarescu et al., 2013). They differ significantly from other encoding schemes used in NLP—e.g., minimal recursion semantics (MRS)—in terms of their expressiveness for several semantic phenomena in natural language (Copestake et al., 2005). Still, in spite of such shortcomings, there is a major attraction to the general philosophy of this approach: by focusing on the predicative core of a sentence, it is an intuitive representation for both interpreting the semantics of a sentence, and perhaps more importantly, for use in annotation efforts.

An AMR represents the meaning of a sentence with a single-rooted, directed, acyclic graph with nodes labeled with concepts and edges labeled with relations. The primary component of an AMR is the predicate-argument structure, with the predicate being a concept that takes a number of

arguments as its children. The predicate and its arguments are represented as nodes in the AMR graph, and the edges represent the relation between the predicate and each of its arguments. As an illustration, the PENMAN notation and graph representation below in (2) represent the AMR for the sentence in (1).

(1) John can't afford a car at the moment.

(2) a.
```
(p / possible-01
    :ARG0 (a / afford-01
        :ARG0 (p2 / person
            :name (n / name
                :op "John"))
        :ARG1 (c /car)
        :time (m / moment))
    :polarity -)
```

b.

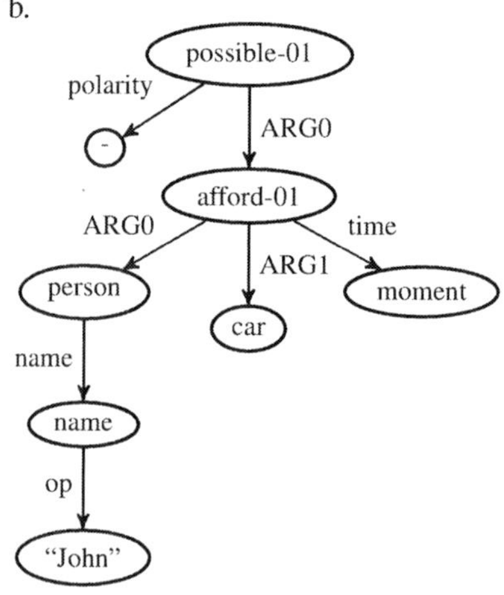

Propositions in an AMR are sense-disambiguated (Palmer et al., 2005). In the example above, "possible-01" refers to the first sense of "possible" while "afford-01" represents the first sense of "afford". A predicate can take a number of core arguments (ARG0, ARG1, etc.) as well as adjunct arguments (e.g., *time*). The semantic roles for the core arguments are defined with respect to each sense of a predicate

Proceedings of the First International Workshop on Designing Meaning Representations, pages 28–33
Florence, Italy, August 1st, 2019 ©2019 Association for Computational Linguistics

and they are drawn from the PropBank frame files [1]. For example, the semantic roles for the core arguments of different senses of "afford" are defined as follows:

(3) a. **afford-01**: be able to spare, have the financial means
ARG0: haver of financial means, agent
ARG2: costly thing, theme

b. **afford-02**: provide, make available
ARG0: provider, agent
ARG1: provided, theme
ARG2: recipient

The attraction of AMR-style representations and annotations is the adoption of a *predicative core* element along with its arguments: e.g., an event and its participants. This, in turn, leads to an event-rooted graph that has many advantages for parsing and matching algorithms. As can be seen from the example, the predicate-argument structure is front and center in AMR, and we consider this to be one of its strengths.

However, as it currently stands, AMR does not represent quantification or its interaction with modality and negation (Bos, 2016). The challenge is to maintain the focus on the predicate-argument structure while also adequately accounting for linguistic phenomena that operate above the level of the core AMR representation, in particular quantification and modality.

2 Quantification and Scope

It can be argued that, besides graph-based matching over predicative structures, AMR does not provide good support for logical inference because it does not yet properly handle scoping and other phenomena. For example, in (4), there is a single talk that everyone in the room is listening to, while in (5), each person has their own coffee. However, AMR does not distinguish between these two cases: it could just as well be that everyone in the room listened to a different talk, or that everyone at noon shared a single cup of coffee.

(4) a. Everyone in the room listened to a talk.
b. $\exists y[\text{talk}(y) \land \forall x \exists e[\text{person}(x) \land \text{inRoom}(x) \to \text{listen}(e, x, y)]]$
c.
```
(l / listen-01
    :ARG0 (p / person
      :mod (a / all)
      :location (r / room))
    :ARG1 (t / talk))
```

[1] https://verbs.colorado.edu/verb-index

(5) a. Everyone drank a coffee at noon.
b. $\forall x[\text{person}(x) \to \exists y \exists e[\text{coffee}(y) \land \text{drink}(e, x, y) \land @(e, \text{noon})]]$
c.
```
(d / drink-01
    :ARG0 (p / person
      :mod (a / all))
    :ARG1 (c / coffee)
    :time (n / noon))
```

In fact, this inability of AMRs to distinguish scoping relations among quantifiers also extends to negation and modality. For example, the AMR for the sentence "Every student did not fail" is given below.

(6) a.
```
(d / fail-01
    :ARG0 (s / student
      :mod (a / all))
    :polarity -)
```
b.

The sentence is ambiguous, however, between the readings "for every student, that student did not fail" and "it is not the case that every student failed".

While MRS and other flattened semantic representations provide a solution to these issues, giving faithful translations of scope with typed expressions, there are several drawbacks to these approaches. Flat representations reveal no semantic core. Hence, as annotations, the resulting structures are difficult to interpret and inspect. Furthermore, quantifier scope is often underspecified even when it can be disambiguated in context. Dependency MRS (DMRS) is one exception to this in the MRS family of representations (Copestake, 2009), where dependency relations link argument heads to the major predicator of the sentence.

In our research, we propose to represent scope relationally, while maintaining both the centrality of the predicative core of the sentence (e.g., *listen*, *drink*), as well as the syntactic integrity of the quantified expression (e.g., *every person*). A relational interpretation for scope provides a first-order interpretation: it references two specific nodes in the graph, and orders one relative to the other. This operates over generalized quantifiers (*some book*, *most people*), negation (*not*, *no*), as well as modals (*possibly*, *likely*, *must*). From an annotation perspective, this is quite different from flat structures, since a human judgment in scope between two elements is directly reflected in the resulting graph. There are complex interactions between negation, modal expressions, and quantified NPs that we will examine, first representationally, and then experimentally with small-scale annotation and testing.

We believe there are advantages to adopting an AMR-style representation for predicate-argument forms of sentences (Banarescu et al., 2013). Given the complexity inherent in the semantics of number, negation, and quantification, we believe that a similar approach to the annotation of scope has some advantages. These include the following:

- It maintains a focus on the *predicative core* of the sentence;

- There is likely a lower *cognitive load* for annotation by non-experts;

- Semantic relations are *transparent* in the graphical representation.

Addressing the problems associated with scope adopting this approach results in a representation we call "Uniform Meaning Representation" (UMR), where the predicative core of AMR is maintained, and embedded under a "scope" graph when required.

3 Towards a Uniform Meaning Representation for Scope

In this section, we illustrate our approach to encoding the expression of quantifier scope in UMR. We draw on some work within the ISO annotation community, where the problem of explicitly annotating scoping relations of events and temporal or spatial quantifiers has been addressed.

To explicitly represent relative scope of quantified expressions, ISO-Space (Pustejovsky, 2017) uses the @quant attribute (adopted from ISO-TimeML), applying it to spatial entities, and in addition uses the attribute @scopes to specify a scoping relation. The following example, taken from ISO 24617-7:2014, illustrates this:

(7) a. A computer$_{se1}$ is on$_{ss1}$ every desk$_{se2}$.
    b. <spatialEntity id="se1" pred="computer"
       quant="1" scopes="∅"/>
       <spatialEntity id="se2"   pred="desk"
       quant="every" scopes="#se1"/>

From a semantic point of view, however, this use of the @scopes attribute is unsatisfactory since the relative scoping of quantifications over different sets of entities is not a local property of one of these quantifications; therefore an annotation such as (7) does not have a compositional semantics. Therefore, we follow (Bunt et al., 2018) and use a link structure, **scopeLink**, to represent scope relations among quantifying NPs, where relType takes a value of 'narrower', 'wider', or 'equal'. For the example in (7), this amounts to marking the universal as taking wide scope over the indefinite.

(8) a. scopeLink($arg_1, arg_2, relType$)
    b. <scopeLink arg1="#se2" arg2="#se1"
    relType="wider"/>

We modify this scoping relation by introducing the predicative domain as an additional argument,

(9) a. $\lambda pred \lambda a_1 \lambda a_0 [\textbf{scope}(a_0, a_1, pred)]$

and model the semantic effect of this relation as similar to the mechanism of Cooper Storage (Cooper, 1975) or a continuation-passing style interpretation of generalized quantifiers (Barker, 2002).

$$[\![a_0]\!]([\![a_1]\!]([\![pred]\!]))$$

For example, consider a relation with two quantifier phrases, and a scoping of the direct object QP_2 over QP_1:

(10) a. $[QP_1]_{arg0}$ pred $[QP_2]_{arg1}$
     b. $\textbf{scope}(QP_1, QP_0, pred)$

The ordering of arguments determines the function application order of each expression, as with continuation-passing style.

This representation is convenient, in that we can maintain a rooted graph structure with the **scope** relation as the root node, as demonstrated below.

```
(11) a. (s / scope
        :pred (b / be-located-at-91
          :ARG0 (c / computer)
          :ARG1 (d / desk
            :quant (e / every)))
        :ARG0 d
        :ARG1 c)
      b.
```

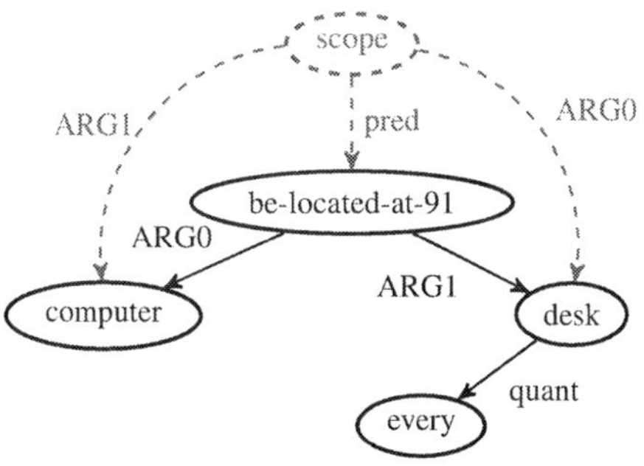

Given the scope-rooted graph above, we apply an interpretation function that translates the graph to an appropriate first-order expression. This gives:

(12) $[\![\text{every desk}]\!]([\![\text{a computer}]\!]([\![\text{be\_located}]\!]))$

For the present annotation, we arrive at the expression in (13).

(13) $\forall y[\text{desk}(y) \rightarrow \exists x[\text{computer}(x) \wedge \text{be-located-at}(x, y)]]$

With the introduction of scope over quantifiers, the annotation provided by a UMR can be compared more directly to the approach and representations deployed in the Groningen Meaning Bank (GMB) and the Parallel Meaning Bank (PMB) projects (Bos et al., 2017; Abzianidze et al., 2017; Van Noord et al., 2018). In this work, sentences are expressed as DRSs within Discourse Representation Theory (Kamp and Reyle, 1993). However, most of the sentences in PMB with potential quantifier scope ambiguities involve temporal expressions and their relative scope over event variables, rather than quantified arguments to the verb. An example is that shown in (14).

(14) a. John golfed every Sunday.
   b. $\forall t[\text{Sunday}(t) \rightarrow \exists e[\text{golf}(e, j) \wedge \text{on}(e, t)]]$

The strategy taken by (Bos et al., 2017), followed here as well, is to scope temporal expressions over the events they govern.

Now let us see how the **scope** relation can be deployed to handle negation and modality in UMR. Consider first the treatment of modals in AMR. As seen in (2) above, modals are treated as predicative nodes. Hence, from `(p / possible-01 :ARG0 phi)`, we can derive the equivalent propositional modal expression, $\Diamond \phi$. However, in (2) we need to translate the polarity over the modal appropriately: $\neg \Diamond \phi$.

In UMR, the **scope** relation acts as a root node assigning the polarity value as taking scope over the modal, along with its body. Consider the UMR graph as shown below. Note that because there may be multiple negations in a sentence, we index negations, e.g., `(n2 / not)`.

(15) a.
```
(s / scope
   :pred (p / possible-01
      :ARG0 (a / afford-01
         :ARG0 (p2 / person
            :name (n / name
               :op "John"))
         :ARG1 (c /car)
         :time (m / moment))
      :polarity (n2 / not))
   :ARG0 n2
   :ARG1 p)
```
b.

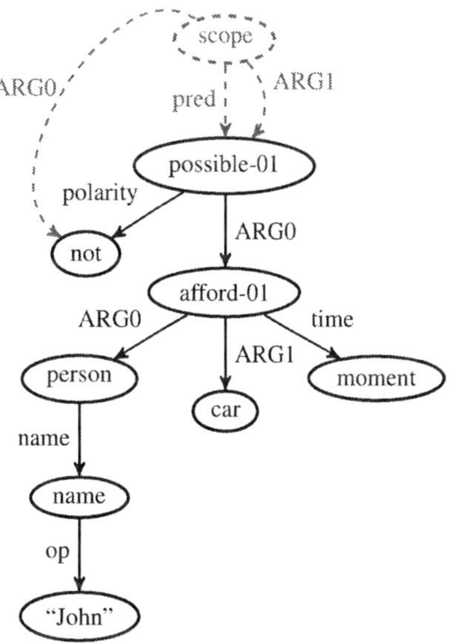

The graph-interpretation function continues walking down the tree, and expands the Skolemized form for 'car' into a quantified expression, inside the scope of the modal, as shown below.

(16) $\neg\Diamond[\exists x[\text{car}(x) \wedge \exists e[\text{afford}(e, j, x) \wedge @(e, \text{N})]]]$

This can be compared to the first-order modal expression generated by (Bos, 2015; Bos et al., 2017) for the sentence as shown below in (17).

(17) $\neg\exists x[\text{car}(x) \wedge \Diamond\exists e[\text{afford}(e, j, x) \wedge @(e, \text{N})]]$

Thus far we have briefly examined the following semantic constructions: quantifier scope for arguments; temporal adjuncts over events; and relative scope of negation and modality.

Now consider the interaction of negation with quantifiers in AMR, as seen in the possible interpretations of (18).

(18)

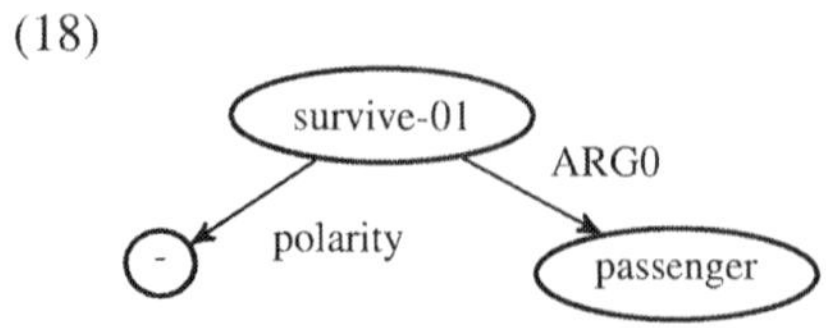

There are two interpretations consistent with this AMR graph.

(19)   a. There is no event of a passenger surviving (no one survived).
$$\neg\exists e\exists x[survive(e,x) \wedge person(x)]$$

   b. There is a passenger who did not survive.
$$\exists x[person(x) \wedge \neg\exists e[survive(e,x)]]$$

With the introduction of the **scope** relation node, we can distinguish these interpretations: for example, the reading in (19a) would be represented as shown below.

(20)

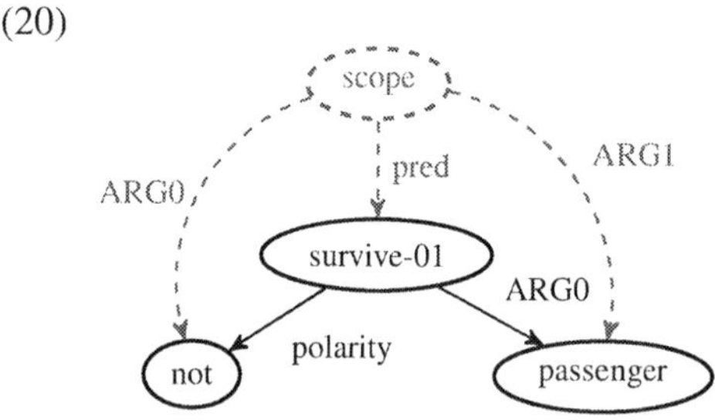

4   Conclusion

In this short note, we introduced a representation and interpretive strategy for capturing scope relations between quantifiers, negation, and modals in AMR. This required an enrichment to the basic vocabulary of AMR that we refer to as a *Uniform Meaning Representation*. The UMR strategy adopts one of the more attractive features of AMR, the predicative core, while increasing the representation language's expressive coverage with the introduction of a **scope** node, determining the relative scope between its two arguments. The interpretation of a specific quantifier or modal is lexically determined. This work is part of a combined effort to enrich the representation of AMRs with tense, (Donatelli et al., 2019), discourse relations (O'Gorman et al., 2018), quantification, and modality.

Acknowledgement

We would like to thank the anonymous reviewers for their helpful comments. This work is supported by the IIS Division of National Science Foundation via Award No. 1763926 entitled "Building a Uniform Meaning Representation for Natural Language Processing". All views expressed in this paper are those of the authors and do not necessarily represent the view of the National Science Foundation.

References

Lasha Abzianidze, Johannes Bjerva, Kilian Evang, Hessel Haagsma, Rik Van Noord, Pierre Ludmann, Duc-Duy Nguyen, and Johan Bos. 2017. The parallel meaning bank: Towards a multilingual corpus of translations annotated with compositional meaning representations. *arXiv preprint arXiv:1702.03964*.

Laura Banarescu, Claire Bonial, Shu Cai, Madalina Georgescu, Kira Griffitt, Ulf Hermjakob, Kevin Knight, Philipp Koehn, Martha Palmer, and Nathan Schneider. 2013. Abstract meaning representation for sembanking. In *Proceedings of the 7th Linguistic Annotation Workshop and Interoperability with Discourse*, pages 178–186.

Chris Barker. 2002. Continuations and the nature of quantification. *Natural language semantics*, 10(3):211–242.

Johan Bos. 2015. Open-domain semantic parsing with boxer. In *Proceedings of the 20th nordic conference of computational linguistics (NODALIDA 2015)*, pages 301–304.

Johan Bos. 2016. Expressive power of abstract meaning representations. *Computational Linguistics*, 42(3):527–535.

Johan Bos, Valerio Basile, Kilian Evang, Noortje J Venhuizen, and Johannes Bjerva. 2017. The groningen meaning bank. In Nancy Ide and James Pustejovsky, editors, *Handbook of linguistic annotation*, pages 463–496. Springer.

Harry Bunt, James Pustejovsky, and Kiyong Lee. 2018. Towards an iso standard for the annotation of quantification. In *Proceedings of the Eleventh International Conference on Language Resources and Evaluation (LREC-2018)*.

Robin Hayes Cooper. 1975. Montague's semantic theory and transformational syntax.

Ann Copestake. 2009. Slacker semantics: why superficiality, dependency and avoidance of commitment can be the right way to go. In *Proceedings of the 12th Conference of the European Chapter of the ACL (EACL 2009)*, pages 1–9.

Ann Copestake, Dan Flickinger, Carl Pollard, and Ivan A Sag. 2005. Minimal recursion semantics: An introduction. *Research on language and computation*, 3(2-3):281–332.

Lucia Donatelli, Nathan Schneider, William Croft, and Michael Regan. 2019. Tense and aspect semantics for sentential amr. *Proceedings of the Society for Computation in Linguistics*, 2(1):346–348.

Hans Kamp and Uwe Reyle. 1993. From discourse to logic, volume 42 of studies in linguistics and philosophy.

Tim O'Gorman, Michael Regan, Kira Griffitt, Ulf Hermjakob, Kevin Knight, and Martha Palmer. 2018. AMR beyond the sentence: the multi-sentence AMR corpus. In *Proceedings of the 27th International Conference on Computational Linguistics*, pages 3693–3702, Santa Fe, New Mexico, USA. Association for Computational Linguistics.

Martha Palmer, Daniel Gildea, and Paul Kingsbury. 2005. The proposition bank: An annotated corpus of semantic roles. *Computational Linguistics*, 31(1):71–106.

James Pustejovsky. 2017. ISO-Space: Annotating static and dynamic spatial information. In *Handbook of Linguistic Annotation*, pages 989–1024. Springer.

Rik Van Noord, Lasha Abzianidze, Hessel Haagsma, and Johan Bos. 2018. Evaluating scoped meaning representations. *arXiv preprint arXiv:1802.08599*.

Parsing Meaning Representations: is Easier Always Better?

Zi Lin[*]
Peking University
zi.lin@pku.edu.cn

Nianwen Xue
Brandeis University
xuen@brandeis.edu

Abstract

The parsing accuracy varies a great deal for different meaning representations. In this paper, we compare the parsing performances between Abstract Meaning Representation (AMR) and Minimal Recursion Semantics (MRS), and provide an in-depth analysis of what factors contributed to the discrepancy in their parsing accuracy. By crystalizing the trade-off between representation expressiveness and ease of automatic parsing, we hope our results can help inform the design of the next-generation meaning representations.

1 Introduction

Meaning representation (MR) parsing is the task of parsing natural language sentences into a formal representation that encodes the meaning of a sentence. As a matter of convention in the field of natural language processing, meaning representation parsing is distinguished from semantic parsing, a form of domain-dependent parsing that analyzes text into executable code for some specific applications. Earlier work in semantic parsing focused on parsing natural language sentences into semantic queries that can be executed against a knowledge base to answer factual questions (Wong and Mooney, 2006; Kate and Wong, 2010; Berant et al., 2013; Artzi and Zettlemoyer, 2013). More recently, this line of work has been extended to parsing natural language text into computer programs (Ling et al., 2016; Yin and Neubig, 2017) and parsing tabular information in texts. Here we focus on the parsing of natural language sentences into domain-independent MRs that are not geared towards any one particular application, but could be potentially useful for a wide range of applications.

The challenge for developing a general-purpose meaning representation is that there is not a universally accepted standard and as a result, existing MRs vary a great deal with respect to which aspects of the linguistic meaning of a sentence are included and how they are represented. For example, existing MRs differ in whether and how they represent named entities, word sense, coreference, and semantic roles, among other meaning components.

These design decisions have consequences for the automatic parsing of these MRs. Among two of the meaning representations for which large-scale manual annotated data exist, the state-of-the-art parsing accuracy for AMR is generally in the high 60s and low 70s (May, 2016; May and Priyadarshi, 2017), while state-of-the-art parsing accuracy for (variations of) MRS is in the high 80s and low 90s (Oepen et al., 2014). Little has been done thus far to investigate the underlying causes for this rather large discrepancy. For purposes of developing the next generation MRs, it is important to know i) which aspects of the MR pose the most challenge to automatic parsing and ii) whether these challenges are "necessary evils" because the information encoded in the MR is important to downstream applications and has to be included, or they can be simplified without hurting the utility of the MR.

To answer these questions, we compare the parsing results between AMR and MRS, two meaning representations for which large-scale manually annotated data sets exist. We use the same parser trained on data sets annotated with the two MRs to ensure that the difference in parsing performance is not due to the difference in parsing algorithms, and we also use the same evaluation metric to ensure that the parsing accuracy is evaluated the same way. The evaluation tool we use is SMATCH (Cai and Knight, 2013), and the

---

[*]Work done during the internship at Brandeis University.

Proceedings of the First International Workshop on Designing Meaning Representations, pages 34–43
Florence, Italy, August 1st, 2019 ©2019 Association for Computational Linguistics

parser we use is CAMR (Wang et al., 2015a,b), a transition-based parser originally developed for AMR that we adapt to MRS. To make CAMR as well as SMATCH work on MRS data, we rewrote the native MRS data in PENMAN notation. Ideally, the parser needs to be trained on the same source text annotated with these two MRs to isolate the contributions of the MR from other factors, but this is not currently possible, so we fall back on the next best thing, and use data sets annotated with AMR and MRS that are similar in size.

Our experimental results show that the SMATCH score for MRS parsing is almost 20% higher than that for AMR. A detailed comparative analysis of the parsing results reveals that the main contributing factors into the lower parsing accuracy for AMR are the following:

- AMR concepts show a higher level of abstraction from surface forms, meaning that AMR concepts bear less resemblance to the word tokens in the original sentence.

- AMR does a much more fine-grained classification for the named entities than MRS, which contributes to errors in concept identification.

- Semantic relations are defined differently in AMR and MRS. While in AMR a semantic role represents a semantic relation between a verbal or nominal predicate and its argument, in MRS the predicate can also be a preposition, adjectives, or adverbs. Another difference is that while in AMR, the semantic roles for the core arguments of a predicate are interpretable with respect to an external lexicon, the semantic roles in MRS reflect the level of obliqueness and are linked to an external lexicon.[1]

We hope that by clearly identifying aspects of the MR that contributed to the challenges in automatic meaning representation parsing, we can help researchers make more informed decisions on

---

[1]These do not necessarily account for all the factors that might contribute to the discrepancy in performance between the two meaning representations. As one reviewer points out, the lack of manual alignment between word tokens in a sentence and the concepts in its AMR graph may also have contributed to challenge in parsing AMRs. Annotation consistency in the data set may also be a contributing factor. There are no obvious way to quantify these factors and we leave these to future research.

the trade-off between representation expressiveness and ease of automatic parsing when developing the next-generation MRs.

The rest of the paper is organized as follows: Section 2 briefly describes the key elements of MRS and AMR; Section 3 reports our experiment setup and main parsing results for the two MRs; Section 4 provides a detailed analysis of the impacts of different aspects of the MR on automatic parsing. Section 5 concludes the paper.

2 Meaning Representations

In this section, we provide a brief description of the meaning representations that we investigate, Minimal Recursion Semantics (MRS) and Abstract Meaning Representation (AMR). Both MRs can be visualized as a graph with labeled nodes and edges. Figure 1 shows the MRS and AMR representations for the sentence "it has no bearing on our work force today", which we will use to illustrate the various aspects of the two meaning representation frameworks.

2.1 Minimal Recursion Semantics

MRS serves as the logical-form semantic representation of the English Resource Grammar (ERG; Flickinger, 2000)[2], a broad-coverage grammar of English and an implementation of the grammatical theory of Head-driven Phrase Structure Grammar (HPSG; Pollard and Sag, 1994). For our experiments, we use a variation of MRS called Elementary Dependency Structures (EDS; Oepen and Lønning, 2006), which retains the structural aspect of MRS that is of interest to us but excludes the morpho-syntactic features and the (underspecified) scopal information.

As can be seen from Figure 1a, nodes in an MRS representation are labeled with semantic predicates (e.g. `_bearing_n_1` and `compound`). MRS makes the distinction between surface and abstract predicates. A surface predicate consists of a lemma followed by (1) a coarse part-of-speech tag and (2) an optional sense label, which can be a number indicating the sense ID, a particle in the verb-particle construction (e.g., look up), or a case-marking prepositions (e.g., rely on). Examples of surface predicates are illustrated below:

- `_look_v_1`: <u>Look</u> how much air is moving around!

---

[2]`http://www.delph-in.net/erg`

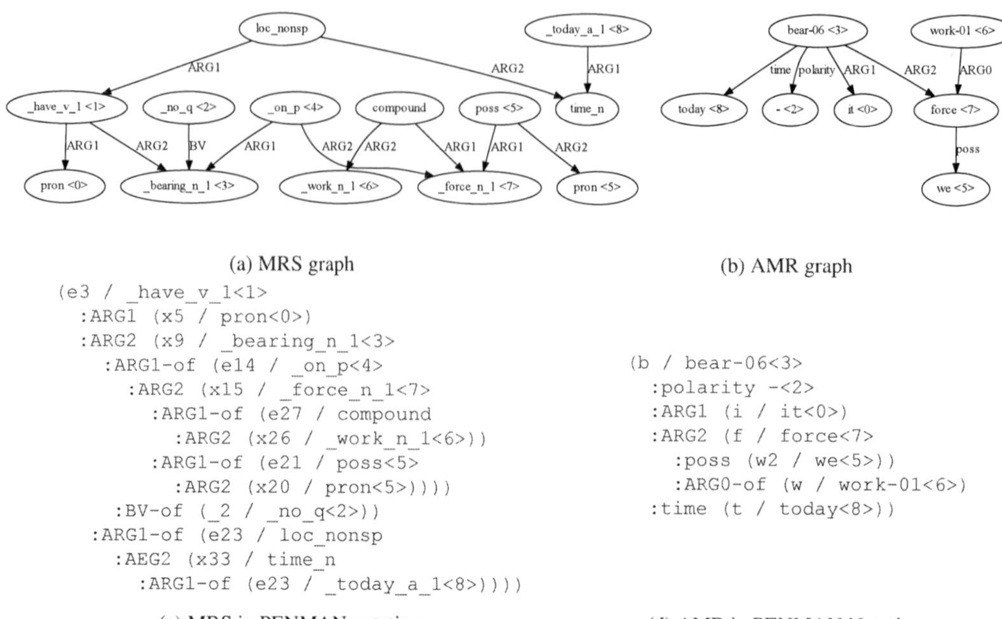

(a) MRS graph   (b) AMR graph

```
(e3 / _have_v_1<1>
  :ARG1 (x5 / pron<0>)
  :ARG2 (x9 / _bearing_n_1<3>
    :ARG1-of (e14 / _on_p<4>
      :ARG2 (x15 / _force_n_1<7>
        :ARG1-of (e27 / compound
          :ARG2 (x26 / _work_n_1<6>))
        :ARG1-of (e21 / poss<5>
          :ARG2 (x20 / pron<5>)))))
    :BV-of (_2 / _no_q<2>))
  :ARG1-of (e23 / loc_nonsp
    :AEG2 (x33 / time_n
      :ARG1-of (e23 / _today_a_1<8>)))))
```

```
(b / bear-06<3>
  :polarity -<2>
  :ARG1 (i / it<0>)
  :ARG2 (f / force<7>
    :poss (w2 / we<5>))
    :ARG0-of (w / work-01<6>)
  :time (t / today<8>))
```

(c) MRS in PENMAN notation   (d) AMR in PENMAN Notation

Figure 1: The graphs and PENMAN notations of MRS and AMR for the sentence "it<0> has<1> no<2> bearing<3> on<4> our<5> work<6> force<7> today<8>" (From `wsj_0003_30`).

- `_look_v_up`: Researchers can look up credit ratings, and even question neighbors.
- `_rely_v_on`: We'll rely very much on their leadership.

No lexical item can be associated with multiple surface predicates in MRS, but some lexical items bring abstract predicates, which is distinguished with no leading underscore. For example, in Figure 1a, the pronouns represented uniformly as `pron`, the `compound` (compounding *work* and *force*), `loc_nonsp` (an implicit locative without a specific preposition), and `time_n` decomposing the lexical item *time* are abstract predicates [3].

The edges in an MRS graph are labeled with a small set of roles that indicate the relation between a predicate and its argument (e.g., `ARG1`, `ARG2`) or between a predicate and a quantifier (e.g., `BV`). These roles are used to provide a numerical ID for the arguments of a predicate that occur in a sentence, and they are not interpretable with respect to an external taxonomy or valency lexicon. As a result, these numerical IDs are ordered and consecutive and it is not possible to have an `ARG3` without an `ARG1` and an `ARG2`. In general, `ARG1` always corresponds to the first (least oblique) argument, `ARG2` the second (next least oblique) argument, and so on.

2.2 Abstract Meaning Representation

AMR represents the meaning of a sentence as a rooted, labeled, directed, and acyclic graph (DAGs), as illustrated in Figure 1b. The nodes in an AMR graph are annotated with AMR concepts, which can also be concrete (surface) or abstract. A concrete concept is "evoked" by one or more lexical items in the sentence, while an abstract concept is inferred from a particular semantic context. A concrete concept can be a sense-tagged predicate (e.g., "bear-06" in Figure 1b) drawn from the Propbank (Palmer et al., 2005), or the lemma of a word in the sentence (e.g., "force" in Figure 1b). In general, only predicates that can be found in the PropBank frame files have their senses defined and annotated in AMR. Here are the four senses defined for the verb "bear" (excluding phrasal verbs)

- `bear-01`: hold, support, endure.
- `bear-02`: bear children.
- `bear-03`: move
- `bear-06`: has relation to

There is also a third type of concrete concepts that diverge further from their corresponding sur-

---

[3]For more details of the abstract predicates, please see: `http://moin.delph-in.net/ErgSemantics/Basics`

face lexical units and as we will show in Section 4, this is one aspect of AMR that poses a great deal of challenge to automatic parsing. For example, the modal verb "can" corresponds to the AMR concept "possible". There are also other cases where a concept corresponds to a morpheme instead of the entire word. For example, the word "investor" is analyzed as

```
(p / person
    :ARG-of (i / invest-01))
```

and the concept "person" corresponds to the suffix "-or".

In addition to concrete concepts, AMR also has abstract concepts that do not correspond to any lexical unit. For example, the concept "have-org-role-91" can be inferred from just the phrase "U.S. President Obama" as it implies that a person named "Obama" holds the position of the "president" in the organization that is the U.S. government:

```
(p / person
    :name (n / name :op1 "Obama")
    :ARG0-of (h / have-arg-role-91
        :ARG1 (c / country
            :name (n2 / name
                :op1 "US"))
        :ARG2 (p2 / president)))
```

The edges in an AMR graph are annotated with AMR relations, most of which can be viewed as semantic roles an argument plays with respect to its predicate. Although the naming convention of the semantic roles defined for the core arguments of a predicate in AMR is very similar to that used in MRS — both use an integer prefixed by "Arg" (e.g., ARG0, ARG1), that's where the similarity ends. Unlike MRS, the semantic role for each core argument is defined for a specific sense of a predicate in the PropBank frame files, and can thus be interpreted. For example, for the predicate `bear-06`, the semantic roles for the core arguments are:

- `ARG1`: topic
- `ARG2`: related topic

In addition to the semantic roles for the core arguments, AMR uses a rather large set of semantic relations for non-core arguments. The semantic relations not tied to a specific predicate and include MANNER, TIME, DEGREE, etc. In total, there are 83 AMR relations.

3 Data preparation and parsing results

3.1 Data Preparation

We conduct the experiments on the dataset SDP2015[4] for MRS parsing and LDC2016E25[5] for AMR parsing. We use the PENMAN notation as the serialization format for both AMR and MRS. The PENMAN notation is the native format for the AMR data set, and we convert the MRS data to the PENMAN notation using the pyDelphin library. We use the training/development/test splits as recommended in the dataset releases. Some key statistics of the two data sets are presented in the top half of Table 1.

As we can see from the table, the number of sentences/graphs in the two data sets is similar in size, and this is important for purposes of comparing the parser performance on the two data sets. The number of nodes per token in MRS is much greater than that in AMR, this is mainly due to (1) the large number of abstract nodes in MRS and (2) the fact that the MRS concepts are much closer to the surface form than AMR (e.g., AMR does not have node representation for determiners, the infinitive marker "to", prepositions that introduce oblique arguments and etc, while for the most cases, MRS does encode information for these function words).

3.2 Choosing a parsing model

Many parsers have been developed recently either for AMR parsing (Lyu and Titov, 2018; Groschwitz et al., 2018; Guo and Lu, 2018; Dozat and Manning, 2018; Wang et al., 2018; Wang and Xue, 2017; Wang et al., 2015a; Flanigan et al., 2014) or MRS parsing (Chen et al., 2018) , but relatively few parsers are capable of parsing both MR formalisms (Buys and Blunsom, 2017). To compare parsing results on MRS and AMR using the same parsing model, we need a parser that can parse another MR with minimal adaptation. In our experiment, we use CAMR, a transition-based parser [6] (Wang et al., 2015a) originally developed for AMR parsing that we also adapt to MRS parsing.

CAMR performs MR parsing in two steps. The first step is to parse a sentence into a dependency

---

[4]`http://sdp.delph-in.net/2015/data.html`
[5]`https://catalog.ldc.upenn.edu/LDC2016E25`
[6]`https://github.com/c-amr/camr`

	MRS			AMR		
	Train	**Dev**	**Test**	**Train**	**Dev**	**Test**
number of graphs/sentences	35,315	1,410	1,410	36,521	1,368	1,371
number of tokens per sentence	22.33	22.92	23.14	17.83	21.59	22.10
number of nodes per token	0.96	0.97	0.93	0.68	0.70	0.70

	Node	**Edge**	**S**MATCH	**Node**	**Edge**	**S**MATCH
CAMR	89.4	81.1	85.3	78.7	57.1	68.0
Buys and Blunsom (2017)	89.1	85.0	87.0	-	-	61.2
Chen et al. (2018)	94.5	87.3	90.9	-	-	-
Lyu and Titov (2018)	-	-	-	85.9	69.8	74.4

Table 1: Statistics and parsing results for MRS and AMR on the test set

tree with an off-the-shelf parser, and the second step is to transform the dependency tree into the target MR graph by performing a series of actions each of which changes a parsing state to a new state. See Wang et al. (2015b,a) for details on how CAMR works.

As we described in Section 2, both AMR and MRS abstract away from the surface lexical units and the nodes in the MR graph are not simply word tokens in the sentence. In order to train CAMR, the word tokens in the sentence need to be aligned with nodes in the meaning representation graph to the extent that is possible. The MRS data comes with manual alignments, but the AMR data set does not, so we utilize the automatic aligner in JAMR (Flanigan et al., 2014) to align the word tokens in the sentence with nodes in the AMR graph.

In our experiment, we use the Stanford CoreNLP toolkit (Manning et al., 2014) to produce the dependency structure that we use as input to CAMR. We also use this toolkit to produce part-of-speech tags and name entity information for use as features. Considering the need for cross-framework MR parsing, we do not make use of a semantic role labeler as the original CAMR does, as semantic role labeling is irrelevant to MRS parsing. This hurts the AMR parsing somewhat but not by too much. When adpating CAMR to MRS, we perform the following post-processing steps: (1) changing the AMR-style naming convention for named entities `name` and `:op` to MRS-style `named` (or other date-entity nodes) and `:carg`; (2) if the word is unknown to the parser, copying the lemma and the predicted POS tag to form an "unknown word"; (3) disabling the functionality for classifying named entities; (4) adding the abstract node "nominalization" if a predicate has been nominalized.

3.3 Parsing Results

The results based on the SMATCH score (Cai and Knight, 2013) are reported in Table 1. We also include the state-of-the-art parsers for each framework (an SHRG-based parser for MRS (Chen et al., 2018) and a neural AMR parser (Lyu and Titov, 2018)) as well as a cross-framework neural parser in Buys and Blunsom (2017). For CAMR, the gap in F1 between the two frameworks is 17.3% and the difference is larger for Buys and Blunsom (2017), which is more than 20%.

4 What makes AMR parsing difficult?

To investigate which aspects of the MRs contribute to the large gap in performance between AMR and MRS parsing, we perform a detailed examination of different aspects of the meaning representation parsing process.

4.1 Concept Detection

The first step in constructing a meaning representation graph is concept identification, or determining the nodes of the meaning representation graph. As should be clear from our description in Section 2, the concepts in an AMR or MRS graph abstract away from the surface lexical units in a sentence, and as a result, it is non-trivial to predict the concepts in a meaning representation graph based on the word tokens in a sentence. This process can be as simple as performing lemmatization, but it can also be as complicated as performing word sense disambiguation or even inferring abstract concepts that do not correspond to a particular word token.

Word sense disambiguation For AMR parsing, word sense disambiguation means recognizing the sense defined in the PropBank frame files (e.g., `bear-01` vs. `bank-06`) and needs to be

MRS						
POS	%	#lemma	#sense	average	score	WSD
n	34.46	1,420	1,434	1.01	95.35	99.76
v	20.37	838	1,010	1.21	85.56	90.58
q	13.97	25	25	1.00	98.22	100.00
p	12.86	96	123	1.28	81.29	76.11
a	11.45	637	648	1.02	90.58	99.90
c	4.20	17	19	1.12	94.46	99.61
x	2.69	80	81	1.01	73.65	99.74
total	100.00	3,113	3,340	1.07	90.78	97.06
AMR						
pred	-	1,292	1,440	1.11	77.93	94.54

Table 2: Node identification and WSD results on MRS in terms of noun (n), verb (v), quantifier (q), preposition (p), adjective (a), conjunction (c), and others (x), and on AMR in terms of predicate (pred). Both are measured on the test set in terms of accuracy based on SMATCH.

performed on verbal, nominal and other predicates. For MRS parsing, word sense disambiguation needs to be performed all the concepts that are not constants (number, date and named entities) or abstract concepts (`compound`, `subord`, etc.).

Table 2 reports the accuracy based on the SMATCH for concept detection in general [7], and concepts that requires word sense disambiguation to identify on the test set. We also present a concept detection accuracy breakdown by the part of speech of the words that they are aligned to. As we can see from the table, the overall concept detection accuracy is much lower for AMR than MRS. However, for concepts that involve word sense disambiguation, the difference is rather small, indicating that word sense disambiguation is not a major contributor in the performance gap.

Concept abstraction Now that we have established that word sense disambiguation is not a major contributor to the difficulty in concept detection for AMR parsing, we take a closer look at how concept detection fared for lexical categories that are known to have a complex mapping to the concepts they "evoke". For lack of a better term, we call this "concept abstraction". We will examine how abstraction of verbs (*v.*), nouns (*n.*), adjectives (*adj.*), adverbs (*adv.*), prepositions (*prep.*), conjunctions (*conj.*), phrasal verbs (*p.v.*) and modal verbs (*mod.*) impact concept detection accuracy.

- **Phrasal verbs** AMR tends to normalize phrasal verbs to single verbs where possible.

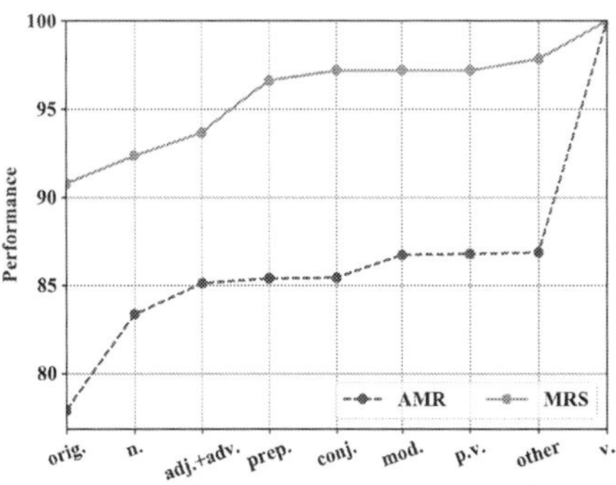

Figure 2: Relative improvement of performance on the test set after correcting each type of POSs or constructions in AMR

For example, the same predicate `bathe-01` is used for both "take a bath" and "bathe".

- **Nouns**. The verb and its nominalization often share the same predicate in AMR. For example, the predicate for both "destruction" and "destroy" is `destroy-01`.

- **Adjectives**. Like nouns, an adjectival predicate is normalized to the same form as that of its verbal counterpart if the adjective is derived from a verb. For example, the predicate for "attractive" is `attract-01`. This obviously does not apply adjectives like "quick" and "tall", which do not have a verbal counterpart.

- **Adverbs with the suffix -ly**. The Predicate of an adverb is often normalized to its adjectival form. For example, for both "quickly" and "quick", the predicate is `quick-01`.

- **Prepositions**. Most prepositions do not map to a concept in AMR except for idiomatic constructions such as "out of mind", whose predicate is `out-06`.

- **Conjunctions**. The concepts for coordinating conjunctions can be very different from their surface form. For example, the concept for "but" is `constrast-01`.

- **Modal verbs**. The AMR concepts for modal verbs are also very different from its surface form. For example, the predicate for the modal verb "can" is `possible-01`, the same as that for the adjective "possible".

type	*n.*	*adj.*	*adv.*	*prep.*	*conj.*	*mod.*	*p.v.*	other	*v.*
%	35.09	10.05	1.87	1.17	1.01	2.59	0.31	0.15	47.76
Performance	83.01	84.44	80.73	73.53	96.61	66.96	83.33	44.44	74.07

Table 3: Individual percentage and score for different types of AMR's predicates

Entity type	Example	AMR	MRS
calendar	lunar calendar	`(d / date-entity :calendar (m / moon))`	–
month	December (8th)	`(d / date-entity :month 12)`	`(x1 / mofy :carg "Dec")`
weekday	Monday	`(d / date-entity :weekday (m / monday))`	`(x1 / dofw :carg "Mon")`
day	(December) 8th	`(d / date-entity :day 8)`	`(x1 / dofm :carg "8")`
dayperiod	night	`(d / date-entity :dayperiod (n / night))`	–

named entity	New York	`(c1 / city`
		`   :name (n1 / name`
		`      :op1 "New" :op2 "York"))`
			`(x1 / named :carg "York"`
			`   :ARG1-of (e1 / compound`
			`      :ARG2 (x2 / named :carg "New")))`

Table 4: Date-entity of AMR and MRS. The `carg` in MRS means "constant argument", which takes as its value a string representing the name of the entity.

To identify the lexical categories or constructions that evoke the concepts, we first extract words or word sequences that are aligned with these concepts, and then use a set of heuristics based on morpho-syntactic patterns to determine the exact type of abstraction in the test set. We measure the improvement in concept detection accuracy if concepts for each additional category are correctly detected. If there is a big improvement in accuracy if we assume the concepts are correctly detected for that category, that means concept detection for that category is a big challenge. The accuracy will remain unchanged if the type is undefined for that MR (e.g. *p.v.* for MRS). MRS labels most of the adverbs as its corresponding adjective form, so we merge these two types together.

The individual result is reported in Table 3 and the improvement is illustraed in Figure 2, which shows that concept detection accuracy in AMR is mainly dragged down by nouns and verbs due to their relatively large proportions. While prepositions play an important role in concept detection in MRS, most prepositions do not map to concepts in AMR and thus do not contribute to the errors in AMR concept detection.The concept detection for modal verbs is also difficult for AMR but not for MRS.

Named and date entities We next examine how well entities are detected in AMR and MRS parsing. Named and date entities are typically multi-Word expressions (MWEs) that do not have a simple mapping between the word tokens in a sentence and the concepts in a meaning representation graph. In AMR, date entities are mapped to a `date-entity` concept with an attribute that

indicates the specific type of entity. Named entities are mapped to a `name` concept with a detailed classification of the named entity type (e.g., `city`, `country`). AMR defines 124 total entity types, a very fine-grained classification. In MRS, date entities map to a date entity type ("season") with an attribute that is a constant ("winter"). Named entities are treated as a type of a `compound` that has a `named` concept as its argument. MRS does not provide a detailed classification of named entities. More examples of AMR and MRS date (the first five rows) and named entities (the last row) are provided in Table 4.

dataset	MRS		AMR	
	#	score	#	score
date entity	266	92.48	273	66.67
NE detection	2,555	81.96	2,065	91.09
NE classification	-	-	-	76.46

Table 5: Results on entity recognition on the test set

The results for detecting date and named entities on the test set are presented in Table 5. A date or named entity is correctly detected if the entire predicted subgraph matches the gold subgraph for the entity. For named entities, we evaluate the named entity detection and named entity classification separately, given the fact that MRS does not classify named entities at all. We can see that the date entity detection accuracy for AMR is much lower than that for MRS, indicating some of the normalization that is needed to map word tokens to AMR concepts is difficult for the parser ("lunar calendar" to `(d/ date-entity`

`:calendar (m / moon))`. For named entities while the named entity detection accuracy is higher for AMR than MRS, but since AMR parsing also requires named entities be correctly classified, overall correctly parsing named entities in AMR is still much harder.

4.2 Relation Detection

In this section, we consider the subtask of relation detection in meaning representation parsing, which involves identifying and labeling the edges in the meaning representation graph. We focus on Semantic Role Labeling (SRL) of the core arguments, arguments that receive the label `ARG-i`, where i is an integer that ranges from 0 to 5. In order to isolate the effect of SRL, we only consider cases where the concepts (nodes) have been correctly detected. The results on the test set are presented in Table 6. The overall results are based on the SRL smatch computed on `:ARG-i` roles using the toolkit `amr-eager`[8]. Here "all matched" refers to complete match, i.e., the predicted subgraph rooted in the predicate [9] match the gold subgraph. Note that both MRS and AMR graphs contain reentrancy, meaning that the same concept can participate in multiple relations, so we also include a separate evaluation of reentrancy.

As we can see, the accuracy for both SRL in general and reentrancy in particular is much lower for AMR than MRS, and the number of reentrancies is much greater for AMR than MRS. [10] A closer look reveals that the main cause for the difference in performance lies in the different ways of how MRS and AMR represent the prepositional phrases and coreferene, as well as how the semantic roles are defined for the two MRs.

Prepositional phrases MRS treats prepositions as predicates, and labels their arguments, while AMR just drops the preposition when it introduces an oblique argument for a verbal predicate so the object of the preposition becomes an argument of the verbal predicate, resulting in non-local rela-

dataset	MRS		AMR	
	#	score	#	score
Overall	-	81.76	-	61.52
All matched	3,398	63.48	4,975	44.77
ARG0	3,087	62.00	3,680	49.43
ARG1	2,985	68.45	5,377	53.97
ARG2	339	35.09	1,614	37.86
ARG3	7	57.13	123	14.63
ARG4	-	-	39	20.51
Reentrancy	807	81.28	1,723	43.91

Table 6: Results on SRL. MRS's argument number begins at 1 so we just move all the argument to begin at 0 to make them comparable.

tions. This explains why SRL is more difficult for AMR than MRS, illustrated in the top example in Figure 3, where there are different representations for the prepositional phrase in the sentence. The MRS design choice, in this case, leads to more structures to predict, compared with just one structure in AMR. Assuming these sub-graphs are comparatively easy to predict, this may contribute to higher scores in MRS parsing.

Coreference AMR resolves sentence-level coreference, i.e., if there is more than one expression in the sentence referring to the same entity, that entity will be an argument for all the predicates that it is an argument of. In contrast, MRS does not resolve coreference and each instance of the same entity will be a separate concept in the MRS graph. This is illustrated in bottom example in Figure 3. The labeled arguments for the predicate "eat" in the two MRs are totally different but actually they refer to the same entities. Not having to do coreference resolution makes MRS parsing easier and this also explains the lower SRL accuracy for AMR.

Interpretability of semantic roles To see the difference in how the semantic roles are defined between MRS and AMR, we conduct a controlled experiment on a subset of 87 graphs in both datasets that all annotate the same source text. After extracting the overlapping predicates (based on the alignments for each MR, gold for MRS and automatic alignment for AMR) and computing the agreement between the semantic roles in the two MRs, we find an interesting fact: the labeled agreement in the subset is rather low ($F1 = 52.22$), but the unlabeled agreement is

---

[8] `https://github.com/mdtux89/amr-eager`

[9] For MRS we only count the verbs, so the number of predicates and arguments is much greater for AMR than MRS.

[10] This may seem to contradict the observation in Kuhlmann and Oepen (2016) where they show MRS has more re-entrancies than AMR. This is because in our experiments we removed the edge linking a conjunction to its conjunct to remove the cycles that would have a negative impact on parsing accuracy but do not offer further information. This accounts for most of the re-entrancies in the EDS variant of MRS.

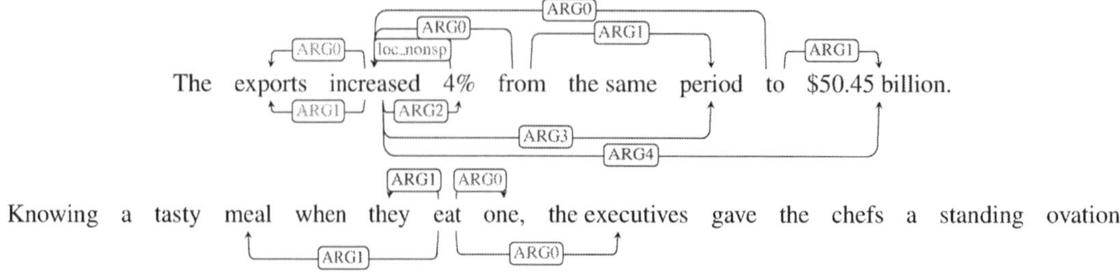

Figure 3: The SRL representations of MRS (edge above) and AMR (edge below) for the sentences "the exports increased 4% from the same period to $50.45 billion" and "knowing a tasty and free meal when they eat one, the executives gave the chefs a standing ovation". For `increase-01`, PropBank defines the `ARG0` and `ARG1` as "cause of increase" and "thing increasing", so "the exports" here will be labeled as `ARG1` instead of `ARG0`.

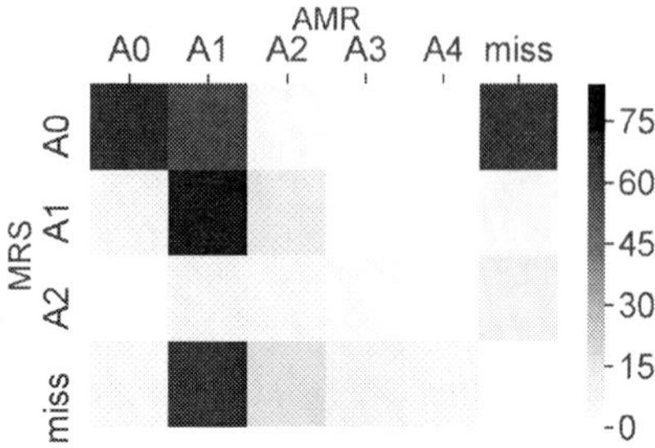

Figure 4: Confusion matrix between MRS and AMR

much higher ($F1 = 77.83$). The low labeled agreement can be explained by the different ways of how semantic roles are defined. We illustrate this difference using the confusion matrix in Figure 4. The numeric value of the semantic roles tends to be smaller in MRS than in AMR. As discussed in Section 2, while the semantic roles in MRS represent the level of obliqueness of arguments realized in a particular sentence, the semantic roles in AMR are defined for the *expected arguments* of a predicate in an external lexicon that is independent of any particular sentence. The semantic roles for the arguments that actually occur in a particular sentence may be discontinuous in a particular context, making them more difficult to predict.

5 Conclusion

In this work, we evaluated the similarities and differences in the semantic content encoded by Minimal Recursion Semantics (MRS) and Abstract Meaning Representation (AMR). After parsing the two MRs using the same parser and evaluating them using the same metric, we provide a detailed analysis of the differences between the two MRs in both substance and style that leads to a large gap in automatic parsing performance. In doing so, we help crystalize the trade-off between representation expressiveness and ease of automatic parsing and hope this study will inform the design and development of next-generation MRs.

Acknowledgement

We thank the anonymous reviewers for their helpful comments, and Junjie Cao for discussing the details of meaning representations with us. This work is supported by a grant from the IIS Division of National Science Foundation (Award No. 1763926) entitled "Building a Uniform Meaning Representation for Natural Language Processing" awarded to the second author. All views expressed in this paper are those of the authors and do not necessarily represent the view of the National Science Foundation.

References

Yoav Artzi and Luke Zettlemoyer. 2013. Weakly supervised learning of semantic parsers for mapping instructions to actions. *Transactions of the Association for Computational Linguistics*, 1:49–62.

Jonathan Berant, Andrew Chou, Roy Frostig, and Percy Liang. 2013. Semantic parsing on freebase from question-answer pairs. In *Proceedings of the 2013 Conference on Empirical Methods in Natural Language Processing*, pages 1533–1544.

Jan Buys and Phil Blunsom. 2017. Robust incremental neural semantic graph parsing. *arXiv preprint arXiv:1704.07092*.

Shu Cai and Kevin Knight. 2013. Smatch: an evaluation metric for semantic feature structures. In *Proceedings of the 51st Annual Meeting of the Association for Computational Linguistics (Volume 2: Short Papers)*, volume 2, pages 748–752.

Yufei Chen, Weiwei Sun, and Xiaojun Wan. 2018. Accurate shrg-based semantic parsing. In *Proceedings of the 56th Annual Meeting of the Association for Computational Linguistics (Volume 1: Long Papers)*, pages 408–418, Melbourne, Australia. Association for Computational Linguistics.

Timothy Dozat and Christopher D Manning. 2018. Simpler but more accurate semantic dependency parsing. *arXiv preprint arXiv:1807.01396*.

Jeffrey Flanigan, Sam Thomson, Jaime Carbonell, Chris Dyer, and Noah A Smith. 2014. A discriminative graph-based parser for the abstract meaning representation. In *Proceedings of the 52nd Annual Meeting of the Association for Computational Linguistics (Volume 1: Long Papers)*, volume 1, pages 1426–1436.

Dan Flickinger. 2000. On building a more effcient grammar by exploiting types. *Natural Language Engineering*, 6(1):15–28.

Jonas Groschwitz, Matthias Lindemann, Meaghan Fowlie, Mark Johnson, and Alexander Koller. 2018. Amr dependency parsing with a typed semantic algebra. *arXiv preprint arXiv:1805.11465*.

Zhijiang Guo and Wei Lu. 2018. Better transition-based amr parsing with a refined search space. In *Proceedings of the 2018 Conference on Empirical Methods in Natural Language Processing*, pages 1712–1722.

Rohit J Kate and Yuk Wah Wong. 2010. Semantic parsing: The task, the state of the art and the future. *Tutorial Abstracts of ACL 2010*, page 6.

Marco Kuhlmann and Stephan Oepen. 2016. Towards a catalogue of linguistic graph banks. *Computational Linguistics*, 42(4):819–827.

Wang Ling, Edward Grefenstette, Karl Moritz Hermann, Tomáš Kočiský, Andrew Senior, Fumin Wang, and Phil Blunsom. 2016. Latent predictor networks for code generation. *arXiv preprint arXiv:1603.06744*.

Chunchuan Lyu and Ivan Titov. 2018. Amr parsing as graph prediction with latent alignment. *arXiv preprint arXiv:1805.05286*.

Christopher Manning, Mihai Surdeanu, John Bauer, Jenny Finkel, Steven Bethard, and David McClosky. 2014. The stanford corenlp natural language processing toolkit. In *Proceedings of 52nd annual meeting of the association for computational linguistics: system demonstrations*, pages 55–60.

Jonathan May. 2016. Semeval-2016 task 8: Meaning representation parsing. In *Proceedings of the 10th international workshop on semantic evaluation (semeval-2016)*, pages 1063–1073.

Jonathan May and Jay Priyadarshi. 2017. Semeval-2017 task 9: Abstract meaning representation parsing and generation. In *Proceedings of the 11th International Workshop on Semantic Evaluation (SemEval-2017)*, pages 536–545.

Stephan Oepen, Marco Kuhlmann, Yusuke Miyao, Daniel Zeman, Dan Flickinger, Jan Hajic, Angelina Ivanova, and Yi Zhang. 2014. Semeval 2014 task 8: Broad-coverage semantic dependency parsing. In *Proceedings of the 8th International Workshop on Semantic Evaluation (SemEval 2014)*, pages 63–72.

Stephan Oepen and Jan Tore Lønning. 2006. Discriminant-based mrs banking. In *LREC*, pages 1250–1255.

Martha Palmer, Daniel Gildea, and Paul Kingsbury. 2005. The proposition bank: An annotated corpus of semantic roles. *Computational linguistics*, 31(1):71–106.

Carl Pollard and Ivan A Sag. 1994. *Head-driven phrase structure grammar*. University of Chicago Press.

Chuan Wang and Nianwen Xue. 2017. Getting the most out of amr parsing. In *Proceedings of the 2017 conference on empirical methods in natural language processing*, pages 1257–1268.

Chuan Wang, Nianwen Xue, and Sameer Pradhan. 2015a. Boosting transition-based amr parsing with refined actions and auxiliary analyzers. In *Proceedings of the 53rd Annual Meeting of the Association for Computational Linguistics and the 7th International Joint Conference on Natural Language Processing (Volume 2: Short Papers)*, volume 2, pages 857–862.

Chuan Wang, Nianwen Xue, and Sameer Pradhan. 2015b. A transition-based algorithm for amr parsing. In *Proceedings of the 2015 Conference of the North American Chapter of the Association for Computational Linguistics: Human Language Technologies*, pages 366–375.

Yuxuan Wang, Wanxiang Che, Jiang Guo, and Ting Liu. 2018. A neural transition-based approach for semantic dependency graph parsing. In *Thirty-Second AAAI Conference on Artificial Intelligence*.

Yuk Wah Wong and Raymond J Mooney. 2006. Learning for semantic parsing with statistical machine translation. In *Proceedings of the main conference on Human Language Technology Conference of the North American Chapter of the Association of Computational Linguistics*, pages 439–446. Association for Computational Linguistics.

Pengcheng Yin and Graham Neubig. 2017. A syntactic neural model for general-purpose code generation. *arXiv preprint arXiv:1704.01696*.

GKR: Bridging the gap between symbolic/structural and distributional meaning representations

Aikaterini-Lida Kalouli
University of Konstanz
aikaterini-lida.kalouli@uni-konstanz.de

Richard Crouch
Chegg

Valeria de Paiva
University of Birmingham

{dick.crouch,valeria.depaiva}@gmail.com

Abstract

Three broad approaches have been attempted to combine distributional and structural/symbolic aspects to construct meaning representations: a) injecting linguistic features into distributional representations, b) injecting distributional features into symbolic representations or c) combining structural and distributional features in the final representation. This work focuses on an example of the third and less studied approach: it extends the Graphical Knowledge Representation (GKR) to include distributional features and proposes a division of semantic labour between the distributional and structural/symbolic features. We propose two extensions of GKR that clearly show this division and empirically test one of the proposals on an NLI dataset with hard compositional pairs.

1 Introduction

Can one combine distributional and structural (symbolic) aspects to construct expressive meaning representations? Three broad approaches have been attempted. First, there is work where linguistic features are used as additional input to systems that create distributional representations, e.g. Padó and Lapata (2007); Levy and Goldberg (2014); Bowman et al. (2015b); Chen et al. (2018). Second, there are approaches where distributional features are used as input to systems that create symbolic representations, e.g. Banarescu et al. (2013); van Noord et al. (2018). Third, and less represented, is the approach attempting to bridge the gap between the other two by combining structural and distributional features in the final representation, e.g. Lewis and Steedman (2013); Beltagy et al. (2016). This paper describes an example of the third approach, and extends the Graphical Knowledge Representation (GKR) (Kalouli and Crouch, 2018) to include distributional features.

We argue for a division of semantic labour. Distributional features are well suited for dealing with conceptual aspects of the meanings of words, phrases, and sentences, such as semantic similarity, and conceivably hypernym and antonym relations (Mikolov et al., 2013a; Pennington et al., 2014; Devlin et al., 2018). But they have yet to establish themselves in dealing with Boolean and contextual phenomena like modals, quantifiers, implicatives, or hypotheticals (Zhu et al., 2018; Dasgupta et al., 2018; Naik et al., 2018; Shwartz and Dagan, 2019). These are phenomena to which more symbolic/structural approaches are well suited. But these approaches have struggled to deal with the more fluid and gradable aspects of conceptual meaning (Beltagy et al., 2016).

Unlike most symbolic meaning representations, GKR does not attempt to push all aspects of meaning into a single uniform logical notation. Nor does it attempt to push all aspects of meaning into a single vector representation, as most distributional meaning representations do. Instead it allows for the separation of, and controlled interaction between, different levels of meaning. In this respect it borrows heavily from the projection architecture of Lexical Functional Grammar (Kaplan, 1995), where constituent and functional structure are seen as two separate but related aspects of syntax, each with their own distinct algebraic characteristics. GKR posits a number of distinct layers of semantic structure, the two principal ones being conceptual, predicate-argument structure, and contextual, Boolean structure. This paper discusses how conceptual structure can be enriched with a distributional sub-layer, while still allowing the contextual layer to continue doing the heavy lifting of dealing with modals, quantifiers, booleans, and the like. Our contributions in this paper are three-fold: Firstly, we briefly describe the construction principles of GKR and show why

Proceedings of the First International Workshop on Designing Meaning Representations, pages 44–55
Florence, Italy, August 1st, 2019 ©2019 Association for Computational Linguistics

it is suitable for bridging the gap between structural and distributional approaches. Secondly, we propose two extensions of GKR that allow for the proposed division of semantic labour. Thirdly, we show how one of the proposals can work in practice, by testing it on a subset of the inference dataset of Dasgupta et al. (2018) containing hard compositional pairs.

2 Relevant Work

Symbolic frameworks for meaning representations such as Discourse Representation Theory (DRT) (Kamp and Reyle, 1993), Minimal Recursion Semantics (MRS) (Copestake et al., 2005; Oepen and Lønning, 2006) or Abstract Knowledge Representation (AKR) (Bobrow et al., 2007) were developed with the goal of supporting natural language inference (NLI) and reasoning, and took special care of complex semantic phenomena such as quantification, negation, modality, factivity, etc. More recent meaning representations such as the Abstract Meaning Representation (AMR) (Banarescu et al., 2013) and the Tectogrammatical Representation (TR) from the Prague Dependency Treebank (Hajič et al., 2012), focus more on lexical semantic aspects, such as semantic roles and word senses, on entities and on relations between them. Automatic parsing of text into these different meaning representations has gained great attention, from early, more rule-based systems like Boxer (Bos, 2008) parsing sentences into DRSs, to more recent, statistical or deep learning systems parsing sentences to AMR e.g. (Flanigan et al., 2014; Wang and Xue, 2017; Ballesteros and Al-Onaizan, 2017) or even to DRSs (van Noord et al., 2018). However, to facilitate annotation and parsing, some of the later automated systems have glossed over many of the more complex semantic phenomena. This has raised questions about their expressive power for hard tasks like NLI, as already critiqued for AMR by Bos (2016) and Stabler (2017).

Distributional meaning representations of sentences range from models that compose representations by operating over word embeddings (Mitchell and Lapata, 2010; Mikolov et al., 2013b; Wieting et al., 2016; Pagliardini et al., 2018) to approaches integrating linguistic/structural features into a learning process (Padó and Lapata, 2007; Levy and Goldberg, 2014; Bowman et al., 2015b) to end-to-end neural network architectures like SkipThoughts (Kiros et al., 2015) and InferSent (Conneau et al., 2017). Already White et al. (2015) and Arora et al. (2017) showed that the more complex architectures do not always outperform simpler vector operations of the former kind, while recently Zhu et al. (2018), Dasgupta et al. (2018) and Naik et al. (2018) argued that current distributional representations fail to capture important aspects of what they call "semantic properties", "compositionality" or "complex semantic phenomena", respectively.[1] This was evaluated based on the task of NLI: the researchers created inference pairs requiring complex semantic knowledge and showed that current sentence representations struggle with them. It could be argued that this can be solved by training on data with more instances of such phenomena. But in the absence of the right kinds of annotation in sufficient volumes, this remains an open question.

Fewer approaches have attempted to bridge the gap between the two ends. Lewis and Steedman (2013) attempted to learn a CCG lexicon which maps equivalent words onto the same logical form, e.g. *author* and *write* map to the same logical form. This is done by first mapping words to a deterministic logical form, using a process similar to Boxer, and then clustering predicates based on their arguments as found in a corpus. The resulting lexicon is used to parse new sentences. Beltagy et al. (2016) present a 3-component system that first translates a sentence to a logical form, also based on Boxer, and then integrates distributional information into the logical forms in the form of weights, e.g. the rule "if x is grumpy, then there is a chance that x is also sad" is weighted by the distributional similarity of the words *grumpy* and *sad*. As a last step, the system draws inferences over the weighted rules using Markov Logic Networks (Richardson and Domingos, 2006), a Statistical Relational Learning (SRL) technique (Getoor and Taskar, 2007) that combines logical and statistical knowledge in one uniform framework, and provides a mechanism for coherent probabilistic inference. Both approaches integrate distribution by clustering or weighting *logical* representations but are still further from the goal to represent the sentence predicate-argument structure as a *distributional* representation suitable for further processing.

---

[1]"Compositionality" is something of a misnomer: basic predicate-argument structure can be compositionally driven by sentence structure.

3   A brief presentation of GKR

The Graphical Knowledge Representation was introduced by Kalouli and Crouch (2018) as a *layered* semantic graph, produced by the open-source semantic parser the researchers make available online.[2] GKR is inspired by Abstract Knowledge Representation (AKR) (Bobrow et al., 2007), the semantic component of the XLE/LFG framework, which was decoupled from XLE/LFG by Crouch (2014) and then revisited in an explicitly graphical form in Boston et al. (2019). Despite important differences between these approaches, the two main principles are common: first, the sentence information is separated in layers/subgraphs/levels and second, there is a strict separation between the conceptual/predicate-argument structure and the contextual/Boolean structure of the sentence.

These two main principles are exactly how GKR lends itself to the blending of structural/symbolic and distributional features. On the one hand, the separation in layers, analogously to the separation into levels in the LFG architecture (Kaplan, 1995), allows for the formulation of modular linguistic generalizations which govern a given level independently from the others. This explicit organization of information exactly allows for the combination of multiple logics and styles of representations, i.e. structural/linguistic and distributional, and contrasts with the "latent" representations used in end-to-end deep learning approaches to sentence representations and in other graph-based approaches like AMR. On the other hand, the division between conceptual and contextual structure already means that boolean, quantificational, and modal structures do not have to be shoe-horned into predicate argument structures. Likewise, there is no reason to try to shoe-horn boolean, quantification, and modal aspects, or predicate argument structure into a distributional vector. The structures can live alongside one another. This still leaves some latitude for how much predicate-argument and contextual structure needs to be injected into vector representations, depending on the task.

The GKR representation, just like its predecessors, is specifically designed for the task of NLI. But the efficacy of layered graphs has also been shown in dialogue management systems by Shen et al. (2018). Precisely, GKR is a rooted,

node-labelled, edge-labelled, directed graph. It currently consists of five sub-graphs, layered on top of a central conceptual (predicate-argument) sub-graph: a dependency sub-graph, a properties sub-graph, a lexical sub-graph, a coreference sub-graph and a contextual sub-graph.

The dependency graph of GKR is straightforwardly rewritten from the output of the Stanford CoreNLP parser (Chen and Manning, 2014) to fit the GKR format. More precisely, the output is obtained from the enhanced++ dependencies of Schuster and Manning (2016). The conceptual graph is the core of the semantic graph and glues all other sub-graphs together. It contains the basic predicate-argument structure of the sentence: what is talked about; the semantic subject or agent, the semantic object or patient, the modifiers, etc. In other words, this graph expresses the basic propositional content of the utterance and thus already captures the "basic", predicate-argument compositionality of the sentence. The graph nodes, which correspond to all *content* words of the dependency graph, assert the existence of the *concepts* described by these words, but do not make claims about the existence of *instances* of those concepts. This means that the nodes represent *concepts* and not individuals and given that, no judgments about truth or entailment can be made from this graph. The edges of the graph encode the semantic relationship between the nodes, as this is translated from the dependency label to a more general "semantic" label.

The properties graph associates the conceptual graph with morphological and syntactical features such as the cardinality of nouns, the kind of quantifiers, the verbal tense and aspect, the finiteness of specifiers, etc., so that crucial information required for tasks like NLI is kept in place. For now, this information is gathered from the surface forms and the POS tags provided by CoreNLP in a rule-based fashion. The lexical graph carries the lexical information of the sentence. It associates each node of the conceptual graph with its disambiguated sense and concept, its hypernyms and its hyponyms, making use of the disambiguation algorithm JIGSAW (Basile et al., 2007), WordNet (Fellbaum, 1998)) and the knowledge base SUMO (Niles and Pease, 2001). The coreference graph resolves coreference and anaphora phenomena between words of the sentence, based on the output of CoreNLP. The edges of this graph model the

---

46

coreferences between the concept nodes.

The contextual graph is also built on top of the conceptual graph and it provides the existential commitments of the sentence: since the conceptual graph only deals with *concepts* and not individuals and thus is incapable on it own to make existential claims and support the attribution of truth and validity, the contextual level is necessary for making such existential commitments and thus support inference. It is also not reducible to some variation of the conceptual layer, because it is exactly this strict separation between the two layers that allows GKR the division of the semantic labour, as it will be shown in the following. The contextual graph introduces a top context (or possible world) which represents whatever the author of the sentence takes the described world to be like; in other words, whatever her "true" world holds, what concepts are instantiated and what are not. Additional contexts can be added, corresponding to any alternative possible worlds introduced in the sentence. Such contexts can be introduced by negation, disjunction, modals, clausal contexts of propositional attitudes (e.g. belief, knowledge, obligation), implicatives and factives, imperatives, questions, conditionals and distributivity. These phenomena are extracted from the sentence in a rule-based manner and their exact conversion into the context graph is defined by a dictionary-like look-up; see Kalouli and Crouch (2018) for more details. This means that the contexts correspond to what we called contextual/Boolean phenomena and what the literature often calls "hard compositionality phenomena". Each of these embedded contexts makes itself commitments about its own state of affairs, also by stating whether a specific concept is instantiated in it or not. As the logic behind this graph is central to our proposal, we show the conceptual and contextual graph of the sentence *The boy faked the illness*, taken from Kalouli and Crouch (2018), in Figure 1. The conceptual graph in blue contains the concepts involved in the sentence and their semantic relations: there is a concept of faking of a concept of illness by a concept of boy. The contextual graph in grey goes further than this to make commitments about the instances of those concepts. The implicative verb *fake* causes the introduction of an additional context (*ctx(illness)*). The top context has an edge (*ctx_hd*) linking it to its head *fake*, which shows

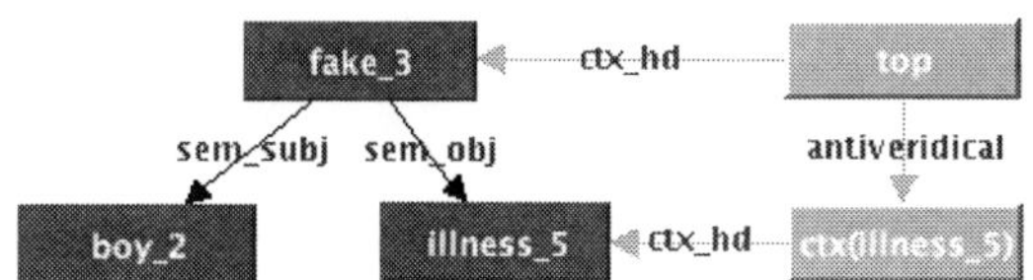

Figure 1: The conceptual graph (left) and the contextual graph (right) of *The boy faked the illness.*

that there is an instance of *faking* in this top context. The top context has a second, *anti-veridical* edge linking it to the context *ctx(illness)* which has *illness* as its head. This head edge asserts that there is an instance of illness in this contrary-to-fact context *ctx(illness)*. But since *ctx(illness)* and top are linked with an anti-veridical edge, it means that there is no instance of *illness* in the top world which is accurate as the illness was faked.

Similar graphs are produced for sentences with negation, e.g. *The dog is not eating the food*: the concepts of *dog*, *food* and *eating* are included in the conceptual graph and the contextual graph contains a top context linking to the embedded context introduced by the negation. The linking is again through an anti-veridical edge, so that the concept of *eating* is not instantiated in the context top. This setting means that negation does not have an impact on the conceptual graph; it is the *contextual* graphs of the positive and negative versions of the sentence that differ. This will prove a very useful feature for our purposes.

An equally useful feature is the treatment of disjunction and conjunction, allowed by the layered nature of GKR. Disjunction and conjunction do have an impact on the conceptual graph. Both introduce an additional *complex* concept that is the combination of the individual disjoined/conjoined concepts (Figure 2, left). The concept graph marks with the edges *is_element* each component concept, of which the complex concept consists (Figure 2, left). However, the difference between conjunction and disjunction is mirrored in the context graph: there, disjunction introduces one additional context for each component of the complex concept (Figure 2, right). These contexts say that in one arm of the disjunct the *walking* concept is instantiated, while in the other arm it is the *driving* concept that is instantiated. The conjunction would instead only contain one top context, in which both concepts are instantiated.

A similar treatment is undertaken for phenomena like modals or quantification. For modals, we

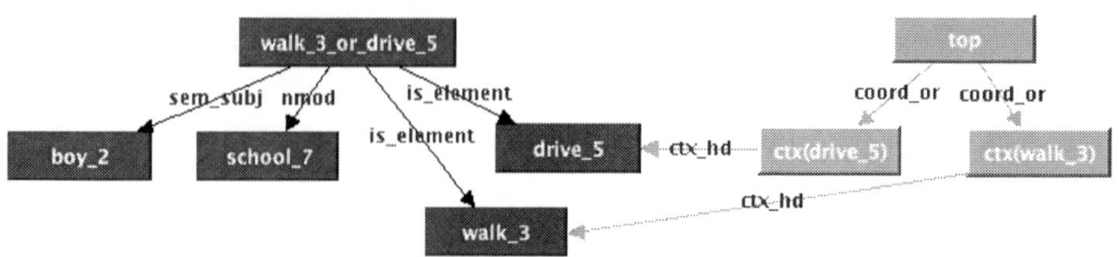

Figure 2: The conceptual graph (left) and the contextual graph (right) of *The boy walked or drove to school.*

can look at the example *Negotiations might prevent the strike* shown in Figure 3. The modal *might* introduces an extra context which is in a "might" relation to top.[3] The implicative *prevent* also introduces an extra context in which the concept of *strike* is not instantiated (anti-veridical relation) because in this context the strike does not take place – since in this context the strike was prevented. If we decide to translate *might* to the averidical relation and by transitive instantiability, we can then conclude that the strike is averidical in top, because in the top world we do not know whether there is a strike or not, which is what the modal *might* conveys.

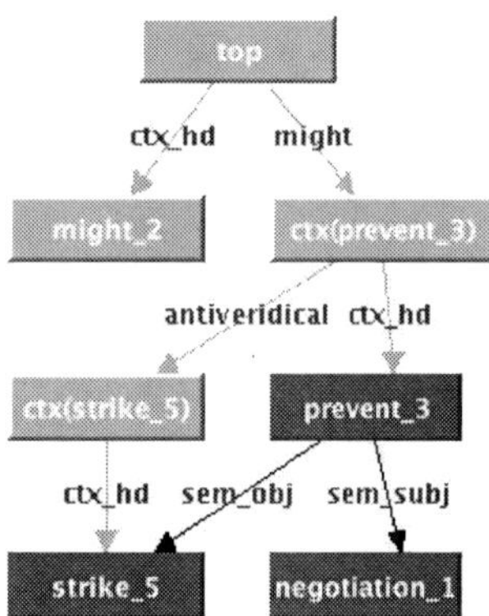

Figure 3: The conceptual graph (bottom) and the contextual graph (top) of *Negotiations might prevent the strike.*

In fact, the interaction between the concept and context graphs implements the "naming" technique of Named Graphs (Carroll et al., 2005), discussed by the creators of GKR in Crouch and Kalouli (2018). A Named Graph, a small extension on top of RDF, associates an extra identifier with a set of triples. For example, a propositional attitude like *Fred believes John does not like Mary*

could be represented as follows:

```
:g1 { :john :like :mary }
:g2 :not :g1
:fred :believe :g2
```

where `:g1` is the name given to the graph expressing the proposition *John likes Mary*, and `:g2` to the graph expressing its negation. But this is also how the context graph works: the contexts are the "names" and the concepts (and their children) associated with them are the "triples" identified by them. For example, in Figure 2, `ctx(drive_5)` is the name given to the subgraph expressing the proposition {boy: drive : school } and `ctx(walk_5)` is the name given to the subgraph expressing the proposition {boy: walk : school}. top is the name given to the graph expressing the disjunction between the two contexts `ctx(drive_5)` and `ctx(walk_5)`. This shows how the "basic" predicate-argument compositionality (concept graph) and the "harder" compositionality (context graph) can be kept apart and foreshadows our proposals: the method of factoring out the "harder" compositionality can lead to better performance for both the symbolic/structural and the distributional systems.

For a more detailed discussion of how the distinct graphs are constructed and how other Boolean/contextual cases can be handled, see Kalouli and Crouch (2018).

4   Our proposal for extension of GKR

The two core principles of GKR, i.e. the strict separation of concepts and contexts, with sentence words representing concepts and not individuals, and the modularity and layer separation of the information, allow us to formulate our proposal for a hybrid meaning representation with symbolic/structural and distributional features.

In this section we show how GKR allows for two different ways of combining symbolic/structural and distributional meaning features, each way involving a different degree of the

---

[3] We can choose to translate each modal to a specific veridicality relation, e.g. *might* to averidical, but the initial graph makes no such translation so that no crucial information gets lost.

contribution of each kind of feature and thus being freely select-able based on the needs of the researcher and of the given application. We present these solutions based on the task of NLI, which has been one of the mostly used tasks for the training and evaluation of meaning representations and is the driving force for the design of GKR.

4.1 More symbolic

This proposal is the closest to the original proposal of Kalouli and Crouch (2018) because it only expands the current lexical graph of GKR but keeps all other linguistic structures in place. In that sense, it is more symbolic/structural than it is distributional: it exploits the distributional strengths for the conceptual meaning of the words but builds both the "basic" (predicate-argument) compositionality as well as the "harder" compositionality phenomena in a symbolic/structural way.

The current GKR lexical graph connects its nodes to hand-curated resources like WordNet and SUMO but it could easily be expanded to also contain links to word embeddings. Given the great success of contextualized word embeddings like ELMo (Peters et al., 2018) and BERT (Devlin et al., 2018), it is promising to expand the graph with such embeddings. With this, each concept node would be further connected to its contextualized word embedding. These contextualized word embeddings can be calculated based on the sentence which is currently modelled or, in the case of NLI, based on both sentences of the pair for a more accurate context.

With such an expanded lexical graph in place, we can proceed to do inference in a similar fashion as the one originally proposed by Kalouli and Crouch (2018): each sentence of the pair is parsed into a GKR graph and then the concepts of the two graphs are matched through specificity relations like the ones proposed in Natural Logic systems (cf. MacCartney and Manning (2007) and Crouch and King (2007)), e.g. that *dog* of the premise is a subclass of *animal* of the hypothesis. So far these relations can only be established based on the human-curated resources, which means that some relations will fail to be captured either because they do not exist in the resources or because the strict, logic-based resources do not allow their associations. For example, as discussed in Kalouli et al. (2018), for a pair like A= *The dog is catching a black frisbee. B= The dog is biting a black frisbee*, the words *catch* and *bite* will not be found related in human-curated resources but given that we are talking about dogs, they should be related. With our proposed extension, such similarities can be captured by *contextualized* word embeddings. By integrating relevant literature attempting to define hypernymy/hyponymy relations between embeddings (e.g. see Yu and Dredze (2015) and Nguyen et al. (2017)), we could even define the exact relation (hypernymy, hyponymy) between two similar embeddings instead of defaulting them to "similar" and thus "entailing". Then, the established specificity judgments are updated with further restrictions imposed by the properties and conceptual graphs. Specifically, the conceptual graph imposes constraints concerning the semantic roles of the concepts, i.e. the "basic" predicate-argument composition, and is thus defining what specificity matches are "compatible" and which have to be removed, e.g. the subject of the one sentence cannot be matched with the object of the other (note that GKR solves active/passive voice and produces the same semantic graph for the active and passive version of a given sentence). Given enough training data, the plausibility of a given match can be estimated through a learning process. After the update of the concept matches, the context graph can determine which of those matched concepts are (un-)instantiated within which contexts, i.e. we now deal with "hard" compositionality cases. This is possible due to the "naming" role that the contexts play: for each concept which we have matched and updated with restrictions, we can find the context it is the head of and look up its instantiation. As a final step for inference, instantiation and specificity are combined to determine entailment relations. A preliminary, experimental version of this proposal is under implementation but its detailed presentation is beyond the scope of this paper.

4.2 More distributional

The previous approach attempts to inject distributional features on the lexical layer of GKR, thus restricting it to the simple contribution of word embeddings. It also integrates a learning process in the match update, but in its core, it solves the "basic" predicate-argument as well as the "harder" boolean/contextual compositionality with symbolic/structural methods, namely through the use of the concept and context graphs. However, for a given application it might be more beneficial to have a stronger distributional effect than the previous approach allows. For this we can still benefit from GKR factoring out the contextual structure, i.e. dealing separately with the "harder" compositionality cases that distributional approaches struggle with, and use the concept graph only in an assisting way.

So, in this approach the merit of the "naming" technique implemented in the context graph shows itself more clearly: we go through the context graph and we collect all contexts being introduced. For each of them we find its head (*ctx_hd*), which leads us back to the node of the concept graph (see Figure 1 and 2). For this node of the concept graph and all of its children (arguments, modifiers), i.e. for the subgraph with this node as the root, we compute a distributional representation with whichever (neural net) approach we want. Now, each context of the context graph, i.e. each "name", is associated with a distributional representation and within the context graph these distributed representations are linked with each other with veridical, anti-veridical or averidical edges, based on the original context graph. After doing this computation for each of the sentences of the inference pair, the resulting "named" graphs can be fed into a subsequent layer function, which matches some or all the representations across graphs/sentences based on a computed similarity. Finally, by look-up of the instantiability of each of the matched representations and, if required, by computation of the result of subsequent instantiabilities, the inference relation is decided.

This simple "trick" of factoring out the "hard" compositionality cases, i.e. packing this information in the context graph, allows us the flexibility of using a variety of options for how word vectors can be composed into phrase vectors. In other words, in this approach the "basic" predicate-argument structure compositionality can be achieved in any (distributional) way a given application requires – independently from the concept graph and not necessarily as a logical form as relevant literature (Lewis and Steedman, 2013; Beltagy et al., 2016) has attempted so far. For example, the researcher could choose a more end-to-end deep architecture, like the one used by Conneau et al. (2017) in InferSent, or train a tree-structured recursive neural model as it is done by

Bowman et al. (2015b), where the tree on which the model is based, is built considering the compositionality principles applying to constituents parsing. No matter the predicate-argument composition approach and the final distributional representation, what is crucial is that Boolean and contextual phenomena can be treated outside this representation and thus distributional approaches can benefit from the precision that symbolic/structural methods achieve in such phenomena. A sample implementation of this proposal is described in Section 5.

5 Proof-of-concept for the "more distributional" approach

Recently, Dasgupta et al. (2018) (DS from now on) experimented with the compositionality of the InferSent (Conneau et al., 2017) embeddings. They created different NLI test sets which contain pairs that cannot be solved with world-knowledge but instead involve some more complex semantic phenomena. They trained a classifier on the inference corpus SNLI (Bowman et al., 2015a), using the state-of-the-art InferSent embeddings, and found that the performance on all of their created sets reaches around 50%, thus proving that such embeddings do not yet capture aspects of "basic" predicate-argument and "harder" compositionality. After including the created test sets into the training data of the classifier, DS show that performance improves. With our "more distributional" proposal, we show that it is not necessary to attempt to adequately include all possible linguistic phenomena in the training data: we choose two of the test sets of DS[4] containing a total of 4800 pairs, where sentence A involves a conjunction of a positive sentence with a negative sentence and sentence B contains one of the conjunct sentences either in its positive or its negative version, as shown below, resulting into entailment or contradiction.

```
A= The boy does frown angrily, but the
girl does not frown angrily.
B= The boy does not frown angrily.
CONTRADICTION
```

For this subset, DS report a performance of 53.2% and 53.8% for *subjv_long* and *subjv_short*, respectively, on the original SNLI trained model.

---

[4]Available from `https://github.com/ishita-dg/ScrambleTests`. Chosen sets: subjv_long and subjv_short.

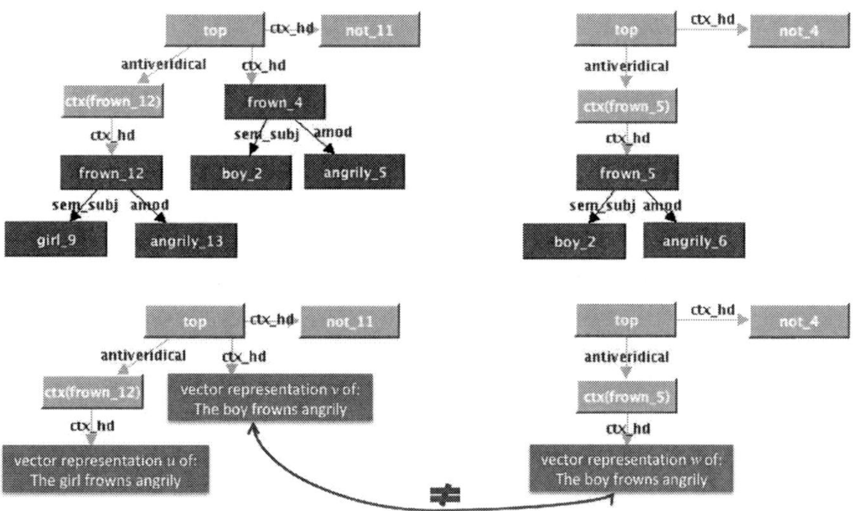

Figure 4: Computation of the "more distributional" proposal. Top: GKR concept and context graphs of the sentences *The boy does frown angrily, but the girl does not frown angrily.* (left) and *The boy does not frown angrily.* (right). Bottom: Injection of the distributional representations in the context graphs for the two sentences, respectively. The red arrow is matching the two similar representations

This set was chosen for three reasons: a) it has one of the lowest performances among DSs' sets, b) it combines two of the most challenging compositionality phenomena contained in DSs' sets altogether, i.e. it requires both the treatment of negation and the distinction between the conjunct sentences/events, and c) the phenomena it deals with are of the type for which GKR's division of semantic labor can show its value and offer a direct solution. Future work can apply the proposed method to the other sets, some of which however, e.g. the scrambled word order sets, might need a stronger symbolic/structural component as presented in our first proposal in Section 4.1.

To test our "more distributional" proposal, we proceed as described in 4.2. We first process both sentences of each pair with GKR and then we go through each sentence to match it to its distributional representation: for each context introduced in the context graph (Figure 4, top, in grey), we retrieve its *cxt_head*, which is a node of the concept graph (Figure 4, top, in blue). For the phrase/sentence consisting of this concept node and all its children, we compute the InferSent representation (Figure 4, bottom, in green). Now, within the context graph, every context ("name") is associated with such a representation, which means that we have the instantiability of each representation. For each pair, we attempt to match

one of the representations of sentence A with the representation of sentence B. In this test set, simple cosine similarities are enough to compute this, because we know that representation B exactly matches one of the A representations. For more complex cases, a trained function should be responsible for the matching, as described above. After a match is found (Figure 4, bottom, red arrow), we look up the instantiability of each of the matched representations in the top context: if one of them is anti-veridical and the other one veridical, there is a contradiction; if both of them have the same veridicality, then we have an entailment. In our example of Figure 4 we have one match between vectors v and w. Vector v is in a veridical relation with the top context (it is in fact the head of the context, thus it is veridical in it), while vector w is in an anti-veridical relation to top. This means that there is a contradiction between the matched representations and thus the whole pair is labelled contradictory.

This process allowed us to achieve 99.5% accuracy on the two test sets. The 24 wrongly labelled pairs were caused by the wrong output of the Stanford Parser, which led to the wrong dependency graph, wrong conceptual graph and finally wrong contextual graph. In fact, there were more cases where the output of the Stanford Parser was incorrect, but if the assignment of concepts to contexts is correct, i.e. a partially wrong conceptual graph is matched to a valid context, those weaknesses might not be crucial for the final result. This additional merit shows how we combine the best of both worlds: the computation can succeed even if the concept graph is erroneous, as long as the contexts assigned to the concepts and the matching between the distributional representations of A and B are good enough. In an erroneous concept graph the concepts acting as context heads might be associated with wrong concepts (children), which in turn means that the distributional representation will also not encode the subgraph that we would ideally want. However, given the robustness of such representations and the fact that they encode world knowledge, the matching between the representations across the two sentences can still succeed if the trained similarity function can recognize two representations as more similar. Then, if the contexts assigned to the concepts and thus the computed representations are correct, the system can still predict the correct relation because it can use the matched representations of the distributional approach and their instantiability of the symbolic/structural approach. This means that we benefit from the robustness of the distributional approaches without sacrificing the precision of the symbolic/structural ones.

Nevertheless, we should also note that the two test sets are artificially simple so that the simple trick of factoring out the contextual structure, i.e. the "hard" compositionality phenomena, performs extremely well in comparison to the purely distributional approaches. Firstly, in this test set, there is little variation between the predicate-argument structures of the sentences of the pairs so that we cannot fully check how the Stanford Parser would perform in other cases and how well the GKR concept and context graphs would then be able to "repair" the mistakes of the parser. Furthermore, in this test set we know that sentence B has only one representation which definitely matches with one of the representations of A. This makes the simple cosine similarity as metric for the matching of the representations efficient enough; however, in a harder data set with no such "patterns", the performance would strongly depend on the quality of the trained matching function, which would have to be more complex than simply the "match with the highest cosine similarity" and thus more error-prone. Despite this grain-of-salt caution, this ap-

proach is expected to perform well for many other complex phenomena apart from negation and conjunction. For example, it will work reasonably well for implicatures such as A = *The boy forgot to close the door.* B= *The boy closed the door.* For sentence A the distributional representations of the subgraph *The boy close the door* will be anti-veridical in the top context of *forget*, while in B the representation of the whole sentence will be veridical in top. These two representations will have the highest similarity in the matching procedure and will thus match. Considering the instatiabilities of this match, the pair will be deemed a contradiction.

Testing this approach with further datasets of complex examples can show potential weaknesses of using GKRs in this way and particularly highlight other aspects where the distributional or the symbolic/structural strengths should be used more or less. For example, as indicated above, testing with sets with scrambled word order pairs (e.g. *The dog is licking the man* vs. *The man is licking the dog*) might show the need for a stronger symbolic/structural component where the predicate-argument structure is considered more, as it is done in the first proposed approach in 4.1. Additionally, it would be interesting to compare this approach to a purely symbolic/structural one to highlight differences in performance. However, to the best of our knowledge, there is no openly-available, purely symbolic NLI system to which we could straight-forwardly compare our results.

6   Conclusions

In this paper we combine symbolic/structural and distributional features for meaning representations and propose that each of them be used in what it is best at: for complex phenomena like quantification, booleans and modality, use structural meaning and for robust, world-knowledge-informed lexical representations, use distributional semantics. We show how GKR could fulfill this role in two different ways and implement one of them to empirically test its adequacy in the setting of simple, but hard problems for distributional approaches. The good performance results make us confident that there is indeed value in combining the merits of distributional and symbolic approaches. Future work will show how the current proposals can be extended to larger scale systems, maybe also in a combined manner.

References

Sanjeev Arora, Yingyu Liang, and Tengyu Ma. 2017. A simple but tough-to-beat baseline for sentence embeddings. In *International Conference on Learning Representations (ICLR)*.

Miguel Ballesteros and Yaser Al-Onaizan. 2017. AMR parsing using stack-LSTMs. In *Proceedings of the 2017 Conference on Empirical Methods in Natural Language Processing*, pages 1269–1275, Copenhagen, Denmark. Association for Computational Linguistics.

Laura Banarescu, Claire Bonial, Shu Cai, Madalina Georgescu, Kira Griffitt, Ulf Hermjakob, Kevin Knight, Philipp Koehn, Martha Palmer, and Nathan Schneider. 2013. Abstract Meaning Representation for Sembanking. In *Proceedings of the 7th Linguistic Annotation Workshop & Interoperability with Discourse*, pages 178–186.

Pierpaolo Basile, Marco de Gemmis, Anna Lisa Gentile, Pasquale Lops, and Giovanni Semeraro. 2007. UNIBA: JIGSAW algorithm for Word Sense Disambiguation. In *Proceedings of the Fourth International Workshop on Semantic Evaluations (SemEval-2007)*, pages 398–401, Prague, Czech Republic. Association for Computational Linguistics.

I. Beltagy, Stephen Roller, Pengxiang Cheng, Katrin Erk, and Raymond J. Mooney. 2016. Representing Meaning with a Combination of Logical and Distributional Models. *Computational Linguistics*, 42(4):763–808.

Daniel G. Bobrow, Bob Cheslow, Cleo Condoravdi, Lauri Karttunen, Tracy Holloway King, Rowan Nairn, Valeria de Paiva, Charlotte Price, and Annie Zaenen. 2007. PARCs Bridge and Question Answering System. In *Proceedings of the Grammar Engineering Across Frameworks Workshop (GEAF 2007)* .

Johan Bos. 2008. Wide-Coverage Semantic Analysis with Boxer. In *Semantics in Text Processing. STEP 2008 Conference Proceedings*, pages 277–286. College Publications.

Johan Bos. 2016. Expressive Power of Abstract Meaning Representations. *Computational Linguistics*, 42(3):527–535.

Marisa Boston, Richard Crouch, Erdem Özcan, and Peter Stubley. 2019. Natural language inference using an ontology. In Cleo Condoravdi and Tracy Holloway King, editors, *Lauri Karttunen Festschrift*. CSLI Publications.

Samuel R. Bowman, Gabor Angeli, Christopher Potts, and Christopher D. Manning. 2015a. A large annotated corpus for learning natural language inference. In *Proceedings of the 2015 Conference on Empirical Methods in Natural Language Processing*, pages 632–642, Lisbon, Portugal. Association for Computational Linguistics.

Samuel R. Bowman, Christopher Potts, and Christopher D. Manning. 2015b. Recursive Neural Networks Can Learn Logical Semantics. In *Proceedings of the 3rd Workshop on Continuous Vector Space Models and their Compositionality*, pages 12–21, Beijing, China. Association for Computational Linguistics.

Jeremy Carroll, Christian Bizer, Pat Hayes, and Patrick Stickler. 2005. Named Graphs. *Web Semantics: Science, Services and Agents on the World Wide Web*, 3(4).

Danqi Chen and Christopher Manning. 2014. A Fast and Accurate Dependency Parser using Neural Networks. In *Proceedings of the 2014 Conference on Empirical Methods in Natural Language Processing (EMNLP)*, pages 740–750. Association for Computational Linguistics.

Qian Chen, Xiaodan Zhu, Zhen-Hua Ling, Diana Inkpen, and Si Wei. 2018. Neural Natural Language Inference Models Enhanced with External Knowledge. In *Proceedings of the 56th Annual Meeting of the Association for Computational Linguistics (Volume 1: Long Papers)*, pages 2406–2417, Melbourne, Australia. Association for Computational Linguistics.

Alexis Conneau, Douwe Kiela, Holger Schwenk, Loïc Barrault, and Antoine Bordes. 2017. Supervised learning of universal sentence representations from natural language inference data. In *Proceedings of the 2017 Conference on Empirical Methods in Natural Language Processing*, pages 670–680, Copenhagen, Denmark. Association for Computational Linguistics.

Ann Copestake, Dan Flickinger, Carl Pollard, and Ivan A. Sag. 2005. Minimal Recursion Semantics: An introduction. *Research on Language and Computation*, 3(2):281–332.

Richard Crouch. 2014. Transfer Semantics for the Clear Parser. In *Proceedings of NLCS 2014*.

Richard Crouch and Aikaterini-Lida Kalouli. 2018. Named Graphs for Semantic Representation. In *Proceedings of the Seventh Joint Conference on Lexical and Computational Semantics*, pages 113–118, New Orleans, Louisiana. Association for Computational Linguistics.

Richard Crouch and Tracy Holloway King. 2007. *Systems and methods for detecting entailment and contradiction*. US Patent 7,313,515.

Ishita Dasgupta, Demi Guo, Andreas Stuhlmüller, Samuel J. Gershman, and Noah D. Goodman. 2018. Evaluating compositionality in sentence embeddings. *CoRR*, abs/1802.04302.

Jacob Devlin, Ming-Wei Chang, Kenton Lee, and Kristina Toutanova. 2018. BERT: Pre-training of deep bidirectional transformers for language understanding. *CoRR*, abs/1810.04805.

C. Fellbaum. 1998. *WordNet: An Electronic Lexical Database (Language, Speech, and Communication)*. The MIT Press.

Jeffrey Flanigan, Sam Thomson, Jaime Carbonell, Chris Dyer, and Noah A. Smith. 2014. A Discriminative Graph-Based Parser for the Abstract Meaning Representation. In *Proceedings of the 52nd Annual Meeting of the Association for Computational Linguistics (Volume 1: Long Papers)*, pages 1426–1436, Baltimore, Maryland. Association for Computational Linguistics.

L. Getoor and B. Taskar. 2007. *Introduction to Statistical Relational Learning*. MIT Press.

Jan Hajič, Eva Hajičová, Jarmila Panevová, Petr Sgall, Ondřej Bojar, Silvie Cinková, Eva Fučíková, Marie Mikulová, Petr Pajas, Jan Popelka, Jiří Semecký, Jana Šindlerová, Jan Štěpánek, Josef Toman, Zdeňka Urešová, and Zdeněk Žabokrtský. 2012. Announcing Prague Czech-English dependency treebank 2.0. In *Proceedings of the Eighth International Conference on Language Resources and Evaluation (LREC-2012)*, pages 3153–3160, Istanbul, Turkey. European Language Resources Association (ELRA).

Aikaterini-Lida Kalouli and Richard Crouch. 2018. GKR: the Graphical Knowledge Representation for semantic parsing. In *Proceedings of the Workshop on Computational Semantics beyond Events and Roles*, pages 27–37, New Orleans, Louisiana. Association for Computational Linguistics.

Aikaterini-Lida Kalouli, Livy Real, and Valeria DePaiva. 2018. WordNet for "Easy" Textual Inferences. In *Proceedings of the Eleventh International Conference on Language Resources and Evaluation (LREC 2018)*, Paris, France. European Language Resources Association (ELRA).

Hans Kamp and Uwe Reyle. 1993. *From Discourse to Logic. Introduction to Modeltheoretic Semantics of Natural Language, Formal Logic and Discourse Representation Theory*. Kluwer, Dordrecht.

Ronald M. Kaplan. 1995. The formal architecture of lexical-functional grammar. In *Formal Issues in Lexical-Functional Grammar*. CSLI Publications, Stanford University.

Ryan Kiros, Yukun Zhu, Ruslan Salakhutdinov, Richard S. Zemel, Antonio Torralba, Raquel Urtasun, and Sanja Fidler. 2015. Skip-Thought vectors. *CoRR*, abs/1506.06726.

Omer Levy and Yoav Goldberg. 2014. Dependency-Based Word Embeddings. In *Proceedings of the 52nd Annual Meeting of the Association for Computational Linguistics (Volume 2: Short Papers)*, pages 302–308, Baltimore, Maryland. Association for Computational Linguistics.

Mike Lewis and Mark Steedman. 2013. Combined Distributional and Logical Semantics. *Transactions of the Association for Computational Linguistics*, 1:179–192.

Bill MacCartney and Christopher D. Manning. 2007. Natural logic for textual inference. In *Proceedings of the ACL-PASCAL Workshop on Textual Entailment and Paraphrasing*, pages 193–200, Prague. Association for Computational Linguistics.

Tomas Mikolov, Kai Chen, Greg Corrado, and Jeffrey Dean. 2013a. Efficient Estimation of Word Representations in Vector Space. *Proceedings of Workshop at ICLR*.

Tomas Mikolov, Ilya Sutskever, Kai Chen, Greg S Corrado, and Jeff Dean. 2013b. Distributed Representations of Words and Phrases and their Compositionality. In C. J. C. Burges, L. Bottou, M. Welling, Z. Ghahramani, and K. Q. Weinberger, editors, *Advances in Neural Information Processing Systems 26*, pages 3111–3119. Curran Associates, Inc.

Jeff Mitchell and Mirella Lapata. 2010. Composition in Distributional Models of Semantics. *Cognitive Science*, 34(8):1388–1429.

Aakanksha Naik, Abhilasha Ravichander, Norman Sadeh, Carolyn Rose, and Graham Neubig. 2018. Stress Test Evaluation for Natural Language Inference. In *Proceedings of the 27th International Conference on Computational Linguistics*, pages 2340–2353, Santa Fe, New Mexico, USA. Association for Computational Linguistics.

Kim Anh Nguyen, Maximilian Köper, Sabine Schulte im Walde, and Ngoc Thang Vu. 2017. Hierarchical Embeddings for Hypernymy Detection and Directionality. In *Proceedings of the 2017 Conference on Empirical Methods in Natural Language Processing*, pages 233–243, Copenhagen, Denmark. Association for Computational Linguistics.

Ian Niles and Adam Pease. 2001. Toward a Standard Upper Ontology. In *Proceedings of the 2nd International Conference on Formal Ontology in Information Systems (FOIS-2001)*, pages 2–9.

Rik van Noord, Lasha Abzianidze, Antonio Toral, and Johan Bos. 2018. Exploring neural methods for parsing discourse representation structures. *Transactions of the Association for Computational Linguistics*, 6:619–633.

Stephan Oepen and Jan Tore Lønning. 2006. Discriminant-based MRS banking. In *Proceedings of the Fifth International Conference on Language Resources and Evaluation (LREC2006)*, Genoa, Italy. European Language Resources Association (ELRA).

Sebastian Padó and Mirella Lapata. 2007. Dependency-Based Construction of Semantic Space Models. *Comput. Linguist.*, 33(2):161–199.

Matteo Pagliardini, Prakhar Gupta, and Martin Jaggi. 2018. Unsupervised learning of sentence embeddings using compositional n-gram features. In *Proceedings of the 2018 Conference of the North American Chapter of the Association for Computational Linguistics: Human Language Technologies, Volume 1 (Long Papers)*, pages 528–540, New Orleans, Louisiana. Association for Computational Linguistics.

Jeffrey Pennington, Richard Socher, and Christopher D. Manning. 2014. Glove: Global Vectors for Word Representation. In *Proceedings of the 2014 Conference on Empirical Methods in Natural Language Processing (EMNLP)*, pages 1532–1543.

Matthew Peters, Mark Neumann, Mohit Iyyer, Matt Gardner, Christopher Clark, Kenton Lee, and Luke Zettlemoyer. 2018. Deep contextualized word representations. In *Proceedings of the 2018 Conference of the North American Chapter of the Association for Computational Linguistics: Human Language Technologies, Volume 1 (Long Papers)*, pages 2227–2237, New Orleans, Louisiana. Association for Computational Linguistics.

Matthew Richardson and Pedro Domingos. 2006. Markov logic networks. *Machine Learning*, 62(1):107–136.

Sebastian Schuster and Christopher D. Manning. 2016. Enhanced English Universal Dependencies: An Improved Representation for Natural Language Understanding Tasks. In *Proceedings of the Tenth International Conference on Language Resources and Evaluation (LREC 2016)*.

Jiaying Shen, Henk Harkema, Richard Crouch, Ciaran O'Reilly, and Peng Yu. 2018. Layered semantic graphs for dialogue management. In *Proceedings of the 22nd workshop on the Semantics and Pragmatics of Dialogue (SemDial)*.

Vered Shwartz and Ido Dagan. 2019. Still a pain in the neck: Evaluating text representations on lexical composition. *CoRR*, abs/1902.10618.

Ed Stabler. 2017. Reforming AMR. In *Formal Grammar 2017. Lecture Notes in Computer Science*, volume 10686. Springer.

Chuan Wang and Nianwen Xue. 2017. Getting the Most out of AMR Parsing. In *Proceedings of the 2017 Conference on Empirical Methods in Natural Language Processing*, pages 1257–1268, Copenhagen, Denmark. Association for Computational Linguistics.

Lyndon White, Roberto Togneri, Wei Liu, and Mohammed Bennamoun. 2015. How well sentence embeddings capture meaning. In *Proceedings of the 20th Australasian Document Computing Symposium*, ADCS '15, pages 9:1–9:8, New York, NY, USA. ACM.

John Wieting, Mohit Bansal, Kevin Gimpel, and Karen Livescu. 2016. Towards Universal Paraphrastic Sentence Embeddings. *CoRR*, abs/1511.08198.

Mo Yu and Mark Dredze. 2015. Learning Composition Models for Phrase Embeddings. *Transactions of the Association for Computational Linguistics*, 3:227–242.

Xunjie Zhu, Tingfeng Li, and Gerard de Melo. 2018. Exploring semantic properties of sentence embeddings. In *Proceedings of the 56th Annual Meeting of the Association for Computational Linguistics (Volume 2: Short Papers)*, pages 632–637, Melbourne, Australia. Association for Computational Linguistics.

Generating Discourse Inferences from
Unscoped Episodic Logical Formulas

Gene Louis Kim, Benjamin Kane, Viet Duong, Muskaan Mendiratta,
Graeme McGuire, Sophie Sackstein, Georgiy Platonov, and Lenhart Schubert
University of Rochester
Department of Computer Science
gkim21,gplatono,schubert@cs.rochester.edu
bkane2,vduong,mmendira,gmcguir2,ssackste@u.rochester.edu

Abstract

Unscoped episodic logical form (ULF) is a semantic representation capturing the predicate-argument structure of English within the episodic logic formalism in relation to the syntactic structure, while leaving scope, word sense, and anaphora unresolved. We describe how ULF can be used to generate natural language inferences that are grounded in the semantic and syntactic structure through a small set of rules defined over interpretable predicates and transformations on ULFs. The semantic restrictions placed by ULF semantic types enables us to ensure that the inferred structures are semantically coherent while the nearness to syntax enables accurate mapping to English. We demonstrate these inferences on four classes of conversationally-oriented inferences in a mixed genre dataset with 68.5% precision from human judgments.

1 Introduction

ULF was recently introduced as a semantic representation that captures the core semantic structure within an expressive logical formalism while staying close enough to the surface language to annotate a dataset that can be used to train a parser (Kim and Schubert, 2019; Kim, 2019). Kim and Schubert (2019) focused on the descriptive power of ULF and its relation to its fully resolved counterpart, Episodic Logic (EL), but the combination of semantic and syntactic information encoded in ULFs should position it to enable certain structurally-driven inferences. In fact, Kim and Schubert (2019) mention some of these inferential classes that they expect ULF will support, but give no description of how to achieve this, nor a demonstration of it in practice.

ULF, being a pre-canonicalized semantic form, makes available many possible structures for similar semantic meanings, which leads to a challenge

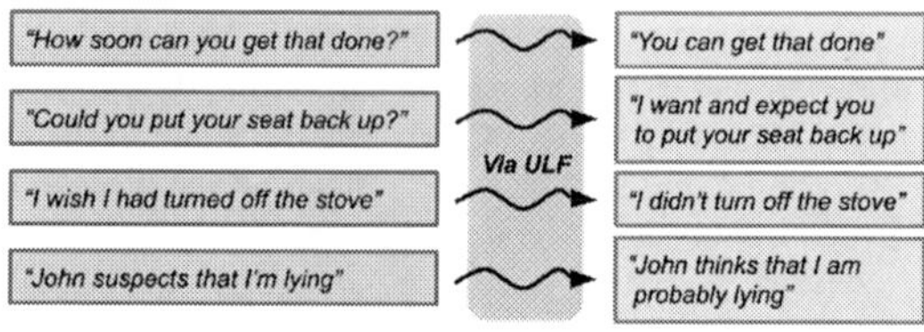

Figure 1: Examples of the sorts of discourse inferences that we generate via ULFs.

in formulating generalizable inferences. This pre-canonicalized nature of ULF, though structurally relatively intricate, has some advantages over fully canonicalized representations for use in natural language tasks. One is that it allows direct translation of intuitions about warranted textual inferences into inference rules (much as in Natural Logic). As well, the ability to accurately generate the English sentences corresponding to a ULF formula and choose how and when to modify the surface form allows a more natural interface with the end task. This feature allows us to evaluate inferences generated by ULF directly over English text rather than using an artificially structured interface, such as classification.

We present a method of generating inferences from ULFs from a small set of interpretable inference rules by first defining general semantic predicates over ULF clauses and tree transformations that correspond to natural semantic operations in ULF. We then evaluate these on four of the five inferential classes presented by Kim and Schubert (2019) over a multi-genre dataset. The ULF structure allows us to incorporate a paraphrase-like rewrite module and then perform direct string comparisons of English generated from ULFs to human generated inferences. Human evaluations show that 68.5% of these generated inferences are acceptable and an error analysis of the system shows that many of the errors can be corrected

Proceedings of the First International Workshop on Designing Meaning Representations, pages 56–65
Florence, Italy, August 1st, 2019 ©2019 Association for Computational Linguistics

with some refinement to the inference rules and the ULF-to-English generation system.

2 Unscoped Episodic Logical Form

ULF is an underspecified variant of EL which captures the predicate-argument structure within the EL type-system while leaving operator scope, anaphora, and word sense unresolved (Kim and Schubert, 2019). All atoms in ULF, with the exception of certain logical functions, syntactic macros, and names are marked with an atomic type, which are written with suffixed tags: `.v`, `.n`, `.a`, `.p`, `.pro`, `.d`, etc. echoing the part-of-speech, such as verb, noun, adjective, preposition, pronoun, determiner, etc., respectively. Some of them contain further specifications as relevant to their entailments, e.g., `.adv-e` for locative or temporal adverbs (implying properties of events). These correspond to particular possible semantic denotations. For example, `.pro` is always an *entity*, `.p` is always a *binary predicate*, and `.v` is an *n-ary predicate*, where *n* can vary. ULF (and EL) uses type-shifting operators to retain type coherence while staying faithful to the semantic types. This is demonstrated in the following example.

(1) *Would you take Tom to Boston with you?*

```
(((pres would.aux-s) you.pro
  (take.v |Tom| (to.p-arg |Boston|)
  (adv-a (with.p you.pro)))) ?)
```

The type shifting operator `adv-a` is necessary in (`adv-a (with.p you.pro)`) since this prepositional phrase is acting as a *predicate modifier* in (1), rather than as a predicate (e.g. *"My daughter is with you"*). Constituents in ULF are combined according to their bracketing and semantic types as ULF does not restrict operator ordering in most constructions.

In order to maintain word order and simplify the explicitly modeled structure, ULF includes syntactic *macros* and *relaxations*. ULF *macros* are marked explicitly and reorganize their arguments in a regular manner. For example, `sub` is a macro for moving topicalized constituents to their semantic positions—see the ULF in Figure 4 for an example. ULF *relaxations* are parts of ULFs that are not required to follow the strict operator-operand syntax because their exact position can be deduced otherwise. The subject-auxiliary inversion in (1) is an example of this.

2.1 Expected Inferences from ULF

Here we briefly describe the classes of inferences that Kim and Schubert (2019) propose could be generated with ULF. [1]

Inferences based on clause-taking verbs – For example, *"She managed to quit smoking"* entails that *"She quit smoking"* and *"John suspects that I am lying"* entails *"John believes that I am probably lying"*. Stratos et al. (2011) have demonstrated such inferences using fully resolved EL formulas.

Inferences based on counterfactuals – For example, *"I wish I hadn't forgotten to turn off the stove"* implicates that *the speaker had forgotten to turn off the stove.*

Inferences from questions – For example, *"How soon can you get that done?"* enables the inference that the addressee is able to get that done (in the foreseeable future), and that the questioner wants to know the expected time of completion, and expects that the addressee probably knows the answer, and will supply it.

Inferences from requests – For example, *"Could you put your seat back up a little?"* implies that the speaker wants the addressee to put their seat back up, and expects he or she will do so.

NLog (Natural Logic) inferences based on generalizations and specializations – For example, *"Every dog in the park chased after the squirrel"*, together with the knowledge that Spot was a dog at the park and that a squirrel is an animal entails that *Spot chased after an animal.*

A common feature among all of these inferences is that they are highly dependent on a combination of the predicate-argument and syntactic structures. Also, these are inferences that come naturally and spontaneously to speakers during conversation and are important for generating natural dialogues by setting up the appropriate conversational context.

---

[1] As ULFs do not resolve operator scope, anaphora, and word sense ambiguity, inferences generated with ULFs will retain these ambiguities. Therefore, the use of these inferences will either need to tolerate such ambiguities, or resolve them in a later step. Later resolution requires keeping track of context of formulas from which conclusions are drawn. For example, say we conclude from *"We know he lied"* that *"He lied"*. Resolving the referent of *"He"* requires the context of the original sentence, which likely disambiguates the person.

"Can somebody help me?"

`(((pres can.aux-v) somebody.pro`
`(help.v me.pro)) ?)`

$\Rightarrow$

"I want somebody to help me."

`(i.pro ((pres want.v) somebody.pro`
`(to (help.v me.pro))))`

Inference Rule

`(∀a,t,v [[[a aux-indicating-request?] ∧ [t request-personal-pronoun?] ∧ [v verb?] ∧`
`(((pres a) t v) ?)]`
`→ (i.pro ((pres want.v) t (to v)))])`

Figure 2: An example of an inference rule for inferring an underlying desire from a request. Infixed notation in the inference rule is marked with square brackets for readability. Generalizations and variants of the rule for handling extraneous sentence modifiers, such as *please*, are omitted for clarity.

3   ULF Inference Rules

The inference rules that we define are tree trans-ductions that respect the EL type system in both the antecedent and consequent clauses, ensuring semantic coherence in the concluded formulas. By using high-level predicates and transformations over ULF expressions, these are simple and inter-pretable at the top level. We use TTT (Purtee and Schubert, 2012) to define our tree-transductions rules as it provides a powerful and flexible way to declare tree transductions and supports custom predicate and mapping functions.

3.1   Named ULF Expression Predicates

The foundation of the interpretable predicates cor-respond to the ULF semantic types with syntac-tic features, e.g. `lex-pronoun?` which is true for any atom with a `.pro` suffix—a ULF pronoun. In line with TTT notation, we indicate predicates by ending the name with a question mark, `?`. These are defined over the possible compositions of ULF expressions which includes, for example, `verb?` and `tensed-verb?` that match arbitrary untensed and tensed verb phrases in ULF. This extends to all distinct ULF constituent types: `noun?`, `adv?`, `term?`, `plural-term?`, `sent?`, etc. We supplement these with predicates that correspond to patterns or enumerations of ULFs that correspond specifi-cally to the inference task in question. For exam-ple, `aux-indicating-request?` is a predicate that is true for eight ULF auxiliary forms that corre-spond to a request.[2]

3.2   Named ULF Expression Transformations

High-level tree transformation rules which cor-respond to natural semantic modifications are also defined and named. These are defined for transformations where the indexical nature and

looser syntactic constraints of ULF lead to non-trivial interactions with the syntactic structure. In other words, these rules are indexical and syntax-sensitive variants of simple EL inference rules. This includes rules such as `non-cf-vp!` which transforms a counterfactual verb phrase (VP) to the corresponding factual VP, `negate-vp!` which negates a VP, and `uninvert-sent!` which trans-forms an subject-auxiliary inverted sentence, e.g. a question, to the uninverted form. We indicate transformation rules by ending the name with an exclamantion mark, `!`. Here are a couple of exam-ples of `negate-vp!` transformations for clarity.

(2) *left the house → did not leave the house*
    `((past leave.v) (the.d house.n))`
  `→((past do.aux-s) not`
    `(leave.v (the.d house.n)))`

(3) *had met before → had not met before*
    `((past perf) meet.v before.adv-e)`
  `→((past perf) not (meet.v before.adv-e))`

Examples (2) and (3) show that the way nega-tion modifies a ULF verb phrase is dependent on the presence or absence of auxiliaries and aspec-tual operators (i.e. perfect and progressive aspect). And if this process results in a new head verb, the tense operator would need to be moved accord-ingly. In order to avoid directly managing these idiosyncratic syntactic phenomena in the inference rules, the VP negation is encapsulated into a single transformation rule.

3.3   Defining Inference Rules

The inferences rules are simple if-then relations defined over a structure where the predicates can appear in the antecedent and the named transfor-mations can appear in the consequent. Figure 2 shows an inference rule for simple requests, writ-ten as a universal quantifier over ULF expressions. In practice, this rule is implemented using a TTT

---

[2]`can.aux-v`, `can.aux-s`, `will.aux-v`, `will.aux-s`, `would.aux-v`, `would.aux-s`, `could.aux-v`, and `could.aux-s`.

58

tree transduction rule. These rules can be formulated as EL meta-axioms (Morbini and Schubert,
2008) generalized with the named ULF expression
predications and transformations to interface with
the looser syntax of ULF and its representational
idiosyncrasies inherited from English. Since the
inferential categories we are exploring are a mix-
ture of entailments, presuppositions, and implicatures their use in a general inference framework
warrants additional management of projecting presuppositions and defusing implicatures.

4   Dataset Construction

We chose a variety of text sources for constructing this dataset to reduce genre-effects and provide good coverage of all the phenomena we are
investigating. Some of these datasets include annotations, which we use only to identify sentence
and token boundaries.

4.1   Data Sources

- **Tatoeba**

  The Tatoeba dataset[3] consists of crowd-sourced
  translations from a community-based educational platform. People can request the translation of a sentence from one language to another on the website and other members will
  provide the translation. Due to this pedagogical
  structure, the sentences are fluent, simple, and
  highly-varied. The English portion downloaded
  on May 18, 2017 contains 687,274 sentences.

- **Discourse Graphbank**

  The Discourse Graphbank (Wolf, 2005) is a
  discourse annotation corpus created from 135
  newswire and WSJ texts. We use the discourse annotations to perform sentence delimit-
  ing. This dataset is on the order of several thousand sentences.

- **Project Gutenberg**

  Project Gutenberg[4] is an online repository of
  texts with expired copyright. We downloaded
  the top 100 most popular books from the 30 days
  prior to February 26, 2018. We then ignored
  books that have non-standard writing styles: po-
  ems, plays, archaic texts, instructional books,
  textbooks, and dictionaries. This collection to-
  tals to 578,650 sentences.

- **UIUC Question Classification**

  The UIUC Question Classification dataset (Li
  and Roth, 2002) consists of questions from the
  TREC question answering competition. It covers a wide range of question structures on a wide
  variety of topics, but focuses on factoid questions. This dataset consists of 15,452 questions.

4.2   Pattern-based Filtering

As the phenomena that we want to focus on are
relatively infrequent, we wrote filtering patterns to
reduce the number of human annotations needed
to get a sufficient dataset for evaluation. Requests,
for example, occur once in roughly every 100 to
1000 sentences, depending on the genre. The filtering is performed by first sentence-delimiting
and tokenizing the source texts then matching
these tokenized sentences over linguistically augmented regular expression patterns. The filtering
patterns are designed for near-full recall of the targeted sentence types by retaining sentences that
superficially look like they could be of those types.

The sentence-delimiters and tokenizers are
hand-built for each dataset for a couple of reasons. First, general purpose models are likely to
fail systematically on our multi-genre dataset and
relatively infrequent phenomena, leading to unin-
tended changes in the dataset distribution. Second,
the datasets have common patterns and existing
annotations which can be exploited in a hand-built
system. For example, the Discourse Graphbank
follows the ends of sentences with a newline and
in the Tatoeba and UIUC datasets each line is a
sentence. The transparency of the rules also have
the benefit that we can interpretably fix errors in
their performance in the future.

These filtering patterns are written in augmented regex patterns. Figure 3 shows two such
augmented regex patterns for plain and inverted
if-then counterfactual constructions. The regexes
are augmented with *tags* written in angle brackets, e.g. <begin?>. These tags refer to regex fragments that are reusable and conceptually coherent
to people. <begin?> matches either the beginning
of the string or space separated from previous text.
<mid> matches words that are padded with spaces
on the sides (i.e. separate tokens from what's defined next to it) and <mid?> is a variant that allows
just a space as well. <past> and <ppart> are alternative lists of past tense and past participle verb
forms. <futr> is an alternatives list of different

Basic if-then `"<begin?>(if|If)<mid>(was|were|had|<past>|<ppart>)<mid?>(<futr>) .+"`

If I thought this would make it difficult for the family , I would n't do it , " he said . – Discourse Graphbank

Inverted if-then `"<begin?>(<futr>)<mid>if<mid>(was|were|had|<past>|<ppart>) .+"`

Tom would n't have married Mary if he 'd known she had spent time in prison . – Tatoeba

Figure 3: Example shorthand regex patterns (Section 4.2) for filtering candidate sentences with matching sentences.

conjugations of *"will"*. Tags for closed classes of words and shorthands for common non-word patterns were hand-curated. Tags for open classes such as `<past>` and `<ppart>` are generated from the XTAG morphological database (Doran et al., 1994) with minor edits during the development process.

4.3 Sentence selection

After performing filtering, we still have far too many sentences to feasibly annotate, so we build a balanced set of 800 sentences split evenly among the four sentence types we filtered for, *clause-taking verbs*, *counterfactuals*, *requests*, and *questions*. For each sentence type, we select the sentence round-robin between the four datasets to balance out the genres. Some types of sentences appear more that 200 times in this sampling because some sentences pass multiple filters. For example, *"Could you open the door?"* passes both the *request* and *question* filters.

4.4 Inference Annotation

As we discuss in Section 7, evaluating automated inferences effectively is a major challenge. Every sentence leads to many inferences at various levels of discourse, certainty, and context-dependence. This is exacerbated by the ability to paraphrase the inferred statements. By limiting ourselves to inferences of particular general structures, we are able to elicit natural responses from people that are restricted to the particular phenomena that we are interested in investigating.

The annotations are separated into the same four categories as the filtering: *clause-taking verbs*, *counterfactuals*, *questions*, and *requests*. The annotator is first asked to select the structural inference pattern that holds for the given sentence and write down the corresponding inferred sentence. For example, say there is the sentence *"If I were rich, I would own a boat"*. The annotator would select an inference template along the lines of `(if <x> were <pred>, <x> would <q>)` → `(<x> is not <pred>)` and write down the inference "I am not rich". This way we can get a

fluent inference, but push the annotator to think about the inferences structurally. The annotators are additionally instructed to keep the inference as fluent as possible, preserve the original sentence as much as possible, and keep the perspective of the speaker of the sentence. We also included an option for annotators to add new rules, to extend the dataset into categories we did not anticipate. This category will be referred to as *Other*.

The annotations were performed by members of our research group, including some of the authors. These were completed before starting the development of the inference system. There is the possibility of development being skewed by knowledge of the annotated data, but we expect this factor to be quite small since the core inference system was built by only a couple of the annotators and the bulk of this development was done several months after completion of the annotations. The annotations totaled 698 inferences from 406 sentences.[5]

5 Evaluation

We developed the inference rules based on a set of 40 sentences randomly sampled from the annotated dataset. The correctness of these inferences is evaluated both through an automatic evaluation over the whole dataset and a human evaluation of a sample of the inferences. Both evaluations are done directly over English sentences by automatically translating the ULF inferences to English sentences. The automatic evaluation also involves a ULF rewriting module to handle semantically equivalent inference variants. All of these components are fine-tuned on the 40 sentence devset. In all of the experiments we start with human ULF annotations as a reliable ULF parser is not yet available.[6]

---

[5]This is half of the original 800 sampled sentence after filtering sentences that had duplicates due to dataset artifacts we failed to notice at the sentence selections stage and sentences that could not be annotated given the current ULF guidelines.

[6]Kim (2019) reports some promising preliminary results on parsing ULFs.

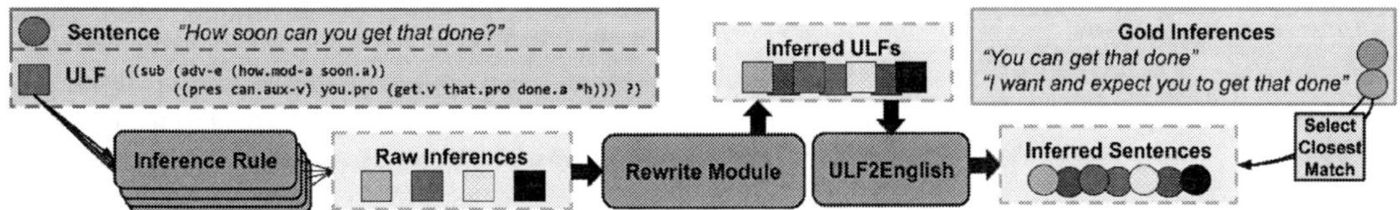

Figure 4: A diagram of the automatic ULF inference evaluation pipeline.

5.1 ULF to English

The ULF-to-English translation is done in a simple multi-stage process of

1. Analyzing the ULF type of each clause,
2. Incorporating morphological inflections based on the type analysis,
3. Filtering out purely logical operators, and
4. Mapping logical symbols to surface form counterparts.

The closeness of ULF to syntax and its preservation of most word-ordering makes hand-building a robust function for this reasonably simple. The verb conjugations and noun pluralizations are performed using the `pattern-en` python package. The code for mapping ULFs to English is available at `https://github.com/genelkim/ulf2english`.

5.2 Rewriting Rules

The rewriting rules capture alternative ways to represent the same sentence without changing the meaning. This includes clausal restructuring (e.g. *"I expect that you come here"* to *"I expect you to come here"* or *"I expect you come here"*), merging inferences (e.g. *"I want you to get that done"* and *"I expect you to get that done"* to *"I want and expect you to get that done"*) and others of this sort that are extremely unlikely to change the meaning of the sentence.

5.3 Automatic Inference Evaluation

A diagram of the automatic evaluation pipeline is presented in Figure 4. The pipeline for a given source sentence and ULF proceeds as follows:

1. Use the inference rules (Section 3) to generate a set of raw inferences from the source ULF.
2. Generate a complete set of possible realizations of the inferred ULFs by rewriting the raw inferences into possible structural variations (Section 5.2).
3. Translate inferred ULFs into English to get a set of inferred sentences (Section 5.1).
4. For each human inference elicited from the current source sentence, find the system-inferred sentence that has the smallest edit distance.
5. Report recall over human inferences with a max edit distance threshold.[7]

We use an edit distance threshold of 3. This allows minor English generation errors such as verb conjugations and pluralizations, but does not allow simple negation insertion/deletion (a difference of a space-separated *"not"* token). Table 1 lists the results of this evaluation. The numerical values are fairly low, but this may be expected given the evaluation procedure. A trivial baseline such as most frequent devset inference or copying the source sentence would lead to a score of 0 or very close to 0 as these are very unlikely to be within a 3-character edit from the inferences in the dataset.

5.4 Human Inference Evaluation

The human inference evaluation was performed over 127 raw ULF inferences. This was built out of 100 randomly sampled inferences with the addition of every counterfactual and clause-taking inference as they are not as common. Each inference was then translated to English, then presented alongside the source sentence to 3 to 4 independent human judges. The judges evaluated correctness of the discourse inference and the grammaticality of the output sentence. Table 2 presents the results of this. 87 of the 127 inferences were marked as correct by a majority of judges and only 21 were marked as incorrect by a majority of judges, for the remaining 19 inferences judges either disagreed completely or a majority judged it as context-dependent. 99 of the 127 inferences were judged grammatical by a majority of judges, which demonstrates the efficacy of the ULF-to-

---

[7]We do not report precision over automatic inferences because missing inferences are common in our dataset. This could be alleviated in the future by explicitly splitting the inference elicitation task into smaller subtasks and/or incorporating a reviewing stage where initial inferences are reviewed, corrected, and possibly added to by a second person.

	cf	cls	req	q	oth	all
Recall	1/13 (8%)	1/33 (3%)	33/97 (34%)	69/316 (22%)	7/130 (5%)	112/662 (18%)

Table 1: Results of automatic inference evaluation described in Section 5.3. **cf** stands for counterfactual inferences, **cls** for clause-taking, **req** for request, **q** for question, **oth** for other.

	cf	cls	req	q-pre	q-act	oth	all
Correct*	11/27	2/5	17/19	13/21	31/39	13/16	68.5%
Incorrect*	9/27	3/5	0/19	3/21	3/39	3/16	16.5%
Context*	7/27	0/5	2/19	5/21	5/39	0/16	15.0%
Grammar	20/27	1/5	19/19	12/21	33/39	14/16	78.0%

Table 2: Results of majority human evaluation of system generated inferences. Evaluation on 127 inferences with from the test set by 3 or 4 people per inference. *Correctness is evaluated on whether the sentence is a reasonable inference in conversation, allowing for some awkwardness in phrasing. Context, means the correctness is highly context-dependent. The inference type labels in the header row are the same as in Table 1 except for the addition of breaking down questions to **q-pre** for question presuppositions and **q-act** for question act inferences.

English translation system.[8] The system seems to struggle most with counterfactual and clause-taking inferences.

5.5 Evaluation of Rewriting Rules

In order to verify that the rewriting rules in fact preserve the semantic meanings, we gathered a sample of 100 system-inferred sentences that were closest to a gold inference (step 4 in Section 5.3). Each inferred sentence is judged as whether it is a valid rewrite of one or more of the raw inferences. A valid rewrite does not introduce new semantic information. 91 out of the 100 were judged as valid by a majority of three human judges. As such, the rewriting system is not abusively over-generating sentences that are semantically different and match to gold inferences, increasing the recall score.

6 Analysis and Discussion

The human inference evaluation (Section 5.4) showed that the system struggles most with counterfactual and clause-taking verb constructions. This is largely because the sampling procedures

for these constructions are not as effective, leading to fewer positive examples in our dataset. In turn, our development set of 40 sentences only included a handful of examples of each inference, so the rules remained brittle after adjusting to the development set. In fact, two of the three incorrect clause-taking verb inferences are a result of a simple mistake of allowing arbitrary terms rather than only reified sentences and verbs in the antecedent.

Some of the automatic inferences were impossible to handle using our inference rules because of disagreements among human elicited inferences on what circumstances warrant particular inferences and how precisely an inference should be expressed. For example, the distinction between the presence or absence of the word "probably" is best handled with a separate confidence metric. In conversations, the distinction between highly probable statements and simply true statements is blurred. One could choose to include or omit "probably" for statements where the possibility of the plain sentence being false is small. Still, we would not want to add this as a rewriting rule since strictly speaking, such hedges do affect the meaning. Similarly, human elicited inferences disagreed on whether requests warrant a question act inference (e.g. *"Could you open the door?"* → *"You know whether you could open the door"*). We opted to avoid generating these inferences in building our rules, which significantly affected the recall score in the automatic evaluation.

The ULF-to-English generation system is remarkably accurate given its fairly simple pipeline approach and given that this is the first real use of this system. 78% grammaticality shows room for improvement and a cursory review of the errors show that there are some ULF macros that still need handling and that verb conjugations need to be made more robust.

Given these results, improvements to the filtering system for counterfactual and clause-taking verb constructions, gathering a larger dataset with a more robust collection procedure, and another set of experiments with the larger dataset would be valuable next steps in more precisely measuring the use of ULF in generating discourse inferences.

7 Related Work

Inference demonstrations have been performed in the past for various semantic representations, showing their respective strengths. Discourse

---

[8] Some inferences marked as ungrammatical were also marked as correct, indicating that the ULF-to-English failures can be minor enough to be easily understood.

Representation Structures and Minimal Recursion Semantics (MRS) can both be mapped to FOL and run on FOL theorem provers (Kamp and Reyle, 1993; Copestake et al., 2005). MRS has been successfully used for the task of recognizing textual entailment (RTE) (Lien and Kouylekov, 2015). Similarly, EL has been shown successful in generating FOL inferences (Morbini and Schubert, 2009) and self-aware metareasoning (Morbini and Schubert, 2011). Abstract Meaning Representation (Banarescu et al., 2013) focuses on event structure, resolution of anaphora, and word senses rather than logical inference and has been demonstrated to support event extraction and summarization (Rao et al., 2017; Wang et al., 2017; Dohare et al., 2017). TRIPS LF (Allen, 1994; Manshadi et al., 2008) is an unscoped modal logic directly integrated with a lexical ontology and has been used for dialogue and biomedical event extraction (Perera et al., 2018; Allen et al., 2015). Distributional representations have been shown to be very effective for RTE, such as in the SNLI and MultiNLI datasets (Bowman et al., 2015; Williams et al., 2018). These datasets are much larger than previous RTE datasets and both provide classification tasks supporting the use of an implicit distributional representation in a neural network system. The discourse inferences we demonstrated with ULFs, which require access to some syntactic information, as well our evaluations based on reliable English generation, are a challenge to all of the semantic representations discussed, because of their relative remoteness from syntax.

In the realm of evaluation methods, our work has similarities with the TAC KBP slot-filling task, which defines specific types of information that the system is meant to extract from the text without knowledge of the possible correct answers (Ellis et al., 2015). But TAC KBP focuses on restricted types of factoids, whereas our evaluation focuses on structure-based sentential inferences. In recent years inference evaluations have typically been posed as either a classification tasks similar to RTE (Bowman et al., 2015; Williams et al., 2018) or multiple-choice question answering (Clark et al., 2018). This knowledge of possible alternatives allows systems to avoid modeling inferences explicitly and to exploit statistical artifacts. The inference model trained on the ATOMIC commonsense dataset was evaluated without providing a set of possible choices by using BLEU (Sap et al., 2019). Though BLEU scores tend to correlate with correct inferences in practice, using it as a metric of evaluation is fraught with danger. Small changes that dramatically alter the meaning of a sentence (e.g., negation) are not reflected in the BLEU scores, and for structurally oriented inferences, incorrect inferences are likely to have misleadingly high scores.

8 Conclusions

We presented the first known method of generating inferences from ULF and an evaluation of inferences, focusing on discourse inferences. We also presented a method of collecting human elicitations of restricted categories of structural inferences, allowing a novel forward inference evaluation. We used these elicited inferences to automatically evaluate the generated inferences with promising results. Human judgments on a sample of generated inferences showed that 68.5% of the inferences are reasonable discourse inferences, 16.5% were unreasonable, and 15% were context-dependent or had disagreements between judges. Our experiments also demonstrate some of the advantages of using a semantic representation closer to the syntactic form such as ULF—reliable translation to English and access to syntactic signals—though this comes at the cost of a more complicated interface with the semantic patterns. There are clear areas of future work on improving the human elicitation collection and the implementation of the inference system. A larger and more refined dataset of inference elicitations will likely allow the development of a robust inference system on the discourse inference categories in question.

References

James Allen, Will de Beaumont, Lucian Galescu, and Choh Man Teng. 2015. Complex event extraction using DRUM. In *Proceedings of BioNLP 15*, pages 1–11, Beijing, China. Association for Computational Linguistics.

J.F. Allen. 1994. *Natural Language Understanding*, second edition. Benjamin Cummings, Redwood City, CA, USA.

Laura Banarescu, Claire Bonial, Shu Cai, Madalina Georgescu, Kira Griffitt, Ulf Hermjakob, Kevin Knight, Philipp Koehn, Martha Palmer, and Nathan Schneider. 2013. Abstract Meaning Representation for sembanking. In *Proceedings of the 7th Linguistic Annotation Workshop and Interoperability with*

Discourse, pages 178–186, Sofia, Bulgaria. Association for Computational Linguistics.

Samuel R. Bowman, Gabor Angeli, Christopher Potts, and Christopher D. Manning. 2015. A large annotated corpus for learning natural language inference. In *Proceedings of the 2015 Conference on Empirical Methods in Natural Language Processing*, pages 632–642, Lisbon, Portugal. Association for Computational Linguistics.

Peter Clark, Isaac Cowhey, Oren Etzioni, Tushar Khot, Ashish Sabharwal, Carissa Schoenick, and Oyvind Tafjord. 2018. Think you have solved question answering? try arc, the ai2 reasoning challenge.

Ann Copestake, Dan Flickinger, Carl Pollard, and Ivan A. Sag. 2005. Minimal Recursion Semantics: An introduction. *Research on Language and Computation*, 3(2):281–332.

Shibhansh Dohare, Harish Karnick, and Vivek Gupta. 2017. Text summarization using abstract meaning representation.

Christy Doran, Dania Egedi, Beth Ann Hockey, B. Srinivas, and Martin Zaidel. 1994. Xtag system - a wide coverage grammar for english. In *COLING 1994 Volume 2: The 15th International Conference on Computational Linguistics*.

Joe Ellis, Jeremy Getman, Dana Fore, Neil Kuster, Zhiyi Song, Ann Bies, and Stephanie Strassel. 2015. Overview of linguistic resources for the TAC KBP 2015 evaluations: Methodologies and results. In *Proceedings of the Eighth Text Analysis Conference (TAC 2015)*.

Hans Kamp and Uwe Reyle. 1993. *From discourse to logic*. Kluwer, Dortrecht.

Gene Kim and Lenhart Schubert. 2019. A type-coherent, expressive representation as an initial step to language understanding. In *Proceedings of the 13th International Conference on Computational Semantics*, Gothenburg, Sweden. Association for Computational Linguistics.

Gene Louis Kim. 2019. Towards parsing unscoped episodic logical forms with a cache transition parser. In *the Poster Abstracts of the Proceedings of the 32nd International Conference of the Florida Artificial Intelligence Research Society*.

Xin Li and Dan Roth. 2002. Learning question classifiers. In *Proceedings of the 19th International Conference on Computational Linguistics - Volume 1*, COLING '02, pages 1–7, Stroudsburg, PA, USA. Association for Computational Linguistics.

Elisabeth Lien and Milen Kouylekov. 2015. Semantic parsing for textual entailment. In *Proceedings of the 14th International Conference on Parsing Technologies*, pages 40–49, Bilbao, Spain. Association for Computational Linguistics.

Mehdi Hafezi Manshadi, James Allen, and Mary Swift. 2008. Toward a universal underspecified semantic representation. In *13th Conference on Formal Grammar (FG 2008), Hamburg, Germany*.

Fabrizio Morbini and Lenhart Schubert. 2008. Metareasoning as an integral part of commonsense and autocognitive reasoning. In *AAAI-08 Workshop on Metareasoning*.

Fabrizio Morbini and Lenhart Schubert. 2009. Evaluation of Epilog: A reasoner for Episodic Logic. In *Proceedings of the Ninth International Symposium on Logical Formalizations of Commonsense Reasoning*, Toronto, Canada.

Fabrizio Morbini and Lenhart Schubert. 2011. Metareasoning as an Integral Part of Commonsense and Autocognitive Reasoning. In Michael T. Cox and Anita Raja, editors, *Metareasoning: Thinking about thinking*. MIT Press.

Ian Perera, James Allen, Choh Man Teng, and Lucian Galescu. 2018. A situated dialogue system for learning structural concepts in blocks world. In *Proceedings of the 19th Annual SIGdial Meeting on Discourse and Dialogue*, pages 89–98, Melbourne, Australia. Association for Computational Linguistics.

Adam Purtee and Lenhart Schubert. 2012. TTT: A tree transduction language for syntactic and semantic processing. In *Proceedings of the Workshop on Applications of Tree Automata Techniques in Natural Language Processing*, ATANLP '12, pages 21–30, Stroudsburg, PA, USA. Association for Computational Linguistics.

Sudha Rao, Daniel Marcu, Kevin Knight, and Hal Daumé III. 2017. Biomedical event extraction using abstract meaning representation. In *BioNLP 2017*, pages 126–135, Vancouver, Canada,. Association for Computational Linguistics.

Maarten Sap, Ronan LeBras, Emily Allaway, Chandra Bhagavatula, Nicholas Lourie, Hannah Rashkin, Brendan Roof, Noah A. Smith, and Yejin Choi. 2019. ATOMIC: An atlas of machine commonsense for if-then reasoning. In *Proceedings of the Thirty-Third AAAI Conference on Artificial Intelligence*. AAAI Press.

Karl Stratos, Lenhart K. Schubert, and Jonathan Gordon. 2011. Episodic Logic: Natural Logic + reasoning. In *Proceedings of the International Conference on Knowledge Engineering and Ontology Development (KEOD)*.

Yanshan Wang, Sijia Liu, Majid Rastegar-Mojarad, Liwei Wang, Feichen Shen, Fei Liu, and Hongfang Liu. 2017. Dependency and amr embeddings for drug-drug interaction extraction from biomedical literature. In *Proceedings of the 8th ACM International Conference on Bioinformatics, Computational Biology,and Health Informatics*, ACM-BCB '17, pages 36–43, New York, NY, USA. ACM.

Adina Williams, Nikita Nangia, and Samuel Bowman. 2018. A broad-coverage challenge corpus for sentence understanding through inference. In *Proceedings of the 2018 Conference of the North American Chapter of the Association for Computational Linguistics: Human Language Technologies, Volume 1 (Long Papers)*, pages 1112–1122. Association for Computational Linguistics.

Florian Wolf. 2005. *Coherence in natural language : data structures and applications*. Ph.D. thesis, Massachusetts Institute of Technology, Dept. of Brain and Cognitive Sciences.

A Plea for Information Structure as a Part of Meaning Representation

Eva Hajičová

Institute of Formal and Applied Linguistics
Faculty of Mathematics and Physics
Charles University, Prague
hajicova@ufal.mff.cuni.cz

Abstract

The view that the representation of information structure (IS) should be a part of (any type of) representation of meaning is based on the fact that IS is a semantically relevant phenomenon (Sect. 2.1). In the contribution, three arguments supporting this view are briefly summarized, namely, the relation of IS to the interpretation of negation and presupposition (Sect. 2.2), the relevance of IS to the understanding of discourse connectivity and for the establishment and interpretation of coreference relations (Sect. 2.3). A possible integration of the description of the main ingredients of IS into a meaning representation is illustrated in Section 3.

1 Introduction

After the more or less isolated (though well substantiated) inquiries into the issues concerning one of the bridges between sentence form and its function in discourse (starting with the pioneering studies by Czech scholars in the first half of the last century followed by such prominent linguists and semanticists as M. A. K. Halliday, B. H. Partee, M. Rooth, E. Prince, K. Lambrecht, M. Steedman, E. Vallduví & E. Engdahl, to name just a few),[1] the last two decades of the last century witnessed an increasing interest of linguists in the study of information structure (IS). These approaches used different terms (theme-rheme, topic-focus, functional sentence perspective, presupposition and focus, background and focus, and a general term information structure (being the most frequent) and claimed to be based on different fundamental oppositions and scales (given - new, aboutness relation, activation or topicality scale) but all were more or less in agreement that this phenomenon, in addition to the syntactic structure of the sentence, is to be taken into account in an integrated description of the sentence and/or discourse, and that it significantly contributes to the study of the functioning of language.

The theory of information structure we subscribe to (cf. e.g. Sgall 1967; 1979; Sgall, Hajičová and Panevová 1986) called Topic-Focus Articulation (TFA) is based on the "aboutness" relation: the Focus of the sentence says something ABOUT its Topic. This dichotomy is based on the primary notion of contextual boundness (see below, Section 3) and its representation is a part of the representation of the sentence on its underlying (deep, tectogrammatical) syntactic level, which is assumed to be a linguistically structured level of meaning. In addition to the basic dichotomy the TFA theory works with a hierarchy of the so-called communicative dynamism, ie. an ordering of the meaningful lexical items (ie. items other than function words) of the sentence from the least communicatively important elements of the sentence to the elements with the highest degree of communicative importance. The TFA is considered to be a recursive phenomenon, which makes it possible to recognize – aside with the global Topic and the global Focus and based on the features of contextual boundness – also local topics and local foci. In this way, the TFA framework offers a possibility, if needed, to recognize more distinctions in addition to the basic dichotomy (as done, e.g. by the focus – background approach of Vallduví and Engdahl (1996), or as needed, according to e.g. Büring (1997) or Steedman (2000), for a proper account of prosody).

---

[1] For the bibliographical references, see the Section References at the end of the paper.

Proceedings of the First International Workshop on Designing Meaning Representations, pages 66–72
Florence, Italy, August 1st, 2019 ©2019 Association for Computational Linguistics

2 Information Structure as a Semantically Relevant Phenomenon

2.1 Basic argument

The crucial argument in support of an inclusion of the representation of information structure into a representation of meaning relates to the fact that IS is *semantically relevant*, as can be documented by examples (1) to (3), taken from early literature on these issues (the capitals denote the intonation center).

(1) (a) Dogs must be CARRIED.

    (a') CARRY dogs.

   (b) DOGS must be carried.

    (b') Carry DOGS. (Halliday 1967)

(2) (a) English is spoken in the SHETLANDS.

   (b) In the Shetlands, ENGLISH is spoken. (Sgall 1967)

(3) (a) Mary always takes John to the MOVIES.

   (b) Mary always takes JOHN to the movies. (Rooth 1985)

For the sake of simplicity, let us reduce here the more differentiated approach of TFA into an articulation of the sentence into its Topic (what is the sentence about) and Focus (what the sentence says about its Topic). Then it can be easily seen that the (a) and (b) sentences in the above sets (capitals indicating the intonation center) differ in this articulation and, correspondingly, differ in their meaning: (1)(b) is non-sensical (one can use the underground elevator also without a dog), (2)(a) even false (English is spoken in other countries as well) and (3)(a) and (b) reflect different situations in the real world (It is always the movies where John is taken vs. It is always John who is taken to the movies). In the surface shape of the sentences, the different interpretations of the (a) and (b) sentences in each set are rendered by different surface means, such as word order or the position of the intonation center, but have to be accounted for in the representation of their meaning if the sentences have to receive the appropriate corresponding reading. For an example from a typologically different language with a rather flexible word order, cf. the Czech equivalents of the sentences (1) through (3), with the assumed prototypical placement of the intonation center at the end of the sentence (indicated again by capitals).

(1') (a) Psy neste v NÁRUČÍ.

   (b) V náručí neste PSY.

(2') (a) Anglicky se mluví na Shetlandských OSTROVECH.

   (b) Na Shetlandských ostrovech se mluví ANGLICKY.

(3') (a) Marie bere Honzu vždy do KINA.

   (b) Marie bere do kina vždy HONZU.

2.2 Negation and presuppostion

Semantic relevance of IS is attested also by the analysis of the semantics of *negation* and of the specification of the notion of *presupposition*. If IS of a sentence is understood in terms of an aboutness relation between the Topic of the sentence, then in the prototypical case of negative sentences, the Focus does not hold about the Topic; in a secondary case, the negative sentence is about a negated topic and something is said about this topic.[2] Thus, prototypically, the sentence (4) is about John (Topic) and it holds *about* John that he didn't come to watch TV (negated Focus).

(4) John didn't come to watch TV.

However, there may be a secondary interpretation of the negative sentence, e.g. in the context of (5).

(5) John didn't come, because he suddenly fell ill.

One of the interpretations of (5) is that the sentence is *about* John's not-coming (Topic) and it says about this negated event that is happened because he suddenly fell ill (Focus).

As Hajičová (e.g.1973; 1984) documented, there is a close relation between IS, negation and presupposition (see the original analysis of presupposition as a specific kind of the entailment

---

[2] An objection that one cannot speak about a non-existent topic does not arise: one can speak about an absence as well as about not-coming, not-visiting (cf. Strawson's example below), etc. See also Heim's treatment of the definite-indefinite noun phrases and her notion of file change semantics in which meanings are analyzed as context-change potentials (Heim 1982; 1983). See also the pioneering study of the relation between theme-rheme and negation by Zemb (1968).

relation by Strawson (1952) and Strawson's (1964) notion of referential availability in his analysis of the sentence *The exhibition was visited by the King of France.* and its negation):

(6) (a) John caused our VICTORY.

   (b) John didn't cause our VICTORY.

   (c) Though he played well as usual, the rest of the team was very weak (and nothing could   have prevented our defeat).

(7) (a) Our victory was caused by JOHN.

   (b) Our victory was not caused by JOHN.

(8) We won.

Both (6)(a) and (7)(a) imply (8). However, it is only the negative counterpart of (7)(a), namely (7)(b), that implies (8), while (6)(b) may appear also in a context suggesting that we were defeated, see (6)(c). In terms of presuppositions, the statement (8) belongs to the presuppositions of (7)(a) since it is entailed both by the positive as well as by the negative sentence, but not to the presuppositions of (6)(a) as it is not entailed by the negative sentence.[3]

2.3   Discourse connectivity

Another phenomenon, though going beyond the interpretation of a single sentence but important for the interpretation of a text (discourse), is *discourse connectivity*. There have been several proposals in literature how to account for these relations, the *centering* theory being one of the most deeply elaborated (cf. Grosz, Joshi and Weinstein, 1983 and its corpus-based evaluation in Poesio et al. 2004). It is based on the model of the local attentional states of speakers and hearers as proposed by Grosz and Sidner (1986). Each utterance in discourse is considered to contain a backward looking center, which links it with the preceding utterance, and a set of entities called forward looking centers; these entities are ranked according to language-specific ranking principles stated in terms of syntactic functions of the

referring expressions. Related treatment rooted in the Praguian traditional account of IS is the idea of so-called thematic progressions (Daneš 1970), explicitly referring to the relation between the theme (Topic) and the rheme (Focus) of a sentence and the theme (Topic) or the rheme (Focus) of the next following sentence (a simple linear thematic progression and a thematic progression with a continuous theme), or to a 'global' theme (derived themes) of the (segment of the) discourse. As demonstrated in Hajičová and Mírovský (2018a), an annotation of a text (corpus) in terms of Topic and Focus makes it possible to find these links between sentences and in this way to account for the structure of discourse. In a similar vein, it has been demonstrated that a meaning representation including some basic attributes of IS serves well for an establishment and interpretation of coreference relations (Hajičová and Mírovský 2018b).

3   Information Structure in an Annotated Corpus

The observations documenting the semantic relevance of the information structure (Sect. 2.1 and 2.2 above) indicate that the information structure (Topic-Focus articulation) of the sentence belongs to the domain of the (syntactico-) semantic structure of the sentence rather than exclusively to the domain of discourse (or, in more general terms, to the domain of pragmatics), as sometimes claimed. However, this is not to deny the interrelation or interaction between the two domains and, as illustrated in Section 2.3, the inclusion of the basic features of IS into the representation of meaning may serve well also for the description of the structure of discourse.

In this final section of our paper we present an example of the annotation scenario illustrating how IS is represented in the Praguian dependency-based sentence representations. For a simplified example of such a representation for sentences in (1), see the Appendix.

The overall annotation scenario includes three levels: (a) morphemic (with detailed part-of-speech tags and rich information on morphological categories), (b) surface shape ("analytical", in the form of dependency-based tree structures with the verb as the root of the tree and with relations labeled by superficial syntactic

---

[3] The specific kind of entailment illustrated here by the above examples was introduced in Hajičová (1972) and called *allegation*: an allegation is an assertion A entailed by an assertion carried by a sentence S, with which the negative counterpart of S entails neither A nor its negation (see also the discussion by Partee 1996).

functions such as Subject, Object, Adverbial, Attribute, etc.), and (c) underlying dependency-based syntactic level (so-called tectogrammatical) with dependency tree structures labeled by functions such as Actor, Patient, Addressee, etc. and including also information on the IS (Topic-Focus articulation) of sentences.[4] For this purpose, a special TFA attribute is established in the scenario for the representation of a sentence on the tectogrammatical level, with three possible values, one of which is assigned to every node of the tree; these values specify, whether the node is contextually bound non-contrastive, contextually bound contrastive, or contextually non-bound. A contextually bound (cb) node represents an item presented by the speaker as referring to an entity assumed to be easily accessible by the hearer(s), i.e. more or less predictable, readily available to the hearers in their memory, while a contextually non-bound (nb) node represents an item presented as not directly available in the given context, cognitively 'new'. While the characteristics 'given' and 'new' refer only to the cognitive background of the distinction of contextual boundness, the distinction itself is an opposition understood as a grammatically patterned feature, rather than in the literal sense of the term. This point is illustrated e.g. by (9).

(9) (Tom entered together with his friends.) My mother recognized only HIM, but no one from his COMPANY.

Both Tom and his friends are 'given' by the preceding context (indicated here by the preceding sentence in the brackets), but in the given sentence they are structured as non-bound (which is reflected in the surface shape of the sentence by the position of the intonation center).

The appurtenance of an item to the Topic or Focus of the sentence is then derived on the basis of the features cb or nb assigned to individual nodes of the tree (see Sgall 1979):

(a) the main verb (V) and any of its direct dependents belong to F iff they carry index nb;

(b) every item that does not depend directly on V and is subordinated to an element of F different from V, belongs to F (where "subordinated to" is defined as the irreflexive transitive closure of "depend on");

(c) iff V and all items directly depending on V are cb, then it is necessary to specify the rightmost k' node of the cb nodes dependent on V and ask whether some of nodes l dependent on k' are nb; if so, this nb node and all its dependents belong to F; if not so, then specify the immediately adjacent (i.e. preceding) sister node of k' and ask whether some of its dependents is cb; these steps are repeated until an nb node depending (immediately or not) on a cb node directly dependent on V is found. This node and all its dependent nodes are then specified as F.

(d) every item not belonging to F according to (a) - (c) belongs to T.

This algorithm has been implemented and is applied in all experiments connected with research questions related to IS.

As described in Zikánová et al. (2009), the SH algorithm was applied to a part of the PDT data (about 11 thousand sentences). The results indicate that a clear division of the sentence into Topic and Focus according to the hypothesized rules has been achieved in 94.28% of sentences to which the procedure has been applied; 4.41% of sentences contained the type of focus referring to a node (or nodes) that belong(s) to the communicatively most dynamic part of the sentence though they depend on a contextually bound node. The real problem of the algorithm then rests with the case of ambiguous partition (1.14%) and cases where no focus was recognized (0.11%). In Rysová et al. (2015) some of the shortcomings of the previous implementation described in Zikánová et al. (2009) were removed and the algorithm was evaluated in a slightly different way: as the gold data we used data annotated by a linguist assuming that the results would better reflect the adequacy of the algorithm for transforming values of contextual boundness into the division of the sentence into the Topic and the Focus. Our gold data consisted of 319 sentences from twelve PDT documents annotated by a single linguistic expert. Without taking into account (already annotated but now hidden) values of contextual boundness, the annotator

---

[4] In addition, two kinds of information are being added in the latest version of PDT, namely annotation of discourse relations based on the analysis of discourse connectors (inspired by the Pennsylvania Discourse Treebank) and information on grammatical and on textual intra- and inter-sentential coreference relations.

marked each node as belonging either to the Topic or to the Focus. On these gold data, the new implementation of the algorithm was evaluated, see Table 1.[5]

Measure	SH Algorithm
F1-measure in topic	0.89
F1-measure in focus	0.95
overall accuracy on tectogrammatical nodes	0.93
overall accuracy on whole sentences	0.75

Table 1: Evaluation of the SH algorithm.

4 Summary

In our contribution we argue that a meaning representation of any type should include information on basic features of information structure. Our argument stems from the fact that information structure (at least the articulation of a sentence into its Topic and Focus) is semantically relevant which is demonstrated on several examples, taking into account also the representation of negation and presupposition. An inclusion of the representation of information structure into an overall representation of meaning also helps to account for some basic features of discourse connectivity and coreference relations. In the Appendix, we have briefly characterized one possible way of representation of the basic features of information structure.

5 Appendix

To attest the plausibility of a representation of IS in an annotated corpus, we present here rather simplified representations of the sentences given above in (1). The symbols ACT, PAT and Gen stand for the deep syntactic functions Actor, Patient and General Actor, respectively, Deb(itive) and Imper stand for deontic and sentential modality, and cb and nb stand for the contextually bound and contextually non-bound values of the TFA attribute. The vertical dotted line denotes the boundary between Topic and Focus.

---

[5] It significantly outperformed the baseline, which was defined as follows: in the linear (surface) form of the sentence, each word before the autosemantic part of the predicate verb belongs to Topic, the rest of the sentence belongs to Focus.

(1) (a) Dogs must be CARRIED.

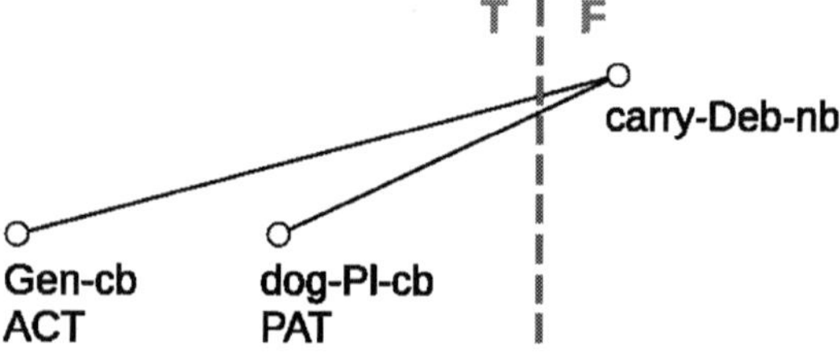

(1) (b) DOGS must be carried.

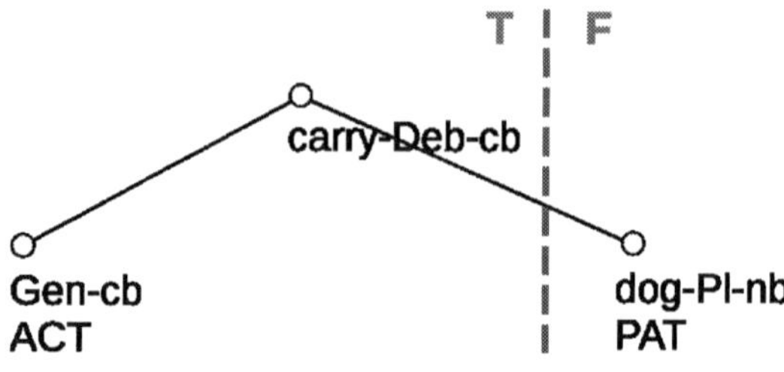

(1) (a') CARRY dogs.

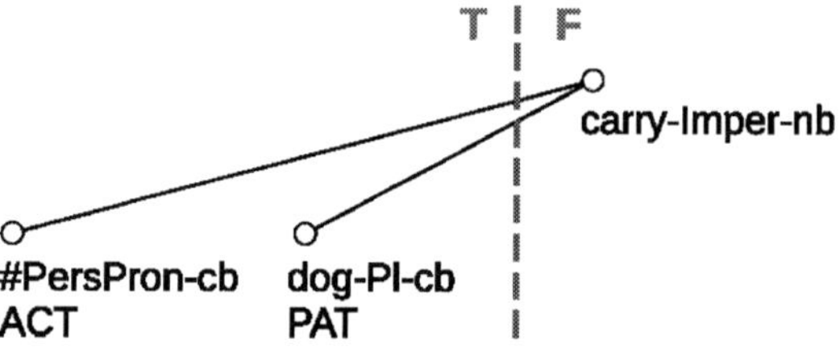

(1) (b') Carry DOGS.

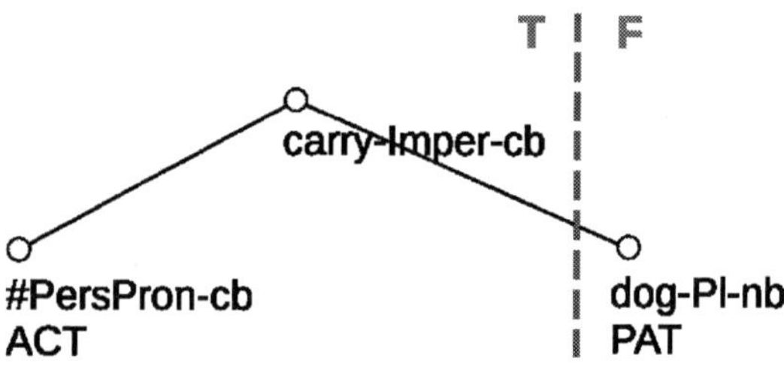

Acknowledgments

The author gratefully acknowledges support from the Ministry of Education of the Czech Republic (project LM2018101 – LINDAT/CLARIAH-CZ). I am also very much grateful to Jiří Mírovský for his help with the formatting of the text.

References

Bäuerle, R., Schwarze C. & A. von Stechow, Eds. (1983), *Meaning, Use and Interpretation of Language.* Berlin: Mouton de Gruyter.

Büring, D. (1997). *The Meaning of Topic and Focus – The 59th Street Bridge Accent.* Londoin: Routledge.

Cole, P., Ed.. (1981*). Radical Pragmatics.* New York: Academic Press.

Daneš, F. (1970). Zur linguistischen Analyse der Textstruktur. *Folia linguistica* 4, 1/2, 72-78.

Grosz, B. & Sidner, C. L. (1986). Attention, Intentions and the structure of discourse. *Computational Linguistics, 12,* 175–204.

Grosz, B. J., Joshi, A. K. & S. Weinstein (1995). Centering: A Framework for modeling the local coherence of discourse. *Computational Linguistics, 21,* 203-225.

Hajič, J., Bejček, E., Bémová, A., Buráňová, E., Hajičová, E., Havelka, J., Homola, P., Kárník, J., Kettnerová, V., Klyueva, N., Kolářová, V., Kučová, L., Lopatková, M., Mikulová, M., Mírovský, J., Nedoluzhko, A., Pajas, P., Panevová, J., Poláková, L., Rysová, M., Sgall, P., Spoustová, J., Straňák, P., Synková, P., Ševčíková, M., Štěpánek, J., Urešová, Z., Vidová Hladká, B., Zeman, D., Zikánová, Š. & Žabokrtský, Z. (2018). Prague Dependency Treebank 3.5. Institute of Formal and Applied Linguistics, LINDAT/CLARIN, Charles University, LINDAT/CLARIN PID: http://hdl.handle.net/11234/1-2621

Hajičová E. (1973), Negation and topic vs. comment. *Philologica Pragensia* 17, 18-25. Reprinted in Hajičová (2017), 50-62.

Hajičová E. (1984), Presupposition and allegation revisited. *Journal of Pragmatics* 8:155-167. Reprinted in Hajičová (2017), 63-77.

Hajičová, E. (2017). *Syntax-Semantics Interface.* Prague: Karolinum

Hajičová E. & J. Mírovský (2018a), Discourse Coherence Through the Lens of an Annotated Text Corpus: A Case Study. In: Proceedings of LREC 2018, Miyazaki, Japan.

Hajičová E. & J. Mírovský (2018b), Topic/Focus vs. Given/New: Information Structure and Coreference Relations in an Annotated Corpus. Presented at the 2018 Annual Conference of Societas Linguistica Europaea, Tallin, Latvia.

Halliday, M. A. K. (1967a). *Intonation and Grammar in British English.* The Hague: Mouton.

Halliday, M. A. K. (1967b). Notes on transitivity and theme in English. Part 2. *Journal of Linguistics* 3, 199-244.

Heim, I. (1982). *The semantics of definite and indefinite noun phrases.* PhD Thesis, Univ. of Massachusetts, Amherst.

Heim, I. (1983). File chnge semantics and the familiarity theory of definiteness. In: Bäuerle, Schwarze & von Stechow, Eds. (1983), 164-189.

Lambrecht, K. (1994). *Information Structure and Sentence Form. Topic, Focus and the Mental Representations of Discourse Referents.* Cambridge: Cambridge University Press.

Partee, B. H. (1996), Allegation and local accommodation. In: Partee & Sgall, Eds. (1996), 65-86.

Partee, B. H. & Sgall, P., Eds. (1996). *Discourse and meaning.* Amsterdam/Philadelphia: John Benjamins.

Prince, E. (1981). Toward a taxonomy of given/new information. In: Cole, Ed.. (1981), 223-254.

Rooth, M. (1985). *Association with focus.* PhD Thesis, Univ. of Massachusetts, Amherst.

Rysová, K.. Mírovský, J. & E. Hajičová (2015). On an apparent freedom of Czech word order. A case study. In: *14th International Workshop on Treebanks and Linguistic Theories (TLT 2015),* IPIPAN, Warszawa, Poland, 93–105.

Sgall P. (1967), Functional Sentence Perspective in a generative description of language. *Prague Studies in Mathematical Linguistics* 2, Prague, Academia, 203-225.

Sgall P. (1979), Towards a Definition of Focus and Topic. *Prague Bulletin of Mathematical Linguistics* 31, 3-25; 32, 1980, 24-32; printed in *Prague Studies in Mathematical Linguistics* 78, 1981, 173-198.

Sgall, P., Hajičová, E. & and J. Panevová (1986). *The Meaning of the Sentence in Its Semantic and Pragmatic Aspects.* Dordrecht: D. Reidel.

Steedman, M. (2000),. Information structure and the syntax-phonology interface. *Linguistic Inquiry* 31, 649-689.

Steinberg, D. D. & Jakobovits, L. A. Eds. (1971). *Semantics. - An interdisciplinary reader.* Cambridge, Mass.: Cambridge University Press.

Strawson, P. (1952). *Introduction to Logical Theory.* London: Methuen

Strawson, P. (1964). Identifying reference and truth values. *Theoria 30,* 96-118. Reprinted in Steinberg & Jakobovits, Eds. (1971), 86-99.

Vallduví, E. & Engdahl, E. (1996). The linguistic realization of information packaging. *Linguistics* 34, 459-519.

Zemb, J-M. (1968). *Les structures logiques de la proposition allemande. Contribution à l'étude des rapports entre la langue et la pensée.* Paris: O.C.D.L.

Zikánová, Š. & M. Týnovský (2009). Identification of Topic and Focus in Czech: Comparative Evaluation on Prague Dependency Treebank. In: Zybatow, G. et al., Eds. *Studies in Formal Slavic Phonology, Morphology, Syntax, Semantics and Information Structure.* Formal Description of Slavic Languages 7, Frankfurt am Main: Peter Lang., 343–353.

TCL - A Lexicon of Turkish Discourse Connectives

Deniz Zeyrek
Graduate School of Informatics
Middle East Technical University
Ankara, Turkey
dezeyrek@metu.edu.tr

Kezban Başıbüyük
Department of Computer Engineering
Middle East Technical University
Ankara, Turkey
kezban.demirtas@metu.edu.tr

Abstract

It is known that discourse connectives are the most salient indicators of discourse relations. State-of-the-art parsers being developed to predict explicit discourse connectives exploit annotated discourse corpora but a lexicon of discourse connectives is also needed to enable further research in discourse structure and support the development of language technologies that use these structures for text understanding. This paper presents a lexicon of Turkish discourse connectives built by automatic means. The lexicon has the format of the German connective lexicon, DiMLex, where for each discourse connective, information about the connective's orthographic variants, syntactic category and senses are provided along with sample relations. In this paper, we describe the data sources we used and the development steps of the lexicon.

1 Introduction

Discourse connectives (alternatively labelled as cue phrases, discourse markers, discourse operators, etc.) are lexical anchors of coherence relations. Such relations (with semantic labels such as expansion, contingency, contrast, concession) can be signalled with discourse connectives, but languages vary in the way they express them. For example, while languages like English and German express discourse relations lexically (with conjunctions and adverbials), Turkish conveys discourse relations through morphological suffixes, as well as lexically. Languages also diverge in the number of connectives that express the same discourse relation. For example, French and Dutch differ in the number of connectives that convey causal relations (Zufferey and Degand, 2017). Finally, discourse connectives are polysemous, expressing several discourse relations. These issues are an obvious challenge for language technologies, translation studies and language learners. What is needed is a resource that goes beyond traditional dictionaries. Our goal in this paper is to reveal the nature of Turkish discourse connectives through discourse-annotated corpora and describe the steps in constructing a discourse connective lexicon that hosts the connectives' various properties. The Turkish Lexicon will ultimately be part of the connective lexicon database (http://connective-lex.info/) that aims to synchronize the lexicons that exist.

The interest in discourse connectives goes hand in hand with the development of discourse-annotated corpora. There are three major approaches that have guided discourse research and inspired other languages to annotate discourse: RST (Mann and Thompson, 1988), SDRT (2012), and the PDTB (Prasad et al., 2014). Our focus in this paper will be the PDTB, one of the best known resources for English discourse. The PDTB takes discourse connectives (henceforth, DCs) as two-place predicates where argumenthood is based on abstract objects (eventualities, facts, propositions, etc.) as in Asher (1993). It annotates the DC together with its binary arguments, which are semantic representations of discourse parts (cf. (Danlos, 2009)). The PDTB-style annotation has been extended to various languages other than English, namely, Arabic (Al-Saif and Markert, 2010), Chinese (Zhou and Xue, 2015), Hindi (Kolachina et al., 2012), and Turkish (Demirşahin and Zeyrek, 2017) as well as a recent multilingual resource, TED-Multilingual Discourse Bank, or TED-MDB (Zeyrek et al., 2019).

In addition to these efforts, there has been an important initiative, namely DiMLex, the discourse connective lexicon first developed for German (Stede and Umbach, 1998; Scheffler and Stede, 2016), which has subsequently been extended to multiple languages, e.g. French (Roze et al., 2012), Italian (Feltracco et al., 2016), Portuguese (Mendes et al., 2018) and recently English-DiMLex for English (Das et al., 2018). Such lex-

Proceedings of the First International Workshop on Designing Meaning Representations, pages 73–81
Florence, Italy, August 1st, 2019 ©2019 Association for Computational Linguistics

icons are sure to complement the ongoing efforts of discourse-annotated corpora, support discourse research and various language technology applications such as discourse parsers.

In this paper, we describe the development of TCL, a lexicon for Turkish discourse connectives, which follows the format of DiMLex. To the best of our knowledge, there is no such resource for Turkish. Thus, our aim is to fill this gap with a resource that covers Turkish discourse connectives with their various properties and a representation of their meanings. This resource will not only benefit discourse studies in Turkish but will also form the basis of future multilingual studies on discourse connectives and their meanings.

In the rest of this paper, we describe the steps in creating the TCL. In Section 2, we provide information about the data sources we used and in Section 3, we discuss the criteria for selecting connectives as TCL entries. Section 4 presents the structure of TCL and Section 5 shows how the lexicon is populated. Section 6 brings the paper to an end and draws some conclusions.

2 Data Sources

In building the TCL, we use three PDTB-inspired annotated corpora to compile explicit DCs, namely, Turkish Discourse Bank or TDB 1.0 (Zeyrek et al., 2013), TDB 1.1 (Zeyrek and Kurfalı, 2017), and the Turkish section of TED-MDB.

- TDB 1.0 is a 400,000-word resource of modern written Turkish containing annotations of explicit DCs and the discourse segments they relate. It also annotates "phrasal expressions" such as *bunun için* 'for this (reason/purpose)', which are linking devices compositionally derived from postpositions (*için* 'since/in order to') and a deictic term. They are a subset of the PDTB's alternative lexicalizations and correspond to "secondary connectives" (Danlos et al., 2018). We used 8439 relations (explicit DCs and "phrasal expressions") from this corpus.

- TDB 1.1 is a 40,000-word-subset of TDB 1.0, where all five relation types of the PDTB are annotated together with their binary arguments (i.e., explicit and implicit relations, alternative lexicalizations, entity relations and no relations). Based on the PDTB-3 relation hierarchy (Lee et al., 2016), the senses of explicit and implicit connectives as well as alternative lexicalizations are annotated. We used 912 explicit relations from this corpus.

- TED-MDB is a corpus of TED talks transcripts in 6 languages (English, German, Polish, European Portuguese, Russian and Turkish). We used 276 explicit relations from the Turkish section of this corpus. TDB 1.0 and TED-MDB annotation files are in pipe-delimited format, the TDB 1.1 annotation files are in XML format.

By using different resources, we take advantage of the different coverage of the three corpora. As expected, while some of the connectives exist in all of the data sources, some connectives (and the information needed for the connective lexicon database) may exist in only one source (see Table 2). Moreover, resorting to different corpora is helpful as different corpora may spot new senses of a DC. For example, different senses of the postpositions *gibi* 'as' and *kadar* 'until/as well as/as much as' have been compiled from different corpora as indicated in Table 1.

3 The criteria for selection of connectives as TCL entries

Turkish is a morphologically rich, agglutinating language with suffixes added to the word root in the order licensed by the morphology and syntax of the language. In this section we describe the major syntactic categories we used to determine DCs, and how we represent suffixal connectives (converbs) in TCL. We also explain our method of determining the syntactic category of other DCs when different POS taggers provide different parses.

TCL only considers explicit discourse connectives annotated in the existing Turkish discourse-annotated corpora. Unlike other DC lexicons such as DimLex and the lexicon of Czech discourse connectives (Mírovský et al., 2017) it does not record non-connective usages.

3.1 Major syntactic categories

DCs are determined on the basis of the following syntactic categories:

- Conjunctions, comprising both the single type *ama* 'but/yet' and the paired or noncontinuous type such as *ne ... ne* 'neither ... nor'.

TCL Entries	TDB 1.1	TED-MDB
gibi 'as'	EXPANSION: Conjunction EXPANSION: Manner: Arg2-as-manner	COMPARISON: Similarity
kadar 'until/as well/much as'	COMPARISON: Degree TEMPORAL: Asynchronous: Precedence	COMPARISON: Similarity CONTINGENCY: Purpose: Arg2-as-goal
artık 'no longer'	EXPANSION: Level-of-detail: Arg2-as-detail TEMPORAL: Synchronous	CONTINGENCY: Cause: Result

Table 1: Different senses of connectives captured via discourse-annotated corpora in Turkish

TCL Entries	Data Sources		
	TDB 1.0	TDB 1.1	TED-MDB
ama 'but/yet'	ama	ama	ama
çünkü 'because'	Çünkü	Çünkü	çünkü
aksine 'in contrast'	aksine		aksine
sadece 'only'			sadece
sayesinde 'thanks to'	sayesinde		
keza 'as well'		Keza	Keza
dahası 'furthermore'	Dahası	Dahası	

Table 2: TCL entries obtained from various discourse-annotated corpora

- Subordinators:
    - Converbs (simplex subordinators), e.g. –sA, 'if', -(y)ArAk 'by means of/ and'.
    - Postpositions (complex subordinators), which involve an accompanying suffix on the (non-finite) verb of the subordinate clause, *gibi* 'as'.

- Adverbs, involving single tokens such as *ayrıca* 'in addition' as well as phrasal tokens, e.g. *ne var ki* 'even so'.[1]

3.2 Representing suffixal connectives

In Turkish, suffixal connectives are essentially converbs forming non-finite adverbial clauses. Converbs have complex allomorphy based on vowel harmony as well as consonant harmony (Zeyrek and Webber, 2008). We decided that such variation has to be represented in TCL. To illustrate, -(y)ArAk 'by means of/and' is a converb shown in the standard morphological notation, where the capital letters indicate alternation (-erek, -arak) and the parentheses show that y is needed if the verb root ends in a vowel (see examples (1), (2), (3)). Other converbs may additionally carry dedicated nominalization markers or person agreement markers, which have different morphological realizations. To identify all occurrences of a converb, the allomorphs need to be specified in the lexicon. By means of the TCL search tool (see 5.1 below), we specified 15 converbs and their allomorphs to be added to TCL. If any allomorph of a specific converb was missing in the corpora we used, those allomorphs were added manually.

(1) **Ali okula gid**-erek *öğretmenle görüştü.* [2]
'*Ali went to school* __and__ **talked with the teacher.**'

(2) **Ali sıkı çalış**-arak *başarı kazandı.*
'*Ali gained success* __by__ **working hard.**'

(3) **Ali şarkı söyle**-yerek *başarı kazandı.*
'*Ali gained success* __by__ **singing.**'

3.3 Noun-based connectives

Turkish has a group of connectives which are the lexicalized forms of nominal roots, e.g. *dahası* 'furthermore', *amacıyla* 'with the aim of', *sonuçta* 'eventually.' For this group of connectives, the available POS taggers sometimes provide incomplete information. Table 3 shows different parses provided by different POS parsers for these connectives.

Connectives	UDPipe	TRmorph
dahası 'furthermore'	Noun	Cnj:adv, Adv
amacıyla 'for the purpose of'	Noun	Noun
sonuçta 'eventually'	Adv	Adv, Noun

Table 3: Different parses for three noun-based DCs

In such cases, we compare different sources to determine the connective's syntactic category for TCL. For example, for the connectives in Table 3, we settled on the syntactic categories provided in Table 4.

---

[1] We note that the TDB's term "phrasal expression" is different from the DimLex term "phrasal connective", which refers to discourse connectives that involve more than one words without specifying the type of words involved in the composition of the connective.

[2] As in the PDTB, Arg2 is the discourse part that hosts the connective and in the examples, it is shown in bold fonts. Arg1 is the other argument and it is rendered in italics. The discourse connective is underlined.

Connectives	TCL
dahası 'furthermore'	Adv
amacıyla 'for the purpose of'	Other
sonuçta 'eventually'	Adv

Table 4: Syntactic categories of three noun-based DCs in TCL

4 The structure of TCL

The TCL structure is based on the structure of the connective lexicon database. Thus, it contains the following components.

- *Orthographical variants:* This criterion specifies whether the connective is a single token (part=single) or a phrasal token (part=phrasal); continuous (orth=cont) or discontinuous (orth=discount). For example, the phrasal connective *ne...ne* 'neither ... nor' is annotated as "discont" while the connective *öte yandan* 'on the other hand' is annotated as "cont". An entry illustrating the orthogrophical variants of the single connective *ama* 'but' is provided in Figure 1.

```
<orths>
  <orth canonical="0" orth_id="16o1" type="cont">
    <part type="single">ama</part>
  </orth>
  <orth canonical="1" orth_id="16o1" type="cont">
    <part type="single">Ama</part>
  </orth>
  <orth canonical="2" orth_id="16o1" type="cont">
    <part type="single">AMA</part>
  </orth>
</orths>
```

Figure 1: Variants of *ama* 'but/yet'

In addition to these, we added the type "suffixal" to TCL to indicate converbs.

- *Canonical Form:* The canonical form of a connective is the most commonly used variant of that connective. For example, the canonical form of *çünkü* 'because' is the sentence-initial *Çünkü*, a property which is determined by the TCL search tool.

- *Frequency:* The frequency of the connective shows both how often it occurs in the corpora and the frequency of each of its sense tags.

- *Syntactic category:* The syntactic category of connectives is assigned using several sources as described in Section 5.1, namely the Turkish section of UDPipe [3], the search tool pro-

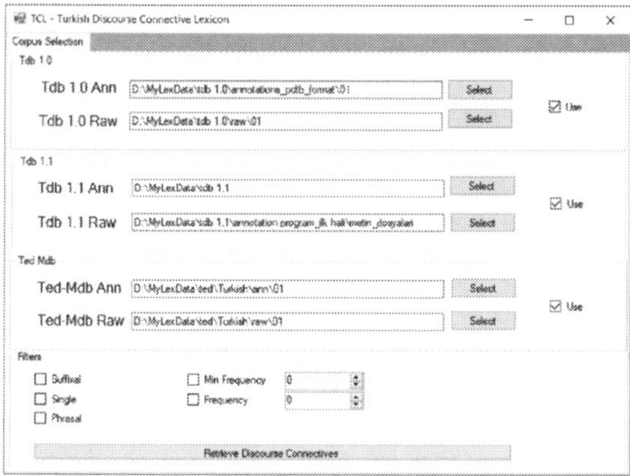

Figure 2: Main window of the TCL search tool

vided in the Turkish Linguistic Society website or TDK [4] and TRmorph [5].

5 Populating the lexicon

5.1 The TCL search tool

We developed a search tool to populate TCL. The search tool was developed using the C# programming language. It is also extendable with new features. The main feature of the tool is that it searches different corpora to retrieve DCs (see Figure 2 for a snapshot of the main window of the tool). In addition, it uses filters for DC types, such as suffixal, single, and phrasal. When the search tool is started, file paths used by the tool are specified in the data path window, namely, the path of the text directory specifying the raw text files that will be searched, and the path of the annotation directory containing the XML or pipe-delimited files storing the annotation information.

5.2 The workflow

Using the search tool, we populated the TCL entries. Our work flow involves several steps, as described below and summarized in Figure 3.

- Firstly, the annotation files of the three corpora are parsed and the relations encoded by explicit connectives are retrieved. For this purpose, an XML parser and a pipe-delimited file parser have been developed.

- *Relation Builder:* The Relation Builder module reads the connective and its sense(s) in each relation directly from the annotation files while it reads the respective relation

<hr>

[3] http://lindat.mff.cuni.cz/services/udpipe/

[4] http://www.tdk.gov.tr

[5] http://coltekin.net/cagri/trmorph/

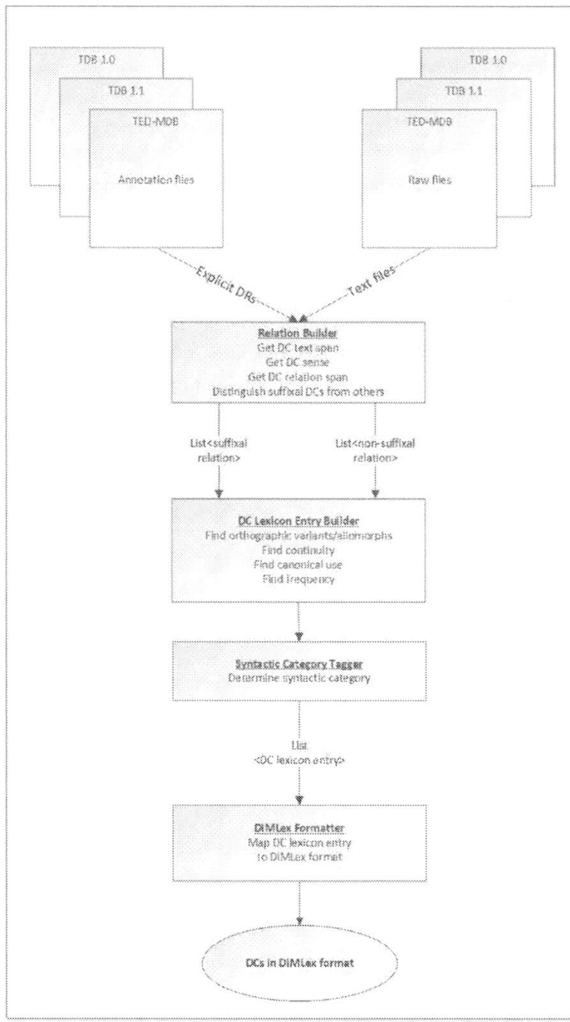

Figure 3: Flow of populating TCL entries

spans from the text files; then it distinguishes suffixal DCs from non-suffixal DCs, i.e. all other types of DCs. To characterize a DC as suffixal, the Relation Builder simply checks the character preceding the DC token. If the previous character is white space, a new line, or a separator (. , : ; ! ? ( ) ' " -), the connective is labeled as *Not Suffixal*; in other cases, it is labeled as *Suffixal*. Hence, two lists of relations are formed, a list of relations containing suffixal connectives and a list of relations containing non-suffixal connectives.

- *DC Lexicon Entry Builder:* Using the two lists of relations from the Relation Builder, this module computes the following properties for each DC to be represented in the lexicon:

  - *Orthographical Variants:* Since suffixal connectives are uniform in terms of orthography, continuity, etc. they do not have variants. Therefore, the DC Lexicon Entry Builder only searches the list of non-suffixal relations to determine the variants of all connectives. Suffixal connectives are simply tagged as "suffixal".

  - *Allomorphs:* To handle the allomorphs of converbs, the list of suffixal relations is used. The entries of this list are analyzed to find out which entries are allomorphs of a suffixal DC.

  - *Continuity:* Phrasal DCs can be continuous or discontinuous. This property is specified automatically by going through the multi-word connectives in the list of non-suffixal relations, and whether there are any words between the two parts of the connective is determined.

  - *Canonical Use:* The DC Lexicon Entry Builder counts the times each variant of a DC occurs in our relation lists and labels the most frequently used variant as canonical.

  - *Frequency:* To set the frequency property, the DC Lexicon Entry Builder uses both lists of relations and computes the number of occurrences of a DC as well as the number of occurrences of each sense of the DC.

- *Syntactic Category Tagger:* This module assigns a syntactic category to each DC. If a connective is suffixal, it is assigned the converb category. The syntactic category of non-suffixal connectives is determined on the basis of the available POS taggers to the extent possible, otherwise by comparing various parses as described in Section 4 above.

Some of the connectives may belong to more than one syntactic category (Zeyrek and Kurfalı, 2018). For such connectives, we provide both of the syntactic categories. E.g. the DC *önce* 'before' is both an adverb (4) and a postposition (5).

(4) *Ali matematiği iyice anladı.* Ama
     <u>daha önce</u> **bir** **problemi** **bile**

Connective-Lex	Syntactic Category of Turkish DCs
cco (Coordinating conjunction)	CCONJ
csu (Subordinating conjunction)	Converb, ADP
adv (Adverb of adverbial)	ADV
other	Secondary connective, Other

Table 5: Mapping of TCL syntactic categories onto Connective-Lex categories

yardımsız çözemezdi.
Ali has now grasped math fully. But
<u>before</u> **he could not solve even one
math problem without help**.'

(5) **Bu filmi görmeden** <u>önce</u> *romanını
okumalısın.*
'<u>Before</u> **seeing this movie,** *you
should read the novel.*'

The syntactic categories we assign to the
DCs are; CCONJ, Converb (Simplex Subordinator), ADP (Postposition, Complex
Subordinator), ADV, Secondary Connective
("phrasal expressions") and Other categories,
such as noun-based connectives. These syntactic categories are mapped onto the categories which the Connective-Lex website offers (cf. Table 5).

- *DiMLex Formatter:* After creating the list of
DC lexicon entries with all the properties described so far, the entries are mapped onto the
DiMLex XML format. Firstly, an XML document is created and for each entry of the lexicon, an XML node is created. The XML elements and attributes are filled with the properties of lexicon entries following the Dim-
Lex format.

- *DCs in the DiMLex format:* At the end of
these steps, we have a list of 180 DCs with
their respective syntactic categories and other
properties.

In Figures 4, 5 and 6, we provide how DCs are represented in the DiMLex format. Figure 4 presents
the entry of a suffixal connective, Figure 5 shows
the entry for a single connective belonging to the
postposition category and Figure 6 illustrates the
entry for a phrasal discontinuous connective.

We computed the sense distribution of Turkish
explicit DCs by using our corpora and compared
the results with the sense distribution of explicits

in the PDTB 2.0 (Prasad et al., 2014). Table 6 displays the distribution of top-level classes comparatively and shows that the PDTB 2.0 displays an
order of Expansion (33%), Comparison (28.8%),
Contingency (19.2%) and Temporal (19%). This
distribution is preserved in Turkish to a great extent in the order of Expansion (36%), Contingency (24.4%), Comparison (22.3%), and Temporal (17.3%).

Sense Class	Turkish corpora	PDTB
TEMPORAL	360	3696
CONTINGENCY	507	3741
COMPARISON	463	5589
EXPANSION	748	6423
TOTAL	2078	19449

Table 6: Distribution of top-level sense classes among explicits in the PDTB 2.0 and discourse-annotated corpora of
Turkish

Table 7 provides the most frequent 15 discourse
connectives and their second-level senses compiled from all data sources.

6 Conclusion

In sum, the major contributions of this paper have
been:

- to characterize various properties of Turkish
discourse connectives including their syntactic categories and the senses they convey via
discourse-annotated corpora,

- to develop a DimLex-style lexicon of discourse connectives to host Turkish discourse
connectives together with their various properties and sample relations retrieved from annotated corpora.

TCL is populated by DCs gleaned from texts belonging to different genres. Given that DCs are
sensitive to genre (Webber, 2009), in future work,
we will compute the distribution of senses in different genres and work on incorporating this information into DiMLex. This aim goes in parallel
with our plan of extending the DC search tool with
new facilities.

DC	Gloss	Senses	Total
ve	and	Conjunction (395), Cause (39), Cause+Belief (2), Asynchronous (24), Synchronous (8), Level-of-detail (3), Conjunction|Level-of-detail (3), Conjunction|Contrast (1), Conjunction|Synchronous (1), Conjunction|Cause (3), Conjunction|Instantiation (1)	480
ama	but/yet	Contrast (92), Concession (135), Exception (8), Concession+SpeechAct (8), Correction (6), Cause+SpeechAct (2), Conjunction (3), Concession|Synchronous (1), Concession|Conjunction (1)	256
için	to/since	Purpose (167), Cause (39), Cause+Belief (3), Degree (2), Level-of-detail (1)	212
sonra	then	Asynchronous (142)	142
çünkü	because	Cause+Belief (17), Cause (76)	85
ancak	however	Concession (36), Exception (4), Contrast (27), Conjunction (1), Exception (1)	69
ayrıca	in addition	Conjunction (41)	41
-ken	while	Synchronous (33), Conjunction (2), Concession+SpeechAct (1), Contrast (1)	37
gibi	as	Conjunction (6), Manner (30), Similarity (1)	37
-(y)HncA	when	Synchronous (19), Cause (6), Asynchronous (10), Level-of-detail (1)	36
-(y)Hp	and	Conjunction (33), Manner (2), Synchronous|Conjunction (1)	36
yani	that is	Equivalence (17), Level-of-detail (4), Cause+Belief (10), Substitution (3), Cause+SpeechAct (1)	35
-sA	if	Condition (23), Concession (2), Negative-condition (4), Condition|Purpose (1), Condition+SpeechAct (3), Substitution (1)	34
-dA	when	Synchronous (29), Condition (1)	30
önce	before	Asynchronous (30)	30

Table 7: 15 most frequent discourse connectives and their second-level sense distribution in discourse-annotated corpora

```xml
<entry id="6" word="-(y)Hp">
  <orths>
    <orth canonical="0" orth_id="6o1" type="cont">
      <part type="suffixal">ıp</part>
    </orth>
    <orth canonical="1" orth_id="6o1" type="cont">
      <part type="suffixal">ip</part>
    </orth>
    <orth canonical="2" orth_id="6o1" type="cont">
      <part type="suffixal">up</part>
    </orth>
    <orth canonical="3" orth_id="6o1" type="cont">
      <part type="suffixal">üp</part>
    </orth>
    <orth canonical="4" orth_id="6o1" type="cont">
      <part type="suffixal">yıp</part>
    </orth>
    <orth canonical="5" orth_id="6o1" type="cont">
      <part type="suffixal">yip</part>
    </orth>
    <orth canonical="6" orth_id="6o1" type="cont">
      <part type="suffixal">yup</part>
    </orth>
    <orth canonical="7" orth_id="6o1" type="cont">
      <part type="suffixal">yüp</part>
    </orth>
  </orths>
  <syn>
    <cat>Converb</cat>
    <sem>
      <pdtb2_relation anno_N="36" freq="33" sense="EXPANSION:Conjunction" />
      <example>hazırlanıp arabaya bindi.</example>
    </sem>
    <sem>
      <pdtb2_relation anno_N="36" freq="2" sense="EXPANSION:Manner:Arg2-as-manner" />
      <example>Oğlum oturup yesene,</example>
    </sem>
    <sem>
      <pdtb2_relation anno_N="36" freq="1" sense="TEMPORAL:Synchronous" />
      <example>bu tarafa çevirip, 6 milyar kilometre öteden Dünya'nın fotoğrafını çektirdiler.</example>
    </sem>
  </syn>
</entry>
```

Figure 4: A suffixal connective -(y)Hp 'and', the senses it conveys and representative examples

```
<entry id="34" word="gibi">
  <orths>
    <orth canonical="0" orth_id="34o1" type="cont">
      <part type="single">gibi</part>
    </orth>
  </orths>
  <syn>
    <cat>ADP</cat>
    <sem>
      <pdtb2_relation anno_N="37" freq="6" sense="EXPANSION:Conjunction" />
      <example>kahve değirmeninin nerede olduğunu bilmediği gibi bulacağını da sanmıyordu.</example>
    </sem>
    <sem>
      <pdtb2_relation anno_N="37" freq="30" sense="EXPANSION:Manner:Arg2-as-manner" />
      <example>beni büyülenmiş gibi dinliyorlardı.</example>
    </sem>
    <sem>
      <pdtb2_relation anno_N="37" freq="1" sense="COMPARISON:Similarity" />
      <example>adeta çok küçük bir kasabada yaşıyormuşuz gibi gözüküyor.</example>
    </sem>
  </syn>
</entry>
```

Figure 5: A single connective *gibi* 'as', the senses it conveys and representative examples

```
<entry id="50" word="ya ... ya da">
  <orths>
    <orth canonical="0" orth_id="50o1" type="discont">
      <part type="phrasal">ya ya da</part>
    </orth>
    <orth canonical="1" orth_id="50o1" type="discont">
      <part type="phrasal">Ya ya da</part>
    </orth>
  </orths>
  <syn>
    <cat>CCONJ</cat>
    <sem>
      <pdtb2_relation anno_N="2" freq="2" sense="EXPANSION:Disjunction" />
      <example>ya tamamen Yok olmuşlar, ya da cins ve tür düzeyinde önemli ölçüde azalmışlardır.</example>
    </sem>
  </syn>
</entry>
```

Figure 6: A phrasal connective *ya ... ya da* 'either ... or', its sense and a representative example

References

Amal Al-Saif and Katja Markert. 2010. The Leeds Arabic Discourse Treebank: Annotating Discourse Connectives for Arabic. In *LREC*, pages 2046–2053.

Nicholas Asher. 1993. Reference to abstract objects in English.

Nicholas Asher. 2012. *Reference to abstract objects in discourse*, volume 50. Springer Science & Business Media.

Laurence Danlos. 2009. D-STAG: a formalism for discourse analysis based on SDRT and using synchronous TAG. In *International Conference on Formal Grammar*, pages 64–84. Springer.

Laurence Danlos, Katerina Rysova, Magdalena Rysova, and Manfred Stede. 2018. Primary and secondary discourse connectives: Definitions and lexicons. *Dialogue and Discourse*, 9:50–78.

Debopam Das, Tatjana Scheffler, Peter Bourgonje, and Manfred Stede. 2018. Constructing a lexicon of English discourse connectives. In *Proceedings of the 19th Annual SIGdial Meeting on Discourse and Dialogue*, pages 360–365.

Işın Demirşahin and Deniz Zeyrek. 2017. Pair annotation as a novel annotation procedure: The case of Turkish Discourse Bank. In *Handbook of Linguistic Annotation*, pages 1219–1240. Springer.

Anna Feltracco, Elisabetta Jezek, Bernardo Magnini, and Manfred Stede. 2016. Lico: A lexicon of Italian connectives. *CLiC it*, page 141.

Sudheer Kolachina, Rashmi Prasad, Dipti Misra Sharma, and Aravind K Joshi. 2012. Evaluation of Discourse Relation Annotation in the Hindi Discourse Relation Bank. In *LREC*, pages 823–828.

Alan Lee, Rashmi Prasad, Bonnie Webber, and Aravind K Joshi. 2016. Annotating discourse relations with the PDTB annotator. In *Proceedings of COLING 2016, the 26th International Conference on Computational Linguistics: System Demonstrations*, pages 121–125.

William C Mann and Sandra A Thompson. 1988. Rhetorical Structure Theory: Toward a functional theory of text organization. *Text-Interdisciplinary Journal for the Study of Discourse*, 8(3):243–281.

Amália Mendes, Iria del Rio, Manfred Stede, and Felix Dombek. 2018. A lexicon of discourse markers for Portuguese–ldm-pt. In *11th International Conference on Language Resources and Evaluation*, pages 4379–4384.

Jiří Mírovskỳ, Pavlína Synková, Magdaléna Rysová, and Lucie Poláková. 2017. CzeDLex–a lexicon of Czech discourse connectives. *The Prague Bulletin of Mathematical Linguistics*, 109(1):61–91.

Rashmi Prasad, Bonnie Webber, and Aravind Joshi. 2014. Reflections on the Penn Discourse Treebank, comparable corpora, and complementary annotation. *Computational Linguistics*, 40(4):921–950.

Charlotte Roze, Laurence Danlos, and Philippe Muller. 2012. Lexconn: a French lexicon of discourse connectives. *Discours. Revue de linguistique, psycholinguistique et informatique. A journal of linguistics, psycholinguistics and computational linguistics*, (10).

Tatjana Scheffler and Manfred Stede. 2016. Adding Semantic Relations to a Large-Coverage Connective Lexicon of German. In *LREC*.

Manfred Stede and Carla Umbach. 1998. Dimlex: A lexicon of discourse markers for text generation and understanding. In *Proceedings of the 36th Annual Meeting of the Association for Computational Linguistics and 17th International Conference on Computational Linguistics-Volume 2*, pages 1238–1242. Association for Computational Linguistics.

Bonnie Webber. 2009. Genre distinctions for discourse in the Penn TreeBank. In *Proceedings of the Joint Conference of the 47th Annual Meeting of the ACL and the 4th International Joint Conference on Natural Language Processing of the AFNLP: Volume 2-Volume 2*, pages 674–682. Association for Computational Linguistics.

Deniz Zeyrek, Isın Demirsahin, A Sevdik-Çallı, and Ruket Çakıcı. 2013. Turkish Discourse Bank: Porting a discourse annotation style to a morphologically rich language. *D&D*, 4(2):174–184.

Deniz Zeyrek and Murathan Kurfalı. 2017. Tdb 1.1: Extensions on Turkish discourse bank. In *Proceedings of the 11th Linguistic Annotation Workshop*, pages 76–81.

Deniz Zeyrek and Murathan Kurfalı. 2018. An assessment of explicit inter-and intra-sentential discourse connectives in Turkish Discourse Bank. In *Proceedings of the Eleventh International Conference on Language Resources and Evaluation (LREC-2018)*.

Deniz Zeyrek, Amália Mendes, Yulia Grishina, Murathan Kurfalı, Samuel Gibbon, and Maciej Ogrodniczuk. 2019. TED Multilingual Discourse Bank (TED-MDB): A parallel corpus annotated in the PDTB style. *Language Resources and Evaluation*, pages 1–27.

Deniz Zeyrek and Bonnie Webber. 2008. A discourse resource for Turkish: Annotating discourse connectives in the METU corpus. In *Proceedings of the 6th workshop on Asian language resources*.

Yuping Zhou and Nianwen Xue. 2015. The Chinese Discourse Treebank: a Chinese corpus annotated with discourse relations. *Language Resources and Evaluation*, 49(2):397–431.

Sandrine Zufferey and Liesbeth Degand. 2017. Annotating the meaning of discourse connectives in multilingual corpora. *Corpus Linguistics and Linguistic Theory*, 13(2):399–422.

Meta-Semantic Representation for Early Detection of Alzheimer's Disease

Jinho D. Choi
Computer Science
Emory University
Atlanta, GA, USA
jchoi31@emory.edu

Mengmei Li
Computer Science
Emory University
Atlanta, GA, USA
kate.li@emory.edu

Felicia Goldstein
Neurology
Emory University
Atlanta, GA, USA
fgoldst@emory.edu

Ihab Hajjar
Neurology
Emory University
Atlanta, GA, USA
ihajjar@emory.edu

Abstract

This paper presents a new task-oriented meaning representation called *meta-semantics*, that is designed to detect patients with early symptoms of Alzheimer's disease by analyzing their language beyond a syntactic or semantic level. Meta-semantic representation consists of three parts, entities, predicate argument structures, and discourse attributes, that derive rich knowledge graphs. For this study, 50 controls and 50 patients with mild cognitive impairment (MCI) are selected, and meta-semantic representation is annotated on their speeches transcribed in text. Inter-annotator agreement scores of 88%, 82%, and 89% are achieved for the three types of annotation, respectively. Five analyses are made using this annotation, depicting clear distinctions between the control and MCI groups. Finally, a neural model is trained on features extracted from those analyses to classify MCI patients from normal controls, showing a high accuracy of 82% that is very promising.

1 Introduction

Our understanding of Alzheimers disease (AD) has evolved over the last few decades. Most notably is the discovery that AD has long latent preclinical and mild cognitive impairment (MCI) stages (Karr et al., 2018; Steenland et al., 2018). These stages are the focus of many prevention and therapeutic interventions. A key limitation in identifying these pre-dementia stages for clinical trial recruitment is the need for expensive or invasive testing like positron emission tomography or obtaining cerebrospinal fluid (CSF) analyses. Traditional cognitive testing is time-consuming and can be biased by literacy and test-taking skills (Fyffe et al., 2011). Recent advances in natural language processing (NLP) offer the unique opportunity to explore previously undetectable changes in the cognitive process of semantics that can be automated in clinical artificial intelligence (Beam and Kohane, 2016).

Limited prior studies have suggested the feasibility of detecting AD by analyzing language variations. One approach includes linguistically motivated analysis extracting lexical, grammatical, and syntactic features to detect language deficits in AD patients (Fraser et al., 2016; Orimaye et al., 2017). The other approach involves deep learning models to extract features from languages used by AD patients (Orimaye et al., 2016; Karlekar et al., 2018). The limitations of these studies are that most were developed based on dementia cases, so their ability to detect pre-dementia is still unknown. The impact of these methods is the highest in the cases where traditional cognitive measures are unable to clarify the patients cognitive status. Hence, we focus on these early MCI stages in this study.

We suggest a new meaning representation called *meta-semantics* that derives a knowledge graph reflecting semantic, pragmatic, and discourse aspects of language spoken by MCI patients. The objective of this representation is not to design yet another structure to capture more information but to sense aspects beyond the syntax and semantic level that are essential for the early detection of MCI patients. We hypothesize that patients in the pre-dementia stage do not necessarily make so much of grammatical mistakes compared to normal people but often have difficulties in elaborating or articulating their thoughts in language. To verify our hypothesis, we collect speeches from 50 normal controls and 50 MCI patients that standardized cognition tests fail to distinguish (Section 2), annotate meta-semantic representation on the transcripts of those speeches (Section 3), make several analyses to comprehend linguistic differences between the control and the MCI groups (Section 4), then develop a neural network model to detect MCI patients from normal controls (Section 5). To the best of our knowledge, this is the first time that a dedicated meaning representation is proposed for the detection of MCI.

Proceedings of the First International Workshop on Designing Meaning Representations, pages 82–91
Florence, Italy, August 1st, 2019 ©2019 Association for Computational Linguistics

2 Data Preparation

We analyzed data from 100 subjects collected as part of the B-SHARP, Brain, Stress, Hypertension, and Aging Research Program.[1] 50 cognitively normal controls and 50 patients with mild cognitive impairment (MCI) were selected based on neuropsychological and clinical assessments performed by a trained physician and a neuropsychologist. The two groups were matched on overall cognitive scores to examine how well our new meta-semantic indices would perform in the setting where standardized tests such as the Montreal Cognitive Assessment (Nasreddine et al., 2005) and the Boston Naming Test (Kaplan et al., 1983) failed to distinguish them. Table 1 shows demographics and clinical features of the control and the MCI groups.

Type	Control	MCI	P-value
Age	65.6 (±6.80)	66.0 (±8.38)	0.809
Race	54%; 44%	58%; 42%	0.840
Sex	62%	60%	1.000
Education	54%	56%	1.000
MoCA	24.2 (±2.15)	23.9 (±2.00)	0.502
BNT	14.0 (±1.43)	13.8 (±1.23)	0.550
CDR	0.01 (±0.07)	0.43 (±0.18)	**<0.001**
FAQ	1.00 (±1.62)	1.71 (±2.57)	0.103

Table 1: Demographics and clinical features of the two groups. Age: avg-years, Race: % African American; % Non-Hispanic Caucasian, Sex: % female, Education: % Bachelor's or above, MoCA (Montreal Cognitive Assessment): avg-score, BNT (Boston Naming Test): avg-score, CDR (Clinical Dementia Rating): avg-score, FAQ (Function Assessment Questionnaire): avg-score. The p-values are evaluated by the t-test except for race, sex, and education which are evaluated by the χ^2 test.

No significant group differences were found in age, race, sex, or education between these two groups. The MCI group performed significantly worse on the Clinical Dementia Rating (Morris, 1994), but did not differ as much on the Function Assessment Questionnaire (Pfeffer et al., 1982) assessing instrumental activities of daily living.

2.1 Speech Task Protocol

We conducted a speech task protocol that evaluated subjects' language abilities on 1) natural speech, 2) fluency, and 3) picture description, and collected audio recordings for all three tasks from each subject. For this study, the audio recordings from the third task, picture description, were used to demonstrate the effectiveness of the meta-semantics analysis on detecting MCI. All subjects were shown the picture in Figure 1, *The Circus Procession*, copyrighted by McLoughlin Brothers as part of the Juvenile Collection, and given the same instruction to describe the picture for one minute. Visual abilities of the subjects were confirmed before recording.

Figure 1: The image of *"The Circus Procession"* used for the picture description task.

2.2 Transcription

Audio recordings for the picture description task (Section 2.1) from the 100 subjects in Table 1 were automatically transcribed by the online tool, Temi,[2] then manually corrected. Table 3 shows transcripts from a normal control and an MCI patient whose MoCA scores are matched to 29 (out of 30 points). For the annotation of meta-semantic representation in Section 3, all transcripts were tokenized by the open-source NLP toolkit called ELIT.[3] Table 2 shows general statistics of these transcripts from the output automatically generated by the part-of-speech tagger and the dependency parser in ELIT.

Type	Control	MCI	P-value
T	174.32 (±40.14)	175.04 (±48.01)	0.936
S	11.34 (±3.08)	11.22 (±3.73)	0.862
N	36.32 (±8.62)	38.06 (±12.25)	0.418
V	27.10 (±7.44)	24.50 (±6.93)	0.077
C	7.74 (±4.25)	7.54 (±4.42)	0.820
RN	2.36 (±1.82)	1.64 (±1.67)	**0.044**
CM	4.52 (±2.74)	4.30 (±2.15)	0.659

Table 2: Statistics of transcripts from the two groups. The avg-count and the stdev are reported for each field. T: tokens, S: sentences, N: nouns, V: verbs, C: conjuncts, RN: relative clauses and non-finite modifiers, CM: clausal modifiers or complements. The p-values are evaluated by the t-test.

---

[1] B-SHARP: http://medicine.emory.edu/bsharp

[2] Temi: https://www.temi.com

[3] ELIT: https://github.com/elitcloud/elit

Control	MCI
This is a what looks like a circus poster. The title is the Circus Procession. There's an off color green background. On the left-hand side is elephant in a costume peddling a tricycle, operating a tricycle. On the right side is another elephant with holding a fan. He's dressed in an outfit with a hat and a cane. There are two people in the background and they could be either men or women. And then there are three, I'll take that back. And then the foreground is a clown in a white suit with red trim. It was copyrighted in 1988 by the McLoughlin Brothers, New York or NY. Um, there's a black border. Um, the, there are shadows represented by some brown color at the bottom.	It's a circus poster. Going left to right is an elephant standing on its side legs, and a, um, vest, a tie and a red Tuxedo coat, and um yellow cap with a black band holding what appears to be a fan in its trunk. The elephant has glasses and a cane. Um, the top, says the Circus Procession. To the left of the elephant is a clown in a white and red costume with red and black paint on his face, red hair or shoes. And there appear to be three like soldiers, um gray suits, yellow trim, um, um, red hair. To the left of them, there's another elephant, riding a bicycle. This elephant has pants to red bicycle. He's got a regular coat of his and a red bow tie.

Table 3: Transcripts from a normal control and an MCI patient whose MoCA scores are 29 points.

No significant group differences were found in text-level counts (tokens and sentences), grammatical categories (nouns and verbs), or syntactic structures (conjuncts, clausal modifiers or complements), except for the relative clauses and non-finite modifiers whose p-value is less than 0.05. The MCI group used notably a fewer number of verbs although the difference to the control group was not significant.

3 Meta-Semantic Representation

We organized a team of two undergraduate students in Linguistics to annotate meta-semantic representation on the transcripts from Section 2.2 such that every transcript was annotated by two people and adjudicated by an expert. The web-based annotation tool called BRAT was used for this annotation (Stenetorp et al., 2012), where the entire content of each transcript was displayed at a time. Figure 2 shows a screenshot of our annotation interface using BRAT on the control example in Table 3.

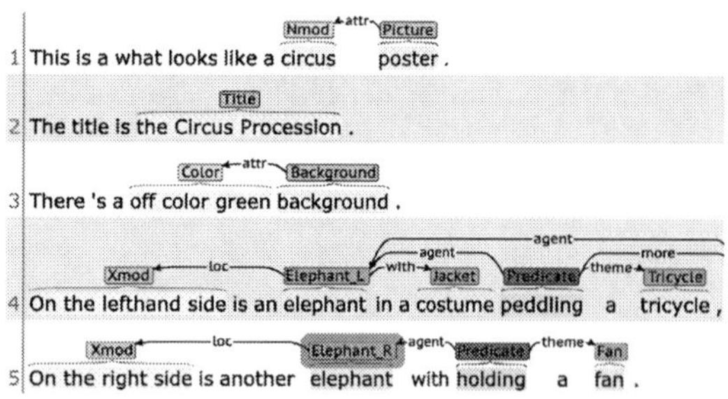

Figure 2: A screenshot of our annotation interface using the web-based tool BRAT on the first five sentences of the control example in Table 3.

Meta-semantic representation involves three types of annotation, entities (Section 3.1), predicate argument structures (Section 3.2), discourse attributes (Section 3.3), as well as few other miscellaneous components (Section 3.4). The following sections give a brief overview of our annotation guidelines.

3.1 Entities

To analyze which and how objects in the picture are described by individual subjects, every object mentioned in the transcript is identified as either a pre-defined entity or an unknown entity. All nominals including pronouns, proper nouns, common nouns, and noun phrases are considered potential mentions. Table 4 shows the list of 50 predefined entities that are frequently mentioned in the transcripts.

Main Entity	Sub Entities
Picture	Background, Border, Copyright, Parade, Shadow, Title
Elephant_L	EL_Beanie, EL_Collar, EL_Head, EL_Jacket, EL_Pants, EL_Tie, EL_Tricycle, EL_Trunk
Elephant_R	ER_Fedora, ER_Coat, ER_Vest, ER_Cane, ER_Fan, ER_Glasses, ER_Head, ER_Collar, ER_Pants, ER_Tie, ER_Hand, ER_Feet, ER_Trunk, ER_Hanky
Men	Man_L, Man_M, Man_R, M_Boots, M_Costume, M_Cross, M_Flag, M_Hat, M_Plume, M_Sword
Clown	CL_Face, CL_Hair, CL_Head, CL_Pants, CL_Ruffle, CL_Shoes, CL_Suit

Table 4: Predefined entities, where the main entities indicate the 5 conspicuous objects in Figure 1 and the sub entities indicate objects that belong to the main entities.

In the example below, five mentions are found and can be linked to four entities as follows:

An *elephant*$_1$ is holding a *fan*$_2$. To the leftside of *him*$_3$, another *elephant*$_4$ is riding a *tricycle*$_5$.

- $\{elephant_1, him_3\} \rightarrow$ `Elephant_R` (elephant on the right)

- $\{elephant_4\} \rightarrow$ `Elephant_L` (elephant on the left)

- $\{fan_2\} \rightarrow$ `ER_Fan`

- $\{tricycle_5\} \rightarrow$ `EL_Tricycle`

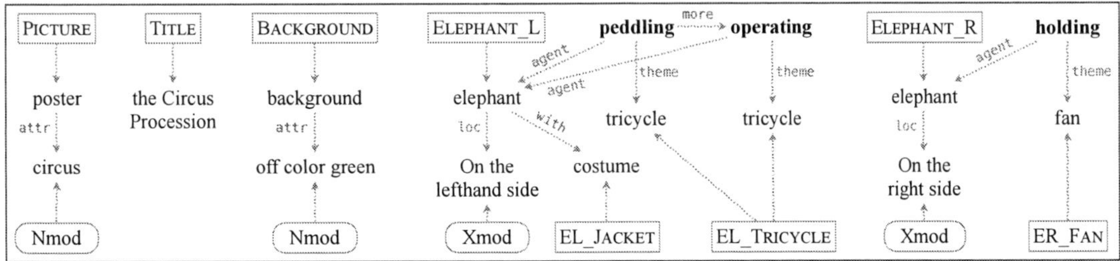

Figure 3: Visualization of meta-semantic representation on the first 5 sentences of the control example in Table 3.

The entity `Men` is a group of three people including `Man_L`, `Man_M`, and `Man_R` (man on the left, middle, and right) as its sub entities. Such a group entity is defined because subjects regularly describe them together as one unit. `Picture` often refers to the types of the picture that subjects view it as (e.g., *poster* in Figure 2). Special kinds of entities, `Title` and `Copyright`, are also defined that are annotated on the literals (e.g., *the Circus Procession* in Figure 2, *McLoughlin Brothers, 1888, N.Y.*) to see if subjects indeed recognize them correctly. Any object that is either ambiguous or not predefined is annotated as an unknown entity.

It is worth mentioning that unlike mention annotation for coreference resolution in OntoNotes (Pradhan et al., 2012) where whole noun phrases are annotated as mentions, function words such as articles or determiners and modifiers such as adverbs or adjectives are not considered part of mentions in our annotation, which is similar to abstract meaning representation (Banarescu et al., 2013). Such abstraction is more suitable for spoken data where the usage of these function words and modifiers is not so consistent.

3.2 Predicate Argument Structures

To analyze semantics of the entities as well as their relations to one another, predicate argument structures are annotated. Note that meta-semantic representation is entity-centric such that expressions that do not describe the picture are discarded from the annotation (e.g., *When I was young, circus came to my town all the time*). Such expressions do not help analyzing subjects' capabilities in describing the picture although they can be used for other kinds of analyses which we will explore in the future.

Following the latest guidelines of PropBank (Bonial et al., 2017), both verbal predicates, excluding auxiliary and modal verbs, and nominal predicates, including eventive nouns and nouns from light-verb constructions, are considered in our representation.

Once predicates are identified, arguments are annotated with the following thematic roles (in the examples, predicates are in italic, arguments are in brackets, and thematic roles are in subscripts):

- `agent`: Prototypical agents
  e.g., An [elephant]$_{agent}$ is *holding* a fan.
- `theme`: Prototypical patients or themes
  e.g., An elephant is *holding* a [fan]$_{theme}$.
- `dative`: Recipients or beneficiaries e.g., The soldier is *bringing* a flag to the [circus]$_{dative}$.
- `adv`: Adverbial modifiers
  e.g., That elephant is [actually]$_{adv}$ *walking*.
- `dir`: Directional modifiers
  e.g., Feathers are *coming* out of the [hat]$_{dir}$.
- `loc`: Locative modifiers e.g., The *clown* is *dancing* in between the [elephants]$_{loc}$.
- `mnr`: Locative modifiers
  e.g., Soldiers are *marching* [proudly]$_{mnr}$.
- `prp`: Purpose or clausal modifiers e.g., The clown is *dancing* to [tease]$_{prp}$ the elephants.
- `tmp`: Temporal modifiers e.g., This seemed to be a poster *made* in the early [1900s]$_{tmp}$.

If an argument is a preposition phrase, the thematic role is annotated on the preposition object such that in the example above, only the head noun [hat] is annotated as `dir` instead of the entire preposition phrase "out of the hat".[4] As shown in the `prp` example, a predicate can be an argument of another predicate. Note that modifiers do not need to be arguments of only predicates but entities as well (e.g., the *elephant* on the [tricycle]$_{loc}$, a *poster* from way back in [1990s]$_{tmp}$).

The choice of these thematic roles are observational to the transcripts. No instance of `dative` is found in our dataset but the role is still kept in the guidelines for future annotation.

---

[4]See the `case` relation in Section 3.4 for more details about how prepositions are handled in our annotation.

3.3 Discourse Attributes

To analyze discourse aspects of the transcripts, six labels and one relation are annotated as follows (in the examples, attributes are indicated in brackets):

ambiguous Objects contextually ambiguous to identify are annotated with this label. For example, both [elephant] and [something] are annotated as ambiguous because it is unclear which elephant and object they refer to. Also, [blue] likely refers to the vest of Elephant_R but not specified in this context; thus, it is also annotated as ambiguous.

> That [elephant] is holding [something].
> The elephant with [blue] on is walking.

opinion Descriptions subjective to that particular subject are annotated with this label. For example, 'red' is considered an objective fact agreed by most subjects whereas [fancy] is considered a subjective opinion, not necessarily agreed by others. Similarly, [like a millionaire] is considered subject's opinion about the elephant's costume.

> The 'red 'tie with the [fancy] shirt.
> That elephant is dressed up [like a millionaire].

emotion Expressions that carry subjects' emotions or their views on objects' emotions are annotated with this label.

> That clown looks [happy].
> The elephant makes me [sad].

certain Adverbials or modals that express certainty are annotated with this label.

> Those people [must] be women.
> This is [obviously] an old poster.

fuzzy Adverbials or modals that express fuzziness are annotated with this label.

> The elephant carries [some kind of] balloon.
> I am [not sure] if the elephant is marching.

emphasis Adverbials used for emphasis are annotated with this label.

> That tricycle is [very] big.
> That clown is [definitely] enjoying this.

more Additional descriptions from appositions and repetitions from repairs are annotated with this relation (in the examples, ones in the brackets have more relations to the ones in italic):

> There are *elephants*, two [elephants]$_{more}$, here.
> This is the Circus *Profession*, [Procession]$_{more}$.
> That one is holding an *umbrella*, or a [fan]$_{more}$.

[elephants] is an apposition that adds more information to *elephants*. [Procession] is a prototypical repair case that fixes the prior mention of *Profession*. [fan] may not be considered a repair in some analysis, but it is in ours because it attempts to fix the earlier mention of *umbrella* in a speech setting.

3.4 Miscellaneous

Two additional modifiers, Nmod and Xmod are annotated. Nmod are modifiers of nominals that modify entities with the attr relation:

> A [polka dot]$_{attr}$ *dress*.
> Very [big]$_{attr}$ [red and yellow]$_{attr}$ *pants*.

Xmod are any other types of modifiers, mostly adverbials and prepositions. If adverbials, they are annotated with the adv relation in Sec 3.2. If prepositions, they are annotated with the case relation:

> There is a [seemingly]$_{adv}$ *dancing* clown.
> Feathers are coming [out of]$_{case}$ the *hat*.

Finally, possessions of entities are annotated with the with relation regardless of verbs such as *have* or *get* for the consistency across different structures. In both of the following sentences, [jacket] has the with relation to the *elephant*.

> The *elephant* with a blue [jacket]$_{with}$.
> The *elephant* has a blue [jacket]$_{with}$.

4 Meta-Semantic Analysis

Given the annotation in Section 3, several analyses are made to observe how effective meta-semantic is to distinguish the control (C) and MCI (M) groups.

4.1 Entity Coverage Analysis

We anticipate that most subjects in C and M would recognize the main entities whereas a fewer number of sub entities would be commonly recognized by M than C. For each entity e_i, that is the i'th entity in Table 4, two counts c_i^c and c_i^m are measured such that they are the numbers of subjects in C and M whose transcripts include at least one mention of e_i. For instance, the entity e_7 = Title is mentioned by $c_7^c = 37$ subjects in C and $c_7^m = 40$ subjects in M in our annotation.

Figure 4 shows how many entities are commonly mentioned by each percentage range of the subjects in C and M. For example, six entities are commonly mentioned by 55~75% of the subjects in C whereas only three entities are commonly mentioned by the same range of the subjects in M. These percentage ranges are analyzed as follows:

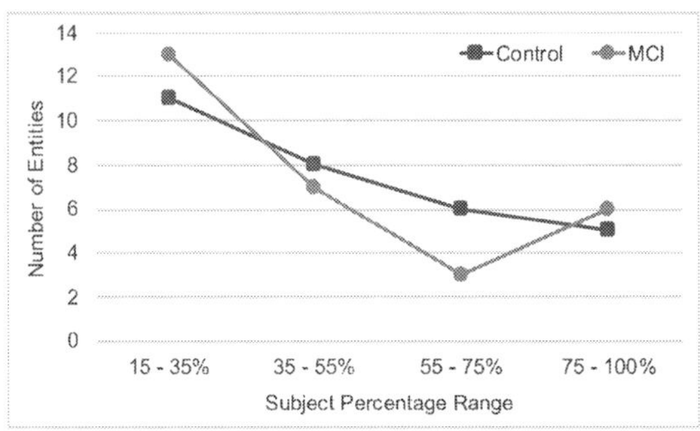

Figure 4: Entity coverage analysis.

High range (75∼100%) No significant group difference is found between C and M. 5 entities, `Elephant_R`, `Elephant_L`, `EL_Tricycle`, `Clown`, and `Men`, are commonly mentioned by C, whereas 6 entities (all of above + `Title`) are commonly mentioned by M in this range.

Mid range (35∼75%) Subjects in M start not recognizing certain entities recognized by subjects in C in this range. 14 entities are commonly mentioned by C whereas 10 entities are mentioned by M. When the range is fine-grained to 45∼75%, the difference becomes even more significant such that 10 entities are commonly mentioned by C whereas only 5 entities are mentioned by M in that range.

Low range (15∼35%) Similar to the high range, no significant difference is found between the two groups. 11 and 13 entities are commonly recognized by C and M, respectively in this range.

For the whole range of 15∼75%, the plot from C can be well fitted to a linear line with $R^2 = 0.9524$, whereas the one from M cannot, resulting significantly lower $R^2 = 0.5924$. The plot from M rather shows an inverted Gaussian distribution, implying that the majority of M tends not to mention about entities that are not immediately conspicuous which is not necessarily the case for subjects in C.

4.2 Entity Focus Analysis

This analysis shows which entities are more frequently mentioned (focused) by what subject group. For each entity e_i and its counts c_i^c and c_i^m in Section 4.1, the proportions p_i^c and p_i^m are measured such that $p_i^c = c_i^c/|C|$ and $p_i^m = c_i^m/|M|$, where $|C| = |M| = 50$ (Table 1). Then, the relative difference d_i^r for the i'th entity is measured as follow:

$$d_i^r = \frac{p_i^c - p_i^m}{\max(p_i^c, p_i^m)}$$

Thus, if d_i^r is greater than 0, e_i is more commonly mentioned by C; otherwise, it is by M. Figure 4 shows the entities that are significantly more mentioned by C (blue) and M (red), where $|d|_i^r \geq 0.2$. 6 entities, `CL_Pants`, `M_Boots`, `ER_Glasses`, `EL_Collar`, `ER_Trunk`, `M_Flag`, `EL_Pants`, `ER_Vest`, and `EL_Jacket`, are noticeably more mentioned by C, whereas only 2 entities, `EL_Tie` and `EL_Hat`, are by M, which are focused on those two small parts of the left elephant. Additionally, M mentions more about the `Background`, which is not a specific object but an abstract environment.

Figure 5: Entity focus analysis. Entities focused by C and M are colored in blue and red, respectively.

4.3 Entity Density Analysis

This analysis shows the proportion of the description used for each object in the transcript. Meta-semantic representation forms a graph comprising many isolated subgraphs. In Figure 3, there are 5 subgraphs, where the largest subgraph has 7 vertices (the one with `Elephant_L`) and the smallest subgraph has only 1 vertex (the one with `Title`).

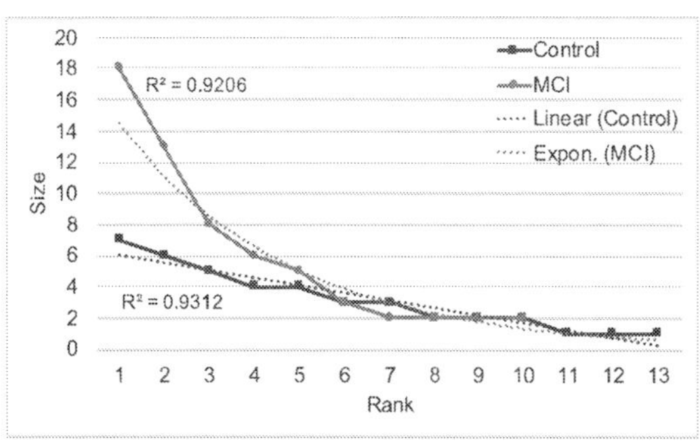

Figure 6: Plots of size lists derived from meta-semantic representation annotated on the control and MCI examples in Table 3, where x and y axises are ranked indices and sizes of the subgraphs, respectively.

Let G^t be a graph derived from meta-semantic representation annotated on the t'th transcript. G^t can be represented by a list of its subgraphs sorted in descending order with respect to their sizes such that $G^t = [g_1^t, \ldots, g_k^t]$ where $|g_i| \geq |g_j|$ for all $0 < i < j \leq k$. The size of a subgraph is determined by the number of vertices. For the graph in Figure 3, $G = [g_1, \ldots, g_5]$ such that $|G| = k = 5$, $|g_1| = 7$, and $|g_5| = 1$. Given G^t, the size list L^t can be derived such that $L^t = [|g_1^t|, \ldots, |g_k^t|]$. Figure 6 shows plots of the size lists from the graphs derived by meta-semantic representation annotated on the control and MCI examples in Table 3. The control plot can be well-fitted to a linear line with $R^2 = 0.9312$, whereas the MCI plot is better fitted to an exponential curve with $R^2 = 0.9206$.

$\overline{SSE}_d$	Control	MCI	P-value
$d = 1$	12.10 (±12.37)	17.50 (±22.43)	0.1394
$d = 2$	5.18 (±4.81)	7.08 (±7.54)	0.1370
$d = 3$	3.03 (±2.44)	4.01 (±3.83)	0.1278
$d = 4$	2.36 (±2.14)	2.55 (±2.12)	0.6661
$d = 5$	1.89 (±1.78)	1.78 (±1.54)	0.7391

Table 5: The average sums of squared errors by fitting each size list to degrees 1-5 of polynomial functions.

Table 5 shows the average sums of squared errors $\overline{SSE}_d$ by fitting each size list $L^t = [l_1^t, \ldots, l_k^t]$ to polynomial functions $f_d(x)$ of degrees $d = [1, .., 5]$ where $n = 50$ for both C and M:

$$\overline{SSE}_d = \frac{1}{n} \sum_{t=1}^{n} \sum_{i=1}^{|L^t|} (f_d(i) - l_i^t)^2$$

The control plots fit to lower degree functions more reliably than the MCI plots, although not statistically significant, implying that subjects in C distribute their time more evenly to describe different entities than subjects in M who tend to spend most of their time to describe a couple of entities but not so much for the rest of the entities.

4.4 Predicate Argument Analysis

Figure 7 shows the average percentages of predicates and their thematic arguments annotated on the transcripts. Subjects in C generally form sentences with more predicate argument structures although the differences are not statistically significant. Not enough instances of the modifiers (e.g., `mnr`, `loc`) are found to make a meaningful analysis for those roles. Although predicate argument structures may not appear useful, these structures make it possible

to perform the entity density analysis in Section 4.3 and potentially other types of analyses, which we will conduct in the future.

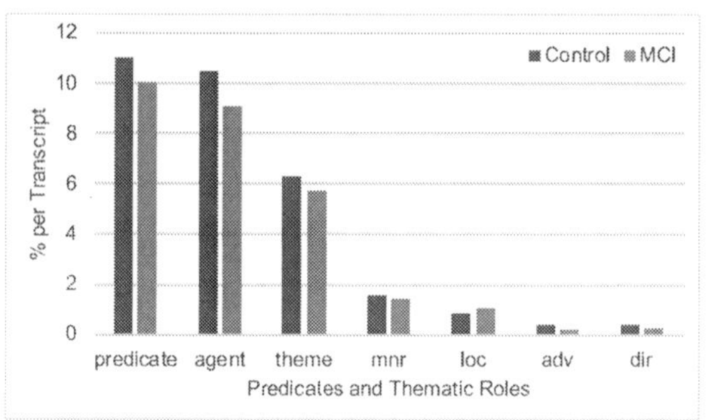

Figure 7: Predicate argument analysis.

4.5 Discourse Attribute Analysis

Figure 8 shows the average percentages of discourse attributes. Notice that M makes over twice more `ambiguous` mentions than C, implying that MCI patients do not elaborate as well. Moreover, M makes more `fuzzy` expressions and frequently uses `more` relations to repair, which makes their speeches less articulated. On the other hand, C makes more subjective `opinion` and `certain` expressions with `emphasis`, which makes their speeches sound more confident. These are essential features to distinguish M from C, makes this analysis more "meta-semantics".

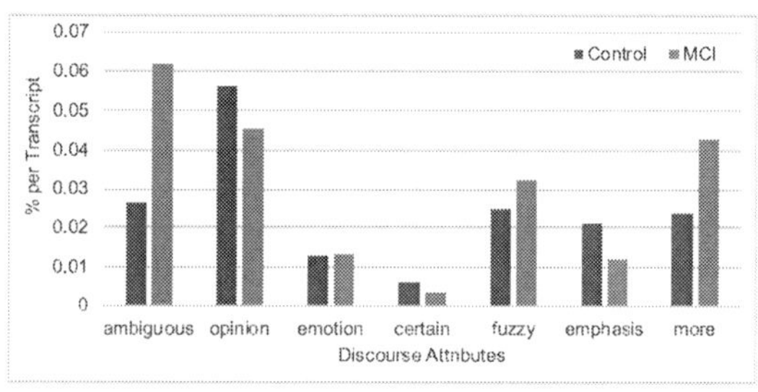

Figure 8: Discourse attribute analysis.

5 Experiments

5.1 Inter-Annotator Agreement

The annotation guidelines summarized in Section 3 are established through multiple rounds of double annotation and adjudication. During the final round, the entity annotation, the predicate argument annotation, and the discourse attribute annotation reach the F1 scores of 88%, 82%, and 89% respectively for the inter-annotator agreement, which yield high-quality data ready for training statistical models.

5.2 Data Split

The 100 transcripts from Section 2 are split into 5 folds where each fold contains 10 transcripts from the control group and another 10 transcripts from the MCI group (so the total of 20 transcripts). To evaluate our model that takes a transcript annotated with meta-semantic representation as input and predicts whether or not it is from the MCI group, 5-fold cross validation is used, which is suitable for experimenting with such a small dataset.

5.3 Features

For each transcript, three types of features are extracted from the meta-semantic analysis in Section 4 for the classifications of Control vs. MCI:

- **Entity Types**: A vector $e \in \mathbb{R}^{1 \times |E|}$ is created where $|E| = 50$ is the total number of predefined entities in Table 4, and each dimension i of e represents the occurrence of the corresponding entity such that $e_i = 1$ if the i'th entity appears in the transcript; otherwise, $e_i = 0$.

- **Entity Densities**: A vector $d \in \mathbb{R}^{1 \times |P|}$ is created where $P = \{1, 2, 3\}$ ($|P| = 3$) consisting of degrees used for the entity density analysis in Section 4.3 (in this case, the polynomial functions with degrees 1, 2, and 3 are used) such that d_i is the sum of the squared error measured by comparing the size list L of this transcript to the fitted polynomial function of the degree i.

- **Labels**: A vector $b \in \mathbb{R}^{1 \times |N|}$ is created where N contains counts of predicates, thematic roles, and discourse attributes in Sections 3.2 and 3.3 ($|N| = 16$) such that b_i is the count of the corresponding component in the transcript.

5.4 Classification

The feature vector $x = e \oplus d \oplus b$ is created by concatenating e, d, and b, and gets fed into a classifier. Figure 9 illustrates the feed-forward neural network used for the classification between the control and the MCI groups. Let the size of the feature vector x be $s = |E| + |P| + |L|$. Then, the input vector $x \in \mathbb{R}^{1 \times s}$ is multiplied by the weight matrix $W_0 \in \mathbb{R}^{s \times d_0}$ and generates the first hidden vector $h_1 = x \cdot W_0$. The hidden vector $h_1 \in \mathbb{R}^{1 \times d_0}$ is multiplied by another weight matrix $W_1 \in \mathbb{R}^{d_0 \times d_1}$ and generates the second hidden vector $h_2 = h_1 \cdot W_1$. Finally, $h_2 \in \mathbb{R}^{1 \times d_1}$ is multiplied by the last weight matrix $W_2 \in \mathbb{R}^{d_1 \times d_2}$ where d_2 is the number of classes to be predicted, and generates the output vector $y = h_2 \cdot W_2 \in \mathbb{R}^{1 \times d_2}$. In our case, the sizes of the hidden vectors are $d_0 = 200$ and $d_1 = 100$, and the size of the output vector is $d_2 = 2$. Note that we have experimented with simpler networks comprising only one or no hidden layer, but the one with two hidden layers shows the best results.

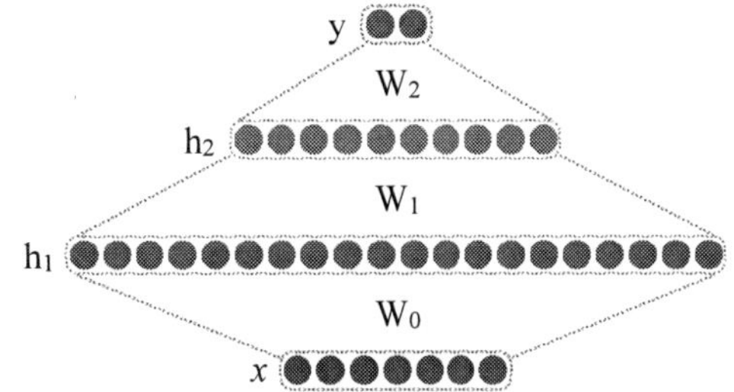

Figure 9: Feed-forward neural network used for the classification of the control vs. MCI group.

The two dimensions y_m and y_c in the output vector are optimized for the likelihoods of the subject being control or MCI, respectively. The average of 82% accuracy is achieved by the 5-fold cross-validation (Section 5.2) with this model. Considering these are subjects that the standardized tests such as MoCA or Boston Naming Test could not distinguish (Table 1), this result is very promising.

6 Related Work

Reilly et al. (2010) found that neurodegenerative disorders could deteriorate nerve cells controlling cognitive, speech and language processes. Verma and Howard (2012) reported that language impairment in AD could affect verbal fluency and naming, that requires integrity of semantic concepts, before breaking down in other facets of the brain. Tillas (2015) showed that linguistic clues captured from verbal utterances could indicate symptoms of AD.

Toledo et al. (2018) investigated the significance of lexical and syntactic features from verbal narratives of AD patients by performing several statistical tests based on 121 elderly participants consisting of 60 patients with AD and 61 control subjects. In this work, immediate word repetitions, word revisions, and coordination structures could be used to distinguish patients with AD from the control group. Mueller et al. (2018) recently found that AD patients often depicted less informative discourse, greater impairment in global coherence, greater modularization, and inferior narrative structure compared to the normal control group.

References

Laura Banarescu, Claire Bonial, Shu Cai, Madalina Georgescu, Kira Griffitt, Ulf Hermjakob, Kevin Knight, Philipp Koehn, Martha Palmer, and Nathan Schneider. 2013. Abstract Meaning Representation for Sembanking. In *Proceedings of the 7th Linguistic Annotation Workshop and Interoperability with Discourse*, LAW-ID'13, pages 178–186.

A. L. Beam and I. S. Kohane. 2016. Translating Artificial Intelligence Into Clinical Care. *Journal of the American Medical Association*, 316(22):2368–2369.

Claire Bonial, Kathryn Conger, Jena D. Hwang, Aous Mansouri, Yahya Aseri, Julia Bonn, Timothy O'Gorman, and Martha Palmer. 2017. Current Directions in English and Arabic PropBank. In Nancy Ide and James Pustejovsky, editors, *Handbook of Linguistic Annotation*, pages 737–769. Springer.

Kathleen C. Fraser, Jed A. Meltzer, and Frank Rudzicz. 2016. Linguistic Features Identify Alzheimer's Disease in Narrative Speech. *Journal of Alzheimer's Disease*, 49(2):407–422.

Denise C. Fyffe, Shubhabrata Mukherjee, Lisa L. Barnes, Jennifer J. Manly, David A. Bennett, and Paul K. Crane. 2011. Explaining Differences in Episodic Memory Performance among Older African Americans and Whites: The Roles of Factors Related to Cognitive Reserve and Test Bias. *Journal of the International Neuropsychological Society*, 17(4):625–638.

Edith Kaplan, Harold Goodglass, and Sandra Weintraub. 1983. *The Boston Naming Test*. Philadelphia: Lea and Febiger.

Sweta Karlekar, Tong Niu, and Mohit Bansal. 2018. Detecting Linguistic Characteristics of Alzheimer's Dementia by Interpreting Neural Models. In *Proceedings of the Conference of the North American Chapter of the Association for Computational Linguistics*, NAACL'18, pages 701–707.

Justin E. Karr, Raquel B. Graham, Scott M. Hofer, and Graciela Muniz-Terrera. 2018. When does cognitive decline begin? A systematic review of change point studies on accelerated decline in cognitive and neurological outcomes preceding mild cognitive impairment, dementia, and death. *Psychology and Aging*, 33(2):195–218.

John C. Morris. 1994. The Clinical Dementia Rating (CDR): current version and scoring rules. *Neurology*, 43(11):2412–2414.

Kimberly Diggle Mueller, Bruce P. Hermann, Jonilda Mecollari, and Lyn Turkstra. 2018. Connected speech and language in mild cognitive impairment and Alzheimer's disease: A review of picture description tasks. *Journal of Clinical and Experimental Neuropsychology*, 40(1):917–939.

Ziad S. Nasreddine, Natalie A. Phillips, Valérie Bédirian, Simon Charbonneau, Victor Whitehead, Isabelle Collin, Jeffrey L. Cummings, and Howard Chertkow. 2005. The Montreal Cognitive Assessment, MoCA: a brief screening tool for mild cognitive impairment. *Journal of the American Geriatrics Society*, 53(4):695–699.

Sylvester O. Orimaye, Jojo S-M. Wong, Karen J. Golden, Chee P. Wong, and Ireneous N. Soyiri. 2017. Predicting probable Alzheimer's disease using linguistic deficits and biomarkers. *BMC Bioinformatics*, 18(34).

Sylvester Olubolu Orimaye, Jojo Sze-Meng Wong, and Judyanne Sharmini Gilbert Fernandez. 2016. Deep-Deep Neural Network Language Models for Predicting Mild Cognitive Impairment. In *Proceedings of the Workshop on Advances in Bioinformatics and Artificial Intelligence: Bridging the Gap*.

R. I. Pfeffer, T. T. Kurosaki, C.H. Jr. Harrah, J. M. Chance, and S. Filos. 1982. Measurement of Functional Activities in Older Adults in the Community. *Journal of Gerontology*, 37(3):323–329.

Sameer Pradhan, Alessandro Moschitti, Nianwen Xue, Olga Uryupina, and Yuchen Zhang. 2012. CoNLL-2012 Shared Task: Modeling Multilingual Unrestricted Coreference in OntoNotes. In *Proceedings of the Sixteenth Conference on Computational Natural Language Learning: Shared Task*, CoNLL'12, pages 1–40.

Jamie Reilly, Amy Rodriguez, Martine Lamy, and Jean Neils-Strunjas. 2010. Cognition, Language, and Clinical Pathological Features of Non-Alzheimer's Dementias: An Overview. *Journal of Communication Disorders*, 43(5):438–452.

Kyle Steenland, Liping Zhao, Samantha E. John, Felicia C. Goldstein, Allan Levey, and Alvaro Alonso. 2018. A 'Framingham-like' Algorithm for Predicting 4-Year Risk of Progression to Amnestic Mild Cognitive Impairment or Alzheimer's Disease Using Multidomain Information. *Journal of Alzheimer's Disease*, 63(4):1383–1393.

Pontus Stenetorp, Sampo Pyysalo, Goran Topić, Tomoko Ohta, Sophia Ananiadou, and Jun'ichi Tsujii. 2012. brat: a Web-based Tool for NLP-Assisted Text Annotation. In *Proceedings of the Demonstrations at the 13th Conference of the European Chapter of the Association for Computational Linguistics*, EACL'12, pages 102–107.

Alexandros Tillas. 2015. Language as Grist to the Mill of Cognition. *Cognitive Processing*, 16(3):219–243.

Cíntia Matsuda Toledo, Sandra M. Aluisio, Leandro Borges dos Santos, Sonia Maria Dozzi Brucki, Eduardo Sturzeneker Trés, Maira Okada de Oliveira, and Letícia Lessa Mansura. 2018. Analysis of macrolinguistic aspects of narratives from individuals with Alzheimer's disease, mild cognitive impairment, and no cognitive impairment. *Alzheimer's Dementia*, 10:31–40.

Myank Verma and Robert J. Howard. 2012. Semantic memory and language dysfunction in early Alzheimer's disease: a review. *International Journal of Geriatric Psychiatry*, 27(12):1209–1217.

Ellipsis in Chinese AMR Corpus

Yihuan Liu[1]   **Bin Li**[1]   **Peiyi Yan**[1]   **Li Song**[1]   **Weiguang Qu**[2]
[1]School of Chinese Language and Literature
Nanjing Normal University
[2]School of Computer Science and Technology
Nanjing Normal University
`lyh.njnu@gmail.com`

Abstract

Ellipsis is very common in language. It's necessary for natural language processing to restore the elided elements in a sentence. However, there's only a few corpora annotating the ellipsis, which draws back the automatic detection and recovery of the ellipsis. This paper introduces the annotation of ellipsis in Chinese sentences, using a novel graph-based representation Abstract Meaning Representation (AMR), which has a good mechanism to restore the elided elements manually. We annotate 5,000 sentences selected from Chinese TreeBank (CTB). We find that 54.98% of sentences have ellipses. 92% of the ellipses are restored by copying the antecedents' concepts. and 12.9% of them are the new added concepts. In addition, we find that the elided element is a word or phrase in most cases, but sometimes only the head of a phrase or parts of a phrase, which is rather hard for the automatic recovery of ellipsis.

1   Introduction

With the rapid development of artificial intelligence (AI), natural language progressing is one of significant applications of AI, and it has made outstanding progress in several basic techniques, such as syntactic analysis and semantic analysis. The former is relatively mature, while the latter needs more efforts (Sun et al., 2014). For example, in the SRL(Semantic Role Labeling)-only task of the CoNLL 2009, the highest score in English is 86.2% and in Chinese it is 78.6% (Hajič et al., 2009). In addition, a common issue for the current semantic parser is that they ignore the elided element which is not overt in the surface form, but necessary in the understanding of the sentence. That elided element is more often referred as ellipsis in linguistic.

Ellipsis is a common linguistic phenomenon across languages. The traditional linguistic researches pay more attention to the formal construction, and don't regard ellipsis as an important factor. Although some theoretical achievements have been made in the classifications and restrictions of ellipsis (Lobeck, 1995; Merchant, 2004, 2007). There are still debates in the definition of ellipsis, the identity constraint between antecedents and the elided element etc. (Phillips and Parker, 2013) .

Most current corpora don't annotate the elided element. A few corpora view ellipsis as an expediency for some irregular sentences, and annotate the elided element roughly. Such as Penn Treebank (PTB for short) (Marcus et al., 1993, 1994), Chinese Treebank (CTB) (Xue et al., 2005), Prague Dependency TreeBank (PDT) (Böhmová et al., 2000; Hajičová et al., 2001) and Universal Treebank (McDonald et al., 2013; Nivre et al., 2016). It is noticeable that Ren et al. (2018) build a treebank with focusing on ellipsis in context for Chinese. But the corpus only contains 572 sentences from a microblog corpus, and the annotations exclude the elided words which can't be said but play an important role in the understanding of the sentence.

This paper uses a novel framework to restore the elided elements in the sentence, which is named Abstract Meaning Representation (AMR)(Banarescu et al., 2013). AMR represents the whole sentence meaning with concepts, which are mainly abstracted from its corresponding words occurring in the sentence. Based on AMR, Chinese AMR (CAMR) makes some adaptations to accommodate Chinese better. What's more, CAMR develops corresponding restoration methods for different types of ellipses, which makes the restoration more reasonable and complete.

The rest of this paper is organized as follows. In Section 2, we discuss the definition of ellipsis and

Proceedings of the First International Workshop on Designing Meaning Representations, pages 92–99
Florence, Italy, August 1st, 2019 ©2019 Association for Computational Linguistics

gives a broader definition, which refers to all phenomena wherein the elided elements are necessary for the meaning of the sentence but not overt in the sentence. In addition, we introduce the representation for ellipsis in PTB, PDT. In Section 3, we describe three methods to restore ellipsis in CAMR. And in Section 4 , we introduce the Chinese AMR corpus which includes 5,000 sentences from the newspaper portion of CTB. and we present some statistics and analysis based on this corpus. Then we conclude our paper with a summary of our contribution in Section 5.

2   Related Work

As we mentioned above, the definition of ellipsis is an unsolved issue. Many linguists have been trying to define it from different aspects.

2.1   Definition of Ellipsis

To improve the agreement and the accuracy of annotation, it is necessary for annotators to understand what is ellipsis. Arnauld and Lancelot (1975) first mentioned ellipsis in their work General and Rational Grammar. And they defined it as a pragmatic phenomenon which omits some redundant words for concision. Jespersen (1924) gave a semantic ellipsis, He assumed that grammarians should always be wary in admitting ellipses except where they are absolutely necessary and where there can be no doubt as to what is understood. Carnie (2013) assumed that ellipses are phenomena where a string that has already been uttered is omitted in subsequent structures where it would otherwise have to be repeated word for word. While Lobeck (1995) viewed ellipsis as a mismatch of phonological content and semantic content, He thought ellipsis means deleting some words which can be inferred from context.

There are other definitions of ellipsis. Quirk et al. (1972) assumed that ellipsis is purely a surface phenomenon. In the strict sense of ellipsis, words are elided only if they are uniquely recoverable. There is no doubt as to what words are to be supplied, and it is possible to add the recovered words to the sentence. The definition was referred to the restraint of ellipsis. Ren et al. (2018) gave a definition of ellipsis in the practice of natural language processing. It views ellipsis as textual omission of words or phrases expressing a semantic role in a sentence, which are optional but not obligatory.

Comparing all definitions above, the consensus is that there are elided elements that are helpful for the understanding of the sentence, and can be recovered from context. This paper follows that consensus and gives a more broad definition for ellipsis. It encompasses all phenomena wherein the elided elements which are necessary for the understanding of the sentence don't refer to a token in the surface form. There are mainly two differences between this definition and others, which are:

- The restoration do not have to be unique and unambiguous.

- The restoration do not have to be written in the surface form.

The traditional theory requires the restoration of ellipsis must be unique and ambiguous. But sometimes the elided words can't not be uniquely and unambiguously restored. For example, in the sentence 1 is a headless nominal, and the subject of 跳舞(dance) is omitted. Due to lack of contextual information, we only know that the elided elements refer to a dancer or some dancers, but we don't know exactly who it is. Since the elided elements are important in the meaning of the sentence, we add a new concept person in the ellipsis site and consider this special headless nominal as ellipsis.

(1) 跳舞 的 走 了
    dance DE go ASP
    "The dancer has gone."

(2) 他 想　吃 苹果
    he want eat apple
    "He wants to eat an apple."

In most cases, The restoration can be said in the surface form, and it makes the sentence regular. But sometimes, the restoration will make the sentence illegal, which means the restoration is only in semantic level. For example, in the sentence 2, the subject of 想(want) and 吃(eat) is 他(he), but 他(he) occurs once in the sentence. According to the theta criterion, each argument is assigned to one and only one theta role, it needs to add another argument to meet the criterion and present the whole sentence meaning. But the recovered sentence "他想他吃苹果。"("He wants him to eat an apple.") is illegal. Considering the semantic importance of the missing argument, we regard this sharing argument as ellipsis, too.

As the goal of the annotation is to present the complete meaning of the sentence, we focus on the semantic aspect than syntactic aspect. And the scope of ellipsis is obviously more extensive than the traditional one. The typical types like VP ellipsis, NP ellipsis and some special phenomena like headless nominal and sharing argument are covered by ellipsis.

2.2 Ellipsis Representation in PTB and PDT

Most current corpora rarely annotate ellipses, only a few corpora have represented part of ellipses with some particular labels, such as PTB, CTB and PDT. Since CTB follows the annotation principles of PTB on the whole, we only describe the representation strategies for ellipsis of PTB and PDT. By comparing the ellipsis representation in these two corpora, we assume that both of them only handle some typical ellipses, and their tree structures are hard to representation ellipsis.

PTB is a large corpus which mainly contains phrase structure annotation. It incorporates the concept of empty category which is introduced in Generative Grammar. Empty category plays a part in syntactic structure and semantic structure, but it has no corresponding phonological content in the sentence, whose performance is similar with ellipsis. In fact, some types of empty categories are covered by ellipsis. So PTB including empty category representation can provide scant help for ellipsis research.

The specific representation method for ellipsis includes two steps. Firstly, PTB annotates the corresponding empty category label in the ellipsis site. Secondly, PTB attaches the id to the labels to contact the empty category and the related elements in the sentence (Xue et al., 2005).

In Figure 1, 公司(company) is a sharing argument, which is shared by the verb 计划(plan) and 增加(increase). PTB regards the elided argument as PRO, and assigns the label NONE - * PRO * to the ellipsis site. The id -1 behind the empty category label corresponds to the superior node NP-PN-SBJ, which indicates that the elided element is 公司(company).

(3) 公司　　计划 增加　产量
　　Company plan increase output
　　"The company plans to increase output."

PDT includes three layers which are morphological layer, syntactic layer and semantic layer.

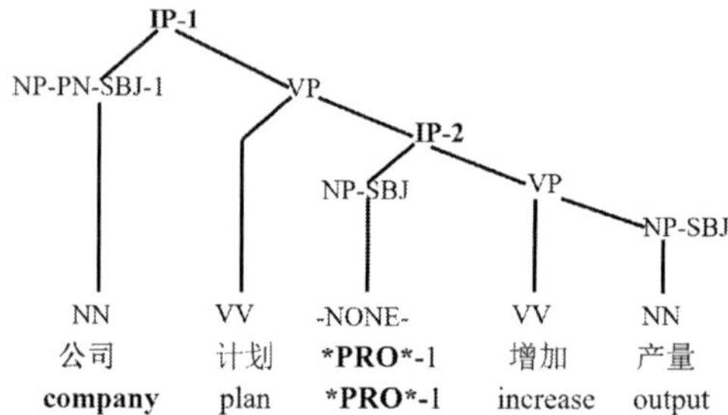

Figure 1: Empty categories in PTB

Each level annotates the morphological, syntactic and semantic information respectively. At the syntactic layer, it annotates the overt words in the sentence, and it restores the elided elements at the semantic layer. The methods of representing ellipsis in PDT are more complex than PTB, which mainly include three steps. Firstly, it adds a new node. Then it judges the category of ellipsis and represent it with corresponding label. At last, if there is an antecedent, it will use the coreference link to associate the new node with its antecedent node (Mikulová, 2014; Hajič et al., 2015).

(4) 公司　　计划 增加　产量
　　Company plan increase output
　　"The company plans to increase output."

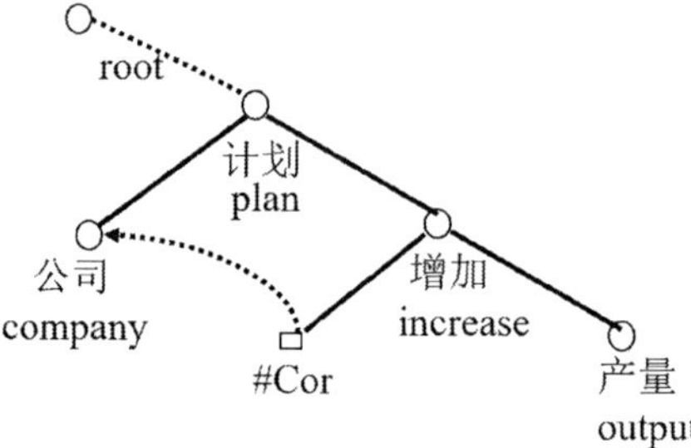

Figure 2: Ellipsis representation in PDT

Figure 2 shows the annotation of Example 3 in PDT. Similar with PTB, PDT also adds a new node for the elided element, and marks it as #Cor, which means the elided element is the subject in the object clause of the control verb 计划(plan). Because of the antecedent 公司(company), coreference link is also added to contact the restored element with its antecedent, as shown by the dotted arrow.

Although PTB and PDT have designed special labels for ellipsis, but they lack complete resolution to deal with some special ellipses. For example, the two corpora have no ability to represent the subtle semantic difference between the elided elements and its antecedent. And both of them restore the elided elements by adding a new node, which make the tree structure more complex, especially when the elided elements occur repeatedly in the same sentence. What's more, to represent the identity of the elided element and its antecedent, a coreference link or other similar marks is added to contact them. In that case, the tree structure is changed into a graph structure.

2.3 Concept-to-word Alignment in CAMR

To represent the whole meaning of the sentence in Chinese, CAMR has made some adaptations to accommodate the linguistic facts of Chinese, and one of the special adaptations is alignment. It uses the sequence number of words in the sentence as the concept id of the notional word, which realizes the concept-to-word alignment in the annotation (Li et al., 2017).And this adaptation helps to represent the elided element more intuitional and convenient.

(5) 他^1 想^2 吃^3 苹果^4
    he want eat apple
    "He want to eat an apple."

```
w/want-01                    x2/想-02
  :arg0() h/he                 :arg0() x1/他
  :arg1() e/eat-01             :arg1() x3/吃-01
    :arg0 h                      :arg0 x1/他
    :arg1 h2/apple               :arg1 x4/苹果
```

As shown on the textual representation on the left, English AMR does not align the concepts with the words, it assigns the first letter of the word to its concept. When the elided element is restored, its antecedent is not very straightforward, especially when the sentence is complex and there are some other words that have same first letter as the antecedent. Specifically, the elided element 他(he) is represented by the initial letter "h" of its antecedent. To annotate and understand the sentence, we need spend time in finding what the initial letter exactly denotes. It is more likely to cause lower efficiency and higher error rate. While CAMR aligns the concepts to their words, and makes the ellipsis representation more clearly.

3 Ellipsis Presentation in CAMR

As we described above, PTB and PDT mainly restore the elided element by referring to its an-

tecedent. CAMR also represents ellipsis with the help of antecedent, but sometimes the sentence has no antecedent, or the reference of the elided element is not identical but similar with its antecedent. Referring to its antecedent is not reasonable any more. Considering these different linguistic performances of ellipsis, CAMR develops corresponding methods to represent them reasonably, which are:

- Copy the antecedent, if there is an antecedent, and the reference of antecedent and the elided element is identical.

- Add a new concept, if there is no antecedent.

- Add a new concept and copy the antecedent, if there is an antecedent, but the reference of antecedent and the elided element is not identical.

3.1 Copy the Antecedent

When the antecedent can be found in context, CAMR directly copies the antecedent's concept and fills the copied concept in ellipsis site to restore the elided element. It is noticeable that CAMR does not increase new concept like PTB and PDT. The concept of the elided element and antecedent will be merged into one concept. In CAMR graph, the concept of the elided element and antecedent share the same concept node. the elided element and its antecedent are dominated by different elements, thus the semantic structure of the sentence becomes a graph.

(6) 公司^1 计划^2 增加^3 产量^4
    Company plan   increase output
    "The company plans to increase output."

```
x2/计划-01
  :arg0() x1/公司
  :arg1() x3/计划-01
    :arg0 x1/公司
    :arg1 x4/产量
```

Comparing Figure 1, Figure 2 and Figure 3 , CAMR does not add a new concept NONE - * PRO * or #Cor for the elided element like PTB and PDT. It copies the node of antecedent 公司(company) directly, and combines the two arguments into one node. The node 公司(company) represents the elided element and its antecedent at the same time. Since the node 计划(plan) and

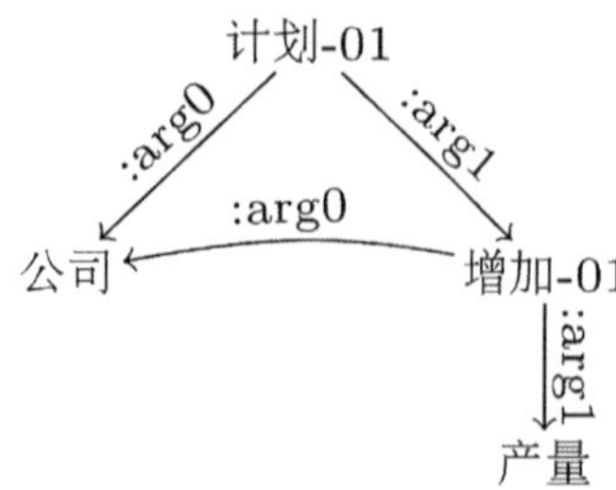

Figure 3: Copy the antecedent in CAMR

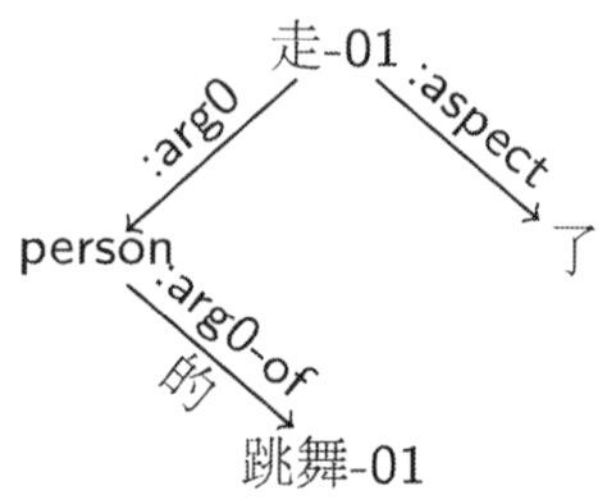

Figure 4: Add a new concept in CAMR

the node 增加(increase) both are fathers of 公司(company), which makes the structure of this sentence a typical graph.

This representation method in CAMR can reduce the total amount of node and make the structure of the whole sentence as clear as possible. The advantage of graph structure benefits when the same elided element occurring repeatedly many times in the sentence. Since no matter how many times the elided element occurs, the number of nodes in the graph will not increase.

3.2 Add New Concepts

When the elided element has no corresponding antecedent in the sentence, the method of copying the concept of antecedent directly is no longer applicable. In this case, CAMR adds a new concept for ellipsis. Specifically, CAMR firstly judges the semantic categories of the elided element and adds an appropriate abstract concepts, such as person and thing. Then it analyses the semantic relationship between the new concept and other concepts. And the whole sentence's meaning is to represent completely.

(7) 跳舞^1 的^2 走^3 了^4
  dance DE go ASP
  "The dancer has gone."

x3/走-01
 :arg0() **x6/person**
  :arg1(x2/的) x1/跳舞-01
 :aspect x4/了

Traditionally, it is assumed that the headless relative construction such as 跳舞的(the dancer), is a contextual variant of the formal nominal structure. When the head is the subject or object of the adjunct in this nominal structure, it can be elided (Huang, 1982). In general, there is no antecedent, and the elided elements are abstract. In Example 7, the elided head of 跳舞的(the dancer) is

vague. It might be a dancer or some dancers. So CAMR adds an abstract concept person to contact 走(walk) and 跳舞(dance), and completes the whole sentence meaning. In these relations, the semantic relation label arg0-of between person and 走(walk) is an inverse relation of arg0, which is used to maintain a single-rooted structure of CAMR graph.

3.3 Add a New Concept and Copy the Antecedent

There is a special ellipsis where the antecedent can be found in the sentence, but the reference of the elided element and its antecedent is not identity. Previous ellipsis researches tend to neglect that semantic nonidentity. Even though PDT has realized that there are differences between the two items in the comparison structure, the annotation schemes can't represent this semantic difference properly. To represent the whole sentence meaning reasonably, CAMR combines the two method described above. That is adding new concepts and then copying the antecedent. Specifically, according to the semantic category of the elided element, CAMR adds a new concept. Then it analyzes the relation between the elided element and its antecedent, and represents this relationship with special semantic relation labels.

(8) 你^1 的^2 收入^3 比^4 我^5 高^6
  you DE income than I high
  "Your income is higher than mine."

x6/高-01
 :arg0() **x3/收入**
  :arg1(x2/的) x1/你
 :compare-to(x4/比) **x8/thing**
  :poss() x5/我
  :dcopy() **x3_s/收入**

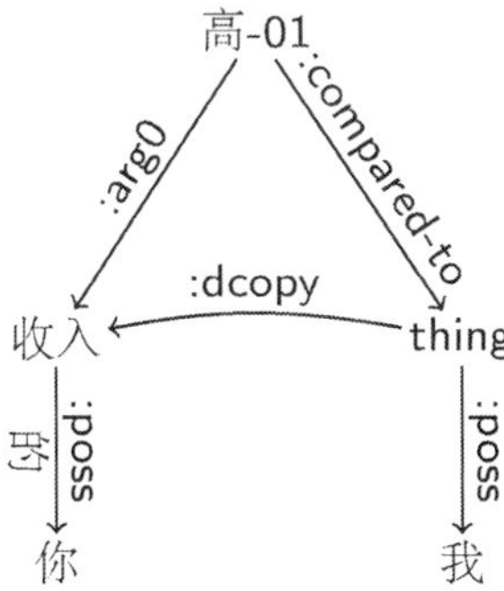

Figure 5: Add a new concept and copy the antecedent

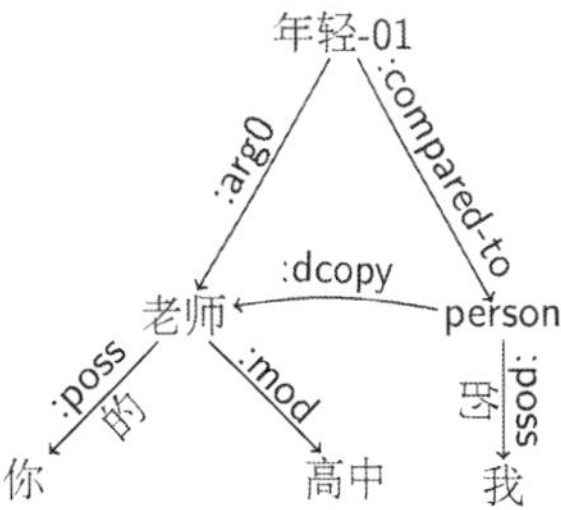

Figure 6: The elided elements are parts of a phrase

The Example 8 is a comparative structure. 你的收入(your income) and 我(I) are asymmetrical in syntactic structure. 我(I) is an incomplete and abbreviated form in semantic expression (Li, 1982). Since the purpose of this sentence is actually to emphasize the difference between the two items 你的收入(Your income) and 我的收入(my income), it is obviously unreasonable to copy the concept directly. So we first add a concept thing and then use a special semantic relation label dcopy, which is added in CAMR to indicate that the elided element and the antecedent belong to the same category, but they refer to different objects in real world.

We further find that there are residual modifiers of the elided elements in Chinese sentence, and these modifiers are the cues which remind us to pay attention to the reference of the elided elements and its antecedent. In Example 6, Example 7, the elided element is a word or a complete phrase exactly. While in Example 8, the elided element is the head of the phrase 我的收入(I income, my income). Sometime it might be more complex. the elided elements are parts of a phrase.

(9) 你[1] 的[2] 高中[3]　老师[4] 比[5] 我[6] 的[7] 年轻[8]
　　you DE high school teacher than I　DE young
　　"Your high school teacher is younger than mine."

x8/年轻-01:
　　:arg0() x4/老师
　　　:arg1(x2/的) x1/你
　　　:mod() x3/高中
　　:compare-to(x5/比) **x10/person**
　　　:poss(x7/的) x4/我
　　　:dcopy() **x3_x4/高中老师**

In Example 9, the elided elements are 高中老师(high school teacher), which are parts of the phrase 我的高中老师(my high school teacher). We are trying to refine the guidelines to represent these different elided elements reasonably, and we will discuss this type of ellipsis in the future.

In conclusion, CAMR can represent the elided element more concisely and show the relationship between the elided element and its antecedent in detail. These three methods can handle most ellipses and represent the semantics of the whole sentence, which determines it is a more reasonable annotation scheme to represent ellipsis.

4 Statistics and Analysis

We annotate 5,000 sentences from Penn Chinese Treebank CTB8.0. Based on this data, we show the proportion of ellipsis and how common it is in Chinese. And we find that the length of the sentence affect the distribution of ellipsis indeed. We also analyze how the added concept work in ellipsis.

4.1 Proportion of Ellipsis in Chinese

As shown in Table 1, the first column **Type** contains three items. Among them, **Overall** means all 5,000 sentences in the corpus. The rest columns represent three statistical indicators,which show the number of tokens, concepts and sentences of ellipsis and overall. In Chinese AMR corpus, we restore 5,787 tokens and 4,178 concepts. And we find that 2,749 sentences are with ellipsis. That is, 54.98% of sentences contain ellipsis, which proves that ellipsis is very common in Chinese.

We further show the proportion of three methods for ellipsis mentioned in Section 3. As shown in Table 2, copying the antecedent is the most popular methods in the corpus, which means that among all elliptical sentences (2,749 sentences), 2,537 sentences appear the identical antecedent. Almost 92% of ellipses can be restored by copy-

Type	Token	Concept	Sentence
Ellipsis	5,787	4,178	2,749
Overall	13,2981	12,0991	5,000
Ratio	4.35%	3.45%	54.98%

Table 1: Proportion of ellipsis in Chinese AMR Corpus

Type	Token	Concept	Sentence
Copy the antecedent	5,143	3,567	2,537
Add a new concept	284	258	230
*Add & Copy	360	353	267

* is the abbreviation of *Add a New Concept and Copy the Antecedent*

Table 2: Frequency of three methods for ellipsis

Type	Token	Concept
Ellipsis	32.58	31.11
Overall	26.6	24.2

Table 3: Average token count and concept count in per sentence

Type	Concept	Frequency	Ratio
Add a new concept	thing	110	38.73%
	person	103	36.27%
	country	8	2.82%
Add & Copy	thing	294	81.67%
	person	35	9.72%
	animal	4	1.11%

Table 4: The added concept for ellipsis

ing its antecedent directly. This high proportion shows that the antecedents are of great importance to restore the elided element, which explains why most current ellipsis models rely on antecedents for ellipsis recognition and restoration.

4.2 The Length of the Elliptical Sentence

The statistics also prove that length of the sentence will affect the distribution of ellipsis. There are two ways to measure the length of a sentence. One is based on words, the length of a sentence refers to the number of words that make up the sentence. The other is based on concepts, the length of a sentence refers to the number of concepts that make up the semantic meaning of a sentence.

The average length of elliptical sentences is about 6 units longer than the regular sentences in the corpus, whether in terms of words or concepts. The reason is that the longer the sentence is, the more complex the semantic structure is and the richer the semantic information is. Therefore, it is more likely to delete some words from the sentence.

4.3 The Added Concept for Ellipsis

CAMR adds new concepts to represent ellipsis when there is no antecedent or the reference of the elided element and its antecedent is different.

CAMR also adds abstract concepts when we annotate proper nouns, special quantity types and special semantic relationships. For example, when annotating quantitative phrases for weight, we first add a concept mass-quantity . These added concepts should be excluded in statistics.

As shown in Table 4, the frequency of thing and person is much higher than other concepts. The reason is mainly that they are more abstract. We usually add *thing* and *person* when the elided element is not clear.

5 Conclusion and Future Work

In this paper, we uses a novel graph-based framework AMR, which mainly represents the elided element by copying its antecedent, adding a new concepts, or we combining the two methods when the reference of the elided elements and its antecedent is not identical. On the basis of Chinese AMR corpus, which contains 5,000 sentences selected from CTB, we show how common ellipsis is in Chinese, and we prove that the length of the sentence affect the distribution of ellipsis indeed. The average length of elliptical sentences is about 6 units longer than the regular. We further show the added concept for ellipsis.

In the future, we will discuss ellipses which are the head of a phrase or just parts of a phrase in detail. And we intend to apply the research result to Chinese AMR parser, to improve its ability to identify and restore ellipsis in Chinese sentences.

Acknowledgments

We are grateful for the comments of the reviewers. This work is the staged achievement of the projects supported by National Social Science Foundation of China (18BYY127) and National Science Foundation of China (61772278).

References

Antoine Arnauld and Claude Lancelot. 1975. *General and Rational Grammar: the Port-royal Grammar*. Mouton Hague, Paris,France.

L Banarescu, C Bonial, S Cai, and et al. 2013. Abstract meaning representation for sembanking. In *Proceedings of the 7th Linguistic Annotation Workshop Interoperability with Discourse*, pages 178–186.

Alena Böhmová, Jan Hajič, Eva Hajičová, and Barbora Hladká. 2000. The prague dependency treebank: a three-level annotation scenario. In *TreeBank: Building and Using Parsed Corpora*.

Andrew Carnie. 2013. *Syntax-a generative introduction*. Wiley Blackwell, London, UK.

Jan Hajič, Massimiliano Ciaramita, Richard Johansson, and et al. 2009. The conll-2019 shared task:syntactic and semantic dependencies in multiple language. In *Proceedings of the 13th Conference on Computational Natural Language Learning (CoNLL): Shared Task*.

Jan Hajič, Eva Hajičová, and et al. 2015. Deletions and node reconstruction a dependency-based multilevel annotation scheme. In *Proceedings of Computational Linguistics and Intelligent Text Processing*, pages 17–31.

Eva Hajičová, Jan Hajič, Barbora Hladká, Martin Holub, and et al. 2001. The current status of the prague dependency treebank. In *Proceedings of the 5th International Conference on Text, Speech and Dialogue*.

G Huang. 1982. The syntactic function and semantic function of ‘de’ structure. *Studies in Language and Linguistics*, 1.

Otto Jespersen. 1924. *The Philosophy of Grammar*. Groge Allen & Unwin LTD, London, UK.

Bin Li, Yuan Wen, Lijun Bu, and et al. Annotating the little prince with chinese amrs.

Bin Li, Yuan Wen, Lijun Bu, and et al. 2017. A comparative analysis of the amr graphs from english and chinese corpus of the little prince. *Journal of Chinese Information Processing*, 31.

L Li. 1982. *The Sentence Pattern in Modern Chinese*. The Commercial Press, Beijing, China.

Anne Lobeck. 1995. *Ellipsis Functional Heads, Licensing, and Identification*. Oxford University Press, New York, US.

Mitchell Marcus, Grace Kim, Mary Ann Marcinkiewicz, and et al. 1994. The penn treebank: annotating predicate argument structure. In *Proceedings of the ARPA Human Language Technology Workshop*.

Mitchell Marcus, Beatrice Santorini, and Mary Ann Marcinkiewicz. 1993. Building a large annotated corpus of english: the penn treebank. *Computational Linguistics*, 19.

Ryan McDonald, Joakim Nivre, Yvonne Quirmbach-Brundage, Yoav Goldberg, and et al. 2013. Universal dependency annotation for multilingual parsing. In *Proceedings of the 51th Annual Meeting of the Association for Computational Linguistics*.

Jason Merchant. 2004. Fragments and ellipsis. *Linguistics and Philosophy*, 27(6):661–738.

Jason Merchant. 2007. There kinds of ellipsis: Syntactic, semantic, pragmatic? In *Semantic Workshop*.

Marie Mikulová. 2014. Semantic representation of ellipsis in the prague dependency treebanks. In *Proceedings of the Conference on Computational Linguistics and Speech Processing*, pages 125–138.

Joakim Nivre, Marie-Catherine de Marneffe, Filip Ginter, Yoav Goldberg, and et al. 2016. Universal dependencies v1: A multilingual treebank collection. In *Proceedings of the Tenth International Conference on Language Resources and Evaluation*.

Colin Phillips and Dan Parker. 2013. The psycholinguistics of ellipsis. *Lingua*, 151.

Randolph Quirk, Sidney Greenbaum, Geoffrey Leech, and Jan Svartvik. 1972. *A Grammar of Contemporary English*. Longman Singapore, Singapore.

Xuancheng Ren, Xu Sun, Bingzhen Wei, Weidong Zhan, and et al. 2018. Building an ellipsis-aware chinese dependency treebank for web text. In *Proceedings of the 12th International Conference on Language Resources and Evaluation*.

Maosong Sun, Ting Liu, Donghong Ji, and et al. 2014. Frontiers of language computing. *Journal of Chinese Information Processing*, 28.

N Xue, F Xia, F Chiou, and et al. 2005. The penn chinese treebank: Phrase structure annotation of a large corpus. *Natural Language Engineering*, 11(2):207–238.

Event Structure Representation: Between Verbs and Argument Structure Constructions

Pavlina Kalm
Dept. of Linguistics
Univ. of New Mexico
pavlinap@unm.edu

Michael Regan
Dept. of Linguistics
Univ. of New Mexico
reganman@unm.edu

William Croft
Dept. of Linguistics
Univ. of New Mexico
wcroft@unm.edu

Abstract

This paper proposes a novel representation of event structure by separating verbal semantics and the meaning of argument structure constructions that verbs occur in. Our model demonstrates how the two meaning representations interact. Our model thus effectively deals with various verb construals in different argument structure constructions, unlike purely verb-based approaches. However, unlike many constructionally-based approaches, we also provide a richer representation of the event structure evoked by the verb meaning.

1 Introduction

Verbal semantics is an area of great interest in theoretical and computational linguistics (e.g. (Fillmore, 1968; Fillmore et al., 2003; Talmy, 1988; Dowty, 1991; Croft, 1991, 2012; Valin and LaPolla, 1997; Levin, 1993; Kipper et al., 2007; Ruppenhofer et al., 2016). It has been widely recognized that verb meaning plays an important role in the syntactic realization of arguments and their interpretation (Levin, 1993). VerbNet (Kipper et al., 2007) and FrameNet (Fillmore et al., 2003; Ruppenhofer et al., 2016) are large online resources on verb meanings that have been developed in recent years. VerbNet, an extensive verb classification system inspired by Levin (1993), defines verb classes based on verbal semantics and the syntactic expression of arguments. FrameNet uses the theory of Frame Semantics (Fillmore, 1982, 1985) to classify lexical units into frames based on their meaning and their semantic and syntactic combinatorial properties with other event participants.

Providing an effective model to represent event structure is essential to many natural language processing (NLP) tasks. Recent meaning representation frameworks employed in NLP (Banarescu et al., 2013; Hajič et al., 2012; Abend and Rappoport, 2013), are largely concerned with identifying event participants and their roles within the event. Most meaning representations use a lexically-based approach that assumes that the lexical semantics of a verb determines the complements that occur with it in a clause.

However, lexically-based models for event structure do not provide a complete representation since verbs can occur in various argument structure constructions (Goldberg, 1995, 2006; Iwata, 2005). Depending on the semantics of the argument structure construction, a verb can be construed in many different ways. For example, a verb such as *kick* can occur in various semantically different constructions, as shown below (Goldberg, 1995, 11).

(1) Pat kicked the wall.

(2) Pat kicked the football into the stadium.

(3) Pat kicked Bob the football.

(4) Pat kicked Bob black and blue.

Kick can be construed as a verb of *contact by impact* when it occurs in the force construction in (1) (Levin, 1993, 148). It can be construed as a verb of *throwing* in the caused motion construction in (2) (Levin, 1993, 146). *Kick* can also be construed as a *transfer* verb in the transfer of possession construction in (3) or a *change of state* verb in the resultative construction in (4).

Goldberg (1995) argues that argument structure constructions carry meanings that exist independently of verbs. She develops a constructional approach in which argument structure meaning and verb meaning combine to specify the event structure. We introduce a model in which event structure is derived from argument structure meaning and verb meaning. The argument structure meaning is based on the semantic annotation scheme

Proceedings of the First International Workshop on Designing Meaning Representations, pages 100–109
Florence, Italy, August 1st, 2019 ©2019 Association for Computational Linguistics

developed in Croft et al. (2016, 2018), which specifies the causal interactions between participants in the event. The verb meaning is a causal network which in many cases is more elaborate than the causal chain specified by the argument structure construction, but uses the same inventory of causal relations as the argument structure meanings. The argument structure meaning is annotated on individual clauses, and the verb meaning is retrieved from a resource based on VerbNet and FrameNet.

Our event structure representation offers a richer model when compared to exclusively lexically-based or constructionally-based resources on verb meaning. We describe below how our representation captures both the constructional meaning and the verb meaning, and how we map the former onto the latter. Having a two-facet representation helps us to effectively deal with verb construals as well as more complex event structures evoked by different event types.

2 Constructional meaning representation

The representation of constructional meaning uses a small set of causal chains that schematically represent the event structure evoked by argument structure constructions. Causal chains consist of event participants, a limited set of force dynamic relations between participants, and information about the participants' subevents. Cross-linguistic evidence indicates that argument realization is best explained by transmission of force relations (Talmy, 1988; Croft, 1991, 2012).

Force-dynamic relations are defined based on existing literature on force dynamic interactions (Talmy, 1988) and event semantics (Dowty, 1991; Tenny, 1994; Hay et al., 1999; Valin and LaPolla, 1997; Verhoeven, 2007; Croft, 2012). Force dynamic relations may be causal (Talmy, 1988) or non-causal (Croft, 1991), such as a spatial relation between a figure and ground in a physical domain. Causal chains represent force dynamic image schemas that correspond to established configurations of causal and non-causal relations between participants and their subevents. The subevents for each participant are specified for qualitative features that describe the states or processes that the participant undergoes over the course of the event (Croft et al., 2017).

2.1 Why constructional causal chains aren't enough

A causal chain model of constructional meaning is not a comprehensive representation of verb meaning. A richer representation of verbal event structure is needed for various event types.

An example of a complex event type that demands a more detailed event structure representation is ingestion. An example with *eat* such as *Jill ate the chicken with chopsticks* illustrates this point. In the causal chain analysis of the argument structure construction depicted in Figure 1, the *chopsticks* are analyzed as an Instrument.

VOL   INTL   COS
Agent $\xrightarrow{Manipulate}$ **Instrument** $\xrightarrow{Force}$ **Patient**

Figure 1: Change of state causal chain

However, the semantic role of the *chopsticks* in an eating event is quite different from that of a more prototypical instrument participant, such as a *hammer* in a breaking event (e.g. *Tony broke the window with a hammer*). In particular, the role of the *chopsticks* in the event structure is more complex. Unlike the *hammer* which *breaks* the window, the *chopsticks* do not *eat* the food. The chopsticks are used to move food to the Agent's mouth rather than eating the chicken. This contrasts with the role of the *hammer* which directly causes the breaking of the window. Consequently, one can use an argument structure construction without an Agent with *break* (*The hammer broke the window*) but not with *eat* (**The chopsticks ate the chicken*). The causal chain in Figure 1 does not capture this fine grained semantic distinction between these two types of instrument roles.

Table 1 contains a list of event types in the physical and mental domains that require a more fine grained event structure representation. A short description of the event structure is provided for each event type to illustrate how the causal relations between participants in these event types are too complex to be accurately represented by causal chains associated with the semantics of argument structure constructions.

In this paper, we present a verb meaning representation that aims to provide a richer model for event structure such that subtle semantic differences between participant roles can be made explicit. We accomplish this by introducing a separate richer representation for the verbal event

Event type	Event description	Example
Ingestion (*e.g. eat, drink*)	An Eater uses a Utensil which moves the Food to the Eater's mouth and the Eater consumes the Food.	*Jill ate the chicken with chopsticks.*
Vehicular motion (*e.g. drive, ride*)	A Rider enters a Vehicle (or a Driver uses a vehicle) which then transports the Rider/Driver to a Destination.	*Brenda went to Berlin by train.*
Perception (*e.g. look, listen*)	A Perceiver uses an Implement which then allows the Perceiver to view a Target.	*They looked at the cranes with binoculars.*
Cooking (*e.g. bake, cook*)	A Cook puts Food in a Cooking_container which then cooks the Food by emitting heat.	*I baked the potatoes in the oven.*
Searching/Finding (*e.g. find, look for*)	A Searcher searches in a Location and mentally attends to a Searched_item by searching for it. The Searched_item is in a spatial relation with the Location.	*I searched the cave for treasure.*
Creation (*e.g. paint, make*)	A Creator has an idea (i.e. mental experience) of a Design which then the Creator creates by producing a Creation using an Instrument.	*Claire drew a picture.*
Emission (*e.g. flash, gush*)	An Emitter creates an Emission with respect to a Ground. The Emission is also in a Path relation with the Emitter.	*The well gushed oil.*
Physical sensation (*e.g. hurt, break*)	An Agent's action results in an effect (e.g. harm) of the Agent, their Body_part, or some other animate entity.	*Tessa sprained her ankle.*

Table 1: Event types with complex event structures

structure.

3 Verbal meaning representation

Our representation of the verbal event structure uses a network model which consists of causal relations between participants and participants' subevents, not unlike causal chains. However, verbal networks contain richer information about the participants' causal relations that are not evoked by the argument structure construction and are therefore not represented in causal chains.

Each causal network is associated with an event type evoked by the verb meaning. For example, an Ingestion network represents the event structure associated with verbs of eating. As shown in Figure 2, the Ingestion network is cyclic and non-branching[1]: the Eater uses the Utensil ("Manipulate" relation) to reach the Food ("Force" relation). The Food moves to the Eater's mouth ("Path" relation) and is subsequently consumed by the Eater ("Force" relation)[2].

Unlike the causal chain representation, the verbal network representation allows for a direct causal relation between the Eater and Food. This

accommodates the semantics of ingestion events in which the Eater, rather than the Utensil, consumes the Food.

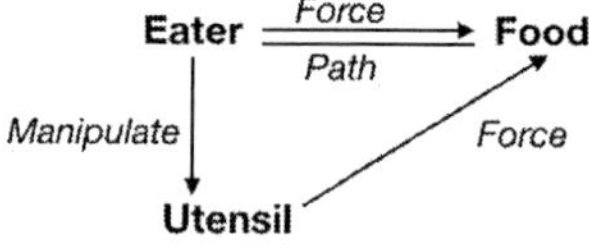

Figure 2: Ingestion network

Two participants in the network are involved in more than one causal relation. The Eater and Food have three distinct roles in the event structure. The Eater is the Agent who initiates the event; it is the ground that is in a Path relation with the Food, and it is also the consumer of the Food. The Food is an endpoint of the Force relation; it is a motion theme that is in a Path relation with the Eater, and it is also a Patient in a Change of State event as it gets consumed.

Since causal networks may be cyclic, the direction and ordering of causal relations within the network is more clearly represented if participants and the relations between them are depicted in a linear fashion, similarly to causal chains. "Unthreading" a linear path in the network represents the sequence of subevents better than a network representation. As shown in Figure 3, the Eater and Food occur twice in the unthreaded version of the causal network.

---

[1]Although the Ingestion network is non-branching, we have not ruled out the possibility of branching in other verbal networks. However, so far we have not come across a verbal network that requires a branching representation.

[2]Following Croft (1991, 2012), causal relations are represented by an arrow and non-causal relations are represented by a straight line in the diagram.

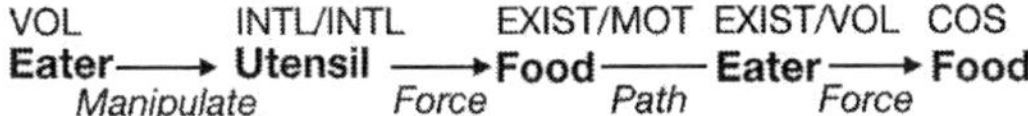

Figure 3: Unthreaded Ingestion network

Since the unthreaded version lays out the participants' relations in a linear chain, this representation also includes information about the change that each participant undergoes in its subevent(s). The network representation in Figure 2 does not include these labels due to a lack of space. We use the unthreaded version of verbal networks in the remainder of this paper to illustrate the mapping of the semantics of argument structure constructions onto the verbal event structure.

3.1 Mapping causal chains into verbal networks

Argument structure constructions may evoke only part of the verbal event structure. That is, causal chains may evoke a subset of participants and the relations between them in the verbal network. Mapping a causal chain into a network allows us to provide a comprehensive event structure representation that accounts for the meaning of the argument structure construction as well as the meaning evoked by the verb.

In many cases, there is a considerable overlap in the two types of representations, i.e. a one-to-one mapping exists between participants and their relations in the causal chain and in the verbal network. This is usually the case with simple event types, e.g. Motion or Force verbs (see Figure 6 in section 3.2 and Figure 11 in section 4). However, the mapping becomes more complicated when a causal chain is mapped into a complex network that contains additional participant relations not present in the causal chain.

Figure 4 demonstrates the mapping between a causal chain associated with the example *Jill ate the chicken with chopsticks* and the Ingestion network. The network representation contains additional participant relations that are not evoked by the causal chain. The correct mapping of participants from the causal chain to the network is achieved by linking participants by their subevents and relations. In addition, the sequence of subevents in the causal chain and in the network must follow the same order. As a result of this constraint, the dotted lines that link participants in causal chains and networks should not cross each other.

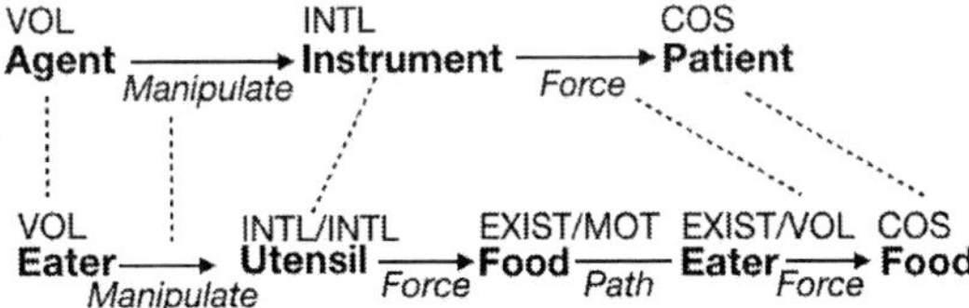

Figure 4: Causal chain (upper part of the diagram) to network (lower part) mapping

The causal chain participants and their relations are mapped into the network as follows: *Jill*, the Agent in the causal chain, is linked to the Eater. Although there are two instances of Eater in the network event structure, the Agent is only linked to the Eater which is the initiator of the causal chain. This is because the Eater must be in a direct Manipulate relation with the Utensil. In addition, both the Agent and the Eater are labeled Volitional (VOL[3]). *Chopsticks* are labeled Internal (INTL[4]) in the causal chain and are therefore linked to the Internal participant in the causal network, which is the Utensil. The Patient, a change of state (COS[5]) theme, is linked to the Food participant at the end of the verbal network which is also labeled COS.

The Food and Eater participants that are in a Path relation with each other constitute a part of the verbal event structure and are therefore represented in the causal network; however, they are not evoked by the argument structure construction. As a result, there is no direct linking of these participants to the causal chain.

3.2 Structure of verbal causal networks

Examining the more complex verbal networks in Table 1 has led us to conclude that networks can be analyzed as a concatenation of less complex event types. Networks can be thought of as being made up of *subchains*. Each subchain denotes a force dynamic image schema that is used to describe the semantics of argument structure constructions. The internal structure of verbal networks is thus composed of subchains that can be used independently as simple networks or concatenated to each other to form complex networks.

---

[3]Volitional describes an entity who exerts volitional force to bring about an event.

[4]Internal is used for participants that undergo internal change.

[5]COS is used for participants that undergo some change of their physical state in the event. In our analysis, a theme in an event of destruction is analyzed as a COS theme.

Subchains are not random subparts of a verbal causal network. A subchain is a subpart of a complex network that can be expressed by itself with a main verb. For example, the Motion subchain can be expressed by a motion verb such as *move* as in *He moved the ball*. The Manipulate network can be expressed by a manipulate verb such as *use* as in *He used the shovel*. The Force network can be expressed with a verb of force such as *hit* as in *He hit the ball*, and the Change of State network can be expressed with a verb of change of state such as *break* as in *The vase broke*.

The concatenation analysis of causal networks can be illustrated on the unthreaded version of the Ingestion network as shown in the bottom part of Figure 5. The event structure for ingestion verbs can be analyzed as being composed of five subchains: (1) a Manipulate image schema between the Eater and the Utensil, (2) a Force image schema between the Utensil and the Food, (3) a Motion image schema between the Food and the Eater, (4) a Force image schema between the Eater and the Food, and (5) a Change of State image schema that contains only one participant, the Food.

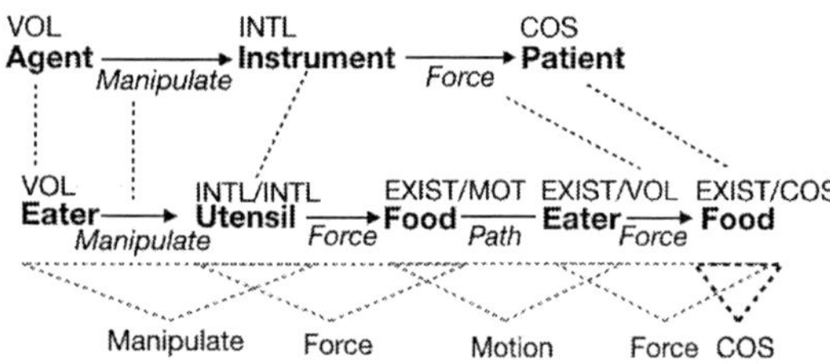

Figure 5: Concatenation of image schemas in the Ingestion network

The Manipulate image schema describes a causal chain in which an Agent uses an Instrument to interact with another physical entity. The physical interaction between an Instrument and Food describes a Force image schema which, in more general terms, denotes an event in which a physical entity interacts with another physical entity (a theme) by exerting physical force and thus causing the theme to undergo some physical change, e.g. a translational motion or a change of state. Alternatively, the physical entity that initiates the Force relation comes into contact with the theme without any physical change taking place. The Motion image schema describes a causal chain in which a motion theme moves along a path with re-

spect to some ground. The Change of State image schema describes a single-participant causal chain in which a theme undergoes a change of state. The change of state event may be initiated by an external entity, such as an Agent in this ingestion example.

Subchains denoting image schemas may be concatenated in various ways to form complex networks; however, they must be connected by one shared participant. Each participant that occurs in two subchains, i.e. as the endpoint of the first subchain and also the initiator of the next subchain in the verbal causal network, has two separate labels that describe the participant's subevent.

To illustrate this point further, let's consider a Motion event. Motion may be concatenated with an external cause (e.g. Force), as in the example *Steve tossed the ball to the garden* (VerbNet). The Agent *Steve* exerts force on the Moved_Entity *ball*, which consequently undergoes motion. The Moved_Entity is in a path relation with the Ground *garden*. The Moved_Entity is both an endpoint of the Force image schema (labeled EXIST[6]) and a motion theme in the Motion image schema (labeled MOT[7]), as shown in Figure 6.

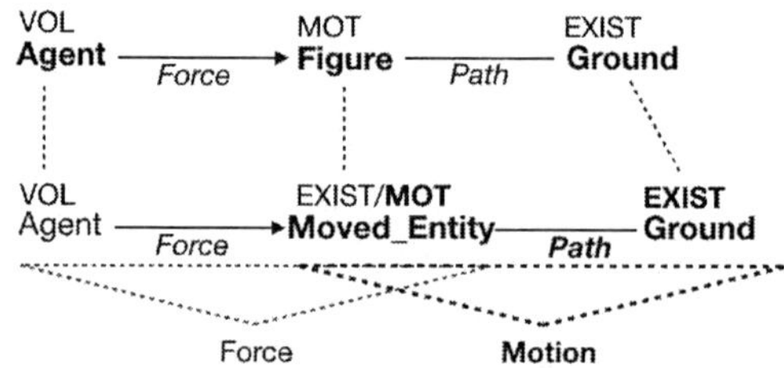

Figure 6: Concatenation of Force and Motion

Each network consists of a *core subchain* which corresponds to a particular event type. For example, in networks with motion verbs, the core subchain consists of two participants: a motion *theme* or *figure* which is in a path relation with a *ground* (Talmy, 1974). To distinguish the core subchain from a concatenated subchain, participants and their relations in the core subchain are highlighted in bold, as shown in Figure 6.

---

[6]EXIST is used to signal the presence of a participant, i.e. that it is part of the event but does not necessarily undergo a change of state or other changes on the qualitative dimension.

[7]MOT is used for themes that undergo motion in motion events.

3.3 Network participants and overlap

Verbal event structure determines the participants and their roles in causal networks. In our network representation, we include all participants that are obligatorily evoked by the verb. To ensure that our networks for event types are comprehensive, we consult VerbNet and FrameNet databases for their semantic identification of event participants (i.e. Roles in VerbNet and Core Frame Elements in FrameNet). Our labels for network participants are chosen based on the participant's role in a given verbal event structure (not unlike Frame Elements in FrameNet); the labels are not meant to be interpreted as semantic role labels.

Including only the participants that are obligatorily evoked by verbal semantics results in causal networks that are closely related but not identical. Consequently, some event types have multiple networks that partially *overlap*. For example, the event structure for vehicular motion (VM) verbs, such as *drive* and *ride*, overlaps since they share event participants, i.e. a Rider, Vehicle, and Destination (see Figure 7). However, their event structure representations are not identical. *Ride* and *drive* evoke different initiators of the causal network, as shown in Figure 7 (cf. FrameNet's Ride_vehicle, Operate_vehicle, and Cause_motion frames).

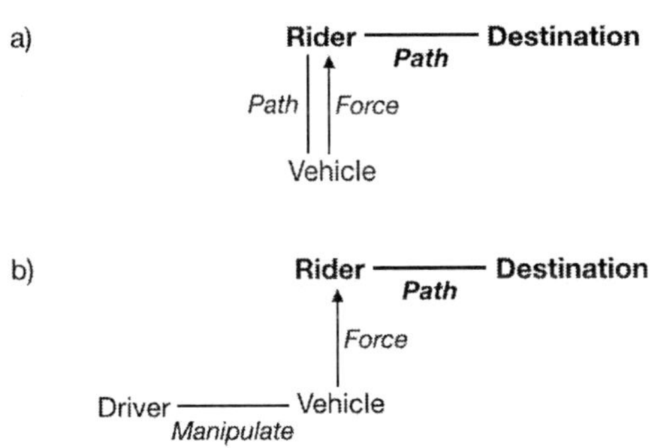

Figure 7: Vehicular Motion network for *ride* (a) and *drive* (b).

The core subchain in both VM networks is a Motion image schema which describes the relation between a Rider and Destination; however, unlike other Motion networks, the VM network is more complex since VM verbs obligatorily evoke a Vehicle as an additional participant in the event structure.

As depicted in Figure 7, the relation between the initiators (i.e. Rider and Driver) and the Ve-

hicle in these two types of VM networks is different. In the Drive network, a Driver drives a Vehicle (Manipulate image schema) to transport a Rider (Force image schema) to a Destination (Motion image schema). Figure 8 shows a mapping of the causal chain associated with the example *He drove him to the hospital* to the Drive verbal causal network[8]. The Vehicle in the network is not linked to any participant in the causal chain since it is not expressed by the argument structure construction. However, it is represented in the causal network because it is evoked by the semantics of *drive*.

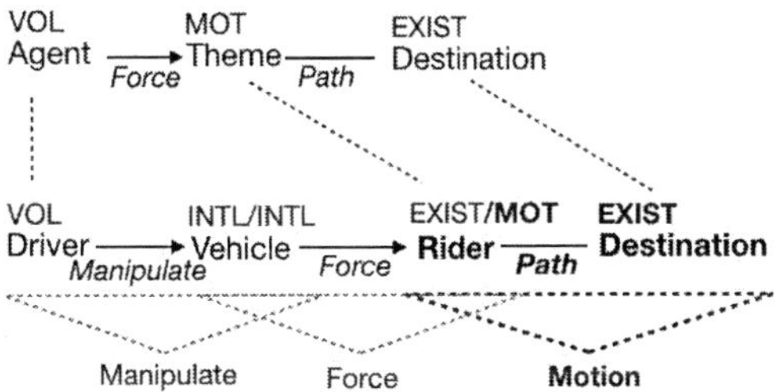

Figure 8: Causal chain to network mapping for *drive*

Ride evokes a similar network representation that partially overlaps with the Drive network. However, in the Ride network, a Rider boards a Vehicle (Motion image schema) which transports the Rider (Force image schema) to a Destination (Motion image schema). Unlike the Drive network, the Ride network is cyclic, i.e. the Rider is involved in more than one relation. This is illustrated on the mapping of the causal chain associated with the example *Brenda went to Berlin by train* to the Ride network in Figure 9.

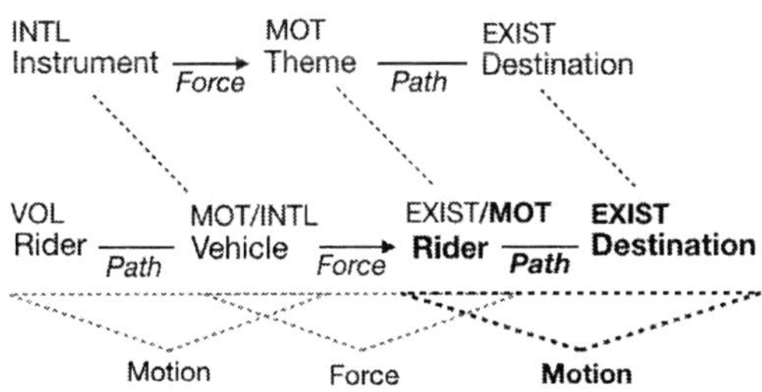

Figure 9: Causal chain to network mapping for *ride*

The Path relation between the Rider and the Ve-

---

[8] *Drive* can also occur in an argument structure construction in which the Agent and the Theme are conflated (e.g. *He drove to Santa Fe*). In this example, the Agent is linked to both the Driver and Rider in the verbal network. A distinct verb for conflated Driver and Rider is used in Dutch (Jens Van Gysel, pers. comm.) and Korean (Sook-kyung Lee, pers. comm.)

hicle is usually not syntactically expressed in argument structure constructions with VM verbs in English; however, it is evoked by the verbal semantics of *ride* verbs. The Instrument is linked to the Vehicle and the Theme to the Rider in the network.

Overlapping of verbal causal networks is common in our event structure representation. Another case of network overlapping can be found with the ingestion verbs *eat* and *feed*, as shown in Figure 10.

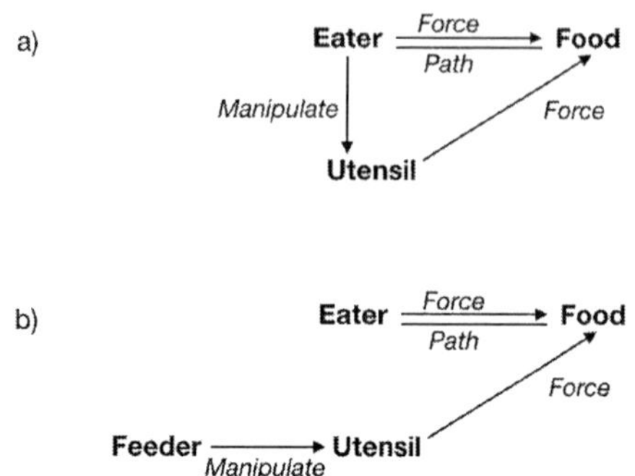

Figure 10: Ingestion network for *eat* (a) and *feed*. (b)

Feed in (b) obligatorily evokes an external initiator, i.e. a Feeder, which is different from an Eater. The Ingestion network for *eat* in (a) does not include a Feeder since *eat* does not obligatorily evoke this participant. The two networks share most of the event participants; however, we provide a separate representation for each event structure since the networks do not overlap fully.

4 Representing construals with causal networks

Using the analysis of image schema concatenation to form complex networks allows us to provide a more comprehensive representation of event structure for examples in which a verb meaning has different construals. As noted in the introductory section of this paper, a verb can have more than one construal depending on the argument structure construction in which it occurs. To demonstrate how our network representation deals with this issue, we will return to the construals of *kick* discussed in the Introduction.

Our causal chain analysis distinguishes the various meanings of *kick* by having a causal chain representation for the constructional semantics. However, an additional layer of information must be included to indicate which part of the event structure is evoked by the verb meaning and which part comes from the meaning of the argument structure construction. In particular, a causal chain analysis of constructional meaning does not convey that *kick* is a Force verb, rather than a Motion verb, when it occurs in a Motion construction or in other construals. Our model pairing constructional meaning (i.e. causal chains) with verb meaning (i.e. verbal networks) provides an event structure representation that accounts for verb construals in various constructions.

4.1 A Motion construal of *kick*

Kick can occur in a caused motion construction, as in *Pat kicked the football into the stadium*. As shown in Figure 11, the core event type in the network representation for this example is identified as Force. The Force image schema describes a causal relation between an Agent and a Force_Theme evoked by the verb *kick*. Since the argument structure construction describes a Motion event, a Motion schema is concatenated onto the Force image schema. That is, the argument structure construction evokes a more complex event structure in which the Force_Theme is also in a Path relation with a Ground. The Force_Theme *football* is both an endpoint of the Force relation as well as a motion theme in the Motion image schema.

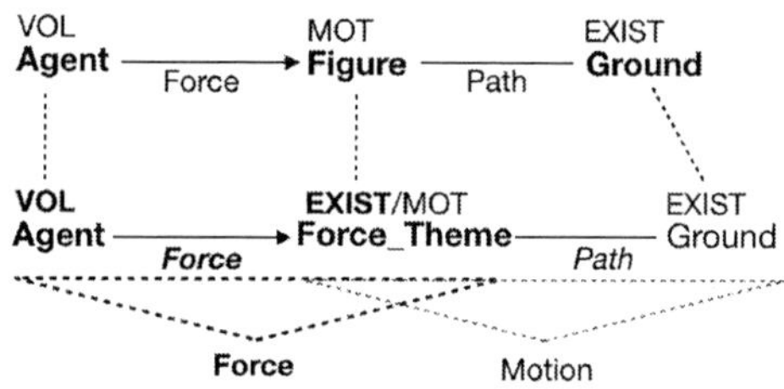

Figure 11: Concatenation of Motion and Force

The two representations for the motion argument structure constructions with *toss* in Figure 6 and *kick* in Figure 11 demonstrate that adding verb meaning to the analysis of event structure allows us to differentiate the semantics of these two examples. In the network representation of *toss*, the core subchain is identified as a Motion image schema since *toss* is a motion verb. As a result, the motion theme is labeled Moved_Entity. The event structure evoked by the construction *Steve tossed the ball to the garden* adds a Force image schema to the Motion subchain.

The network representation of the motion example with *kick* in Figure 11 is different. Force is identified as the core subchain since *kick* is a Force verb. The motion theme is labeled Force_Theme. The event structure evoked by the construction *Pat kicked the football into the stadium* adds a Motion image schema to the Force subchain. The distinct labels for participants in each network are motivated by the core subchain which is evoked by the verb meaning.

4.2 COS and Transfer construals of *kick*

Our representation also allows us to differentiate the event structure evoked by the COS argument structure construction *Pat kicked Bob black and blue* from the verbal semantics of *kick*. The core event type profiles a causal relation between an Agent and a Force_Theme. As shown in Figure 12, the Force_Theme is identified as both the endpoint of the Force image schema as well as a COS theme in the COS image schema evoked by the constructional semantics.

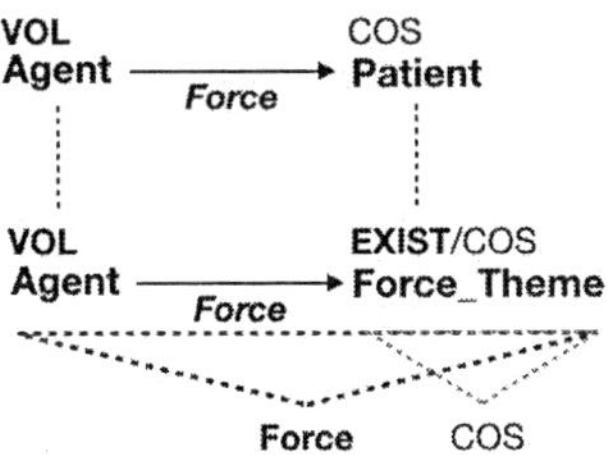

Figure 12: Concatenation of Change of State and Force

Figure 13 shows our event structure representation for *kick* in a Transfer construction as in *Pat kicked Bob the football*. Similarly to the network representation in Figure 11 and 12, the core event type in the network is Force. The Transfer argument structure construction adds a Recipient *Bob* who is in a Control relation with the Force_Theme *football*.

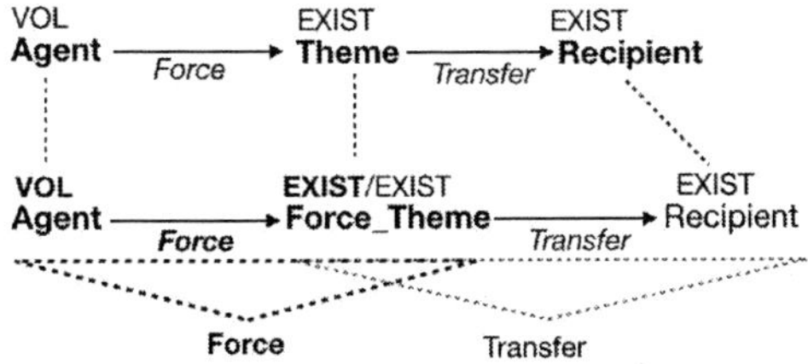

Figure 13: Concatenation of Transfer and Force

As these examples demonstrate, verbal causal networks provide more detailed information about the event structure than causal chains. Using the notion of image schema concatenation allows us to deal with various verb construals in different argument structure constructions. Our event structure representation represents verb meaning and constructional meaning, and distinguishes one from the other.

5 Conclusion

In this paper, we present a model of verb meaning representation that accounts for the semantics of argument structure constructions as well as verbal event structures associated with event types. Our proposed causal networks for verb meanings represent richer event structures associated with complex event types. Our network representations can also deal with verb construals in various argument structure constructions.

The verbal causal networks are more general than VerbNet classes and subclasses which are based on Levin (1993) argument structure constructions. As a result, they subsume more than one VerbNet class. The networks are also more general than frames in FrameNet. In some cases, our networks link to higher order non-lexical frames in FrameNet. However, this is not always the case. In many cases, our networks link to multiple less schematic lexical frames.

Verbal networks will be stored with verbs in VerbNet in the relevant classes. For example, the Ingestion network will be linked to the following VerbNet classes: chew-39.2, dine-39.5, eat-39.1, gobble-39.3.-1, and gorge-39.6. Given the direct correspondence between verbal networks and VerbNet classes, our verbal analysis provides the same verb coverage of corpus data as VerbNet (cf. Palmer et al. (2005) for VerbNet's coverage of the Penn Treebank II). An automated analysis and linking of networks to verbal entries in corpora will use existing computational methods for verb sense disambiguation (Loper et al., 2007; Chen and Palmer, 2009; Brown et al., 2011; Peterson et al., 2016) to accomplish a correct match of verb senses to verbal networks.

A near-term objective of our work is to design a computational model that automates the mapping between the participants in the different networks. Given a causal chain, a verbal event network, and a set of possible links, the task is to determine the path through the network that describes an event. Developing such a computational model will be complicated by the multiple possible interactions of verb meaning and accompanying argument structure construction, the many possible concatenations of image schemas, the need to respect the dimensionality of the links in the causal representations, as well as how to account for coercion and construal. A starting point is to recognize that argument structure constructions are defined by a small set of force dynamic relations, and these relations also define verbal networks. The next step toward a computational model will be to extract constructional meaning from raw text, to be reported on in future work.

Currently, our event structure representation covers physical and mental domains. However, there are many complex event types in the social domain that need to be analyzed. Among others, verbs of transfer of possession and communication, which make up a large portion of the verbal lexicon in the social domain, all involve complex cyclic networks which will benefit from a semantic representation that is separate from the argument structure construction meaning.

6 Acknowledgments

This research was partly funded by grant number HDTRA1-15-0063 from the Defense Threat Reduction Agency to the last author.

References

Omri Abend and Ari Rappoport. 2013. Universal conceptual cognitive annotation (ucca). In *Proceedings of the 51st Annual Meeting of the Association for Computational Linguistics*, volume 1, pages 228–238.

Laura Banarescu, Claire Bonial, Shu Cau, Madalina Georgescu, Kira Griffitt, Ulf Hermjakob, Kevin Knight, Phillipp Koehn, Martha Palmer, and Nathan Schneider. 2013. Abstract meaning representation for sembanking. In *Proceedings of the 7th Linguistic Annotation Workshop*.

Susan Windisch Brown, Dmitriy Dligach, and Martha Palmer. 2011. VerbNet class assignment as a WSD task. In *Proceedings of the Ninth International Conference on Computational Semantics. Association for Computational Linguistics*.

Jinying Chen and Martha S. Palmer. 2009. Improving English verb sense disambiguation performance with linguistically motivated features and clear sense distinction boundaries. *Language Resources and Evaluation*, 43(2):181–208.

William Croft. 1991. *Syntactic categories and grammatical relations: the cognitive organization of information.* Chicago: University of Chicago Press.

William Croft. 2012. *Verbs: aspect and causal structure.* Oxford University Press.

William Croft, Pavlína Pešková, and Michael Regan. 2016. Annotation of causal and aspectual structure of events in RED: a preliminary report. In *4th Events Workshop, 15th Annual Conference of the North American Chapter of the Association of Computational Linguistics: Human Language Technologies*, NAAACL-HLT 2016, pages 8–17. Stroudsburg, Penn: Association for Computational Linguistics.

William Croft, Pavlína Pešková, and Michael Regan. 2017. Integrating decompositional event structure into storylines. In *Proceedings of the Workshop on Events and Stories in the News*, pages 98–109.

William Croft, Pavlína Pešková, Michael Regan, and Sook-kyung Lee. 2018. A rich annotation scheme for mental events. In *Proceedings of the Workshop on Events and Stories in the News*, pages 7–17.

David Dowty. 1991. Thematic proto-roles and argument selection. *Language*, 67:547–619.

Charles J. Fillmore. 1968. Lexical entries for verb. *Foundations of Language*, 4(4):373–393.

Charles J. Fillmore. 1982. Frame semantics. In The Linguistic Society of Korea, editor, *Linguistics in the morning calm*, pages 111–137. Seoul: Hanshin.

Charles J. Fillmore. 1985. Frames and the semantics of understanding. *Quaderni di semantica*, 6:622–54.

Charles J. Fillmore, Christopher R. Johnson, and Miriam R. Petruck. 2003. Background to FrameNet. *International Journal of Lexicography*, 16:235–50.

Adele E. Goldberg. 1995. *Constructions: A Construction Grammar Approach to Argument Structure.* Chicago: University of Chicago Pres.

Adele E. Goldberg. 2006. *Constructions at work: the nature of generalization in language.* Oxford: Oxford University Press.

Jan Hajič, Eva Hajičová, Jarmila Panevová, Petr Sgall, Ondřej Bojar, Silvie Cinková, Eva Fucíková, Marie Mikulová, Petr Pajas, Jan Popelka, Jiří Semecký, Jana Šindlerová, Jan Štěpánek, Josef Toman, Zdeňka Urešová, and Zdeněk Žabokrtský. 2012. Announcing prague czech-english dependency treebank 2.0. In *LREC*, pages 3153–3160.

Jennifer Hay, Christopher Kennedy, and Beth Levin. 1999. Scalar structure underlies telicity in "degree achievements". In Tanya Matthews and Devon Strolovitch, editors, *Proceedings of SALT*, volume 9, pages 127–144. Ithaca: Cornell University Press.

Seizi Iwata. 2005. Locative alternation and two levels of verb meaning. *Cognitive Linguistics*, 16(2):355–407.

Karin Kipper, Anna Korhonen, Neville Ryant, and Martha Palmer. 2007. A large-scale classification of English verbs. *English Resources and Evaluations*, 42:21–40.

Beth Levin. 1993. *English verb classes and alternations: a preliminary investigation*. Chicago: University of Chicago Press.

Edward Loper, Szu-Ting Yi, and Martha Palmer. 2007. Combining lexical resources: mapping between Propbank and VerbNet. In *Proceedings of the 7th International Workshop on Computational Linguistics, Tilburg, the Netherlands*.

Martha Palmer, Daniel Gildea, and Paul Kingsbury. 2005. The proposition bank: an annotated corpus of semantic roles. *Computational linguistics*, 31(1):71–106.

Daniel Peterson, Jordan Boyd-Graber, Martha Palmer, and Daisuke Kawahara. 2016. Leveraging verbnet to build corpus-specific verb clusters. In *Proceedings of the Fifth Joint Conference on Lexical and Computational Semantics*, pages 102–107.

Josef Ruppenhofer, Michael Ellsworth, Miria R. L. Petruck, Christopher R. Johnson, Collin F. Baker, and Jan Scheffczyk. 2016. *FrameNet II: Extended Theory and Practice*. http://framenet.icsi.berkeley.edu.

Leonard Talmy. 1974. Semantics and syntax in motion. In John Kimball, editor, *Syntax and Semantics 4*, pages 181–238. New York: Academic Press.

Leonard Talmy. 1988. Force dynamics in language and cognition. *Cognitive Science*, 2:49–100.

Carol L. Tenny. 1994. *Aspectual roles and the syntax-semantics interface*. Dordrech: Kluwer.

Robert D. Van Valin and Randy J. LaPolla. 1997. *Syntax: structure, meaning, and function*. Cambridge University Press.

Elisabeth Verhoeven. 2007. *Experiential Constructions in Yucatec Maya: a typologically based analysis of a function domain in a Mayan language*. John Benjamins Publishing Company.

Distributional Semantics Meets Construction Grammar.
Towards a Unified Usage-Based Model of Grammar and Meaning

Giulia Rambelli
University of Pisa
giulia.rambelli@phd.unipi.it

Emmanuele Chersoni
The Hong Kong Polytechnic University
emmanuelechersoni@gmail.com

Philippe Blache
Aix-Marseille University
blache@lpl-aix.fr

Chu-Ren Huang
The Hong Kong Polytechnic University
churen.huang@polyu.edu.hk

Alessandro Lenci
University of Pisa
alessandro.lenci@unipi.it

Abstract

In this paper, we propose a new type of semantic representation of Construction Grammar that combines constructions with the vector representations used in Distributional Semantics. We introduce a new framework, Distributional Construction Grammar, where grammar and meaning are systematically modeled from language use, and finally, we discuss the kind of contributions that distributional models can provide to CxG representation from a linguistic and cognitive perspective.

1 Introduction

In the last decades, usage-based models of language have captured the attention of linguistics and cognitive science (Tommasello, 2003; Bybee, 2010). The different approaches covered by this label are based on the assumptions that linguistic knowledge is embodied in mental processing and representations that are sensitive to context and statistical probabilities (Boyland, 2009), and that language structures at all levels, from morphology to syntax, emerge out of facts of actual language usage (Bybee, 2010).

A usage-based framework that turned out to be extremely influential is **Construction Grammar** (CxG) (Hoffman and Trousdale, 2013), a family of theories sharing the fundamental idea that language is a collection of form-meaning pairings called *constructions* (henceforth *Cxs*) (Fillmore, 1988; Goldberg, 2006). Cxs differ for their degree of schematicity, ranging from morphemes (e.g., *pre-*, *-ing*), to complex words (e.g., *daredevil*) to filled or partially-filled idioms (e.g., *give the devil his dues* or *Jog (someones) memory*) to more abstract patterns like the ditransitive Cxs `[Subj V Obj1 Obj2]`. It is worth stressing that, even if the concept of construction is based on the idea that linguistic properties actually emerge from language *use*, CxG theories have typically preferred to model the semantic content of constructions in terms of hand-made, formal representations like those of Frame Semantics (Baker et al., 1998). This leaves open the issue of how semantic representations can be learned from empirical evidence, and how do they relate to the usage-based nature of Cxs. In fact, for a usage-based model of grammar based on a strong syntax-semantics parallelism, it would be desirable to be grounded on a framework allowing to learn the semantic content of Cxs from language use.

In this perspective, a promising solution for representing constructional semantics is given by an approach to meaning representations that has gained a rising interest in both computational linguistics and cognitive science, namely **Distributional Semantics** (henceforth DS). DS is a usage-based model of word meaning, based on the well-established assumption that the statistical distribution of linguistic items in context plays a key role in characterizing their semantic behaviour (*Distributional Hypothesis* (Harris, 1954)). More precisely, Distributional Semantic Models (DSMs) represent the lexicon in terms of vector spaces, where a lexical target is described in terms of a vector (also known as *embedding*) built by identifying in a corpus its syntactic and lexical contexts (Lenci, 2018). Lately, neural models to learn distributional vectors have gained massive popularity: these algorithms build low-dimensional vector representations by learning to optimally predict the contexts of the target words (Mikolov et al., 2013). On the negative side, DS lacks a clear

Proceedings of the First International Workshop on Designing Meaning Representations, pages 110–120
Florence, Italy, August 1st, 2019 ©2019 Association for Computational Linguistics

connection with usage-based theoretical frameworks. To the best of our knowledge, existing attempts of linking DS with models of grammar have rather targeted formal theories like Montague Grammar and Categorial Grammar (Baroni et al., 2014; Grefenstette and Sadrzadeh, 2015).

To sum up, both CxG and DS share the assumption that linguistic structures naturally emerge from language usage, and that a representation of both form and meaning of any linguistic item can be modeled through its distributional statistics, and more generally, with the quantitative information derived from corpus data. However, these two models still live in parallel worlds. On the one hand, CxG is a model of grammar in search for a consistent usage-based model of meaning, and, conversely, DS is a computational framework to build semantic representations in search for an empirically adequate theory of grammar.

As we illustrate in Section 2, occasional encounters between DS and CxG have already happened, but we believe that new fruitful advances could come from the exploitation of the mutual synergies between CxG and DS, and by letting these two worlds finally meet and interact in a more systematic way. Following this direction of research, we introduce a new representation framework called **Distributional Construction Grammar**, which aims at bringing together these two theoretical paradigms. Our goal is to integrate distributional information into constructions by completing their semantic structures with distributional vectors extracted from large textual corpora, as samples of language usage.

These pages are structured as follows: after reviewing existing literature on CxG and related computational studies, in Section 3 we outline the key characteristics of our theoretical proposal, while Section 4 provides a general discussion about what contributions DSMs can provide to CxG representation from a linguistic and cognitive perspective. Although this is essentially a theoretical contribution, we outline ongoing work focusing on its computational implementation and empirical validation. We conclude by reporting future perspectives of research.

2 Related Work

Despite the popularity of the constructional approach in corpus linguistics (Gries and Stefanowitsch, 2004), computational semantics research has never formulated a systematic proposal for deriving representations of constructional meaning from corpus data. Previous literature has mostly focused either on the automatic identification of constructions on the basis of their formal features, or on modeling the meaning of a specific CxG.

For the former approach, we should mention the works of Dunn (2017, 2019) that aim at automatically inducing a set of grammatical units (Cxs) from a large corpus. On the one hand, Dunn's contributions provide a method for extracting Cxs from corpora, but on the other hand they are mainly concerned with the formal side of the constructions, and especially with the problem of how syntactic constraints are learned. Some sort of semantic representation is included, in the form of semantic cluster of word embeddings to which the word forms appearing in the constructions are assigned. However, these works do not present any evaluation of the construction representations in terms of semantic tasks.

Another line of research has focused in using constructions for building computational models of language acquisition. Alishahi and Stevenson (2008) propose a model for the representation, acquisition and use of verb argument structure by formulating constructions as probabilistic associations between syntactic and semantic properties of verbs and their arguments. This probabilistic association emerges over time through a Bayesian acquisition process in which similar verb usages are detected and grouped together to form general constructions, based on their syntactic and semantic properties. Despite the success of this model, the semantic representation of argument structure is still symbolic and each semantic category of input constructions are manually compiled, in contrast with the usage-based nature of constructions.

Other studies used DSMs to model constructional meaning, by focusing on a specific type of Cx rather than on the entire grammar. For example, Levshina and Heylen (2014) build a vector space to study Dutch causative constructions with *doen* ('do') and *laten* ('let'). They compute several vector spaces with different context types, both for the nouns that fill the Causer and Causee slot and for the verbs that fill the Effected Predicate slot. Then, they cluster these nouns and verbs at different levels of granularity and test which classification better predicts the use of *laten* and *doen*.

A recent trend in diachronic linguistics investigates linguistic change as a sequence of gradual changes in distributional patterns of usage (Bybee, 2010). For instance, Perek (2016) investigates the productivity of the *V the hell out of NP* construction (e.g., *You scared the hell out of me*) from 1930 to 2009. On one side, he clusters the vectors of verbs occurring in this construction to pin point the preferred semantic domains of the Cx in its diachronic evolution. Secondly, he computes the density of the semantic space of the construction around a given word in a certain period to be predictive of that word joining the construction in the subsequent period. A similar approach is applied to study changes in the productivity of the *Way*-construction over the period 1830-2009 (Perek, 2018). Perek's analysis also proves that distributional similarity and neighbourhood density in the vector space can be predictive of the usage of a construction with a new lexical item. Other works have followed this approach, demonstrating the validity of DSMs to model the semantic change of constructions in diachrony. Amato and Lenci (2017) examine the Italian Gerundival Periphrases *stare* (to stay) *andare* (to go), *venire* (to come) followed by a gerund. As in previous works, they uses DSMs to i) identify similarities and differences among Cxs clustering the vectors of verbs occurring in each Cx, and ii) investigate the changes undergone by the semantic space of the verbs occurring in the Cxs throughout a very long period (from 1550 to 2009).

Lebani and Lenci (2017) present an unsupervised distributional semantic representation of argument constructions. Following the assumption that constructional meanings for argument Cxs arise from the meaning of high frequency verbs that co-occur with them (Goldberg, 1999; Casenhiser and Goldberg, 2005; Barak and Goldberg, 2017), they compute distributional vectors for CxS as the centroids of the vectors of their typical verbs, and use them to model the psycholinguistic data about construction priming in Johnson and Goldberg (2013). This representation of construction meaning has also been applied to study valency coercion by Busso et al. (2018).

Following a parallel research line on probing tasks for distributed vectors, Kann et al. (2019) investigate whether word and sentence embeddings encode the grammatical distinctions necessary for inferring the idiosyncratic frame-selectional properties of verbs. Their findings show that, at least for some alternations, verb embeddings encode sufficient information for distinguishing between acceptable and unacceptable combinations.

3 Distributional CxG Framework

We introduce a new framework aimed at integrating the computational representation derived from distributional methods into the explicit formalization of Construction Grammars, called **Distributional Construction Grammar** (DisCxG).

DisCxG is based on three components:

- **Constructions**: stored pairings of form and function, including morphemes, words, idioms, partially lexically filled and fully general linguistic patterns (Goldberg, 2003);

- **Frames**: schematic semantic knowledge describing scenes and situations in terms of their semantic roles;

- **Events**: semantic information concerning particular event instances with their specific participants. The introduction of this component, which is a novelty with respect to traditional CxG frameworks, has been inspired by cognitive models such as the *Generalized Event Knowledge* (McRae and Matsuki, 2009) and the *Words-as-Cues* hypothesis (Elman, 2014).

The peculiarity of DisCxG is that we distinguish two layers of semantic representation, referring to two different and yet complementary aspects of semantic knowledge. Specifically, frames define a prototypical semantic representation based on the different semantic roles (the *frame elements*) defining argument structures, while events provide a specialization of the frame by taking into account information about specific participants and relations between them. Crucially, we assume that *both these layers have a DS representation in terms of distributional vectors learned from corpus co-occurrences*.

Following the central tenet of CxGs, according to which linguistic information is encoded in similar way for lexical items as well as for more abstract Cxs (e.g., *covariational-conditional* Cx, *ditransitive* Cx etc.), the three components of DisCxG are modeled using the same type of formal representation with recursive feature-structures, which is inspired by Sign-Based Construction Grammar (SBCG) (Sag, 2012; Michaelis, 2013).

3.1 Constructions

In DisCxG, a construction is represented by form and semantic features. The following list presents the set of main features of Cxs adapting the formalization in SBCG:

- The FORM feature contains the basic formal characteristics of constructions. It includes the (i) PHONological/SURFACE form, (ii) the (morpho)syntactic features (SYN), i.e part-of-speech (TYPE), CASE (nominal, accusative), the set of elements subcategorized (VAL), and (iii) PROPERTIES representing explicitly the syntactic relations among the elements of the Cx.

- The ARGument-STructure implements the interface between syntactic and semantic roles. The arguments are in order of their accessibility hierarchy (subj $\prec$ d-obj $\prec$ obl...), encoding the syntactic role. Each argument specifies the case, related to the grammatical function, and links to the thematic role.[1]

- The SEMantic feature specifies the properties of Cx's meaning (Section 3.2).

Unlike SGBG or other CxG theories, we include inside FORM a new feature called PROPERTIES, borrowed from *Property Grammars* (Blache, 2005). Properties encode syntactic information about the components of a Cx, and they play an important role in its recognition. However, the discussion of this linguistic aspect is not presented here, as the focus of this paper is on the semantic side of constructions.[2]

As said above, a Cx can describe linguistic objects of various levels of complexity and schematicity: words, phrases, fully lexicalized idiomatic patterns, partially lexicalized schemas, etc. Thus, the attribute-value matrix can be applied to lexical entries, as the verb *read* in Figure 1, as well as to abstract constructions that do not involve lexical material. Figure 2 depicts the *ditransitive* Cx. The semantic particularity of this construction is that whatever the lexicalization of the verb, this construction always involve a possession interpretation (more precisely the transfer of something to somebody), represented in the TRANSFER frame.

Differently from standard SBCG formalization of Cxs, we add the distributional feature DSVECTOR into the semantic layer in order to integrate lexical distributional representations. The semantic structure of a lexical item can be associated with its distributional vector (e.g., the embedding of *read)*, but we can also include a distributional representation of abstract syntactic constructions following the approach of Lebani and Lenci (2017) we have illustrated in Section 2.

3.2 Frames

A frame is a schematic representation of an event or scenario together with the participating actors/objects/locations and their (semantic) role (Fillmore, 1982). For instance, the sentences

1. (a) *Mary bought a car from John (for 5000$).*
   (b) *John sold a car to Mary (for 5000$).*

activate the same COMMERCIAL_TRANSACTION frame, consisting of a SELLER (*John*), a BUYER (*Mary*), a GOOD which is sold (*car*), and the MONEY used in the transaction (*5000$*).

Semantic frames are the standard meaning representation in CxG, which represent them as symbolic structures. The source of this information is typically FrameNet (Ruppenhofer et al., 2016), a lexical database of English containing more than 1,200 semantic frames linked to more than 200,000 manually annotated sentences. The not negligible problem of FrameNet is that entries must be created by expert lexicographers. This has lead to a widely recognized coverage problem in its lexical units (Baker, 2012).

In DisCxG, semantic frames are still represented as structures, but the value of semantic roles consists of distributional vectors. As for the COMMERCIAL_TRANSACTION frame in Figure 3, each frame element has associated a specific embedding. It is worth noting that in this first version of the DisCxG model, frame representations are still based on predefined lists of semantic roles, as defined in FrameNet (e.g., BUYER, SELLER, etc.). However, some works have recently attempted to automatically infer frames (and their roles) from distributional information[3]. Woodsend and Lap-

---

[1]SGCG distinguishes between valence and argument structure: the ARG-ST encodes overt and covert arguments, including extracted (non-local) and unexpressed elements, while VAL in the form description represents only realized elements. When no covert arguments occur, these features are identical.

[2]For more details on the Propery Grammar framework, see Blache (2016).

[3]Lately, SemEval 2019 proposed a task on unsupervised

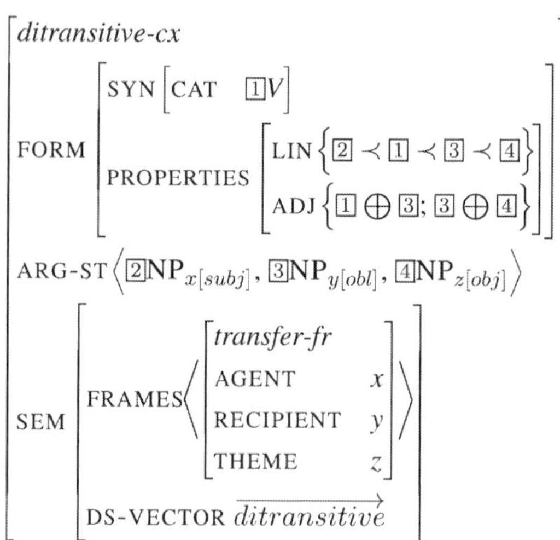

Figure 1: Description of *read* verb

Figure 2: Description of *ditransitive* Cx

ata (2015) use distributional representations to induce embeddings for predicates and their arguments. Ustalov et al. (2018) propose a different methodology for unsupervised semantic frame induction. They build embeddings as the concatenations of subject-verb-object triples and identify frames as clustered triples. Of course, a limit of this approach is that it only uses subject and object arguments, while frames are generally associated with a wider variety of roles. Lebani and Lenci (2018) instead provide a distributional representation of verb-specific semantic roles as clusters of features automatically induced from corpora.

In this paper, we assume that at least some aspects of semantic roles can be derived from combining (e.g., with summation) the distributional vectors of their most prototypical fillers, following an approach widely explored in DS (Baroni and Lenci, 2010; Erk et al., 2010; Sayeed et al., 2016; Santus et al., 2017). For instance, the $\overrightarrow{buyer}$ role in the COMMERCIAL_TRANSACTION frame can be taken as a vector encoding the properties of the typical nouns filling this role. We are aware that this solution is just an approximation of the content of frames elements. How to satisfactorily characterize semantic frames and roles using DS is in fact still an open research question.

3.3 Events

Neurocognitive research has brought extensive evidence that stored world knowledge plays a key role in online language production and compre-

lexical semantic frame induction (http://alt.qcri.org/semeval2019/index.php?id=tasks)

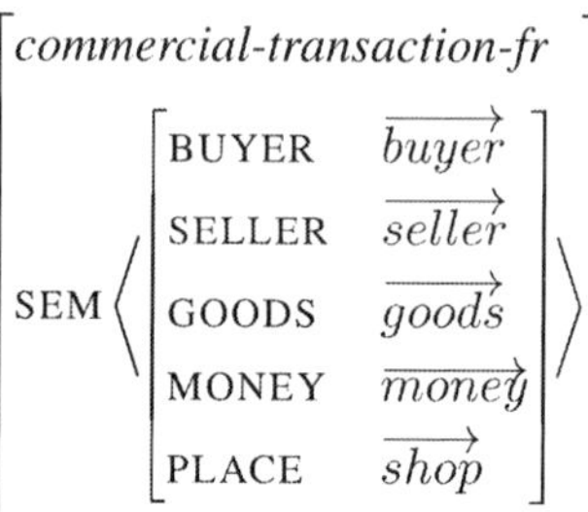

Figure 3: The COMMERCIAL_TRANSACTION frame containing the distributional representation of the semantic roles

hension. An important aspect of such knowledge consists of the events and situations that we experience under different modalities, including the linguistic input. McRae and Matsuki (2009) call it Generalized Event Knowledge (GEK), because it contains information about prototypical event structures. Language comprehension has been characterized as a largely predictive process (Kuperberg and Jaeger, 2015). Predictions are memory-based, and experiences about events and their participants are used to generate expectations about the upcoming linguistic input, thereby minimizing the processing effort (Elman, 2014; McRae and Matsuki, 2009). For instance, argument combinations that are more 'coherent' with the event scenarios activated by the previous words are read faster in self-paced reading tasks and elicited smaller N400 amplitudes in ERP experiments (Paczynski and Kuperberg, 2012).

In DisCxG, events have a crucial role: they

bridge the gap between the concrete instantiation of a Cx in context and its conceptualized meaning (conveyed from frames). For example, let's consider the verb *read*. We know that this verb subcategorizes for two noun phrases (form) and involves a generic READING frame in which there is someone who reads (READER) and something that is read (TEXT). This frame only provides an abstract, context-independent representation of the verb meaning, and the two roles can be generally defined as clusters of properties derived from singular subjects and objects of *read*. However, the semantic representation comprehenders build during sentence processing is influenced by the specific fillers that instantiate the frame elements. If the input is *A student reads..*, the fact that the word *student* appears as the subject of the verb activates a specific scenario, together with a series of expectations about the prototypicality of other lexical items. Consequently, the object of the previous sentence is more likely to be *book* rather than *magazine* (Chersoni et al., 2019). Accordingly, in DisCxG events are considered as functions that specialize the semantic meaning encoded in frames. The word *student* specializes the READING frame into a specific event, triggering expectations about the most likely participants of the other roles: the READER is encoded as a lexical unit vector, and the distributional restriction applied to the TEXT is represented by a subset of possible objects ordered by their degree of typicality in the event. Figure 4 gives a simple example of the specialization brought out by event knowledge.

$$\left[\begin{array}{l} \textit{student-read-event} \\ \text{SPECIALIZE } \textit{reading-fr} \\ \text{SEM} \left\langle \left[\begin{array}{ll} \text{READER} & \overrightarrow{student} \\ \text{TEXT} & \{\overrightarrow{book}, \overrightarrow{paper}..\} \end{array} \right] \right\rangle \end{array} \right]$$

Figure 4: *Student-read* event as the specialization of READING frame

In a similar way, events can instantiate an abstract construction dynamically, according to the context. The different lexicalization of the AGENT and the RECIPIENT in the ditransitive construction causes a different selection of the THEME. For example, the fact that the sentence fragment *The teacher gives students ...* could be completed as in (2) expresses a distributional restriction that can be encoded as an event capturing the co-occurrences

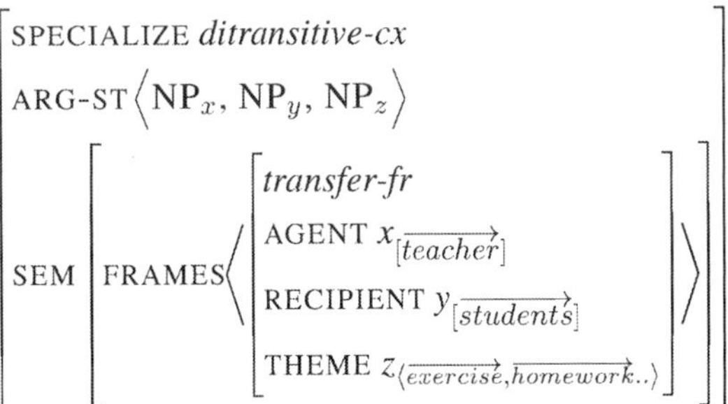

Figure 5: *Ditransitive* event specialization

teacher/student/exercises (Figure 5).

2. *The teacher gives students ... → The teacher gives students exercises*

Any lexical item activate a portion of event knowledge (Elman, 2014): in fact, if verbs evoke events, nouns evoke entities that participate into events. Thus, events and entities are themselves interlinked: there is not a specific feature EVENT in the description of the lexical entry *teacher*, but events are activated by the lexical entry, generating a network of expectations about upcoming words in the sentence (McRae and Matsuki, 2009).

Given this assumption, Chersoni et al. (2019) represent event knowledge in terms of a Distributional Event Graph (DEG) automatically built from parsed corpora. In this graph, nodes are embeddings and edges are labeled with syntactic relations and weighted using statistic association measures (Figure 6). Each event is a a path in DEG. Thus, given a lexical cue *w*, it is possible to identify the events it activates (together with the strength of its activation, defined as a function of the graph weights) and generate expectations about incoming inputs on both paradigmatic and syntagmatic axes. With this graph-based approach, Chersoni et al. (2019) model sentence comprehension as the dynamic and incremental creation of a semantic representation integrated into a semantically coherent structure contributing to the sentence interpretation.

We propose to include in our framework the information encoded in DEG. Each lexical entry contains a pointer to its corresponding node in the graph. Therefore, the *frame specialization* we have described above corresponds to an event encoded with a specific path in the DEG. Event information represents a way to unify the schematic descriptions contained in the grammar with the world knowledge and contextual information progressively activated by lexical items and integrated during language processing.

4 Some Other Arguments in Favor of a Distributional CxG

As we said in Section 2, few works have tried to use distributional semantic representations of constructions and existing studied have focused more on applying DS to a particular construction type, instead of providing a general model to represent the semantic content of Cxs. We argue that DSMs could give an important contribution in designing representations of constructional meaning. In what follows, we briefly discuss some specific issues related to Construction Grammars that could be addressed by combining them with Distributional Semantics.

Measuring similarity among constructions and frames The dominant approaches like frame semantics and traditional CxGs tend to represent entities and their relations in a formal (hand-made) way. A potential limitation of these methods is that it is hard to assess the similarity between frames or constructions, while one advantage of distributional vectors is that one can easily compute the degree of similarity between linguistic items represented in a vector space. For example, Busso et al. (2018) built a semantic space for several Italian argument constructions and then computed the similarity of their vectors, observing that some Cxs have similar distributional behaviour like Caused-Motion and Dative.

As for frames, there has been some work on using distributional similarity between vectors for their unsupervised induction (Ustalov et al., 2018), for comparing frames across languages (Sikos and Padó, 2018), and even for the automatic identification of the semantic relations holding between them (Botschen et al., 2017).

Identifying idiomatic meaning Many studies in theoretical, descriptive and experimental linguistics have recently questioned the *fregean* principle of compositionality, which assumes that the meaning of an expression is the result of the incremental composition of its sub-constituents. There is a large number of linguistic phenomena whose meaning is accessed directly from the whole linguistic structure: this is typically the case with idioms or multi-word expressions, where the figurative meaning cannot be decomposed. In computational semantics, a large literature has been aiming at modeling idiomaticity using DSMs. Senaldi et al. (2016) carried out an idiom type identification task representing Italian V-NP and V-PP Cxs as vectors. They observed that the vectors of VN and AN idioms are less similar to the vectors of lexical variants of these expressions with respect to the vectors of compositional constructions. (Cordeiro et al., 2019) realized a framework for predict compound compositionality using DSMs, evaluating to what extent they capture idiomaticity compared to human judgments. Results revealed a high agreement between the models and human predictions, suggesting that they are able to incorporate information about idiomaticity.

In future works, it would be interesting to see if DSMs-based approaches can be used in combination with methods for the identification of the formal features of constructions (Dunn, 2017, 2019), in order to tackle the task of compositionality prediction simultaneously with syntactic and semantic features.

Modeling sentence comprehension A trend in computational semantics regards the application of DSMs to sentence processing (Mitchell et al., 2010; Lenci, 2011; Sayeed et al., 2015; Johns and Jones, 2015, i.a.).

Chersoni et al. (2016, 2017) propose a Distributional Model of sentence comprehension inspired by the general principles of the Memory, Unification and Control framework (Hagoort, 2013, 2015). The memory component includes events in GEK with feature structures containing information directly extracted from parsed sentences in corpora: attributes are syntactic dependencies, while values are distributional vectors of dependent lexemes. Then, they model semantic composition as an event construction and update function F, whose aim is to build a coherent semantic representation by integrating the GEK cued by the linguistic elements.

The framework has been applied to the logical metonymy phenomenon (e.g, *The student begins the book*), using the semantic complexity function to model the processing costs of metonymic sentences, which was shown to be higher compared to non-coercion sentences (McElree et al., 2001; Traxler et al., 2002). Evaluation against psycholinguistic datasets proves the linguistic and

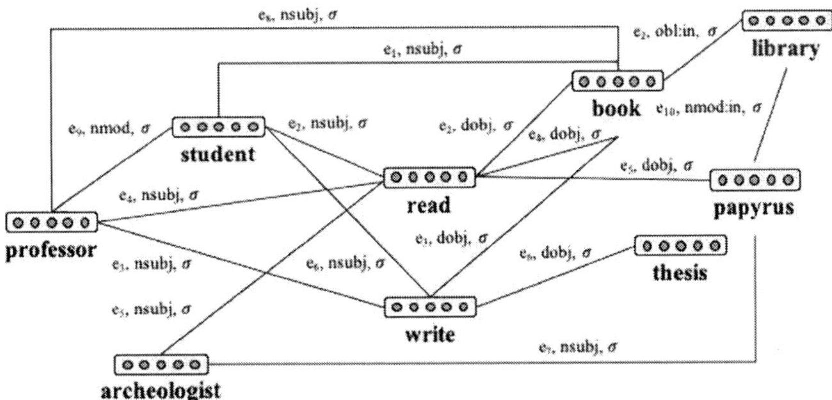

Figure 6: An extract of DEG showing several instances of events (Chersoni et al., 2019)

psycholinguistic validity of using embeddings to represent events and including them in incremental model of sentence comprehension.

Evaluations based on experimental evidence DSMs have proved to be very useful in modeling human performance in psycholinguistic tasks (Mandera et al., 2017). This is an important finding, since it allows to test the predictions of Construction Grammar theories against data derived from behavioral experiments.

To cite an example from the DS literature, the models proposed by Lebani and Lenci (2017) replicated the priming effect of the lexical decision task by Johnson and Goldberg (2013), where the participants were asked to judge whether a given verb was a real word or not, after being exposed to an argument structure construction in the form of a Jabberwocky sentence. The authors of the study created distributional representations of constructions as combinations of the vectors of their typical verbs, and measured their cosine similarity with the verbs of the original experiment, showing that their model can accurately reproduce the results reported by Johnson and Goldberg (2013).

5 Conclusion

In this paper, we investigated the potential contribution of DSMs to the semantic representation of constructions, and we presented a theoretical proposal bringing together vector spaces and constructions into a unique framework. It is worth highlighting our main contributions:

- We built a unified representation of grammar and meaning based on the assumption that language structure and properties emerge from language use.

- We integrated information about events to build a semantic representation of an input as an incremental and predictive process.

Converging different layers of meaning representation into a unique framework is not a trivial problem, and in our future work we will need to find optimal ways to balance these two components: semantic vectors derived from corpus data on the one hand, and a possibly accurate formalization of the internal structure of the constructions on the other hand. In this contribution, we hoped to show that merging the two frameworks would be worth the efforts, as they share many theoretical assumptions and complement themselves on the basis of their respective strengths.

Our future goal is the automatic building and inclusion of a distributional representation of frames and event in DisCxG; our aim is to exploit the final formalism to build for the first time a *Distributional Construction Treebank*. Moreover, we are planning to apply this framework in a predictive model of language comprehension, defining how a Cx is activated by the combination of syntactic, lexical and distributional cues occurring in DisCxG. We believe this framework could be a starting point for applications in NLP such as Knowledge representation and reasoning, Natural Language Understanding and Generation, but also a potential term of comparison for psycholinguistic models of human language comprehension.

References

Afra Alishahi and Suzanne Stevenson. 2008. A Computational Model of Early Argument Structure Acquisition. *Cognitive Science*, 32(5):789–834.

Irene Amato and Alessandro Lenci. 2017. Story of a Construction: Statistical and Distributional Analysis of the Development of the Italian Gerundival Construction. In G. Marotta and F. S. Lievers, editors, *Strutture Linguistiche e Dati Empirici in Diacronia e Sincronia*, pages 135–158. Pisa University Press.

Collin F Baker. 2012. FrameNet, Current Collaborations and Future Goals. *Language, Resources and Evaluation*, 46(2):269–286.

Collin F. Baker, Charles J. Fillmore, and John B. Lowe. 1998. The Berkeley FrameNet project. In *Proceedings of COLING-ACL*, pages 86–90, Montreal, Canada. ACL.

Libby Barak and Adele Goldberg. 2017. Modeling the Partial Productivity of Constructions. In *Proceeedings of the 2017 AAAI Spring Symposium Series on Computational Construction Grammar and Natural Language Understanding*, pages 131–138.

Marco Baroni, Raffaela Bernardi, and Roberto Zamparelli. 2014. Frege in Space: A Program of Compositional Distributional Semantics. *Linguistic Issues in Language Technology*, 9(6):5–110.

Marco Baroni and Alessandro Lenci. 2010. Distributional Memory: A General Framework for Corpus-Based Semantics. *Computational Linguistics*, 36(4):673–721.

Philippe Blache. 2005. Property Grammars: A Fully Constraint-Based Theory. In Skadhauge P. R. Christiansen, H. and J. Villadsen, editors, *Constraint Solving and Language Processing. CSLP 2004*, volume 3438 of *LNAI*, pages 1–16. Springer, Berlin, Heidelberg.

Philippe Blache. 2016. Representing Syntax by Means of Properties: A Formal Framework for Descriptive Approaches. *Journal of Language Modelling*, 4(2):183–224.

Teresa Botschen, Hatem Mouss**elly Sergieh, and Iryna Gurevych. 2017. Prediction of Frame-to-Frame Relations in the FrameNet Hierarchy with Frame Embeddings. In *Proceedings of the ACL Workshop on Representation Learning for NLP*, pages 146–156.

Joyce Tang Boyland. 2009. Usage-Based Models of Language. In D. Eddington, editor, *Experimental and Quantitative Linguistics*, pages 351–419. Lincom, Munich.

Lucia Busso, Ludovica Pannitto, and Alessandro Lenci. 2018. Modelling Italian Construction Flexibility with Distributional Semantics: Are Constructions Enough? In *Proceedings of the Fifth Italian Conference on Computational Linguistics (CLiC-it 2018)*, pages 68–74.

J. Bybee. 2010. *Language, Usage and Cognition.* Cambridge University Press.

Devin Casenhiser and Adele E Goldberg. 2005. Fast Mapping Between a Phrasal Form and Meaning. *Developmental science*, 8(6):500–508.

Emmanuele Chersoni, Philippe Blache, and Alessandro Lenci. 2016. Towards a Distributional Model of Semantic Complexity. In *Proceedings of the COLING Workshop on Computational Linguistics for Linguistic Complexity (CL4LC)*, pages 12–22.

Emmanuele Chersoni, Alessandro Lenci, and Philippe Blache. 2017. Logical Metonymy in a Distributional Model of Sentence Comprehension. In *Proceedings of *SEM*, pages 168–177.

Emmanuele Chersoni, Enrico Santus, Ludovica Pannitto, Alessandro Lenci, Philippe Blache, and Chu-Ren Huang. 2019. A Structured Distributional Model of Sentence Meaning and Processing. *Journal of Natural Language Engineering*. To Appear.

Silvio Cordeiro, Aline Villavicencio, Marco Idiart, and Carlos Ramisch. 2019. Unsupervised Compositionality Prediction of Nominal Compounds. *Computational Linguistics*, 45:1–57.

Jonathan Dunn. 2017. Computational Learning of Construction Grammars. *Language and Cognition*, 9(2):254–292.

Jonathan Dunn. 2019. Frequency vs. Association for Constraint Selection in Usage-Based Construction Grammar. In *Proceedings of the NAACL Workshop on Cognitive Modeling and Computational Linguistics.*

Jeffrey L. Elman. 2014. Systematicity in the Lexicon: On Having Your Cake and Eating It Too. In Paco Calvo and John Symons, editors, *The Architecture of Cognition*, pages 115–145. The MIT Press.

Katrin Erk, Sebastian Padó, and Ulrike Padó. 2010. A Flexible, Corpus-Driven Model of Regular and Inverse Selectional Preferences. *Computational Linguistics*, 36(4):723–763.

Charles J. Fillmore. 1982. Frame Semantics. *Linguistics in the Morning Calm*, pages 111–37.

Charles J Fillmore. 1988. The Mechanisms of Construction Grammar. *Annual Meeting of the Berkeley Linguistics Society*, 14:35–55.

Adele E. Goldberg. 1999. The Emergence of the Semantics of Argument Structure Constructions. In B. MacWhinney, editor, *The Emergence of Language*, pages 197–212. Lawrence Erlbaum Publications, Hillsdale, NJ.

Adele E. Goldberg. 2003. Constructions: A New Theoretical Approach to Language. *Trends in Cognitive Sciences*, 7(5):219–224.

Adele E Goldberg. 2006. *Constructions at Work: The Nature of Generalization in Language.* Oxford University Press on Demand.

Edward Grefenstette and Mehrnoosh Sadrzadeh. 2015. Concrete Models and Empirical Evaluations for the Categorical Compositional Distributional Model of Meaning. *Computational Linguistics*, 41(1):71–118.

Stefan Th. Gries and Anatol Stefanowitsch. 2004. Extending Collostructional Analysis. A Corpus-Based Perspective on 'Alternations'. *International Journal of Corpus Linguistics*, 9(1):97–129.

Peter Hagoort. 2013. MUC (Memory, Unification, Control) and Beyond. *Frontiers in Psychology*, 4:1–13.

Peter Hagoort. 2015. MUC (Memory, Unification, Control): A Model on the Neurobiology of Language Beyond Single Word Processing. In *Neurobiology of language*, pages 339–347. Elsevier.

Zellig S. Harris. 1954. Distributional Structure. *Word*, 10:146–62.

Thomas Hoffman and Graeme Trousdale, editors. 2013. *The Oxford Handbook of Construction Grammar*. Oxford University Press, Oxford.

Brendan T Johns and Michael N Jones. 2015. Generating Structure from Experience: A Retrieval-Based Model of Language Processing. *Canadian Journal of Experimental Psychology*, 69(3):233–251.

Matt A. Johnson and Adele E. Goldberg. 2013. Evidence for Automatic Accessing of Constructional Meaning: Jabberwocky Sentences Prime Associated Verbs. *Language and Cognitive Processes*, 28(10):1439–1452.

Katharina Kann, Alex Warstadt, Adina Williams, and Samuel R Bowman. 2019. Verb Argument Structure Alternations in Word and Sentence Embeddings. In *Proceedings of the Society for Computation in Linguistics (SCiL) 2019*, pages 287–297.

Gina R. Kuperberg and T. Florian Jaeger. 2015. What Do We Mean by Prediction in Language Comprehension? *Language Cognition & Neuroscience*, 3798.

Gianluca E Lebani and Alessandro Lenci. 2017. Modelling the Meaning of Argument Constructions with Distributional Semantics. In *Proceedings of the AAAI 2017 Spring Symposium on Computational Construction Grammar and Natural Language Understanding*, pages 197–204.

Gianluca E. Lebani and Alessandro Lenci. 2018. A Distributional Model of Verb-Specific Semantic Roles Inferences. In Thierry Poibeau and Aline Villavicencio, editors, *Language, Cognition, and Computational Models*, pages 118–158. Cambridge University Press, Cambridge.

Alessandro Lenci. 2011. Composing and Updating Verb Argument Expectations: A Distributional Semantic Model. In *Proceedings of the ACL Workshop on Cognitive Modeling and Computational Linguistics*, pages 58–66.

Alessandro Lenci. 2018. Distributional Models of Word Meaning. *Annual Review of Linguistics*, 4(1):151–171.

Natalia Levshina and Kris Heylen. 2014. A Radically Data-Driven Construction Grammar: Experiments with Dutch Causative Constructions. In R. Boogaart, T. Colleman, and Rutten G., editors, *Extending the Scope of Construction Grammar*, pages 17–46. Mouton de Gruyter, Berlin.

Paweł Mandera, Emmanuel Keuleers, and Marc Brysbaert. 2017. Explaining Human Performance in Psycholinguistic Tasks with Models of Semantic Similarity Based on Prediction and Counting: A Review and Empirical Validation. *Journal of Memory and Language*, 92:57–78.

Brian McElree, Matthew J Traxler, Martin J Pickering, Rachel E Seely, and Ray Jackendoff. 2001. Reading Time Evidence for Enriched Composition. *Cognition*, 78(1):B17–B25.

Ken McRae and Kazunaga Matsuki. 2009. People Use their Knowledge of Common Events to Understand Language, and Do So as Quickly as Possible. *Language and Linguistics Compass*, 3(6):1417–1429.

Laura A Michaelis. 2013. Sign-Based Construction Grammar. In *The Oxford Handbook of Construction Grammar*, pages 133–152, Oxford. Oxford University Press.

Tomas Mikolov, Ilya Sutskever, Kai Chen, Greg Corrado, and Jeffrey Dean. 2013. Distributed Representations of Words and Phrases and their Compositionality. In *Advances in Neural Information Processing Systems (NIPS 2013)*, pages 3111–3119.

Jeff Mitchell, Mirella Lapata, Vera Demberg, and Frank Keller. 2010. Syntactic and Semantic Factors in Processing Difficulty: An Integrated Measure. In *Proceedings of ACL*, pages 196–206, Uppsala, Sweden. ACL.

Martin Paczynski and Gina R. Kuperberg. 2012. Multiple Influences of Semantic Memory on Sentence Processing: Distinct Effects of Semantic Relatedness on Violations of Real-World Event/State Knowledge and Animacy Selection Restrictions. *J Memory and Language*, 67(4).

Florent Perek. 2016. Using Distributional Semantics to Study Syntactic Productivity in Diachrony: A Case Study. *Linguistics*, 54(1):149–188.

Florent Perek. 2018. Recent Change in the Productivity and Schematicity of the Way-Construction: A Distributional Semantic Analysis. *Corpus Linguistics and Linguistic Theory*, 14(1):65–97.

Josef Ruppenhofer, Michael Ellsworth, Myriam Schwarzer-Petruck, Christopher R Johnson, and Jan Scheffczyk. 2016. *FrameNet II: Extended Theory and Practice*.

Ivan A Sag. 2012. Sign-Based Construction Grammar: An Informal Synopsis. In *Sign-based construction grammar*, volume 193, pages 69–202. CSLI: CSLI Publications.

Enrico Santus, Emmanuele Chersoni, Alessandro Lenci, and Philippe Blache. 2017. Measuring Thematic Fit with Distributional Feature Overlap. In *Proceedings of EMNLP*, pages 648–658.

Asad Sayeed, Stefan Fischer, and Vera Demberg. 2015. Vector-Space Calculation of Semantic Surprisal for Predicting Word Pronunciation Duration. In *Proceedings of ACL-IJCNLP*, pages 763–773, Beijing, China. ACL.

Asad Sayeed, Clayton Greenberg, and Vera Demberg. 2016. Thematic Fit Evaluation: An Aspect of Selectional Preferences. In *Proceedings of the ACL Workshop on Evaluating Vector-Space Representations for NLP*, pages 99–105.

Marco Silvio Giuseppe Senaldi, Gianluca E Lebani, and Alessandro Lenci. 2016. Lexical Variability and Compositionality: Investigating Idiomaticity with Distributional Semantic Models. In *Proceedings of the ACL Workshop on Multiword Expressions*, pages 21–31.

Jennifer Sikos and Sebastian Padó. 2018. Using Embeddings to Compare FrameNet Frames Across Languages. In *Proceedings of the COLING Workshop on Linguistic Resources for Natural Language Processing*, pages 91–101.

Michael Tommasello. 2003. *Constructing a Language: A Usage-Based Theory of Language Acquisition*. Harvard University Press, Cambridge, MA.

Matthew J Traxler, Martin J Pickering, and Brian McElree. 2002. Coercion in Sentence Processing: Evidence from Eye-Movements and Self-Paced Reading. *Journal of Memory and Language*, 47(4):530–547.

Dmitry Ustalov, Alexander Panchenko, Andrei Kutuzov, Chris Biemann, and Simone Paolo Ponzetto. 2018. Unsupervised Semantic Frame Induction Using Triclustering. In *Proceedings of ACL*, pages 55–62.

Kristian Woodsend and Mirella Lapata. 2015. Distributed Representations for Unsupervised Semantic Role Labeling. In *Proceedings of EMNLP*, pages 2482–2491.

Meaning Representation of Null-Instantiated Semantic Roles in FrameNet

Miriam R. L. Petruck
International Computer Science Institute
Berkeley, CA 94704
`miriamp@icsi.berkeley.edu`

Abstract

Humans have the unique ability to infer information about participants in a scene, even if they are not mentioned in a text about that scene. Computer systems cannot do so without explicit information about those participants. This paper addresses the linguistic phenomenon of null-instantiated frame elements, i.e., implicit semantic roles, and their representation in FrameNet (FN). It motivates FN's annotation practice, and illustrates the three types of null-instantiated arguments that FrameNet tracks, noting that other lexical resources do not record such semantic-pragmatic information, despite its need in natural language understanding (NLU), and the elaborate efforts to create new datasets. It challenges the community to appeal to FN data to develop more sophisticated techniques for recognizing implicit semantic roles, and creating needed datasets. While the annotation of null-instantiated roles was lexicographically motivated, FN provides useful information for text processing, and therefore it must be considered in the design of any meaning representation for NLU.

1 Introduction

Null instantiation as a linguistic phenomenon has received much attention in the literature on verbal argument structure. Fillmore (1986) identified idiosyncrasies of lexically licensed null arguments in near-synonymous verbs. Resnik (1996) explained the phenomenon in terms of selectional restirictions; Rapaport Hovav and Levin (1998) invoke Aktionsart. Others (Ruppenhofer and Baker 2003, Ruppenhofer and Michaelis 2014) appeal to frames or constructions.

Aside from verbal argument structure, the discourse in which a sentence occurs also may license an omission. Ruppenhofer et al. (2010) initiated the task of linking events and their participants in discourse, with participating systems yielding different degrees of success. Roth and Lapata (2015) introduced techniques for semantic role labeling that use various discourse level features in an effort to identify implicit roles. With semantic role labeling (SRL) usually limited to sentence level analysis, the conundrum of identifying something absent from a text is clear, more so when the major resources do not identify or record information about implicit roles.

Efforts to create resources to use in work on developing techniques for recognizing implicit semantic roles have not yielded large datasets. For the SemEval task, Ruppenhofer et al. (2010) annotated 500 sentences from a novel. Studying nominal predicates, Gerber and Chai (2010, 2012) created a dataset of 1000 examples from NomBank (Meyers et al. 2004). Roth and Frank (2015) aligned monolingual comparable texts to obtain implicit arguments, resulting in a dataset similar in size to previous datasets. Recently, Cheng and Erk (2018) used coreference information to generate additional training data; Cheng and Erk (2019) addressed the problem using an approach to generate data that scales.

Despite the need, no work addresses resources that record null instantiations (because most do not), or the representation of null-instantiated semantic roles.[1] This paper begins to fill the gap by bringing attention to FrameNet's practice of recording information about null-instantiated semantic roles, i.e., representing the meaning of omitted arguments, a practice that no other major lexical resource observes. It also challenges the broad NLP/NLU community of resource builders, designers of linguistic annotation and meaning

---

[1] The call for papers for this workshop did not mention FrameNet, even though its a recognized resource in NLP precisely because of the way that it represents meaning, i.e. via frames and various frame features (e.g., Smith 2017).

Proceedings of the First International Workshop on Designing Meaning Representations, pages 121–127
Florence, Italy, August 1st, 2019 ©2019 Association for Computational Linguistics

representation schemes, as well as developers of SRL systems to exploit and expand the data that FrameNet already provides.

The rest of the paper proceeds as follows: Section 2 provides background to FN, and describes the goals of the projects meaning representation; Section 3 covers null instantiation in FN, provides example sentences including annotation, illustrating how FN implements its desiderata; Section 4 presents a challenge to the NLP community; and Section 5 summarizes the paper, addressing some limitations of FrameNet.

2 Background to FrameNet

2.1 General Information

FrameNet (Ruppenhofer et al. 2016) is a research and resource development project in corpus-based computational lexicography project based on the principles of Frame Semantics (Fillmore 1985), whose goal is documenting the valences, i.e., the syntactic and semantic combinatorial possibilities of each item analyzed. These valence descriptions provide critical information on the mapping between form and meaning that NLP and NLU require. At the heart of the work is the semantic frame, a script-like knowledge structure that facilitates inferencing within and across events, situations, states-of-affairs, relations, and objects. FN defines a semantic frame in terms of its frame elements (FEs), or participants in the scene that the frame captures; a lexical unit (LU) is a pairing of a lemma and a frame, characterizing that LU in terms of the frame that it evokes.

To illustrate, FrameNet has defined `Revenge` as a situation in which an AVENGER[2] performs a PUNISHMENT on an OFFENDER as a response to a PUNISHMENT, inflicted on an INJURED_PARTY; and these core frame elements uniquely define the frame. Among the LUs in `Revenge` are *avenge.v, avenger.n, get even.v, retributory.a, revenge.v, revenge.n, vengeance.n, vengeful.a, and vindictive.a*, where nouns, verbs, and adjectives are included. The linguistic realization of each frame element highlights different participants of the frame, as shown in sentence #1, where the target of the analysis is the verb *avenge*.[3]

____

[2]Frame names appear in `Typewriter` font; and frame element names appear in SMALL CAPS.

[3]For convenience only, examples in this paper are of verbs as predicators, which appear in **bold** font.

1. (Peter AVENGER) **avenged** (the attack on the boys PUNISHMENT).

Sentence #1 illustrates the instantiation of two of the frames core frame elements: the proper noun *Peter* is the AVENGER and the NP *the attack on the boys* is the PUNISHMENT. No other core FEs of the `Revenge` frame is instantiated in the sentence.

2.2 Meaning Representation in FrameNet

FrameNet's ultimate goal is the representation of the lexical semantics of every sentence in a text based on the relations between predicators and their dependents, which include clauses and phrases that also include predicators (Fillmore and Baker 2001, Baker et al. 2007: 100). FrameNet's meaning representation for these predicators was designed in accord with the principles of Frame Semantics (Fillmore 1985). For each LU that FN analyzes (annotates), the goal is to identify the linguistic material that instantiates the frame elements of the given frame, and then characterize the grammatical function and phrase type of that material. Note that annotated FEs are actually triples of information about the annotated constituent, not simply information about the constituent's semantic role. Importantly, meaning and form are inextricably tied together, where each contributes its part to characterization of the whole. Table 1 shows the FE identified as PUNISHMENT (example # 1), as a triple of information.

the attack on the boys	
Frame Element (FE)	PUNISHMENT
Grammatical Function	Object
Phrase Type	NP

Table 1: FE as Triple of Information

The goal of providing a valence description for each lexical unit that FN analyzes necessitates recording information about omitted arguments. FN characterizes the syntactic and semantic conditions under which an omission is possible. For sentence # 1, FrameNet's lexicographic purposes require recording information about OFFENDER and PUNISHMENT, two *lexically* licensed null-instantiations (Fillmore 2007).[4]

____

[4]FN supports second layer annotation, and in this case would annotate the PP *on the boys* as the INJURED_PARTY.

3 Null-Instantiation (NI) in FrameNet

FN annotates information about the conceptually required semantic roles, i.e., the core FEs of a frame, even if absent from the text. FN records three types of null-instantiation, one licensed by a construction, and the others licensed lexically. FrameNet includes approximately 55,700 NI labels in its annotations; and some 26% of the omissions are licensed consturctionally, with the remaining 76% licensed lexically.[5] This section very briefly addresses the first type, and then presents *lexically* licensed omissions.[6]

3.1 Constructional Null Instantiation

Constructional Null Instantiations are licensed by grammatical constructions. Examples of CNI are the omitted agent in a passive sentence (# 2), or the omitted subject in an imperative (# 3).

2. Sue was **avenged** by killing her assailant.
3. **Get even** with that bum.

In both sentences, the AVENGER is understood as a participant in the event, although not mentioned in the relevant clause (# 2) or sentence (# 3).

3.2 Definite Null Instantiation (DNI)

Definite Null Instantiation (DNI) identifies those missing core FEs that were mentioned previously in the text or can be understood, that is, inferred from the discourse. Consider examples # 4–5 as two contiguous lines of text, where information about a null-instantiated core FE appears in the context of the relevant piece of text, allowing the language user to infer the missing argument. Encountering # 5 signals the language user to refer back to information in # 4.

4. Wendy was **astonished** (at the killing of the pirate PUNISHMENT).
5. (Peter AVENGER) had **avenged** (the attack on the boys PUNISHMENT).

Ziem (2013, 2014) demonstrated that DNIs in spoken discourse tend to be specified in adjacent sentences, and thus also showed the relevance of frames to text coherence.

3.3 Indefinite Null Instantiation (INI)

Indefinite Null Instantiation (INI) is the other lexically specific licensed omission, and it is illustrated with the missing objects of verbs such as eat, bake, and sew. These verbs are usually transitive, but can be used intransitively (# 6–# 7).

6. Let's go out to **eat**.
7. Sam took his time **baking**.

With such verbs, language users understand the nature of the missing material without referring back to any previously mentioned entity in the discourse. In # 6 speakers will understand that the omitted object is consumable food. Cheng and Erks (2019) recent study about implicit arguments draws on event knowledge to predict the semantic roles of omitted arguments. The work also relies upon the (psycho-linguistic) notions of entity salience and text coherence for building a computational model.

Recording null instantiation offers the ability to distinguish multiple senses of a lemma, as is apparent with different senses of the verb *give*, as 8b and 9b show.[7]

8. **GIVE** as donate
   (a) Let's talk to the Red Cross.
   (b) I already **gave**.

9. **GIVE** as gift
   (a) I **gave** Sue a birthday present.
   (b) *I already **gave**.

Thus, only the donation sense of *give* allows omitting the object; but *give* meaning gift someone a present does not. Only for the donation sense of *give* does FN record example 8b as having a null-instantiated object.

3.4 Complicating Factors

FN's concept of a CoreSet adds to the challenge of automatically recognizing null instantiations. Given a set of two or more core FEs in a frame, annotating just one of them satisfies FN's requirements. For example, SOURCE, PATH, and GOAL are core FEs in motion-related frames; however not all of these FEs always manifest in every sentence that describes a motion event.

Consider example 10, an instance of the Self_motion frame, which defines a scene in

---

[5]Clearly, providing the total number of sentences would be ideal; obtaining that number is not straightforward.

[6]A full treatment of grammatical constructions is well beyond the scope of this paper. Explicit grammatical information, some of which a syntactically-parsed corpus might provide, would aid in the identification of CNIs. Still, the automatic recognition of constructions is in a relatively early stage of development (e.g., Dunietz 2018, Dunietz et al. 2017).

[7]These data derive from a presentation by Fillmore at Boeing in 2001.

which the SELF-MOVER, a living being, moves under its own direction along a PATH.

10. (Chuck SELF-MOVER) walked (to the BART station GOAL).

In 10, of the CoreSet FEs, only the GOAL is realized; FN annotates the PP *to the BART station* as the GOAL, along with *Chuck* as the SELF-MOVER, and considers its job done (for that sentence).

Given a CoreSet, annotating just one of its members is legitimate; however, it does not preclude annotating more than one of the FEs. Thus, FN would annotate the PATH and the GOAL FEs in 11.

11. (Chuck SELF-MOVER) walked (along Center Street PATH) (to the BART station GOAL).

This state-of-affairs complicates matters for the recognition of null instantiations, as (so far) other than listing CoreSet FEs in the frame definition, FN does not directly record null-instantiated CoreSet FEs with its annotated data. although the information is available via the frame element-to-frame element relations within a frame.

Additionally, lexical semantic and pragmatic phenomena contribute to the way that FrameNet distinguishes between **INI**) and (**DNI**), as Ruppenhofer et al. (2010) among others have noted. To illustrate, sentence 12 exemplifies the `Similarity` frame, in which ENTITY_1, ENTITY_2, and DIMENSION are core FEs. While FN records ENTITY_2 as DNI, it records DIMENSION as INI. Since the interpretation of the sentence relies on the accessibility of ENTITY_2 to the language user, that FE is a DNI.

12. The split went in a **different** direction.... (ENTITY_2 DNI) (DIMENSION INI)

In contrast, simply knowing that ENTITY_1 and ENTITY_2 differ along some DIMENSION, a specific prior mention in the text or surrounding discourse is not necessary to interpret the sentence. As such, FN records DIMENSION as an INI.

Furthermore, (assumed) prior mention in a text, i.e., beyond the boundary of the single sentence, might suggest the likelihood of a DNI interpretation. However, not all lexical items will license the same FE omission. For example, although both are defined in terms of the `Arriving` frame, *arrive*.v licenses the omission of the GOAL, while *reach*.v does not, as examples 14 and 13 show.

13. Seymour **arrived** [DNI GOAL]

14. * Seymour **reached**

3.5 Other Lexical Resources

The comparison with other lexical resources is warranted given the impetus to feature one of FN's many differentiating characteristics. No major lexical resource records information about lexically licensed implicit semantic roles.

PropBank (Palmer et al. 2005) has annotated a corpus of text with information about basic semantic propositions, also adding predicate-argument relations to the syntactic trees of the Penn Treebank. PropBank also created parallel PropBank resources for other languages and genres. It then moved on to annotate light verb constructions in multiple languages (Hwang et al. 2010). Note that PropBanks traces only record syntactically motivated omissions, not lexically licensed ones (Ellsworth et al. 2004). VerbNet (Kipper-Schuler 2005, Kipper et al. 2006) is a very large lexicon of verbs in English that extends Levin (1993) with explicitly stated syntactic and semantic information. It provides mapping to other resources, including to WordNet senses (Fellbaum 1998) and FrameNet frames. However, it does not include any information on null-instantiated arguments.

In short, the well-known and oft-used resources for text processing simply do not include the requisite information, and hence the ongoing need for researchers to construct new datasets.

4 A Challenge for the Community

Recent advances in the development of semantic role labeling (SRL) systems (e.g., Swayamdipta et al. 2018) offer the prospect of automating more of FrameNet's process (than at present), specifically the annotation of frame elements (i.e., semantic roles). Such SRL systems are based on existing annotated FN data, and exploit a range of different machine learning techniques (Das et al., 2014, Hermann et al. 2014, Kshirsagar et al., 2015, Tckstrm et al., 2015, among others). Not surprisingly, none of these systems attempt recognizing null-instantiated frame elements, not least in part due to the difficulty of the task. Still the needed data for doing so is available in the FN database, even if limited. Instead, these systems quietly ignore the presence of the null-instantiated information.

Efforts to identify implicit semantic roles, whether definite or indefinite null instantiations, tend to create limited data sets and focus on the different and new computational techniques that (may) improve the results (as briefly characterized in 1). Nevertheless, the need remains for more data on implicit semantic roles, both to facilitate the ability to recognize these null instantiated elements and to advance the goals of SRL, as well as those of FrameNet in the long term.

As a consequence, the current work calls for the community to partner with FrameNet with the goal of designing a task that exploits the recorded NI information in the database. For example, the task might include developing a new data set that distinguishes null-instantiated CoreSet FEs from other core FEs, thereby eliminating one of the complicating factors in using the FN corpus. Also, comparing results (of NI-recognition) between the new corpus and the existing corpus (of FN's NI data) may yield useful information for future investigation. Of course, the technical details of such a task have yet to be specified. However, by garnering the collective experience of the broad NLP and NLU community, especially those who work with FN data already, FrameNet will be poised to investigate the potential benefit of using the data and to measure that benefit to determine its value.

5   Summary

This paper has focused on the representation of the linguistic phenomenon of null-instantiated core frame elements, i.e., implicit semantic roles, and their representation in FN. It introduced the basic concepts of FrameNet, illustrated the types of null instantiation for which FN provides information, acknowledging the lexicographically motivated annotation practice, and urged the community to leverage existing data in the FN database. Finally, it also advocates for the design of meaning representations explicitly reference null instantiation. The ubiquity of the phenomenon in language language demands doing so.[8]

FrameNet's developers are not impervious to the complexities and FN-specific data format and annotation practice that resulted in an apparently inhospitable resource. Recall the concept of a CoreSet, which interacts with FN's annotation of NIs (as illustrated in 3.4). Also, while the NLTK FrameNet API allows access to NI information by annotation set in a given frame, it does not have a built-in function to query the database by valence pattern (Schneider and Wooters 2017). As a consequence, actually finding NIs is not as easy as would be desirable. Also, as others have indicated already, gaps in coverage play a role in the performance of systems that use FrameNet for different applications (e.g., Palmer and Sporleder 2010).

The design of meaning representations for achieving natural language understanding must include the representation of null-instantiated roles. Exploiting an existing semantically rich resource to jump-start a critical aspect of the work is expedient; appealing to FrameNet is essential.

Acknowledgements

The author is grateful to Collin Baker, Michael Ellsworth, and Dmetri Hayes, current members of the FrameNet team, for their helpful input, as well as to a few *honorary* members of the team, specifically Josef Ruppenhofer, Nathan Schneider, and Swabha Swayamdipta. The current version of this work also benefited from reviewer feedback.

References

Collin Baker, Michael Ellsworth, and Katrin Erk. 2007. Semeval'07 task 19: Frame semantic structure extraction. In *Proceedings of the 4th International Workshop on Semantic Evaluations*, SemEval '07, pages 99–104, Stroudsburg, PA, USA. Association for Computational Linguistics.

Collin F. Baker and Josef Ruppenhofer. 2002. FrameNet's frames vs. levin's verb classes. In *Proceedings of 28th Annual Meeting of the Berkeley Linguistics Society*, pages 27–38.

Pengxiang Cheng and Katrin Erk. 2018a. Implicit argument prediction as reading comprehension. *CoRR*, abs/1811.03554.

Pengxiang Cheng and Katrin Erk. 2018b. Implicit argument prediction with event knowledge. In *Proceedings of the 2018 Conference of the North American Chapter of the Association for Computational Linguistics: Human Language Technologies, Volume 1 (Long Papers)*, pages 831–840, New Orleans, Louisiana. Association for Computational Linguistics.

Dipanjan Das, Desai Chen, Andr F. T. Martins, Nathan Schneider, and Noah A. Smith. 2014. Frame-semantic parsing. *Computational Linguistics*, 40(1):9–56.

Jesse Dunietz. 2018. *Annotating and Automatically Tagging Constructions of Causal Language*. Ph.D. thesis, Carnegie Mellon University, Pittsburgh, PA.

---

[8]For example, Ruppenhofer et al. 2010 reported that null-instantiated FEs constituted nearly 20% of the data.

Jesse Dunietz, Lori Levin, and Jaime Carbonell. 2017. The BECauSE corpus 2.0: Annotating causality and overlapping relations. In *Proceedings of the 11th Linguistic Annotation Workshop*, pages 95–104, Valencia, Spain. Association for Computational Linguistics.

M. Ellsworth, K. Erk, P. Kingsbury, and S. Pado. 2004. PropBank, SALSA and FrameNet: How design determines product. In *Proceedings of the Workshop on Building Lexical Resources From Semantically Annotated Corpora, LREC-2004*, Lisbon.

Christiane Fellbaum, editor. 1998. *WordNet: an electronic lexical database*. MIT Press, Cambridge.

C. J. Fillmore. 2007. Valency issues in framenet. In *Valency: Theoretical, Descriptive and Cognitive Issues*, pages 29–160. Mouton de Gruyter, Berlin and New York.

Charles J. Fillmore. 1985. Frames and the semantics of understanding. *Quaderni di Semantica*, 6(2):222–254.

Charles J. Fillmore. 1986. Pragmatically controlled zero anaphora. In *Proceedings of the Twelfth Annual Meeting of the Berkeley Linguistics Society*, pages 95–107.

Charles J. Fillmore and Collin F. Baker. 2001. Frame semantics for text understanding. In *Proceedings of WordNet and Other Lexical Resources Workshop*, Pittsburgh. NAACL, NAACL.

Matthew Gerber and Joyce Y. Chai. 2012. Semantic role labeling of implicit arguments for nominal predicates. *Computational Linguistics*, 38(4):755–798.

Matthew Gerber and Joyce Yue Chai. 2010. Beyond nombank: A study of implicit arguments for nominal predicates. In *ACL 2010, Proceedings of the 48th Annual Meeting of the Association for Computational Linguistics, July 11-16, 2010, Uppsala, Sweden*, pages 1583–1592.

Karl Moritz Hermann, Dipanjan Das, Jason Weston, and Kuzman Ganchev. 2014. Semantic frame identification with distributed word representations. In *Proceedings of the 52nd Annual Meeting of the Association for Computational Linguistics, ACL 2014, June 22-27, 2014, Baltimore, MD, USA, Volume 1: Long Papers*, pages 1448–1458.

Jena D. Hwang, Archna Bhatia, Claire Bonial, Aous Mansouri, Ashwini Vaidya, Nianwen Xue, and Martha Palmer. 2010. Propbank annotation of multilingual light verb constructions. In *Proceedings of the Fourth Linguistic Annotation Workshop, LAW 2010, Uppsala, Sweden, July 15-16, 2010*, pages 82–90.

Karin Kipper, Anna Korhonen, Neville Ryant, and Martha Palmer. 2006. Extending verbnet with novel verb classes. In *Proceedings of the Fifth International Conference on Language Resources and Evaluation, LREC 2006, Genoa, Italy, May 22-28, 2006.*, pages 1027–1032.

Meghana Kshirsagar, Sam Thomson, Nathan Schneider, Jaime G. Carbonell, Noah A. Smith, and Chris Dyer. 2015. Frame-semantic role labeling with heterogeneous annotations. In *Proceedings of the 53rd Annual Meeting of the Association for Computational Linguistics and the 7th International Joint Conference on Natural Language Processing of the Asian Federation of Natural Language Processing, ACL 2015, July 26-31, 2015, Beijing, China, Volume 2: Short Papers*, pages 218–224.

Beth Levin. 1993. *English Verb Classes and Alternations: A Preliminary Investigation*. University of Chicago Press, Chicago, IL.

Adam Meyers, Ruth Reeves, Catherine Macleod, Rachel Szekely, Veronika Zielinska, Brian Young, and Ralph Grishman. 2004. Annotating noun argument structure for nombank. In *Proceedings of the Fourth International Conference on Language Resources and Evaluation, LREC 2004, May 26-28, 2004, Lisbon, Portugal*.

Alexis Palmer and Caroline Sporleder. 2010. Evaluating framenet-style semantic parsing: the role of coverage gaps in framenet. In *COLING 2010, 23rd International Conference on Computational Linguistics, Posters Volume, 23-27 August 2010, Beijing, China*, pages 928–936.

Martha Palmer, Paul Kingsbury, and Daniel Gildea. 2005. The proposition bank: An annotated corpus of semantic roles. *Computational Linguistics*, 31(1):71–106.

Philip Resnik. 1996. Selectional constraints: an information-theoretic model and its computational realization. *Cognition*, 61:127–159.

Michael Roth and Anette Frank. 2015. Inducing implicit arguments from comparable texts: A framework and its applications. *Computational Linguistics*, 41(4):625–664.

Michael Roth and Mirella Lapata. 2015. Context-aware frame-semantic role labeling. *TACL*, 3:449–460.

Josef Ruppenhofer and Laura A. Michaelis. a. Building verb meanings. In *The Projection of Arguments: Lexical and Compositional Factors*, pages 97–134. CSLI Publication, Stanford, CA.

Josef Ruppenhofer and Laura A. Michaelis. b. Frames and the interpretation of omitted arguments. In *Linguistic Perspectives on Structure and Context: Studies in Honor of Knud Lambrecht*, pages 57–86. John Benjamins, Amsterdam and Philadelphia.

Josef Ruppenhofer, Caroline Sporleder, Roser Morante, Collin Baker, and Martha Palmer. 2010. Semeval-2010 task 10: Linking events and their participants in discourse. In *Proceedings of the 5th International Workshop on Semantic Evaluation, SemEval@ACL 2010, Uppsala University, Uppsala, Sweden, July 15-16, 2010*, pages 45–50.

Karin Kipper Schuler. 2005. *VerbNet: A broad-coverage, comprehensive verb lexicon*. Ph.D. thesis, University of Pennsylvania, Philadelphia.

Swabha Swayamdipta, Sam Thomson, Kenton Lee, Luke Zettlemoyer, Chris Dyer, and Noah A. Smith. 2018. Syntactic scaffolds for semantic structures. In *Proceedings of the 2018 Conference on Empirical Methods in Natural Language Processing, Brussels, Belgium, October 31 - November 4, 2018*, pages 3772–3782.

Oscar Täckström, Kuzman Ganchev, and Dipanjan Das. 2015. Efficient inference and structured learning for semantic role labeling. *TACL*, 3:29–41.

Alexander Ziem. 2013. Beyond the sentence: towards a cognitive-linguistic approach to textual reference. In *Yearbook of the German Cognitive Linguistic Association*, volume 1, pages 39–58, Berlin and New York. Mouton de Gruyter.

Alexander Ziem. 2014. *Frames of Understanding in Text and Discourse: Theoretical Foundations and Descriptive Applications*. John Benjamins, Amsterdam and Philadelphia.

Copula and Case-Stacking Annotations for Korean AMR

Hyonsu Choe[1], Jiyoon Han[1], Hyejin Park[2], Hansaem Kim[3†]

[1]Interdisciplinary Graduate Program of Linguistics and Informatics, Yonsei University, Seoul, South Korea
[2]Department of Korean Language and Literature, Yonsei University, Seoul, South Korea
[3]Institution of Language and Information Studies, Yonsei University, Seoul, South Korea
`{choehyonsu, clinamen35, hjp1010, khss}@.yonsei.ac.kr`

Abstract

This paper concerns the application of Abstract Meaning Representation (AMR) to Korean. In this regard, it focuses on the copula construction and its negation and the case-stacking phenomenon thereof. To illustrate this clearly, we reviewed the `:domain` annotation scheme from various perspectives. In this process, the existing annotation guidelines were improved to devise annotation schemes for each issue under the principle of pursuing consistency and efficiency of annotation without distorting the characteristics of Korean.

1 Introduction

Abstract Meaning Representation (AMR) (Banarescu et al., 2013) is a framework suitable for integrated semantic annotation. When localizing AMR annotation guidelines (Banarescu et al., 2018) for Korean, it is vital to maximize the use of existing annotation conventions widely accepted in English, Chinese, and other languages to ensure high compatibility between the AMR corpora of each language.

However, current AMR annotation guidelines are geared to English vocabulary and grammatical phenomena. Therefore, it is necessary to devise semantic annotation schemes for Korean AMR that reflect existing annotation guidelines as much as possible while accurately representing the characteristics of Korean. This paper reviews annotation methods for several grammatical phenomena that are the characteristics of Korean and presents guidelines thereof. Section 3 presents an annotation method for consistently representing the copula '-이-(-i-)' in the Korean

copula construction and the lexical negation '아니-(ani-; *to be not*)'. Copula constructions in Korean are formed through the copula '-이-(-i-)'; in this regard, it is necessary to establish annotation guidelines considering its negation, relativization, and complementization. Section 4 presents a case-stacking annotation method representing two or more subjects or objects. Case-stacking in Korean is a phenomenon in which several nominative or accusative words are licensed to a single predicate, and they have a pragmatic and semantic relationship with each other.

Regarding such issues, it would be helpful to boost Korean sembanking by properly adjusting AMR annotation standards and Korean-specific grammar phenomena to increase annotation efficiency.

2 Predicate Annotation

The first problem to consider for representing Korean sentences through AMR is determining what language resources to use in the annotation of core semantic roles. AMR uses the frameset of the Proposition Bank (PropBank) (Palmer et al., 2005) to represent the meaning of sentences, while Chinese AMR (CAMR) uses the Chinese PropBank (Xue & Palmer, 2009) frameset (Li et al., 2016). Brazil-Portuguese AMR (AMR-BR) uses the VerboBrasil dataset (Duran et al., 2013) as its annotation resource, which was built through the PropBank-BR project (Duran & Aluˊısio, 2012) promoted after the PropBank initiative. (Anchiêta & Pardo, 2018)

The Korean PropBank (Palmer et al., 2006) consists of the Virginia corpus and the Newswire corpus; the Newswire corpus comprises 2,749 predicates attached to more than 23,000 semantic roles. (Bae & Lee, 2015) Given that most languages, including Spanish (Migueles-Abraira

---

† corresponding author

Proceedings of the First International Workshop on Designing Meaning Representations, pages 128–135
Florence, Italy, August 1st, 2019 ©2019 Association for Computational Linguistics

et al., 2018), have adopted the PropBank, the use of the Korean PropBank is a top priority when representing Korean AMR. Most importantly, annotating frame-arguments according to the PropBank convention facilitates alignment with AMRs in other languages; compatibility with AMR corpora in many languages is advantageous.

However, as the lists of predicates and predicate senses in each language do not coincide with each other, detailed annotation guidelines may vary. For example, when applying the way of representing copula constructions and its negation with AMR in other languages to Korean copula constructions, problems arise in case of dealing with the predicate '아니-(ani-)', which is the lexicalized form of '-이-(-i-)' and means *"to be not."* Therefore, it is necessary to present a rational guideline considering the annotation methods of the general copula construction in Korean.

3 Copula Constructions

As AMR strives to represent the abstract meaning of language expressions, it is recommended to annotate the actual meaning of the copula construction to clarify the actual meaning rather than annotate the syntactic structure. Most copula constructions can be annotated using existing frames with well-defined arguments and semantic roles. For example, (1) is an annotation of the "NP is NP" construction using `work-01` to place the focus on meaning.

(1) *The boy is a hard worker.*

```
(w / work-01
    :ARG0 (b / boy)
    :manner (h / hard-02))
```

However, for annotating some "Noun is noun" constructions or predicate adjectives with no available frame, the English specification proposes an annotation using `:domain` and its inverse role, `:mod`, for unspecified modification (often modifying a noun) and the like by relativization. In these cases, as there is no frame available, it is difficult to represent the meaning of the expression clearly. Annotating with `:domain` and `:mod` is a simpler and more efficient way to handle the cases for which annotators cannot

decide a proper way of representation, while it is a less interpretive representation.

(2) a. *The man is a lawyer.*

```
(l / lawyer
    :domain (m / man))
```

b. *The man who is a lawyer*

```
(m / man
    :mod (l / lawyer))
```

In (2), the annotation of "The man is a lawyer" and its relativization is shown. Here, as there is no frame for 'lawyer', `:domain` and its inverse role, `:mod`, are used for annotation.

In reality, AMR for several languages makes limited use of `:domain` only if there is no available frame. In CAMR, when representing the sentences with the main verb "是," which functions as a copula, `:domain` is defined as a non-core role relation used in attribution and jurisdiction as in (3). However, as representing meaning by `:domain` is more ambiguous, it was found that the use of `:domain` gradually decreased as the labeling process continued. Thus, as the labeling process proceeded, the emphasis was placed on annotations that clearly reveal the semantic relationship rather than those close to the sentence format.

(3) *他是班长。*
'He is a leader.'

```
(x0 / 班长
    :domain (x1 / 他)
```

The annotation of the Korean copula construction should also clearly reveal the meaning of the sentence. In subsequent sections, we will examine the usage of the copula '-이-(-i-)' in Korean and briefly propose a proper way to annotate each usage. We will also examine cases in which we are forced to annotate with `:domain` and discuss special considerations for these cases. Next, we examine cases in which the negation of the copula construction is realized through the predicate *ani-*, and how to deal with the cases where the conceptual annotation is difficult.

3.1 Annotation of Copula *-i-*

Korean copula '-이-(-i-)', unlike "be", which is a verb in English sentences, combines directly with the content word to form the predicate and is conjugated. In Korean, the usage of the copula '-이-(-i-)' is largely classified into the following: i) class membership (ascriptive), ii) identity and identification, iii) locational, iv) existential, v) presentational, vi) temporal, vii) quantificational, viii) cleft sentence and ix) relatedness and illogical usage. (Park, 2012)

Most of these uses can be represented through verbalization, non-core roles, special frames, and the like. For example, in the case of i), it can be represented through :subset, :consist-of, and have-org-role-91; :location for iii) and iv); first-class concept and date-entity for v) and vi); and :quant for vii). Further, (4a) is an AMR using frame 담당-01 (*to be in charge of*), and (4b) is simply represented with non-core roles.

(4) a. *그 부분이 내 담당이다.*

    geu bubun-i   nae damdang-i-da.
    that part-NOM   my charge-COP-DECL
    'I am in charge of that part.'

```
(담 / 담당-01|to be in charge of
    :ARG0 (나 / 나|I)
    :ARG1 (부 / 부분|part
        :mod (그 / 그|that)))
```

  b. *사무실에 프린터가 세 대다.*

    samusil-e peulinteo-ga se dae-(i)-da.
    office-in   printer-NOM   three unit-COP-DECL
    'There are three printers in the office.'

```
(프 / 프린터|printer
    :location (사 / 사무실|office)
    :quant 3)
```

The relativization of the copula construction annotated using :domain is annotated with :mod, the inverse role of :domain (as shown in (5)).

(5) *변호사인 그는 아직 미혼이다.*

    byeonhosa-i-n   geu-neun ajik mihon-i-da.
    lawyer-COP-PART   he-ADP   yet unmarried-COP-DECL
    'The man who is a lawyer is not married yet.'

```
(결 / 결혼-01|marry
    :polarity -
    :mod (아 / 아직|yet)
    :ARG0 (그 / 그|the man
        :mod (변 / 변호사|lawyer)))
```

However, interpretive annotation is not possible in all cases. In certain cases of i), ii), viii), and ix), annotations by :domain may be inevitable. Types i) and ii) roughly correspond to cases where there is no available frame, while viii) and ix) correspond to cases where there is a presupposed context or it is a focus construction. In these cases, :domain is used. In (6), as there is no way of knowing the "best option" is for what, there is a limit to fully revealing the meaning.

(6) *정직하게 얘기하는 것이 최선의 선택이다.*

    jeongjik-ha-ge yaegi-ha-neun geos-i   choeseon-ui
    seontaeg-i-da.
    honest-do-PART talk-do-PART   thing-NOM best-GEN
    options-COP-DECL
    'That talking honestly is the best option.'

```
(선 / 선택|option
    :mod (최 / 최선|best)
    :domain (이 / 이야기-01|to talk
        :manner (정 / 정직-01|to be honest)))
```

3.2 Copula *-i-* with *ani-* Negation

Korean copula '-이-(-i-)' does not function as an independent morpheme but constitutes a predicate with preceding words. In contrast, the negation of '-이-(-i-)' is realized by lexical negation with the adjective predicate '아니-(ani-)' or syntactically realized with '-(이)지 않- (-(i)ci anh-)'.[‡] If the difference in the meaning of the proposition of the copula construction and its negation is the presence or absence of negation, then in general situations, it is desirable to annotate negation only with :polarity -.

[‡] Syntactic negation '-(이)지 않- (-(i)ci anh-)' is not mentioned in this paper. Further works will be followed on the negation of Korean.

Below, (7) is a representation of a sentence in which the negation of (4a) is realized through '아니-(ani-)'. Compared to (4a), the only difference is the presence or absence of the :polarity - annotation.

(7) 그 부분은 내 담당이 아니다.
   geu bubun-eun nae damdang-i ani-da.
   that part-ADP my charge-ADP NEG-DECL
   'I am not in charge of that part.'

```
(담 / 담당-01|
    :polarity -
    :ARG0 (나 / 나|I)
    :ARG1 (부 / 부분|part
        :mod (그 / 그|that)))
```

Even if the representation of the copula construction uses :domain, the :polarity - annotation can be used. For example, (8b) shows a sentence in which the negation of (8a) is realized through '아니-(ani-)'. Similarly, compared to (8a), the only difference is the presence or absence of the :polarity - annotation. (Note that there is no frame unavailable for predication, "문제(이)다(munje-(i^cop)-da; *to be problematic*)"

(8) a. 빙하가 녹는 것은 문제다.
   bingha-ga nog-neun geos-eun munje-(i)-da.
   glacier-NOM melt-PART thing-ADP problem-COP-DECL
   'That glaciers are melting is a problem.'

```
(문 / 문제|problem
    :domain (녹 / 녹-01|to melt
        :ARG1 (빙 / 빙하|glacier)))
```

  b. 빙하가 녹는 것은 문제가 아니다.
   bingha-ga nog-neun geos-eun munje-ga ani-da.
   glacier-NOM melt-PART thing-ADP problem-ADP NEG-DECL
   'That glaciers are melting is not a problem.'

```
(문 / 문제|problem
    :polarity -
    :domain (녹 / 녹-01|to melt
        :ARG1 (빙 / 빙하|glacier)))
```

However, there are cases in which the meaning changes when the core frame arguments of predicate '아니-(ani-)' are inverted. For example, (9b) is a sentence in which the argument from 9(a) is simply replaced, which can change the meaning of the sentence. Here, simply annotating with :polarity - can pose a problem. It is difficult to view (9b) as the negative construction of (8a).

(9) a. 빙하가 녹는 것은 문제가 아니다. → *'That glaciers are melting is not a problem. (~ is not problematic.)'*

  b. 문제는 빙하가 녹는 것이 아니다. → *'The problem is not (the event) that glaciers are melting. (The problem is the other one.)'*

In addition, if the meaning of (9b) differs from that of (9a), then the representations should not be the same. To represent (9b) as a trial, (10) assigns :polarity - to "빙하가 녹는 것 (*That glaciers are melting*)," a thing in a predicate. However, the annotation of (10) is closer to "문제는 빙하가 녹지 않는 것이다. (*The problem is (the event) that glaciers are NOT melting*)" rather than the meaning of (9b).

(10) An inappropriate representation of (9b):
   문제는 빙하가 녹는 것이 아니다.
   munje-neun bingha-ga nog-neun geos-i ani-da.
   problem-ADP glacier-NOM melt-PART thing-ADP NEG-DECL
   'The problem is not (the event) that glaciers are melting.'

```
(녹 / 녹-01|to melt
    :polarity -
    :ARG1 (빙 / 빙하|glacier)
    :domain (문 / 문제|problem))
```

In this case, annotation with :polarity - is not appropriate. The Korean PropBank provides the frame 아니-01 (*to be not*) for the predicate *ani-*, whose usage seems appropriate. 아니-01 has two core semantic roles; :ARG1(subj) is assigned to "*thing in focus*" and :ARG2(comp) is assigned to "*thing in predication.*" This method is an appropriate alternative when it is not enough to only add the `:polarity -` to the AMR of the copula construction to represent the meaning of the *ani-* construction. Example (11) is an annotation of (9b) using frame 아니-01. The representation of (11) is not the same as that of (10).

(11) More appropriate representation of (9b) with frame 아니-01:

> 문제는 빙하가 녹는 것이 아니다.
> munje-neun   bingha-ga   nog-neun   geos-i   ani-da.
> problem-ADP   glacier-NOM   melt-PART   thing-ADP   NEG-DECL
> 'The problem is not (the event) that glaciers are melting.'

```
(아 / 아니-01|to be not
   :ARG1 (문 / 문제|problem)
   :ARG2 (녹 / 녹-01|to melt
       :ARG1 (빙 / 빙하|glacier)))
```

Moreover, when the '아니-(ani-)' construction is relativized, the annotation standard of the copula construction is considered. However, it should be noted that during complementation, frame 아니-02 (*besides that*) is used as in (12b).

(12) a. 전혀 문제가 아닌 상황
> jeonhyeo   munje-ga   ani-n   sanghwang
> totally   problem-ADP   NEG-PART   situation
> 'The situation that is not an issue at all.'

```
(상 / 상황|situation
   :mod (문 / 문제|problem
       :polarity -
       :mod (전 / 전혀|totally)))
```

b. 억울한 사람은 다른 사람이 아닌 바로 나다.
> eogul-han   salam-eun   daleun   salam-i   ani-n   balo   na-(i)-da.
> wrong-PART person-ADP different person-ADP NEG-PART exactly me-COP-DECL
> 'The wronged person is none other than me.'

```
(억 / 억울-01|to feel wronged
  :ARG1 (나 / 나|I
    :mod (아 / 아니-02|besides that
      :ARG0 (사 / 사람|person
        :ARG1-of (다 / 다르-01|to be
                           different
)))))
```

It is preferable to annotate the presence or absence of `:polarity -` based on the same proposition of the copula construction and its negation. This will ensure that the propositions of the affirmative and negative constructions are aligned with one another. In addition, when the copula construction or its negated sentence is relativized, the propositions must also be aligned with each other. The use of the frames 아니-01 or 아니-02 is highly limited to cases in which the meaning of the sentence changes, which is due to the characteristics of the predicate '아니-(ani-)'.

4 Case-stacking

Korean is a SOV (subject-object-verb) language with case markers. The agent and patient are placed before the predicate, and word order constraints are loose because of the presence of case markers. Therefore, Korean sentences generally rely on the case markers to encode and decode the grammatical relationships and semantic roles of the arguments.

Korean has sentence types including the so-called double nominative construction (DNC) and double accusative construction (DAC). (Brown & Yeon, 2015) In DNC and DAC, the nominative marker '-이(-i)`가(-ga)' or the accusative marker '-을(-eul)/-를(-leul)' is licensed to two or more constituents in a sentence.

There are several types of double case marker construction. DNC can be classified as embedded sentences, psychological adjective constructions, numeral phrase constructions, complement constructions, complex predicate constructions, etc. (Lee, 2018) As for complement constructions, specific predicates such as '되-(*become*)' and '아니-(*be not*)' constitute 'NP1-이/가(-i/ga) NP2-이/가(-i/ga) V' sentence structure. In this structure, 'NP2' can be classified as a complement (not the subject), and second '-이/가(-i/ga)' as a complementary case marker.

In the case of DAC, it can be classified as possessive constructions, locative alternation constructions, change-of-state constructions, numeral phrase constructions, support verb constructions, etc. (Shin, 2016)

The numeral phrase construction is included in both DNC and DAC, which can be represented in AMR easily by `:quant`. Two constituents which are marked by the same case marker generally have different grammatical and semantic relation.

These double case marker constructions are conventionally called 'double subject/object construction', while there is still room for argument about whether both constituents with the same marker are both subject or object.

In DNC and DAC, the two subjects or two objects are usually divided into "inner-nominative and accusative" and "outer-nominative and accusative," with a semantic and discourse relationship therebetween. As a result, there is generally a word order constraint between the two constituents.

In Korean, the predicate of a double nominative construction is often an adjective. Although there are various types of Korean nominative case-stacking constructions, (Wunderlich, 2014) this paper discusses only those for predicate clause and psychological adjective constructions. (Yoo, 2000) Korean also has several types of accusative case-stacking constructions. However, this paper discusses only the annotations of constructions corresponding to two objects with a whole-part relationship or dative verb constructions.[§] (Yeon, 2010)

First, this section analyzes the sentence structure of DNC through the major subject (outer-nominative) and sentential predicate (a clause in which inner-nominative and predicate are embedded). We propose using :domain for the major subject that is the topic of a discourse of the sentential predicate. This annotation method is very efficient because it can be applied repeatedly, even when the subject appears more than once. A frame 좋-01 (*to be good*) in (13) takes only one subject that stands for "*thing being good*"; two or more subjects appear in real text. Here, the outer nominative was annotated with :domain as the main subject.

(13) *기계가 상태가 좋다.*
    gigye-ga   *sangtae-ga*   *joh-da.*
    machine-NOM   condition-NOM   good-DECL
    'The condition of the machine is fine.'

```
(좋 / 좋-01|to be good
    :ARG1 (상 / 상태|condition)
    :domain (기 / 기계|machine))
```

However, the use of :domain still needs to be limited in double nominative constructions. A better representation with :time clearly reveals the meaning as in (14).

(14) *어제가 날씨가 더웠다.*
    eoje-ga   *nalssi-ga*   *deo-woss-da.*
    yesterday-NOM   weather-NOM   hot-PAST-DECL
    'The weather of yesterday was hot.'

```
(덥 / 덥-01|to be hot
    :ARG1 (날 / 날씨|weather)
    :time (어 / 어제|yesterday))
```

In adjective constructions in which nominative case-stacking occurs, attention should be paid to the annotation according to predicate sense. In (15), which uses a psychological adjective rather than a qualifying adjective, while nominative case-stacking occurs, the semantic role of each constituent corresponds to agent and patient. If predicate senses vary, the core argument annotation should differ, corresponding to a role set of the frame.

(15) *나는 그가 좋다.*
    na-neun   *geu-ga*   *joh-da.*
    I-ADP   he-NOM   like-DECL
    'I like him.'

```
(좋 / 좋-02|to like
    :ARG0 (나 / 나|I)
    :ARG1 (그 / 그|he))
```

Multiple accusative case licensing in DAC usually involves paraphrasing adnominal possessive structures; there are many cases in which possessor raising occurs. (Nakamura, 2002) If it is difficult to clarify the relationship between two accusatives, it is convenient to use :domain as in (16), but if not, it is important to clarify the meaning. Example (17) annotates the relationship between "발톱 (*claw*)" and "고양이 (*cat*)" using :part-of, without using :domain.

(16) *제비를 꽝을 뽑았다.*
    jebi-leul   *kkwang-eul*   *ppob-at-da.*
    lot-ACC   blank-ACC   draw-PAST-DECL
    'I drew a blank lot.'

```
(뽑 / 뽑-01|to draw
    :ARG1 (꽝 / 꽝|blank)
    :domain (제 / 제비|lot))
```

133

(17) 그녀는 고양이를 발톱을 잘라 주었다.

    geunyeo-neun goyangi-leul baltob-eul jal-la ju-eot-da.
    she-ADP   cat-ACC   claw-ACC   cut-PART AUX-PAST-DECL
    'She cut the cat's claws.'

```
(자 / 자르-01|to cut
   :ARG0 (그 / 그녀|she)
   :ARG1 (발 / 발톱|claw
      :part-of (고 / 고양이|cat)))
```

However, in dative constructions in which the dative case or accusative case appears, the annotation of the frame argument must be noted.

(18) 할머니는 아끼던 구두를 나를 주셨다.

    halmeoni-neun akki-deon gudu-leul na-leul ju-sy-eot-da.
    grandmother-ADP   spare-PART shoes-ACC me-ACC give-HON-PAST-DECL
    'My grandmother gave me the shoes I loved.'

```
(주 / 주-01|to give
   :ARG0 (할 / 할머니|grandmother)
   :ARG1 (구 / 구두|shoes
      :ARG1-of (아 / 아끼-01|spare)
   :ARG2 (나 / 나|I))
```

5   Conclusion and Further Works

This paper discussed consistent annotation methods for the Korean copula construction, its negation, complementation, and relativization with focus on the copula '-이-(-i-)' and the predicate '아니-(ani-)'. In this process, we also demonstrated cases in which annotation must be performed using the frames 아니-01 and 아니-02.

In addition, we proposed a new usage for :domain with regard to case-stacking, which occurs in Korean sentences frequently. While its limited usage is recommended, in cases in which there are two or more subjects or objects when there is no available frame for the sentential predicate, it can be used repeatedly.

The annotation guideline of the Korean copula construction presented in this paper is essentially based on the copula construction annotation standards of other languages. However, as indicated in the limited discussion of the predicate '아니-(ani-)', devising consistent annotation

principles for scopal polarity remains a topic for future discussion. Accordingly, it is necessary to examine various aspects of negative representation more broadly than those discussed in this paper. Besides, as the usage of :domain slightly expands, the usage of :domain and :mod label in terms of the determination of a topic of discourse and modifications should also be considered. This discussion will enable the AMR scheme to represent the semantics of Korean more explicitly.

In the future, we aim to build a Korean AMR corpus reflecting these discussions. For this task, the consistency and efficiency of the annotation guidelines need to be improved. Also, well-established language resources are required to reduce cost and efforts to build an actual Korean AMR corpus.

Currently, the following language resources which are labeled with semantic roles are available in Korean: UCorpus-DP/SR & UPropBank of Ucorpus (Released by KLPLAB, University of Ulsan) and SRL datasets of Exobrain Language Analysis Corpus v4.0 (Released by Seoul SW-SoC Convergence R&BD Center, ETRI). The UCorpus uses an extended set of theta roles from Sejong Electronic Dictionary and The Exobrain Corpus follows the annotation system of Korean Proposition Bank.

The next step of this research is to construct a Korean AMR corpus by converting the existing Korean semantic resources followed by correcting it manually. This further work to construct Korean AMR corpus would provide detailed guidelines, which could stimulate future studies in Korean sembanking.

References

Anchiêta, R., & Pardo, T., 2018, Towards AMR-BR: A SemBank for Brazilian Portuguese Language. In *Proceedings of the Eleventh International Conference on Language Resources and Evaluation (LREC-2018)*.

Bae, J., & Lee, C., 2015, Extending Korean PropBank for Korean Semantic Role Labeling and Applying Domain Adaptation Technique. *Korean Journal of Cognitive Science*, 26(4), 377-392.

Banarescu, L., Bonial, C., Cai, S., Georgescu, M., Griffitt, K., Hermjakob, U., ... & Schneider, N., 2013, Abstract meaning representation for sembanking. In *Proceedings of the 7th Linguistic*

Annotation Workshop and Interoperability with Discourse, 178-186.

Banarescu, L., Bonial, C., Cai, S., Georgescu, M., Griffitt, K., Hermjakob, U., Knight, K., Koehn, P., Palmer, M., Schnetder, N., 2018. Abstract Meaning Representation (AMR) 1.2.6 Specification. Accessed: 1 may 2019. Available at: https://github.com/amrisi/amr-guidelines/blob/master/amr.md

Brown, L., & Yeon, J. (Eds.)., 2015, *The handbook of Korean linguistics*. John Wiley & Sons.

Duran, M. S. and Aluísio, S. M., 2012. Propbank-br: a brazilian treebank annotated with semantic role labels. In *Proceedings of the 8th international conference on Language Resources and Evaluation*, pages 1862–1867.

Duran, M. S., Martins, J. P., and Aluísio, S. M., 2013. Um repositorio de verbos para a anotaç˜ao de pap˜eis´ semanticos dispon^´ıvel na web. In *Proceedings of the 9th Brazilian Symposium in Information and Human Language Technology*, pages 168–172.

Lee, Y., 2018, A syntactic analysis of so-called double-subject construction, *Morphology*, 20.2, 202-231.

Li, B., Wen, Y., Weiguang, Q. U., Bu, L., & Xue, N., 2016, Annotating the little prince with chinese AMRs. In *Proceedings of the 10th linguistic annotation workshop held in conjunction with ACL 2016 (LAW-X 2016)*, 7-15.

Migueles-Abraira, N., 2017, A Study Towards Spanish Abstract Meaning Representation. MSc thesis, University of the Basque Country.

Migueles-Abraira, N., Agerri, R., & de Ilarraza, A. D., 2018, Annotating Abstract Meaning Representations for Spanish. In *Proceedings of the Eleventh International Conference on Language Resources and Evaluation (LREC-2018)*.

Nakamura, H., 2002, Double subject, double nominative object and double accusative object constructions in Japanese and Korean. In *Proceedings of the 16th Pacific Asia Conference on Language, Information and Computation*, 358-369.

Palmer, M., Gildea, D., & Kingsbury, P., 2005, The proposition bank: An annotated corpus of semantic roles. *Computational linguistics, 31*(1), 71-106.

Palmer, M., Ryu, S., Choi, J., Yoon, S., & Jeon, Y., 2006, Korean propbank. *LDC Catalog No.: LDC2006T03 ISBN*, 1-58563.

Park, J., 2012, Semantic description of lexical and grammatical elements in Korean using semantic map model. *Journal of Korean Linguistics, 63*, 459-519.

Shin, S., 2016, A study on the functions of eul/reul through examining double accusative constructions: focusing on transitivity, *Urimalgeul: The Korean Language and Literature*, 68, 1-35.

Wunderlich, D., 2014, Variations of double nominative in Korean and Japanese. *Studies in Language and Cognition*, 339.

Xue, N., Palmer, M., 2009, Adding semantic roles to the Chinese Treebank. *Natural Language Engineering*, 15(1):143-172.

Yeon, J., 2010, Constraints on double-accusative external possession constructions in Korean: A cognitive approach. In: Yeon, Jaehoon and Kiaer, Jieun, (eds.), *Selected Papers from the 2nd European Conference on Korean Linguistics*. Lincom Europa. (Lincom Studies in Asian Linguistics)

Yoo, H., 2000. A study on the classification of Korean adjectives. *Journal of Korean Linguistics, 36*, 221-258.

ClearTAC: Verb Tense, Aspect, and Form Classification Using Neural Nets

Skatje Myers
University of Colorado at Boulder
Boulder, CO, USA
skatje.myers@colorado.edu

Martha Palmer
University of Colorado at Boulder
Boulder, CO, USA
martha.palmer@colorado.edu

Abstract

This paper proposes using a Bidirectional LSTM-CRF model in order to identify the tense and aspect of verbs. The information that this classifier outputs can be useful for ordering events and can provide a pre-processing step to improve efficiency of annotating this type of information. This neural network architecture has been successfully employed for other sequential labeling tasks, and we show that it significantly outperforms the rule-based tool TMV-annotator on the Propbank I dataset.

1   Introduction

Identifying the tense and aspect of predicates can provide important clues to the sequencing and structure of events, which is a vital part of numerous down-stream natural language processing applications.

Our long term goal is to augment Abstract Meaning Representations (Banarescu et al., 2013) with tense and aspect information. With the assumption that an automatic pre-processing step could greatly reduce the annotation effort involved, we have been exploring different options for English tense and aspect annotation.

In this paper we compare two approaches to automatically classifying tense (present, past, etc.), aspect (progressive, perfect, etc.), and the form of verb (finite, participle, etc.). Our own work trains a BiLSTM-CRF NN, ClearTAC, on the PropBank annotations (Palmer et al., 2005) for the form, tense, and aspect of verbs. We compare the results to TMV-annotator, a rule-based system developed by (Ramm et al., 2017). Not surprisingly, we find our NN system significantly outperforms the rule-based system on the Propbank test data. In Section 2 we discuss related work and provide background information on TMV-annotator. Section 3 reviews the PropBank annotation and our modifications to

the test data aimed at ensuring an apples to apples comparison with TMV-annotator. Section 4 describes the system architecture for ClearTAC, and Section 5 presents the experimental results for both systems, a comparison, and error analysis. We conclude in Section 6 and outline our plans for further development.

2   Background

Abstract Meaning Representations (AMRs) (Banarescu et al., 2013) are a graph-based representation of the semantics of sentences. They aim to strip away syntactic idiosyncrasies of text into a standardized representation of the meaning. The initial work on AMRs left out tense and aspect as being more syntactic features than semantic, but the absence of this feature makes generation from AMRs and temporal reasoning much more difficult. Very recently there have been efforts underway to extend AMRs to incorporate this type of temporal information (Donatelli et al., 2018). Since existing AMR corpora will need to be revised with annotations of this type of information, automatically classifying the tense and aspect of verbs could provide a shortcut. Annotators can work much more efficiently by only checking the accuracy of the automatic labels instead of annotating from scratch. Availability of automatic tense and aspect tagging could also prove useful for any system interested in extracting temporal sequences of events, and has been a long-standing research goal.

Much of the previous work on tense classification has been for the purpose of improving machine translation, including (Ye and Zhang, 2005) and (Ye et al., 2006), which explored tense classification of Chinese as a sequential classification task, using conditional random fields and a combination of surface and latent features, such as verb

Proceedings of the First International Workshop on Designing Meaning Representations, pages 136–140
Florence, Italy, August 1st, 2019 ©2019 Association for Computational Linguistics

telicity, verb punctuality, and temporal ordering between adjacent events.

The NLPWin pipeline (Vanderwende, 2015) consists of components spanning from lexical analysis to construction of logical form representations to collecting these representations into a knowledge database. Tense is included as one of the attributes of the declension of a verb. This system is a rule-based approach, as is TMV-annotator described below.

Other recent work on tense classification includes (Reichart and Rappoport, 2010) attempting to distinguish between the different word senses within a tense/aspect. (Ferreira and Pereira, 2018) performed tense classification with the end goal of transposing verb tenses in a sentence for language study.

2.1 TMV-annotator

TMV-annotator (Ramm et al., 2017) is a rule-based tool for annotating verbs with tense, mood, and voice in English, German, and French. In the case of English, it also identifies whether the verb is progressive.

Although the rules were hand-crafted for each language, they operate on dependency parses. The authors specifically use the Mate parser (Bohnet and Nivre, 2012) for their reported results, although the tool could be used on any dependency parses that use the same part of speech and dependency labels as Mate. The first step of their tool is to identify verbal complexes (VCs), which consist of a main verb and verbal particles and negating words. Subsequent rules based on the words in the VC and their dependencies make binary decisions about whether the VC is finite, progressive, active or passive voice, subjunctive or indicative, as well as assign a tense. A subset of output for an example sentence is shown in Table 1.

For tense tagging, the authors report an accuracy of 81.5 on randomly selected English sentences from Europarl. In Section 5.2, we evaluate TMV-annotator on the Propbank I data and compare it to ClearTAC.

3 Data

3.1 Propbank I

The first version of Propbank, PropBank I, (Palmer et al., 2005) annotated the original Penn Treebank with semantic roles, roleset IDs, and inflection of each verb.

Sentence	The finger-pointing has already begun.
Verbal complex	has begun
Main	begun
Finite?	yes
Tense	present perfect
Progressive?	no

Table 1: Partial output of TMV-annotator for an example verbal complex, showing the fields relevant to this work.

The information in the inflection field consists of form, tense, aspect, person, and voice. We trained our model to predict form, tense, and aspect, which were labeled in the dataset with the following possible values:

- Form:

    - infinitive (i)
    - finite (v)
    - gerund (g)
    - participle (p)
    - none (verbs that occur with modal verbs)

- Tense:

    - present (n)
    - past (p)
    - future (f)
    - none

- Aspect:

    - perfect (p)
    - progressive (o)
    - both (b)
    - none

Not all combinations of these fields are valid. For instance, gerunds, participles that do not occur with an auxiliary verb, and verbs that occur with a modal verb are always tenseless and aspectless. Table 2 shows example Propbank I annotations.

We removed 13 files from our training/development sets, which seem to have been overlooked during original annotation. In total, the data contains 112,570 annotated verb tokens, of which the test set consists of 5,273 verb tokens.

Roleset ID	Form	Tense	Aspect
come.01	finite	past	-
halt.01	participle	past	progressive
trade.01	gerund	-	-

Table 2: Example Propbank I annotation for the sentence: At 2:43 p.m. EDT, came the sickening news: The Big Board was halting trading in UAL, "pending news."

3.2 Reduced Propbank I

The goals of the TMV-annotator tool (described in Section 2) do not perfectly match with the annotation goals of Propbank I. Therefore, we created a reduced version of the Propbank I data to avoid penalizing the tool for using a different annotation schema. The changes are as follows:

- Remove gerunds.

- Ignore tense for participles that occur with an auxiliary verb. TMV-annotator assigns only aspect, whereas Propbank assigns both.

- Remove standalone participles that occur without an auxiliary verb. For example: "Some circuit breakers **installed** after the October 1987 crash failed their first test."

This reduces the number of verbs in the dataset to 92,686, of which 4,486 are in the test set.

4 ClearTAC System Architecture

Bidirectional LSTM-CRF models have been shown to be useful for numerous sequence labeling tasks, such as part of speech tagging, named entity recognition, and chunking (Huang et al., 2015). Based on these results, we expected good performance on classification of tense and aspect. Our neural network consists of a Bi-LSTM layer with 150 hidden units followed by a CRF layer. The inputs to the NN were sentence-length sequences, with each token represented by pretrained 300-dimension GloVe embeddings (Pennington et al., 2014). No part-of-speech or syntactic pre-processing was used. Classifying form, tense, and aspect was treated as a joint task.

5 Results

Our model was evaluated on both the full and reduced Propbank I datasets, as described in Section 3. The results are presented in Table 3.

Full Propbank I			
	P	R	F1
Verb identification	94.30	97.25	95.75
Form	92.61	95.51	94.03
Tense	92.66	95.56	94.09
Aspect	93.88	96.81	95.32
Form + tense + aspect	92.04	94.92	93.46
Reduced Propbank I			
	P	R	F1
Verb identification	96.20	97.10	96.65
Form	95.36	96.26	95.81
Tense	95.30	96.19	95.74
Aspect	96.05	96.95	96.49
Form + tense + aspect	95.19	96.08	95.63

Table 3: Evaluation of our system on Propbank I.

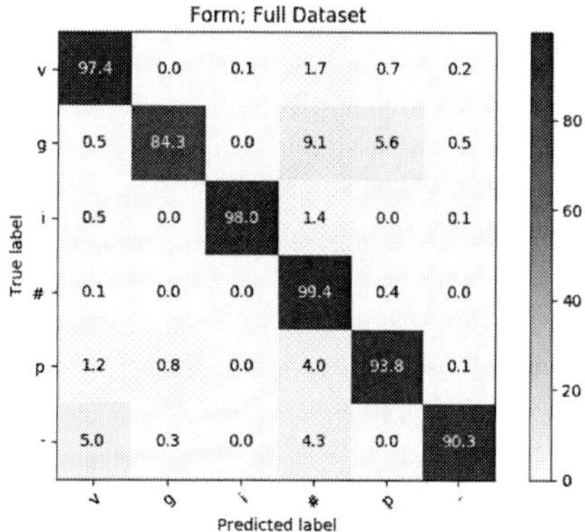

Figure 1: Confusion matrix of our model output for verb **form** on the full Propbank dataset. See Section 3.1 for a legend. '#' is the label for a non-verb token.

Performance across the board for the various subtasks on both datasets was consistently in the mid-90's. The more challenging task of tagging all forms, tenses, and aspects in Propbank I saw a performance decrease of only 2 points compared to the reduced dataset.

5.1 Error Analysis

Overall, the model had the most challenges with gerunds and verbs with modals, often predicting them not to be a verb. With these forms also being tenseless, the effect can also be seen in the high number of gold "no tense" labels being misclassified as not a verb.

Figures 1, 2, and 3 show confusion matrices for the model's output for each of the three subtasks on the full Propbank I dataset.

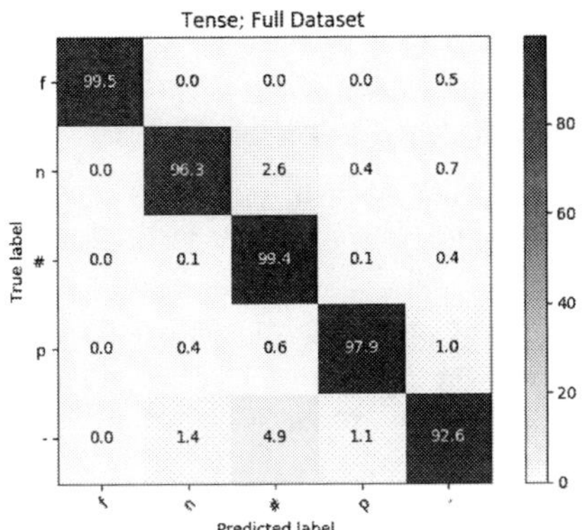

Figure 2: Confusion matrix of our model output for verb **tense** on the full Propbank dataset. See Section 3.1 for a legend. '#' is the label for a non-verb token.

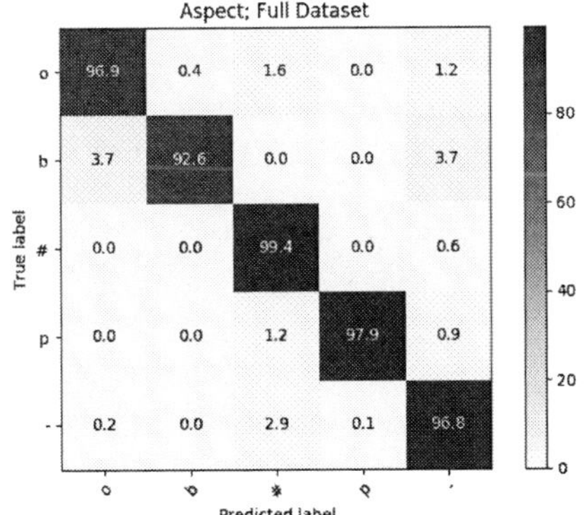

Figure 3: Confusion matrix of our model output for verb **aspect** on the full Propbank dataset. See Section 3.1 for a legend. '#' is the label for a non-verb token.

Full Propbank I			
	P	R	F1
Verb identification	95.68	77.77	85.80
Form	76.46	62.15	68.56
Tense	85.74	69.69	76.89
Aspect	93.56	76.05	83.90
Form + tense + aspect	70.79	57.54	63.48
Reduced Propbank I			
	P	R	F1
Verb identification	94.14	89.95	92.00
Form	76.22	72.83	74.49
Tense	76.43	73.03	74.69
Aspect	92.70	88.56	90.58
Form + tense + aspect	75.64	72.27	73.92

Table 4: Evaluation of TMV-annotator on the complete and reduced Propbank I test sets.

5.2 Comparison with TMV

As described in Section 2, the TMV-annotator tool (Ramm et al., 2017) is a rule-based tool for annotating tense, aspect, and mood in English, French, and German. We ran this tool on the output of the Mate dependency parser (Bohnet and Nivre, 2012) (which the tool was designed in mind of) using a pre-trained model and evaluated on both the complete Propbank I test data, which includes verb forms that TMV-annotator was never intended to annotate, such as gerunds, as well as the reduced Propbank I test set as described in Section 3.2, which only contains the intersection of TMV-annotator and Propbank I annotations. The results of this are presented in Table 4.

Unsurprisingly, TMV-annotator is only able to reach a F-score of 63.48 on the whole task on the full dataset. As would be expected in this circumstance, the recall is much lower than precision.

On the Reduced Propbank I dataset, TMV-annotator performs significantly better, but still falls over 20 points shy of our NN system. Simply the misidentification of verbs in the data, likely due to parsing errors, drops the F-score a full 8 points. Notably, TMV-annotator achieves an F-score in the 90s on the subtask of classifying aspect, while form and tense prove to be more challenging, with F-scores near 75.

6 Conclusions and Future Work

Our NN model outperformed the rule-based TMV-annotator when annotating the same subset of verb form, tense, and aspect by 21.71 points. Furthermore, this model achieved a F-score of 93.46 on the more challenging task of classifying the full label set of form, tense, and aspect present in Propbank I. The performance of this model makes it a feasible pre-processing step to add tense annotation to Abstract Meaning Representations.

There are a number of architectural or feature improvements left for future work. Embeddings such as ELMo or Bert could possibly help with performance on out-of-vocabulary words as well as help distinguish between identical verb forms, such as gerunds and present-tense verbs, due to incorporating context. Better performance may also be possible by dividing the subtasks of classifying form, tense, and aspect, rather than treating it as a single joint task.

Another dataset which has been annotated with tense and aspect is TimeML (Pustejovsky et al., 2003). Evaluation of our system on this data would be complementary to this work and is planned for future work.

Acknowledgments

We gratefully acknowledge the support of NSF 1764048 RI: Medium: Collaborative Research: Developing a Uniform Meaning Representation for Natural Language Processing. Any opinions, findings, and conclusions or recommendations expressed in this material are those of the authors and do not necessarily reflect the views of DTRA or the U.S. government.

References

Laura Banarescu, Claire Bonial, Shu Cai, Madalina Georgescu, Kira Griffitt, Ulf Hermjakob, Kevin Knight, Philipp Koehn, Martha Palmer, and Nathan Schneider. 2013. Abstract meaning representation for sembanking. In *Proceedings of the 7th Linguistic Annotation Workshop and Interoperability with Discourse*, pages 178–186.

Bernd Bohnet and Joakim Nivre. 2012. A transition-based system for joint part-of-speech tagging and labeled non-projective dependency parsing. In *Proceedings of the 2012 Joint Conference on Empirical Methods in Natural Language Processing and Computational Natural Language Learning*, pages 1455–1465. Association for Computational Linguistics.

Lucia Donatelli, Michael Regan, William Croft, and Nathan Schneider. 2018. Annotation of tense and aspect semantics for sentential AMR. In *Proceedings of the Joint Workshop on Linguistic Annotation, Multiword Expressions and Constructions (LAW-MWE-CxG-2018)*, pages 96–108, Santa Fe, New Mexico, USA. Association for Computational Linguistics.

Kledilson Ferreira and Jr Álvaro R Pereira. 2018. Verb tense classification and automatic exercise generation. In *Proceedings of the 24th Brazilian Symposium on Multimedia and the Web*, pages 105–108. ACM.

Zhiheng Huang, Wei Xu, and Kai Yu. 2015. Bidirectional lstm-crf models for sequence tagging. *arXiv preprint arXiv:1508.01991*.

Martha Palmer, Daniel Gildea, and Paul Kingsbury. 2005. The proposition bank: An annotated corpus of semantic roles. *Computational linguistics*, 31(1):71–106.

Jeffrey Pennington, Richard Socher, and Christopher Manning. 2014. Glove: Global vectors for word representation. In *Proceedings of the 2014 conference on empirical methods in natural language processing (EMNLP)*, pages 1532–1543.

James Pustejovsky, José M Castano, Robert Ingria, Roser Sauri, Robert J Gaizauskas, Andrea Setzer, Graham Katz, and Dragomir R Radev. 2003. Timeml: Robust specification of event and temporal expressions in text. *New directions in question answering*, 3:28–34.

Anita Ramm, Sharid Loáiciga, Annemarie Friedrich, and Alexander Fraser. 2017. Annotating tense, mood and voice for english, french and german. *Proceedings of ACL 2017, System Demonstrations*, pages 1–6.

Roi Reichart and Ari Rappoport. 2010. Tense sense disambiguation: A new syntactic polysemy task. In *Proceedings of the 2010 Conference on Empirical Methods in Natural Language Processing*, pages 325–334, Cambridge, MA. Association for Computational Linguistics.

Lucy Vanderwende. 2015. Nlpwin–an introduction. Technical report, Microsoft Research tech report no. MSR-TR-2015-23.

Yang Ye, Victoria Li Fossum, and Steven Abney. 2006. Latent features in automatic tense translation between chinese and english. In *Proceedings of the fifth SIGHAN workshop on Chinese language processing*, pages 48–55.

Yang Ye and Zhu Zhang. 2005. Tense tagging for verbs in cross-lingual context: A case study. In *International Conference on Natural Language Processing*, pages 885–895. Springer.

Preparing SNACS for Subjects and Objects

Adi Shalev
Hebrew University of Jerusalem
`adi.bitan@mail.huji.ac.il`

Jena D. Hwang
IHMC
`jhwang@ihmc.us`

Nathan Schneider
Georgetown University
`nathan.schneider@georgetown.edu`

Vivek Srikumar
University of Utah
`svivek@cs.utah.edu`

Omri Abend   Ari Rappoport
Hebrew University of Jerusalem
`{oabend, arir}@cs.huji.ac.il`

Abstract

Research on adpositions and possessives in multiple languages has led to a small inventory of general-purpose meaning classes that disambiguate tokens. Importantly, that work has argued for a principled separation of the *semantic role* in a scene from the *function* coded by morphosyntax. Here, we ask whether this approach can be generalized beyond adpositions and possessives to cover all scene participants—including subjects and objects—directly, without reference to a frame lexicon. We present new guidelines for English and the results of an interannotator agreement study.

1 Introduction

Studies of verbal argument structure have established some clear semantic correlations of syntactic relations like subject and object, and there are various approaches to expressing these generalizations using categorical semantic roles (Fillmore, 1968, 1982; Levin, 1993) or bundles of proto-properties (Dowty, 1991; Reisinger et al., 2015) that generalize across verbs. A parallel line of work (§2) has looked at the meanings coded by grammatical phrase-markers such as prepositions and possessives and how to disambiguate them. These inquiries necessarily overlap because many prepositions mark verb arguments or modifiers. Consequently, insights from the study of prepositions/ case may improve the meaning representation of core syntactic arguments, or vice versa.

In this paper, we investigate whether SNACS (Schneider et al., 2018b), an approach to semantic disambiguation of adpositions and possessives, can be adapted to cover syntactically core grammatical relations (subjects and objects). We believe this may have several practical advantages for NLP.

First, many of the semantic labels in SNACS derive from VerbNet (Kipper et al., 2008) role labels.

However, VerbNet and other frame-semantic approaches like FrameNet (Fillmore and Baker, 2009) and PropBank (Palmer et al., 2005) *assume a lexicon* as a prerequisite for semantic role annotation. This can be an obstacle to comprehensive corpus annotation when out-of-vocabulary predicates are encountered. But is a lexicon really necessary for role annotation? A general-purpose set of role labels with detailed criteria for each can potentially bypass coverage limitations of lexicon-based approaches, while still supporting some degree of generalization across grammatical paraphrases.

Second, the nonreliance on a lexicon potentially *simplifies the annotation process* in some respects. For example, no explicit predicate disambiguation step is necessary, and the annotator does not need to consult frame-specific role definitions.[1]

Third, the semantic criteria for SNACS labels are designed to be *language-neutral*, and investigations thus far suggest that they can be generalized to languages besides English (Hwang et al., 2017; Zhu et al., 2019). While this paper focuses on English, we see the future opportunity for cross-lingual extension without the construction of new lexicons as a major advantage.

Finally, SNACS is unique in allowing *two* semantic labels per target, one reflecting a level of meaning closer to the grammatical coding, and the other at a deeper level associated with the predicate scene type (§3). We show below that the SNACS analysis, while designed for PPs, can be extended to subjects and objects, to the extent that the coarse-grained inventory distinguishes roles in the scene.

We summarize SNACS in §2, and in §3 propose a strategy for adapting SNACS for English subjects

---

[1] On the other hand, consulting a frame-specific set of core roles may simplify the role labeling task for an annotator, producing higher-quality annotations. In the future it may be worth exploring a hybrid solution that maps lexicon-defined roles to supersenses and asks the annotator to apply supersenses directly only for out-of-vocabulary predicates.

Proceedings of the First International Workshop on Designing Meaning Representations, pages 141–147
Florence, Italy, August 1st, 2019 ©2019 Association for Computational Linguistics

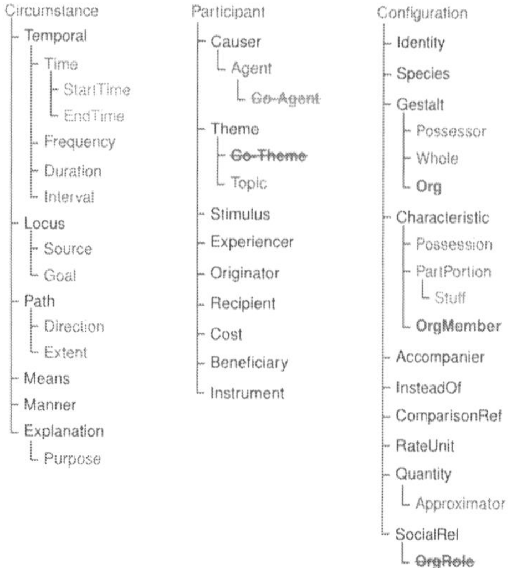

Figure 1: Modified inventory of supersenses based on the SNACS hierarchy (additions and removals in bold).

and objects. This involves minor changes to the label inventory and new annotation guidelines for a variety of challenging phenomena. We conduct a pilot interannotator agreement study on Wikipedia articles (§4) and release the annotations.[2]

2 Background

The SNACS[3] hierarchy is a taxonomy of coarse-grained supersenses developed to mark semantic relations as expressed by adpositions (prepositions + postpositions) and possessives (Schneider et al., 2018b). The complete SNACS hierarchy is shown in figure 1 with our modifications highlighted.

SNACS includes the usual thematic relations (e.g., AGENT, THEME, RECIPIENT) and adjunct relations (e.g., TIME, LOCUS including locations, PURPOSE) used by most resources designed for SRL annotation. SNACS diverges from the general predicate-argument labeling standards in its inclusion of non-standard roles such as ORIGINATOR in creation (creator), transfer (giver) and communication (speaker) events, and labels regarding properties involved in a static relationship to one another (e.g., POSSESSION in "owner **of** the car").

Unlike labels used by efforts such as PropBank and FrameNet, SNACS labels are highly coarse-grained and generalize across various scenes and situations. This approach also differs from frame-alternation–based lexicons like VerbNet, which defines classes of verbs whose members exhibit similar syntactic alternations involving the same subset

of roles. Instead, SNACS places the burden of semantics directly on a fixed set of **supersenses**, forgoing the use of frame (or class) definitions. The supersenses can be thought of as disambiguating coarse-grained adposition senses. The supersense labels effectively encapsulate—at a highly abstract/ schematic level—various basic scenarios that are important to language and grammar, such as transitive action, motion, unidirectional transfer/communication, and psychological events, as well as stative relations like possession, quantity, comparison, and identity. SNACS does not formalize a semantic core/non-core or argument/adjunct distinction, though roles in the PARTICIPANT hierarchy are typically core and roles in the CIRCUMSTANCE hierarchy are typically non-core in predicate-argument annotation schemes like PropBank and FrameNet.

SNACS further adopts a device called *construal* (Hwang et al., 2017), explained below.

3 Applying SNACS

We adopt the SNACS labels originally developed for disambiguating adpositions and possessives as exemplified in (1) and extend their use to annotate the subject and object of a verb as seen in (2).

(1) a. The bagel was eaten **by**$_{\text{AGENT}}$ Jane.

  b. Jane dined **on**$_{\text{THEME}}$ a bagel.

(2) [Jane]$_{\text{AGENT}}$ ate [a bagel]$_{\text{THEME}}$.

Following the construal approach, which is illustrated in table 1 for adpositions, we separate two semantic dimensions of an annotation target: **Scene Role**: What semantic role is most closely associated with the type of scene (typically indicated by the verb/predicate)? **Function**: What semantic role is most salient in the morphosyntactic coding of the phrase (with a grammatical relation like subject or object, or overt marking with closed-class morphology like adpositions and case)? Consider the following examples. Construal is notated by SCENE ROLE↝FUNCTION.

(3) [Jane]$_{\text{RECIPIENT↝AGENT}}$ bought [the book]$_{\text{POSSESSION↝THEME}}$.

(4) [Bingley]$_{\text{SOCIALREL↝THEME}}$ married [Jane]$_{\text{SOCIALREL↝THEME}}$.

The scene role indicates the participation role of the target in the scene described by the verb. Jane is the RECIPIENT in a transfer scene in (3), and she is in a certain social relationship with Bingley (i.e., SOCIALREL) given the marriage scene in (4). The function label, on the other hand, captures the

---

[2] https://github.com/adishalev/SNACS_DMR_IAA

[3] Semantic Network of Adposition and Case Supersenses

Phrase	Scene Role	Coding	Function	Congruent?
The ball was hit **by** the batter	AGENT	**by**	AGENT	✓
Put the book **on** the shelf	GOAL	**on**	LOCUS	✗
Put the book **onto** the shelf	GOAL	**onto**	GOAL	✓
I talked **to** her	RECIPIENT	**to**	GOAL	✗
I heard it **in** my bedroom	LOCUS	**in**	LOCUS	✓
I heard it **from** my bedroom	LOCUS	**from**	SOURCE	✗
John**'s** death	THEME	**'s**	GESTALT	✗
the windshield **of** the car	WHOLE	**of**	WHOLE	✓

Table 1: SNACS for adpositions/possessives (Schneider et al., 2018b,a). The scene role and function annotations are labels from figure 1 and are often but not always congruent for a particular token. The function annotation reflects the semantics of the morphosyntactic coding (such as the choice of adposition). Note that, especially for adnominal PPs and genitives, the governor sometimes does not lexically denote an event or state; rather, a semantic relation such as possession or part-whole is indicated by the morphosyntax.

orthogonal dimsension of agency which is more closely tied to syntactic realization: Jane is the AGENT of the buying action, while the book is the THEME in (3); Jane and Bingley are the THEMEs of the marriage in (4). Further examples are shown in figure 2. In many cases, the scene role will be identical to the function. These are called **congruent construals**. But in other cases, they can differ, as illustrated in table 1.

In the rest of the section, we discuss a few difficult cases while assessing SNACS labels for the annotation of subject and objects, and decisions made regarding these challenges including slight deviations from the latest SNACS standards.

Scene role prioritization. In some cases, multiple supersenses are equally applicable at the scene level. In such cases, we give highest priority to more complex and less frequent scene types such as transfer (ORIGINATOR, RECIPIENT) or employee-organization (or social) relations (ORGMEMBER, ORG, SOCIALREL). The causal roles (AGENT, INSTRUMENT, THEME), if appearing in the scene position, are prioritized next. The highly frequent locative scenes (LOCUS, SOURCE, GOAL) are given the lowest priority. In example (10), the subject "I" could be considered either a metaphorical source location of the recommendation (i.e., SOURCE) or can be considered the speaker in a communication event (i.e., ORIGINATOR). The latter scene is prioritized, and the scene roles ORIGINATOR, TOPIC (i.e., the message), and RECIPIENT reflect the prioritized choice.

(10) [I]ORIGINATOR↝AGENT recommended [the book]TOPIC↝TOPIC [to him]RECIPIENT↝GOAL.

Transfer of possession often implies change of location, and being a part of something often implies being located in it. If both are salient, for the scene role annotation, we prioritize the more

complex scene over the locative semantics:

(11) [Jane]RECIPIENT↝AGENT took the book from me.

(12) I relinquished the book [to Jane]RECIPIENT↝GOAL.

(13) At the play, he spotted Mary [in the cast]ORG↝LOCUS.

In (11, 12), Jane is arguably a GOAL of motion by virtue of being a RECIPIENT of something physical. We do not use GOAL as the scene role, however, if RECIPIENT applies. In (13), Mary can be understood as part of the cast (which is an organization) or as located within the cast. We prioritize the former. Other pairs that tend to overlap include: RECIPIENT/BENEFICIARY, closely correlated when someone is given or told something for their benefit or harm—we prioritize RECIPIENT for the scene role; and STIMULUS/TOPIC, closely correlated when a thought or message triggers an emotional reaction—we prioritize STIMULUS for the scene role.

If two equally prioritized scenes are in conflict with one another, we rely on the semantics of the predicate to disambiguate the scene. Note that in (14), CJ is likely an employee of the White House. However, CJ is not considered the ORGMEMBER as the verb "brief" does not intrinsically conventionalize the employee-organization relationship in its semantics. With a predicate that conventionally encodes employment or some other stable relationship—*employ*, *hire*, *work **for/at***, etc.— ORGMEMBER would be annotated.

(14) [CJ]ORIGINATOR↝AGENT briefs the press [for the White House]ORG↝BENEFICIARY.

Role duplication. The latest version of SNACS we adopt for our study does not allow participant

(5) a. [Rachel]_{AGENT↝AGENT} opened [the door]_{THEME↝THEME} [**with** the remote control]_{INSTRUMENT↝INSTRUMENT}.

    b. [The remote control]_{INSTRUMENT↝INSTRUMENT} opened [the door]_{THEME↝THEME}.

    c. [I]_{AGENT↝AGENT} used [the remote control]_{INSTRUMENT↝INSTRUMENT} [**to** open the door]_{PURPOSE↝PURPOSE}.

    d. [The door]_{THEME↝THEME} opened.

(6) [Rachel]_{THEME↝THEME} sneezed.

(7) [Rachel]_{EXPERIENCER↝AGENT} watched [the children playing]_{STIMULUS↝THEME}.

(8) [Rachel]_{EXPERIENCER↝THEME} heard [the noise]_{STIMULUS↝THEME}.

(9) [Rachel]_{AGENT↝AGENT} spent [$5]_{COST↝COST} [**on** coffee]_{POSSESSION↝THEME}.

Figure 2: Annotated examples from our guidelines.

labels such as AGENT or THEME to appear multiple times in a given scene, opting for the use of a "Co-" label for the second participant sharing the same role (e.g., CO-AGENT). In applying SNACS guidelines for subjects and objects, this became untenable, as "Co-" prefixation could apply to a good majority of the PARTICIPANT labels, threatening a quick proliferation of the supersenses. E.g., (4) would require CO-SOCIALREL, (16) would require CO-EXPERIENCER, and so forth. In an effort to keep the supersense inventory limited, we diverge from the latest SNACS standards to allow role duplication in a scene. This is allowed even when targets assigned the same role are not fully symmetric or are qualitatively distinct as in (17).

(15) [A reception]_{THEME↝THEME} will precede [the dinner]_{THEME↝THEME}.

(16) [He]_{EXPERIENCER↝THEME} heard the news [**with** a stranger]_{EXPERIENCER↝ACCOMPANIER}.

(17) Replace [the old one]_{THEME↝THEME} [**with** the new one]_{THEME↝ACCOMPANIER}.

Thematic hierarchy. As discussed above, the function label generally reflects AGENT-THEME relations of a proposition. More specifically, we annotate all subjects and *direct* objects with a function in the following thematic hierarchy: {AGENT, CAUSER} > {INSTRUMENT, MEANS} > {THEME, TOPIC, COST}. In a transitive clause, the supersense of the subject cannot be ranked lower than the direct object (e.g., a subject construed as a THEME cannot have a direct object construed as an AGENT). Indirect objects in the English double object construction[4] are treated as RECIPIENT construals.

(18) I sent [John]_{RECIPIENT↝RECIPIENT} a cake.

(19) I sent a cake [**to** John]_{RECIPIENT↝GOAL}.

(20) I baked [John]_{RECIPIENT↝RECIPIENT} a cake.

(21) I paid [John]_{RECIPIENT↝RECIPIENT} [$10]_{COST↝COST}.

Copular sentences. These are treated differently from non-copular sentences. The English copula relates a subject to an object in what is semantically an identificational (22a) or predicational (22b) relationship. To these cases we assign IDENTITY-IDENTITY or GESTALT-CHARACTERISTIC at the scene level, respectively. Roughly speaking, IDENTITY indicates the identified or identifying category or referent, and CHARACTERISTIC indicates a property being ascribed to the GESTALT:

(22) a. [John]_{IDENTITY↝IDENTITY} is [a man]_{IDENTITY↝IDENTITY}.

    b. [John]_{GESTALT↝THEME} is [tall]_{CHARACTERISTIC↝CHARACTERISTIC}.

Open issues. The unresolved problem of causatives and caused-motion constructions is discussed in appendix A.

4 Interannotator Agreement Study

Data. We piloted our guidelines using a sample of 100 scenes from the English UCCA-annotated Wiki corpus[5] as detailed by Abend and Rappoport (2013). UCCA is a scheme for annotating coarse-grained predicate-argument structure such that syntactically varied paraphrases and translations should receive similar analyses. It captures both static and dynamic scenes and their participants, but does not mark semantic roles.

Annotators. Four annotators (A, B, C, D), all authors of this paper, took part in this study. All are computational linguistics researchers.

Datasets. Prior to development of guidelines for subjects and objects, one of the annotators (Annotator A) sampled 106 Wiki documents (44k tokens) and tagged all 10k instances of UCCA Participants[6] with a supersense based on the existing guidelines

---

[4] If there is a single overt object, we treat it as an indirect object if what would normally be a direct object is implicit: e.g., *John* is treated as an indirect object in *I told John.* (where the content of what is told is implicit).

[5] http://cs.huji.ac.il/~oabend/ucca.html; the Wikipedia corpus contains 369 documents (biographies of entertainment industry figures) with 159k tokens and 36k Participant units.

[6] The UCCA category Participant is broader than the PARTICIPANT supersense, also including locations, for example.

Subjects/Objects (N=57)				
κ	A	B	C	D
A		.75	.38	.72
B	.64		.42	.83
C	.50	.63		.54
D	.68	.83	.65	

(Lower triangle = Scene Role; upper triangle = Function.)

PPs (N=42)				
κ	A	B	C	D
A		.68	.68	.68
B	.54		.79	.84
C	.57	.64		.92
D	.60	.75	.75	

(Lower triangle = Scene Role; upper triangle = Function.)

Table 2: Cohen's Kappa scores for interannotator agreement for all pairings of four annotators.

for adpositions. This preliminary dataset was used to stimulate discussion for developing guidelines for subjects and objects. Once the new guidelines were written, four annotators first annotated a practice dataset of 48 UCCA Participant tokens, then adjudicated disagreements through discussion and clarified certain policies before annotating a final sample of 100 tokens for measuring agreement.[7] Participant units were sampled based on the preliminary annotation, stratified across subtypes of PARTICIPANT and CONFIGURATION to ensure diversity. In the final sample, the syntactic distribution is as follows: 31 subjects (including 4 passive subjects and 6 copular subjects); 26 objects (including 1 indirect object and 2 copular complements); 42 PPs; and 1 possessive.

Coverage of the hierarchy. Under the PARTICIPANT tree in the hierarchy, there are 12 supersenses, of which 11 were used as scene roles and 9 as functions. (By design, PARTICIPANT itself is never used and exists only to organize the hierarchy.) The CONFIGURATION tree includes 19 supersenses, of which 14 were used as scene roles and 10 as functions. In the CIRCUMSTANCE tree—which primarily applies to syntactic adverbials—GOAL, LOCUS, SOURCE, MANNER, MEANS, and CIRCUMSTANCE were all used as functions, and all but SOURCE also appeared as a scene role.

Quantitative IAA results. We first compare agreement on two subsamples: the subject/object Participants, and the prepositional phrase Participants. Pairwise Cohen's κ scores appear in table 2.

Subjects/objects: For the scene role, all annotators agree on 46% of items (26/57), and at least 3 annotators on 84%. For the function, 51% have total agreement, and 86% have a majority. Average pairwise κ is 0.66 for scene and 0.61 for function.

PPs: At the scene level, 48% (20/42) have total agreement, and 71% have a majority. For the function, 64% have total agreement, and 88% have a majority. Average pairwise κ is 0.64 for scene and 0.77 for function.

Thus subjects/objects (SOs) receive higher scene role agreement than PPs—somewhat surprising given that the labels were originally designed for prepositions! This may be an artifact of the particular sample, or may indicate that the scene role is more intuitive for SOs than for PPs. PPs have higher agreement than SOs with respect to function; this may be due to some difficulty deciding between AGENT and THEME for the function of SOs, plus the availability of extensive guidelines/examples for prepositional SNACS annotation.[8]

Disagreements involving agentivity. We found it can be difficult to choose between AGENT and THEME for the function of a subject with borderline agentivity, e.g., in scenes of *befriending* someone or *forming* a musical group with others. Likewise, the line between AGENT and THEME for the function can be unclear in cognition/perception scenes like *[She] enjoyed the fame* and *[She] saw the social scene as tedious and superficial*. We decided the annotator should consider whether the scene involves judgment or is more of a passive experience; EXPERIENCER⤳THEME would thus apply to the first example and EXPERIENCER⤳AGENT to second.[9] Finally, the line between CAUSER and INSTRUMENT can be unclear in sentences like *I was hit [**by** a car]* and *I was quoted [**by** a magazine]*.

UCCA issues. We found a handful of UCCA annotation errors—primarily where two verbs were analyzed as separate scenes but the first ought to be considered a light verb. A more interesting case was the relation between the two bolded expressions in *William S. Paley set terms that included… **ownership** of the negative at the end of the contract*. The UCCA annotation treats *William S. Paley* as a Participant of *ownership* (i.e., the owner). Though POSSESSOR is a natural scene role for the owner of something, we concluded that this was an indirect inference not suitable for annotating with a function.

5 Conclusion

We explored whether a system for semantic relation annotation can be extended beyond prepositions and possessives to cover English subjects and objects. While initial annotation results are promising, further work is needed to substantiate the approach on a larger scale, and ideally in multiple languages.

---

[7] 4 tokens where annotators noticed a problem with the UCCA annotation were discarded and replaced.

[8] Raw agreements are higher than kappa, but the same trends hold.

[9] There is precedent for this distinction in FrameNet's Perception_active vs. Perception_experience frames.

Acknowledgments

We would like to thank Jakob Prange and anonymous reviewers for their feedback. This research was supported in part by NSF award IIS-1812778 and grant 2016375 from the United States–Israel Binational Science Foundation (BSF), Jerusalem, Israel.

References

Omri Abend and Ari Rappoport. 2013. Universal Conceptual Cognitive Annotation (UCCA). In *Proc. of ACL*, pages 228–238, Sofia, Bulgaria.

David Dowty. 1991. Thematic proto-roles and argument selection. *Language*, 67(3):547–619.

Charles J. Fillmore. 1968. The case for case. In Emmon Bach and Robert Thomas Harms, editors, *Universals in Linguistic Theory*, pages 1–88. Holt, Rinehart, and Winston, New York.

Charles J. Fillmore. 1982. Frame Semantics. In *Linguistics in the Morning Calm*, pages 111–137. Hanshin Publishing Co., Seoul, South Korea.

Charles J. Fillmore and Collin Baker. 2009. A frames approach to semantic analysis. In Bernd Heine and Heiko Narrog, editors, *The Oxford Handbook of Linguistic Analysis*, pages 791–816. Oxford University Press, Oxford, UK.

Adele E. Goldberg. 2006. *Constructions at work: the nature of generalization in language*. Oxford University Press, Oxford.

Jena D. Hwang, Archna Bhatia, Na-Rae Han, Tim O'Gorman, Vivek Srikumar, and Nathan Schneider. 2017. Double trouble: the problem of construal in semantic annotation of adpositions. In *Proc. of *SEM*, pages 178–188, Vancouver, Canada.

Karin Kipper, Anna Korhonen, Neville Ryant, and Martha Palmer. 2008. A large-scale classification of English verbs. *Language Resources and Evaluation*, 42(1):21–40.

Beth Levin. 1993. *English verb classes and alternations: a preliminary investigation*. University of Chicago Press, Chicago.

Martha Palmer, Daniel Gildea, and Paul Kingsbury. 2005. The Proposition Bank: An annotated corpus of semantic roles. *Computational Linguistics*, 31(1):71–106.

Drew Reisinger, Rachel Rudinger, Francis Ferraro, Craig Harman, Kyle Rawlins, and Benjamin Van Durme. 2015. Semantic proto-roles. *Transactions of the Association for Computational Linguistics*, 3:475–488.

Nathan Schneider, Jena D. Hwang, Archna Bhatia, Na-Rae Han, Vivek Srikumar, Tim O'Gorman, Sarah R. Moeller, Omri Abend, Austin Blodgett, and Jakob Prange. 2018a. Adposition and Case Supersenses v2: Guidelines for English. *arXiv:1704.02134 [cs.CL]*.

Nathan Schneider, Jena D. Hwang, Vivek Srikumar, Jakob Prange, Austin Blodgett, Sarah R. Moeller, Aviram Stern, Adi Bitan, and Omri Abend. 2018b. Comprehensive supersense disambiguation of English prepositions and possessives. In *Proc. of ACL*, pages 185–196, Melbourne, Australia.

Yilun Zhu, Yang Liu, Siyao Peng, Austin Blodgett, Yushi Zhao, and Nathan Schneider. 2019. Adpositional supersenses for Mandarin Chinese. In *Proc. of SCiL*, volume 2, pages 334–337, New York, NY, USA.

A   Open Issues

Sometimes a sentence will construe a scene as involving more arguments than a predicate normally licenses, as in the following causative or caused-motion examples (Goldberg, 2006):

(23) $[\text{Rachel}]_{\text{THEME}\rightsquigarrow?}$ sneezed (implicit: blew) $[\text{the napkin}]_{\text{THEME}\rightsquigarrow\text{THEME}}$ $[\text{off the table}]_{\text{PATH}\rightsquigarrow\text{SOURCE}}$.

(24) $[\text{Rachel}]_{\text{AGENT}\rightsquigarrow?}$ (implicit: caused) jumped $[\text{the horse}]_{\text{AGENT}\rightsquigarrow\text{THEME}}$ $[\text{over the fence}]_{\text{PATH}\rightsquigarrow\text{PATH}}$.

So far, we have posited the scene to be the situation or event described by the predicate. The problem is that in addition to the scene evoked by the verb (sneezing in (23) and jumping in (24)), there is an added caused-motion scene whose semantics derives from the construction. Should there be an indication that the sneezer is also the causer of motion, and that the ultimate causer of jumping is separate from the impelled jumper? One possible solution would be to add implicit predicates so the verb- and construction-triggered scenes would be annotated separately. A different solution may be to relax the definition of what constitutes a scene to allow for non-predicate-driven scenes as well.

A Case Study on Meaning Representation for Vietnamese

Hà Mỹ Linh
VNU University of Science, Vietnam
halinh.hus@gmail.com

Nguyễn Thị Minh Huyền
VNU University of Science, Vietnam
huyenntm@hus.edu.vn

Abstract

This paper presents a case study on meaning representation for Vietnamese. Having introduced several existing semantic representation schemes, we select AMR (Abstract Meaning Representation) as a basis for our work on Vietnamese. From it, we define a meaning representation label set by adapting the English schema and taking into account the specific characteristics of Vietnamese.

1 Introduction

Semantic parsing, the task of assigning to a natural language expression a machine-interpretable meaning representation, is one of the most difficult problems in NLP. A meaning representation of a document will describe who did what to whom, when, where, why and how in the context. This problem is well studied in NLP, and many methods have been proposed to solve semantic parsing, such as rule-based (Popescu et al., 2003), supervised (Zelle, 1995), unsupervised (Goldwasser et al., 2011), *etc*. Some applications of semantic parsing include machine translation (Andreas et al., 2013), question-answering (He and Golub, 2016), and code generation (Ling et al., 2016). Current research on open-domain semantic parsing focuses on supervised learning methods, using large semantic annotated corpus as training data. However, few annotated corpora are available.

Semantic representations have been developed from different linguistic perspectives, in relation with diverse practical problems. Previously, meaning representation frameworks such as Minimum Recursive Semantics (MRS) (Copestake et al., 2005) and Discourse Representation Theory (Kamp et al., 2010) were developed with the aim of accounting for a variety of linguistic phenomena including anaphora, presupposition, temporal expressions, *etc*. Some recent meaning representations (Abstract Meaning Representation (AMR) (Banarescu et al., 2013), Universal Conceptual Cognitive Annotation (UCCA) (Abend and Rappoport, 2013), Dependency based Compositional Semantics (Liang et al., 2013), Treebank Semantics System (Alastair and Yoshimoto, 2012)) have been designed to focus on presenting semantic information such as semantic role and word meaning, or entities and relationships.

This paper focuses on Abstract Meaning Representation (AMR) to design a meaning representation for Vietnamese. In the next section, we discuss in greater detail the existing semantic representations for other languages and some dictionaries and corpora in Vietnamese that are useful for meaning representation. We then delve into the semantic research that has been developed for Vietnamese. Finally, we introduce our own work on building a meaning representation for Vietnamese based on AMR, and highlight the characteristics and the difficulties met when expressing semantics for Vietnamese text.

2 Related works

2.1 Meaning representation

Typically, semantic representations for a sentence often focuses on the predicate (usually verb) and its arguments. Researchers have been developing meaning representations for a sentence or paragraph to maximally exploit the semantics of each context.

One of the most common meaning representations is the "logical form", which is based on predicates and lambda calculus. When a sentence or paragraph has been fully parsed and all ambiguities resolved, its meaning will be represented in a unique logical form. However, this only fully solves a few simple cases. In contrast, in seman-

Proceedings of the First International Workshop on Designing Meaning Representations, pages 148–153
Florence, Italy, August 1st, 2019 ©2019 Association for Computational Linguistics

tic analysis, we often encounter complex structures that cannot be captured in tree structures or simple logical expressions, requiring the development of more advanced semantic representations.

In Dependency-Based Compositional Semantics (Liang et al., 2013), the authors present a representation of formal semantics using trees. The full version of this model can handle linguistic phenomena such as quantification or comparison. For their part, the authors of Treebank Semantics System (Alastair and Yoshimoto, 2012) [1] describe a method to convert existing treebanks with syntactic information into banks of meaning representation. Inputs to the system are expressions of the formal language obtained from the conversion of parsed treebank data, and outputs are predicate logic-based meaning representations.

Universal Conceptual Cognitive Annotation (UCCA) (Abend and Rappoport, 2013), based on Basic Linguistic Theory (Genetti, 2011), denotes semantic differences and aims to abstract specific syntax structures. It includes a rich set of semantic distinctions. UCCA contains a set of scenes which includes: relationships, argument structures of verbs, nouns and adjectives.

In this section, we focus more on two meaning representations: Abstract Meaning Representation (AMR) and Groningen Meaning Bank (GMB).

2.1.1 Abstract Meaning Representation (AMR)

AMR, built in 2013 by (Banarescu et al., 2013), is a logic-labeled semantic data warehouse (sembank) for English. AMR captures the information: "Who did what to whom?". Each sentence is represented by a directional non-cyclic graph whose labeled arcs represent relations and leaf nodes represent concepts (Figure 1). AMR semantic information is captured through events and concepts described as predicates with their arguments. AMR concepts are either English words, Prop-Bank framesets, or special keywords.

AMR is used in many NLP tasks, and much research has been dedicated to automatically generating AMR for various languages. This requires several pre-processing tasks such as named entity recognition, semantic role labeling, word sense disambiguation, *etc*. Some AMR parsing tools use stack-lstms (Miguel and Yaser, 2017), recurrent neural networks (Foland and Martin, 2017), or

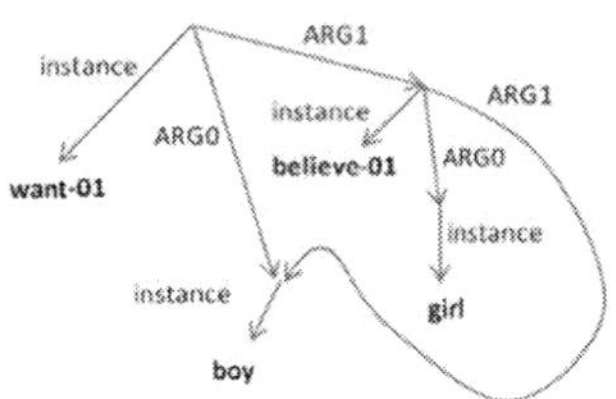

Figure 1: An example of a graph in AMR

transition-based parsing (Wang et al., 2015). Most of those methods are very recent and experimental. Besides, AMR has some limitations: it does not present quantifier scope, co-references, tense, aspect, or quotation marks.

2.1.2 Groningen Meaning Bank (GMB)

GMB (Bos, 2013) is a crowdsourced semantic resource. Its aim is to provide a large collection of semantically annotated English texts with formal rather than shallow semantics. It also focuses on annotating texts, not isolated sentences, and can integrate various semantic phenomena such as predicate argument structure, scope, tense, thematic roles, rhetorical relations and presuppositions into a single semantic formalism: Discourse Representation Theory (Kamp et al., 2010).

Annotations in GMB are introduced in two main ways: direct edition is done by experts, while a game called Wordrobe lets anyone enrich it indirectly. A first release of GMB contains 1,000 texts with 4,239 sentences and 82,752 tokens. The final version includes 10,000 documents with more than 1 million words.

All those semantic corpora rely on the existence of resources such as dictionary, constituency treebank, dependency treebank, Verbnet, Wordnet, Propbank, *etc*. In the next section, we discuss the necessary resources towards meaning representation for Vietnamese.

2.2 Resources for Vietnamese

Vietnamese language has received the attention of many NLP research groups in recent years, and many basic problems of parsing and semantic analysis have been solved, but they generally only revolve around simple vocabulary and syntactic issues. Some notable efforts to build data for Vietnamese NLP are:

- Dictionary: the largest dictionary built according to the Lexical Markup Framework

---

[1] http://www.compling.jp/ajb129/ts.html

(LMF) standard is the Vietnamese Computational Lexicon - VCL (Huyen et al., 2006), (Luong and Huyen, 2008). Built in the framework of a Vietnam national project, it contains about 42,000 word entries. Its initial goal is to serve for Vietnamese syntax processing, and each item is described along three dimensions: morphology, syntax, and semantics.

- VietTreebank is a corpus containing about 10,000 syntactically annotated sentences in Penn treebank format. As for English, the label set of VietTreeBank includes part-of-speech labels, phrase labels, and functional syntactic labels.

- vnPropbank: the authors of (Linh et al., 2015) have applied semantic role labeling to build a vnPropbank that contains over 5000 sentences from VietTreeBank. Contrary to the English Propbank, Vietnamese framesets are not connected with any other resource, since there is no Vietnamese lexicon similar to VerbNet.

- Vietnamese dependency treebank: in (Thi et al., 2013), the authors define a dependency label set based on the English dependency schema. Next, they propose an algorithm to transform more than 10000 sentences from VietTreebank into a dependency treebank (Phuong et al., 2015), (T-L et al., 2016). 3000 sentences from the Vietnamese dependency treebank were integrated into Stanford University's Universal Dependency project (Luong Nguyen Thi and Le-Hong, 2018).

In addition, (Nguyen et al., 2016) introduces a lexicon enriched with syntactic and semantic information, based on the VCL. This lexicon is designed to serve for a syntactic and semantic parser using the TAG (tree adjoining grammar) formalism. The authors have assigned 23826 of the 44812 entries in the VCL lexicon to TAG elementary trees and logical semantic representations. This allows us to be able to make the inference of new knowledge from the original sentence. It can be considered as a work of great significance for analyzing Vietnamese semantics based on the predicate frames and lexicons.

Thus, a number of dictionaries and corpora which are useful for meaning representation exist for Vietnamese. However, these corpora have limitations, and Vietnamese still lacks lexical resources comparable to VerbNet, FrameNet or WordNet for English, making the building of a good semantic representation a difficult problem and that will take a lot of time and effort.

3 A case study: Vietnamese meaning representation

3.1 Annotation model

For Vietnamese, we have chosen to base our work on AMR, which is a flexible and easy to understand semantic representation, and benefits from many AMR analysis algorithms developed for English. However, we identify some differences between ways of expressing meaning in English and Vietnamese, and therefore need to design some additional components.

Our goal is not only to answer the simple question "Who is doing what to whom", but also to add other information such as: where, when, why and how. We want to show the relationship between entities in the sentence in the most complete and understandable way. In addition, we would like to overcome some limitations of AMR such as adding co-reference, tense and some labels to express function words and extra words, which are very important in Vietnamese since they carry all the information about gender, tense, time, *etc*.

3.2 Data

Vietnamese text: the data we use to test semantic representation is a Vietnamese translation of Saint-Exupéry's *The Little Prince*. An AMR version of it exists for English, which will provide us with a reference for design, discussion and comparison.

We first implement a number of pre-processing steps such as: word segmentation, part of speech tagging and dependency parsing. These pre-processing steps are necessary because they allow us to identify what the sentence components are, their meanings, and the relationships between them.

For example, the sentence "**Nó** [*It*] **vẽ** [*draw*] **một** [*one*] **con** [*animal classifier*[2]] **trăn** [*boa*] **đang** [*present continuous tense*] **nuốt** [*swallow*] **một** [*one*] **con** [*animal classifier*] **thú** [*animal*]" (*It was a picture of a boa constrictor in the act*

---

[2]Vietnamese, like many Asian languages, has noun classifiers

of swallowing an animal) is pre-processed as follows:

1	nó	P	2	nsubj
2	vẽ	V	0	root
3	một	M	5	nummod
4	con	Nc	5	compound
5	trăn	N	7	nsubj
6	đang	R	7	advmod
7	nuốt	V	2	dobj
8	một	M	10	nummod
9	con	Nc	10	compound
10	thú	N	7	dobj
11	.	PUNCT	2	punct

In which the third, fourth and fifth columns are respectively the POS label[3], the word from which the current word depends on (head of a word), and the dependency label.

We then build a meaning representation for this sentence and conduct a comparison with the original sentence in the AMR corpus:

```
(v / vẽ-01
     :domain (n / nó)
     :topic (t / trăn
              :Arg0-of (n2 / nuốt-01
                   :tense (d / đang)
                   :Arg1 (t2 / thú))))

(p / picture
     :domain (i / it)
     :topic (b2 / boa
              :mod (c2 / constrictor)
              :ARG0-of (s / swallow-01
                   :ARG1 (a / animal))))
```

In this example, English uses the copula verb (*was*) while the Vietnamese version use a normal verb (*vẽ - draw*). Therefore, the main event in the English sentence is *p / picture*, while in Vietnamese we have *v / vẽ-01*. The word *"constrictor"* is not translated in the Vietnamese sentence, so there is no *mod* relation. In addition, as we want to keep trace the tense information, we add the new label *"tense"* to indicate the present continuous tense in this sentence.

Vietnamese computational lexicon (VCL): we rely on the aforementioned VCL (Huyen et al., 2006) to extract the necessary Vietnamese semantic information. Each of its 42,000 entries contains information such as definition, POS, examples,

synonyms, antonyms, as well as some very useful (albeit incomplete) information such as predicate frameset, semantic tree, semantic role [4].

3.3 Discussion

We developed an application to assist the manual annotation process, allowing us to choose, for an input text, the meaning of words in the VCL dictionary, add or update semantic labels. The output is a meaning representation of the sentence.

We perform the labeling and build the AMR label set for single sentences in the text of The Little Prince. In addition to using the English labels already in AMR, mapping 193 kinds of semantic categories in VCL to entities in AMR, we have introduced specific labels for Vietnamese to overcome some limitations of AMR. While this is an ongoing work, we can already present a few first remarks on the application of AMR to Vietnamese:

- **Syntactic modals**: we do not group words like in AMR English. For example: "obligate-01" instead of "must", "obligate"... In Vietnamese, there is not yet a list of synonyms that could be helpful for this grouping, as in English. For now, we still keep original syntactic modals in the sentence such as: "phải" (*must*), "nên" (*should*), "có_thể" (*can*)...

- **Adverbs with -ly**: in Vietnamese, these words do not exist. But we still use the *"manner"* for adjectives that act as adverbs in a sentence (which is similar to English, since adverbs normally get stemmed to the adjective form). For example: "nhanh" (*quickly - quick*), chậm (*slowly - slow*)...

- **Adjectives that invoke predicates**: there is a syntactic difference between English and Vietnamese. In a sentence such as "Cô ấy rất đẹp" (She is very beautiful), in Vietnamese, "đẹp" (beautiful) is a predicate without "be" as in English. However, they have the same meaning representation because AMR leaves out the "be" information in this case.

- **Noun classifiers**: in Vietnamese, a noun classifier is used before common nouns in the noun phrase. They are generally referred to as "individual classifier" such as: "cái nhà" (*house*), "cái mũ" (*hat*), "con chó" (*dog*), *etc.*

---

[3]P: pronoun, V: verb, N: noun, M: numeral, Nc: noun classifier, R: adverb, PUNC: punctuation

[4]https://vlsp.hpda.vn/demo/?page=vcl

Similar to Chinese (Li et al., 2016), we leave out this word in the meaning representation. There is, however, a special case: if a noun classifier stands alone in a sentence, we need to show its co-reference in the previous sentence. For example: "Tôi có hai **cái** mũ. Tôi thích **cái** màu xanh." (*I have two hats. I like the blue one.*). In this sentence, "cái" indicates "cái mũ" which is mentioned before.

- **Tenses**: the Vietnamese tenses are often described by using function words such as "đã" (*in past*), "đang" (*in present*), "sẽ" (*in future*).

4   Conclusion

We have presented some ways to represent semantic information, and have further studied the application of the AMR formalism to the representation of Vietnamese semantics. Currently, we are conducting AMR-based labeling of the text *The Little Prince* using the VCL dictionary. As this task progresses, we will keep refining and proposing further improvements to the semantic representation schema for Vietnamese.

In the future, after completing the data labeling, we hope to build an alignment tool between AMR in English and AMR in Vietnamese so that we can make a comparison between the two languages. Besides, we would like to build a converter across semantic representations such as from AMR to GMB or UCCA.

References

Omri Abend and Ari Rappoport. 2013. Universal conceptual cognitive annotation (ucca). In *Proceedings of the 51st Annual Meeting of the Association for Computational Linguistics (Volume 1: Long Papers)*, pages 228–238, Sofia, Bulgaria. Association for Computational Linguistics.

Butler Alastair and Kei Yoshimoto. 2012. Banking meaning representations from treebanks. *Linguistic Issues in Language Technology - LiLT*, 7:1–22.

Jacob Andreas, Andreas Vlachos, and Stephen Clark. 2013. Semantic parsing as machine translation. *Association for Computational Linguistics*, 2:47–52.

Laura Banarescu, Claire Bonial, Shu Cai, Madalina Georgescu, Kira Griffitt, Ulf Hermjakob, Kevin Knight, Philipp Koehn, Martha Palmer, and Nathan Schneider. 2013. Abstract meaning representation for sembanking. In *Proceedings of the 7th Linguistic Annotation Workshop and Interoperability with Discourse*, pages 178–186, Sofia, Bulgaria. Association for Computational Linguistics.

Johan Bos. 2013. The groningen meaning bank. In *Proceedings of the Joint Symposium on Semantic Processing. Textual Inference and Structures in Corpora*, page 2, Trento, Italy.

Ann Copestake, Dan Flickinger, Carl Pollard, and Ivan A. Sag. 2005. Minimal recursion semantics: An introduction. *Research on Language and Computation*, 3(2):281–332.

William Foland and James H. Martin. 2017. Abstract meaning representation parsing using lstm recurrent neural networks. In *Proceedings of the 55th Annual Meeting of the Association for Computational Linguistics (Volume 1: Long Papers)*, pages 463–472, Vancouver, Canada. Association for Computational Linguistics.

Carol Genetti. 2011. Basic linguistic theory. vol. 1: Methodology. vol. 2: Grammatical topics by r. m. w. dixon. *Language*, 87:899–904.

Dan Goldwasser, Roi Reichart, James Clarke, and Dan Roth. 2011. Confidence driven unsupervised semantic parsing. In *Proceedings of the 49th Annual Meeting of the Association for Computational Linguistics: Human Language Technologies*, pages 1486–1495, Portland, Oregon, USA. Association for Computational Linguistics.

Xiaodong He and David Golub. 2016. Character-level question answering with attention. *Proceedings of the 2016 Conference on Empirical Methods in Natural Language Processing*, pages 1598–1607.

Nguyen Thi Minh Huyen, Laurent Romary, Mathias Rossignol, and Xuan Luong Vu. 2006. A lexicon for vietnamese language processing. *Language Resources and Evaluation*, 40(3/4):291–309.

Hans Kamp, Josef Genabith, and Uwe Reyle. 2010. *Discourse Representation Theory*, pages 125–394.

Bin Li, Yuan Wen, Weiguang Qu, Lijun Bu, and Nianwen Xue. 2016. Annotating the little prince with chinese amrs. In *LAW@ACL*.

Percy Liang, Michael I. Jordan, and Dan Klein. 2013. Learning dependency-based compositional semantics. *Computational Linguistics*, 39(2):389–446.

Wang Ling, Phil Blunsom, Edward Grefenstette, Karl Moritz Hermann, Tomas Kocisky, Fumin Wang, and Andrew Senior. 2016. Latent predictor networks for code generation. *Proceedings of the 54th Annual Meeting of the Association for Computational Linguistics (Volume 1: Long Papers)*, 1:599–609.

H. M. Linh, N. T. Lương, N. V. Hùng, N. T. M. Huyền, L. H. Phương, and P. T. Hue. 2015. Xây dựng kho ngữ liệu mẫu có gán nhãn vai nghĩa cho tiếng việt. In *Proceedings of the National Symposium on Research, Development and Application of Information and Communication Technology*, pages 409–414.

Vu Xuan Luong and Nguyen Thi Minh Huyen. 2008. Building a vietnamese computational lexicon. In *Proceedings of the National Symposium on Research, Development and Application of Information and Communication Technology*, pages 283–292.

Thi Minh Huyen Nguyen Luong Nguyen Thi, Linh Ha My and Phuong Le-Hong. 2018. Using bilstm in dependency parsing for vietnamese. *Computación y Sistemas*, 22:853–862.

Ballesteros Miguel and Al-Onaizan Yaser. 2017. Amr parsing using stack-lstms. In *Proceedings of the 2017 Conference on Empirical Methods in Natural Language Processing*, pages 1269–1275, Copenhagen, Denmark. Association for Computational Linguistics.

Thi Huyen Nguyen, Nguyen Thi Minh Huyen, Quyen The Ngo, and Minh Hai Nguyen. 2016. Towards a syntactically and semantically enriched lexicon for vietnamese processing. In *The 2013 RIVF International Conference on Computing and Communication Technologies - Research, Innovation, and Vision for Future (RIVF)*, pages 187–192.

Le-Hong Phuong, Huyen Nguyen, Thi-Luong Nguyen, and My-Linh Ha. 2015. Fast dependency parsing using distributed word representations. volume 9441.

Ana-Maria Popescu, Oren Etzioni, and Henry Kautz. 2003. Towards a theory of natural language interfaces to databases. In *Proceedings of the 8th International Conference on Intelligent User Interfaces*, IUI '03, pages 149–157. ACM.

Nguyen T-L, Ha M-L, Le-Hong P, and Nguyen T-M-H. 2016. Using distributed word representations in graph-based dependency parsing for vietnamese. In *The 9th National Conference on Fundamental and Applied Information Technology (FAIR'9)*, pages 804–810.

Luong Nguyen Thi, Linh Ha My, H. Nguyen Viet, Huyền Nguyễn Thị Minh, and Phuong Le Hong. 2013. Building a treebank for vietnamese dependency parsing. *The 2013 RIVF International Conference on Computing and Communication Technologies - Research, Innovation, and Vision for Future (RIVF)*, pages 147–151.

Chuan Wang, Nianwen Xue, and Sameer Pradhan. 2015. A transition-based algorithm for amr parsing. In *Proceedings of the 2015 Conference of the North American Chapter of the Association for Computational Linguistics: Human Language Technologies*, pages 366–375, Denver, Colorado. Association for Computational Linguistics.

John M. Zelle. 1995. *Using Inductive Logic Programming to Automate the Construction of Natural Language Parsers*. Ph.D. thesis, Department of Computer Sciences, The University of Texas at Austin, Austin, TX.

VerbNet Representations: Subevent Semantics for Transfer Verbs

Susan Windisch Brown
University of Colorado
brownsw@colorado.edu

Julia Bonn
University of Colorado
bonnj@colorado.edu

James Gung
University of Colorado
james.gung@colorado.edu

Annie Zaenen
Stanford University
azaenen@stanford.edu

James Pustejovsky
Brandeis University
jamesp@cs.brandeis.edu

Martha Palmer
University of Colorado
mpalmer@colorado.edu

Abstract

This paper announces the release of a new version of the English lexical resource VerbNet with substantially revised semantic representations designed to facilitate computer planning and reasoning based on human language. We use the transfer of possession and transfer of information event representations to illustrate both the general framework of the representations and the types of nuances the new representations can capture. These representations use a Generative Lexicon-inspired subevent structure to track attributes of event participants across time, highlighting oppositions and temporal and causal relations among the subevents.

1 Introduction

Many natural language processing tasks have seen rapid advancement in recent years using deep learning methods; however, those tasks that require precise tracking of event sequences and participants across a discourse still perform better using explicit representations of the meanings of each sentence or utterance. To be most useful for automatic language understanding and generation, such representations need to be both automatically derivable from text and reasonably formatted for computer analysis and planning systems. For applications like robotics or interactions with avatars, commonsense inferences needed to understand human language directions or interactions are often not derivable directly from the utterance. Tracking intrinsic and extrinsic states of entities, such as their existence, location or functionality, currently requires explicit statements with precise temporal sequencing.

In this paper, we describe new semantic representations for the lexical resource VerbNet that provide this sort of information for thousands of verb senses and introduce a means for automatically translating text to these representations. We explore the format of these representations and the types of information they track by thoroughly examining the representations for transfer of possessions and information. These event types are excellent examples of complex events with multiple participants and relations between them that change across the time frame of the event. By aligning our new representations more closely with the dynamic event structure encapsulated by the Generative Lexicon, we can provide a more precise subevent structure that makes the changes over time explicit (Pustejovsky, 1995; Pustejovsky et al., 2016). *Who has what when* and *who knows what when* are exactly the sorts of things that we want to extract from text, but this extraction is difficult without explicit, computationally-tractable representations. These event types also make up a substantial portion of VerbNet: 37 classes of verbs deal with change of possession and transfer of information out of VerbNet's 300+ classes, covering 810 verbs.

2 Background

The language resource VerbNet (Kipper et al., 2006) is a hierarchical, wide-coverage verb lexicon that groups verbs into classes based on similarities in their syntactic and semantic behavior (Schuler, 2005). Each class in VerbNet includes a set of member verbs, the thematic roles used in the predicate-argument structure of these members (Bonial et al., 2011), and the class-specific selectional preferences for those roles. The class also provides a set of typical syntactic patterns and corresponding semantic representations. A verb can be a member of multiple classes; for example, *run* is a member of 8 VerbNet classes, including the run-51.3.2 class (*he ran to the store*)

Proceedings of the First International Workshop on Designing Meaning Representations, pages 154–163
Florence, Italy, August 1st, 2019 ©2019 Association for Computational Linguistics

and the function-105.2.1 class (*the car isn't running*). These memberships usually correspond to coarse-grained senses of the verb. The resource was originally based on Levin's (1993) analysis of English verbs but has since been expanded to include dozens of additional classes and hundreds of additional verbs and verb senses.

VerbNet representations previously formed the basis for Parameterized Action Representation (PAR) providing a conceptual representation of different types of actions (Badler et al., 1999). These actions involve changes of state, changes of location, and exertion of force and can be used to animate human avatars in a virtual 3D environment (R. Bindiganavale and Palmer, 2000). They are particularly well suited for motion and contact verb classes, providing an abstract, language-independent representation (Kipper and Palmer, 2000). The more precise temporal sequencing described here is even more suitable as a foundation for natural language instructions and human-robot or human-avatar interactions.

2.1 VerbNet

VerbNet has long been used in NLP for semantic role labeling and other inference-enabling tasks (Shi and Mihalcea, 2005; Giuglea and Moschitti, 2006; Loper et al., 2007; Bos, 2008). In addition, automatic disambiguation of a verb's VerbNet class has been used as a stand-in for verb sense disambiguation (Abend et al., 2008; Brown et al., 2014; Croce et al., 2012; Kawahara and Palmer, 2014).

VerbNet's semantic representations use a Davidsonian first-order-logic formulation that incorporates the thematic roles of the class. Each frame in a class is labeled with a flat syntactic pattern (e.g., NP V NP). The "syntax" that follows shows how the thematic roles for that class appear in that pattern (e.g., Agent V Patient), much like the argument role constructions of Goldberg (2006). A previous revision of the VerbNet semantic representations made the correspondence of these patterns to constructions more explicit by using a common predicate (i.e., path_rel) for all caused-motion construction frames(Hwang, 2014). At the request of some users, we are substituting more specific predicates for the general path_rel predicate, such as has_location, has_state and has_possession, although the subevent patterns continue to show the commonality across these caused-motion frames.

Each frame also includes a semantic representation that uses basic predicates to show the relationships between the thematic role arguments and to track any changes over the time course of the event. Thematic roles that appear in the "syntax" should always appear somewhere in the semantic representation. Overall, this linking in each frame of the syntactic pattern to a semantic representation is a unique feature of VerbNet that emphasizes the close interplay of syntax and semantics.

2.2 Revision of the Semantic Representations

VerbNet's old representations included an event variable E as an argument to the predicates. Representations of states were indicated with either a bare E, as for the own-100 class: **has_possession**(E, Pivot, Theme), or During(E), as for the contiguous_location-47.8 class (*Italy borders France*): **contact**(During(E), Theme, Co-Theme). Most classes having to do with change, such as changes in location, changes in state and changes in possession, used a **path_rel** predicate in combination with Start(E), During(E), and End/Result(E) to show the transition from one location or state to another (1).

(1) *The rabbit hopped across the lawn.*
Theme V Trajectory
motion(during(E), Theme)
path_rel(start(E), Theme, ?Initial location[1],
CH_OF_LOC, prep)
path_rel(during(E), Theme, Trajectory,
CH_OF_LOC, prep)
path_rel(end(E), Theme, ?Destination,
CH_OF_LOC, prep)

Efforts to use VerbNet's semantic representations (Zaenen et al., 2008; Narayan-Chen et al., 2017), however, indicated a need for greater consistency and expressiveness. We have addressed consistency on several fronts. First, all necessary participants are accounted for in the representations, whether they are instantiated in the syntax, incorporated in the verb itself (e.g., *to drill),* or simply logically necessary (e.g., all entities that change location begin in an initial location, whether it is commonly mentioned or not).

---

[1]A question mark in front of a thematic role indicates a role that appears in the syntax in some frames for the class but not in this particular frame.

Second, similar event types are represented with a similar format; for example, all states are represented with E, never with During(E). Finally, predicates are given formal definitions that apply across classes.

In order to clarify what is happening at each stage of an event, we turned to the Generative Lexicon (Pustejovsky, 1995) for an explicit theory of subevent structure. Classic GL characterizes the different Aktionsarten in terms of structured subevents, with states represented with a simple e, processes as a sequence of states characterizing values of some attribute, $e_1...e_n$, and transitions describing the opposition inherent in achievements and accomplishments. In subsequent work within GL, event structure has been integrated with dynamic semantic models in order to more explicitly represent the attribute modified in the course of the event (the location of the moving entity, the extent of a created or destroyed entity, etc.) as a sequence of states related to time points or intervals. This Dynamic Event Model (Pustejovsky and Moszkowicz, 2011; Pustejovsky, 2013) explicitly labels the transitions that move an event from frame to frame.

Applying the Dynamic Event Model to Verb-Net semantic representations allowed us refine the event sequences by expanding the previous tripartite division of Start(E), During(E), and End(E) to an indefinite number of subevents. These numbered subevents allow very precise tracking of participants across time and a nuanced representation of causation and action sequencing within a single event. In the general case, e_1 occurs before e_2, which occurs before e_3, and so on. We've introduced predicates that indicate temporal and causal relations between the subevents, such as **cause**(e_i, e_j) and **co-temporal**(e_i, e_j).

We have made other refinements suggested by the GL Dynamic Event Model. For example, we greatly expanded the use of negated predicates to make explicit the opposition occurring in events involving change: e.g., *John died* is analyzed as the opposition $\langle$**alive**(e_1,Patient), $\neg$**alive**(e_2,Patient)$\rangle$. Compare the new representation for changes of location in (2) to (1) above. In (2), we use the opposition between **has_location** and $\neg$**has_location** to make clear that once the Theme is motion (in e_2), it is no longer in the Initial_location. In order to distinguish the event type associated with a semantic predicate, we in-

troduced a new event variable, $\ddot{e}$, to distinguish a process from other types of subevents, such as states. For example, see the motion predicate in (2).

(2) *The rabbit hopped across the lawn.*
Theme V Trajectory
has_location(e_1, Theme, ?Initial_Location)
motion($\ddot{e}_2$, Theme, Trajectory)
$\neg$**has_location**(e_2, Theme, ?Initial_location)
has_location(e_3, Theme, ?Destination)

Although people infer that an entity is no longer at its initial location once motion has begun, computers need explicit mention of this fact to accurately track the location of an entity. Similarly, some states hold throughout an event, while others do not. Our new representations make these distinctions clear, where *pre-event*, *while-event*, and *post-event* conditions are distinguished formally in the representation.

Elsewhere (Brown et al., 2018), we discuss in more detail the Dynamic Event Model, show the effect of the new subevent structure on the interpretation of the role of the Agent, and give further examples of the new change of location and change of state representations.

3 Change of Possession

In this section, we closely examine the representations for events involving changes in possession. These representations illustrate the greater clarity and flexibility we have gained by adopting the conventions described in section 2. They also show some of the choices we have made to capture the underlying semantics while maintaining a connection to the varying surface forms. We discuss both one-way transfers (*give*) and two-way transfers (*sell*). We also address the different perspectives verbs can impose on a transfer event, such as the difference between *Mary gave John the book* and *John obtained the book from Mary*, in which the Agent of the event is the Source or the Recipient of the item, respectively. These variations have interesting analogs in the Transfer of Information classes (Fig. 1), which we discuss in Section 4.

The semantic representations for changes of possession in VerbNet assume a literal, non-metaphoric use of the verbs in question. Metaphor may select only some of the source domain's participants or entailments. For example, *She stole*

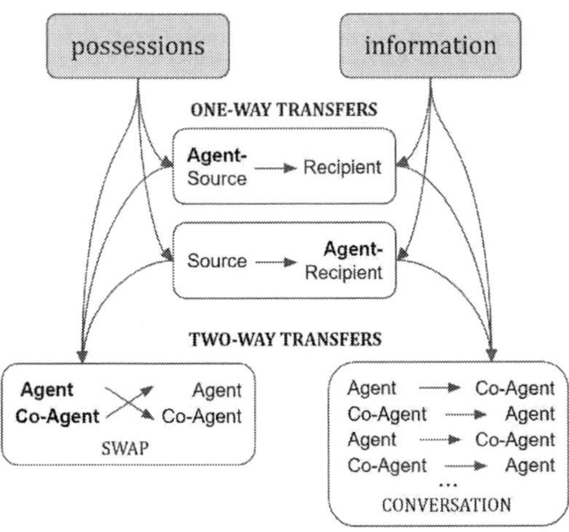

Figure 1: Primary distinctions made in the VerbNet representations for events involving transfer

John's car entails that John no longer has possession of his car, whereas *She stole John's heart* does not entail his loss of a vital organ. An analysis of VerbNet classes in terms of their application to figurative language (Brown and Palmer, 2012) showed that some classes concern only metaphoric uses of their member verbs (e.g., calibratible_cos-45.6.1), with semantic representations that directly represent the figurative meaning without reference to the source domain. Many classes, however, were shown to refer to literal uses of the verbs, although it was suggested that transformations or re-interpretations of the semantic representations could be possible.

3.1 Previous Representations

The previous model allowed only three temporal subevent periods: Start, During, and End. For both Change of Possession and Transfer of Information classes, each possession received one **path_rel** for the Start period and one for the End period, allowing one clear owner per period. For Change of Possession, it was reasonable to assume that possession transferred fully during the event, and as such, information about who did not possess a thing at any point could have been inferred through a rule. This model was sufficient for Change of Possession classes in and of themselves, but failed to capture any contrast with Transfer of Information classes, for which this assumption does not hold.

The **cause** predicate included arguments for an Agent or Causer (no other thematic roles were allowed), and the overall event E. This was sufficient

for one-way transfers in which one party was responsible for initiating the entire change, but was insufficient when more than one transfer occurred. There was no way to show that one party could initiate one transfer while another party initiated another. Two-way transfer representations either attributed all causation to one party, or omitted the **cause** predicate entirely. The ability to omit the predicate led one to wonder why it was ever necessary to include it.

3.2 New Representations

Three predicates form the core of the change of possession representations:

- **has_possession**(e, [slot-1], [slot-2])
- **transfer**(e, [slot-1], [slot-2], [slot-3])
- **cause**(e_i, e_j)

We define **has_possession** broadly as involving ownership or control over a thing; e.g., *I have a pencil* can mean either you own a pencil or you (possibly temporarily) have use of a pencil. Within the predicate, slot-1 is reserved for the possessor and can take thematic roles Source, Recipient, Goal, Agent, and Co-Agent. Slot-2 is reserved for the possession, and can take roles Theme and Asset.

Transfer is now a causative predicate, describing an event in which possession of a thing transfers from one possessor to another. All three participants are given as arguments. Slot-1 is reserved for the possessor who initiates the transfer, and can take thematic roles Agent and Co-Agent. Slot-2 is reserved for the possession (Theme or Asset), and slot-3 is reserved for the other possessor (Source, Recipient/Goal, Agent, and Co-Agent).

The order of arguments within this predicate often aligns with the temporal order of possession, but this is incidental. Sometimes, an Agent who is initiating a **transfer** is the recipient of that transfer; in these cases, the Agent will still occupy slot-1, even though they end up with possession last. It is also possible for an Agent to occupy slot-3 if another party (Co-Agent) is initiating the **transfer**. The subevent numbering of the **has_possession** predicates before and after the **transfer** provide a full description of the temporal order of possession.

The new basic representation is shown in (3).

(3) **has_possession**(e_1, Source, Theme)
   ¬**has_possession**(e_1, Recipient, Theme)

transfer(e_2, Source, Theme, Recipient)
has_possession(e_3, Recipient, Theme)
¬**has_possession**(e_3, Source, Theme)
cause(e_2, e_3)

This representation contains an initial state subevent, a **transfer** subevent, and a resulting state subevent. **Cause**(e_2, e_3) tells us that the **transfer** triggers the resulting state. The opposing ¬**has_possession** predicates show without a doubt that the Source stops having possession as soon as the transfer occurs, and the Recipient does not take possession until then. This allows for clear automatic tracking of an entity's ownership status and provides an important contrast with the new Transfer of Information representations. It will also allow coverage of cases of shared ownership of possessions, if VerbNet expands in that direction.

3.3 Change of Possession Variations

Agents as Sources or Recipients: Depending on the class, an Agent may function as Source or Recipient. In the old representations, some classes ended up including as core roles both an Agent and a Recipient, or an Agent and a Source, even if those roles always overlapped in the syntax. This was likely due to pressure to include in the class thematic roles that were projected by the main predicates, **path_rel**, **cause** and **transfer**. In the new model, we let Agent stand in for whichever role it overlaps throughout the representation. This eliminates the need for the **equals** predicate, and has allowed us to eliminate syntactically redundant roles from the class role inventories.

Six classes demonstrate one-way transfers in which the entity who starts with possession initiates giving that possession away: cheat-10.6.1, contribute-13.2, equip-13.4.2, fulfilling-13.4.1, future_having-13.3, and give-13.1-1. In example (4) from fulfilling-13.4.1, Agent replaces Source throughout.

(4) *Brown presented a plaque to Jones*
Agent V Theme Recipient
has_possession(e_1, Agent, Theme)
¬**has_possession**(e_1, Recipient, Theme)
transfer(e_2, Agent, Theme, Recipient)
has_possession(e_3, Recipient, Theme)
¬**has_possession**(e_3, Agent, Theme)
cause(e_2, e_3)

Five classes demonstrate one-way transfers in which an entity who does not have possession of

a thing initiates taking that thing from the original possessor: berry-13.7, deprive-10.6.2, obtain-13.5.2, rob-10.6.4, and steal-10.5. The example from steal-10.5 in (5) shows how Agent replaces Recipient.

(5) *They stole the painting from the museum*
Agent V Theme Source
has_possession(e_1, Source, Theme)
¬**has_possession**(e_1, Agent, Theme)
transfer(e_2, Agent, Theme, Source)
has_possession(e_3, Agent, Theme)
¬**has_possession**(e_3, Source, Theme)
cause(e_2, e_3)

Four main classes and two additional subclasses belonging to classes listed above demonstrate two-way transfers: exchange-13.6.1, get-13.5.1, invest-13.5.4, and pay-68, as well as give-13.1-1 and obtain-13.5.2-1. In the following example from exchange-13.6.1, note the new handling of subevents, **cause**, and the argument structure of **transfer**. In e_2, the Agent initiates the transfer of the Theme, and in e_3, the Co-Agent initiates the transfer of the Co-Theme. Subevent e_2 causes the resulting possession states of the Theme, and e_3 causes the resulting possession states of the Co-Theme.

(6) *Gwen exchanged the dress for a shirt*
Agent V Theme Co-Theme
has_possession(e_1, Agent, Theme)
¬**has_possession**(e_1, ?Co-Agent, Theme)
has_possession(e_1, ?Co-Agent, Co-Theme)
¬**has_possession**(e_1, Agent, Co-Theme)
transfer(e_2, Agent, Theme, ?Co-Agent)
transfer(e_3, ?Co-Agent, Co-Theme, Agent)
has_possession(e_4, ?Co-Agent, Theme)
¬**has_possession**(e_4, Agent, Theme)
has_possession(e_5, Agent, Co-Theme)
¬**has_possession**(e_5, ?Co-Agent, Co-Theme)
cause(e_2, e_4)
cause(e_3, e_5)

Substitute-13.6.2 used to be included in this group, but since it was specifically split off from exchange-13.6.1 to deal with a two-way exchange of location (i.e., two entities change places with each other), we are now treating it purely as a Change of Location class rather than Change of Possession. When compared with (6), example (7) from substitute-13.6.2 highlights the distinctions we are able to achieve using the new Change of Location vs. Change of Possession treatments.

(7) *One bell ringer swapped places with another*
    Theme V Location Co-Theme
    has_location$(e_1$, Theme, Location_I)
    has_location$(e_2$, Co-Theme, Location_J)
    motion$(\ddot{e}_3$, Theme, Trajectory)
    ¬**has_location**$(\ddot{e}_3$, Theme, Location_I)
    motion$(\ddot{e}_4$, Co-Theme, Trajectory)
    ¬**has_location**$(\ddot{e}_4$, Co-Theme, Location_J)
    has_location$(e_5$, Theme, Location_J)
    has_location$(e_6$, Co-Theme, Location_I)
    cause$(\ddot{e}_3, e_5)$
    cause$(\ddot{e}_4, e_6)$

Additional predicates: Several subgroups within Change of Possession use additional predicates to depict additional semantics. Future-having-13.3 and berry-13.7 both take an **irrealis**(e) predicate to show that the **transfer** and resulting states are intended, but not guaranteed to have taken place yet. **Irrealis**'s single argument is a subevent number, and one predicate is given per qualifying subevent. Another additional predicate is used in the get-13.5.1, give-13.1-1, obtain-13.5.2, and pay-68 classes. These all involve two-way transfers in which a Theme is exchanged for an Asset, where the Asset is the cost of the Theme, represented as **cost**(Theme, Asset). Finally, rob-10.6.4 and steal-10.5 both involve an Agent/Recipient who initiates taking a possession in an illegal manner. The representations include a **manner**(e, Illegal, Agent) predicate which, for this usage, takes Illegal as a constant.

4 Transfer of Information

4.1 Previous Representations

In the old model, the only consistent difference between Transfer of Information and Change of Possession in terms of predicates and representation structure lay within **path_rel**, which contained a constant called either TR_OF_INFO or CH_OF_POSS, respectively. Like Change of Possession, only one **path_rel** was provided per temporal period, allowing only one clear possessor per period. Unfortunately, this failed to capture the important distinctions that knowledge is generally not lost when communicated, and one party's possession and communication of knowledge is no guarantee that another party doesn't already possess it too.

4.2 New Representations

Two new predicates describe Transfer of Information:

- **has_information**(e, [slot-1], [slot-2])
- **transfer_info**(e, [slot-1], [slot-2], [slot-3])

These mirror the predicates used in Change of Possession in terms of their argument slots and functions, excepting that slot-2 may take Theme or Topic but not Asset. Topic is used most commonly for verbal information, while Theme is reserved for non-verbal information, which often reflects assent or emotional states.

The basic representation in (8) differs from Change of Possession in terms of the boundaries on possession before and after the **transfer_info** subevent. Here, by leaving the Recipient's possession status underspecified in e1, we make no claims about whether or not the Recipient already knew the information at the beginning of the event. By marking the Source's possession status with a big E, we assert that the Source maintains possession of the information throughout the event, even after the **transfer_info** communication subevent.

(8) **has_information**(E, Source, Topic)
    transfer_info$(e_1$, Source, Topic, Recipient)
    has_information$(e_2$, Recipient, Topic)
    cause(e_1, e_2)

4.3 Transfer of Information Variations

One-way transfers: Just as with Change of Possession, Transfer of Information classes may involve an Agentive Source or Agentive Recipient. The basic representations for these types alternate from the basic Transfer of Information representation in the same way demonstrated above, with Agent replacing either Source or Recipient throughout. The vast majority of Transfer of Information classes are of the Agentive Source type, including advise-37.9, complain-37.8, confess-37.10, crane-40.3.2, curtsey-40.3.3, initiate_communication-37.4.2, inquire-37.1.2, instr_communication-37.4.1, interrogate-37.1.3, lecture-37.11, manner_speaking-37.3, nonverbal_expression-40.2, overstate-37.12, promise-37.13, say-37.7, tell-37.2, transfer_mesg-37.1.1, and wink-40.3.1. Just one class, learn-14, features an Agentive Recipient.

Two-way transfers: The two-way Transfer of Information classes, chit_chat-37.6 and talk-37.5, differ from the two-way Change of Possession classes in several ways. Most notably, they are not limited to a single transfer in each direction; instead, a sequence of transfers repeats back and forth between the two participants an unspecified number of times. The subevent ordering is changed so that the state resulting from one **transfer_info** occurs before the next **transfer_info** begins. The repeated turn-taking is expressed using the **repeated_sequence** predicate, which may take as many subevent arguments as necessary to capture the full span of the repeated behavior. The example in (9) is from chit_chat-37.6.

(9) *Susan chitchatted with Rachel about the problem*
Agent V Co-Agent Topic
has_information(E, Agent, Topic_I)
has_information(E, Co-Agent, Topic_J)
transfer_info(e_1, Agent, Topic_I, Co-Agent)
has_information(e_2, Co-Agent, Topic_I)
transfer_info(ee_3, Co-Agent, Topic_J, Agent)
has_information(e_4, Agent, Topic_J)
cause(e_1, e_2)
cause(e_3, e_4)
repeated_sequence(e_1, e_2, e_3, e_4)

Additional predicates and selectional restrictions: Several subgroups within Transfer of Information capture further semantic details using either additional predicates or specialized selectional restrictions on class roles. Two classes feature verbs of asking: inquire-37.1.2 and interrogate-37.1.3. These classes take a Topic role with a selectional restriction [+question], which helps clarify that the communication event taking place regards the question and never the response. Manner_speaking-37.3 and nonverbal_expression-40.2 both feature verbs that describe the manner of communication. The representations use another **manner** predicate, this time with a verb-specific role V_Manner in place of a constant. Instr_communication-37.4 features verbs that describe an instrument used to communicate (e.g., *phone*), and uses **utilize**(e, Agent, V_Instrument) to convey this.

Two subgroups use Theme with selectional restriction [+nonverbal_information]. The first group involves communication via some sort of voluntary bodily motion named by the verb, including classes crane-40.3.2, curtsey-40.3.3, and wink-40.3.1. In addition to the basic **transfer_info** predicates, these classes take a Patient role that is shown to be a body part of the Agent with a **part_of**(Patient, Agent) predicate. During the course of the **transfer_info** subevent, the Agent moves the Patient into a verb-specific position, represented using **has_position**(e, Patient, V_Position) and **body_motion**(ë, Agent). These classes have a more nuanced take on the possession boundaries than the basic representation in (8). In example (10) from wink-40.3.1, the Theme is a nonverbal emotional state conveyed through a bodily motion. We can generally assume that the Recipient does not have prior access to this type of information, and we make this explicit in e1.

(10) *Linda nodded her agreement*
Agent V Theme
has_information(E, Agent, Theme)
¬**has_information**(e_1, ?Recipient, Theme)
¬**has_position**(e_1, ?Patient , V_Position)
transfer_info($ë_2$, Agent, Theme, ?Recipient)
body_motion($ë_2$, Agent)
has_position(e_2, ?Patient , V_Position)
has_information(e_3, ?Recipient, Theme)
part_of(?Patient , Agent)
cause($ë_2$, e_3)

The second group involves potentially involuntary nonverbal expressions of an internal state, and includes classes animal_sounds-38 and nonverbal_expression-40.2 (11). As part of this release, we have added a new Stimulus thematic role to these classes. The previous release included frames for constructions using a Recipient, like *Paul laughed at Mary* and *The dog barked at the cat,* but didn't cover possible constructions like *Paul laughed at Mary to his friends* or *The dog whimpered to its owner about the rabbit in the yard.* Adding Stimulus and its usual predicate **in_reaction_to**(e, Stimulus) to these representations aligns them with the other Stimulus/Experiencer classes and expands the range of frames they cover. These classes reflect the same assumptions about boundaries on possession shown in (10).

(11) *The dog whimpered to its owner at the sight of the rabbit in the yard*

Agent   V   Recipient   Stimulus
has_information(E, Agent, ?Theme)
¬**has_information**(e_1, Recipient, ?Theme)
transfer_info(e_2, Agent, ?Theme, Recipient)
manner(e_2, Agent, V_Manner)
in_reaction_to(e_2, Stimulus)
has_information(e_3, Recipient, ?Theme)
cause(e_2, e_3)

5   Automatic VerbNet Parsing

To facilitate immediate use of the new VerbNet semantic representations, we are releasing a semantic parser that predicts the updated semantic representations from events in natural language input sentences. For a given predicative verb in a sentence, we define VerbNet semantic parsing as the task of identifying the VN class, associated thematic roles, and corresponding semantic representations linked to a frame within the class.

We approach VerbNet semantic parsing in three distinct steps: 1. Sense disambiguation to identify the appropriate VN class, 2. PropBank semantic role labeling (Gildea and Jurafsky, 2002; Palmer et al., 2005) to identify and classify arguments, and 3. Alignment of PropBank semantic roles with VN thematic roles within a frame belonging to the predicted VN class. After aligning arguments from the PropBank SRL system's output with the thematic roles in a particular VN frame, the frame's associated semantic predicates can be instantiated using the aligned arguments.

For sense disambiguation, we use a supervised verb sense classifier trained on updated VN class tags (Palmer et al., 2017). For semantic role labeling, we use a variation of the system described in He et al. (2017) and Peters et al. (2018) using solely ELMo embeddings (without any pre-trained or fine-tuned word-specific vectors) trained on a combination of three PropBank annotated corpora described in (O'Gorman et al., 2019): OntoNotes (Hovy et al., 2006), the English Web TreeBank (Bies et al., 2012), and the BOLT corpus (Garland et al., 2012). For alignment, we begin by applying updated SemLink mappings (Palmer, 2009) to map PropBank roles to linked VN thematic roles for the identified VN class. Remaining arguments are then mapped using heuristics based on the syntactic and selectional restrictions defined in the VN class. To select among multiple valid frames, we select the frame with highest total number of roles among the VN frames with the fewest unmapped roles.

This approach to VN parsing using multiple independent systems represents a simple baseline approach. We leave a more sophisticated, unified approach to VN semantic parsing to future work.

6   Conclusion

The fine-grained semantic representations presented here improve the consistency and precision of VerbNet's verb semantics, offering a more useful modeling for the subevent structure of particular event types. This should improve VerbNet's utility for human-robot and human-avatar interaction, and lend enhanced richness to applications aimed at temporal event sequencing.

All of the resources described in this paper are freely available. An online, browsable version of all the semantic representations is available through the Unified Verb Index at https://uvi.colorado.edu/uvi_search. A downloadable version can be accessed at https://uvi.colorado.edu/nlp_applications. A demo of the VerbNet Parser is at http://verbnet-semantic-parser.appspot.com/.

Acknowledgments

We gratefully acknowledge the support of DTRAl -16-1-0002/Project 1553695, eTASC - Empirical Evidence for a Theoretical Approach to Semantic Components and DARPA 15-18-CwC-FP-032 Communicating with Computers, C3 Cognitively Coherent Human-Computer Communication (sub from UIUC) and Elementary Composable Ideas (ECI) Repository (sub from SIFT). Any opinions, findings, and conclusions or recommendations expressed in this material are those of the authors and do not necessarily reflect the views of DTRA or the U.S. government.

In addition, we thank our anonymous reviewers for their constructive feedback.

References

Omri Abend, Roi Reichart, and Ari Rappoport. 2008. A supervised algorithm for verb disambiguation into verbnet classes. In *Proceedings of the 22nd International Conference on Computational Linguistics-Volume 1*, pages 9–16. Association for Computational Linguistics.

Norm Badler, Martha Palmer, and Rama Bindiganavle. 1999. Animation control for real-time virtual humans. *Communications of the ACM*, 42(7):65–73.

Ann Bies, Justin Mott, Colin Warner, and Seth Kulick. 2012. English web treebank. *Linguistic Data Consortium, Philadelphia, PA*.

Claire Bonial, Susan Windisch Brown, William Corvey, Martha Palmer, Volha Petukhova, and Harry Bunt. 2011. An exploratory comparison of thematic roles in verbnet and lirics. In *Workshop on Interoperable Semantic Annotation*, page 39.

Johan Bos. 2008. Wide-coverage semantic analysis with boxer. In *Proceedings of the 2008 Conference on Semantics in Text Processing*, pages 277–286. Association for Computational Linguistics.

Susan Windisch Brown, Dmitriy Dligach, and Martha Palmer. 2014. Verbnet class assignment as a wsd task. In *Computing Meaning*, pages 203–216. Springer.

Susan Windisch Brown and Martha Palmer. 2012. Semantic annotation of metaphorical verbs with verbnet: A case study of climband poison. In *Workshop on interoperable semantic annotation*, page 72.

Susan Windisch Brown, James Pustejovsky, Annie Zaenen, and Martha Palmer. 2018. Integrating generative lexicon event structures into verbnet. In *Proceedings of the Eleventh International Conference on Language Resources and Evaluation (LREC-2018)*.

Danilo Croce, Roberto Basili, Alessandro Moschitti, and Martha Palmer. 2012. Verb classification using distributional similarity in syntactic and semantic structures. In *Proceedings of the 50th Annual Meeting of the Association for Computational Linguistics: Long Papers-Volume 1*, pages 263–272. Association for Computational Linguistics.

Jennifer Garland, Stephanie Strassel, Safa Ismael, Zhiyi Song, and Haejoong Lee. 2012. Linguistic resources for genre-independent language technologies: user-generated content in bolt. In *Workshop Programme*, page 34.

Daniel Gildea and Daniel Jurafsky. 2002. Automatic labeling of semantic roles. *Computational Linguistics*, 28(3):245–288.

Ana-Maria Giuglea and Alessandro Moschitti. 2006. Semantic role labeling via framenet, verbnet and propbank. In *Proceedings of the 21st International Conference on Computational Linguistics and the 44th annual meeting of the Association for Computational Linguistics*, pages 929–936. Association for Computational Linguistics.

Adele E Goldberg. 2006. *Constructions at work: The nature of generalization in language*. Oxford University Press on Demand.

Luheng He, Kenton Lee, Mike Lewis, and Luke Zettlemoyer. 2017. Deep Semantic Role Labeling: What Works and What's Next. *Proceedings of the 55th Annual Meeting of the Association for Computational Linguistics (Volume 1: Long Papers)*.

Eduard Hovy, Mitchell Marcus, Martha Palmer, Lance Ramshaw, and Ralph Weischedel. 2006. OntoNotes: the 90% solution. In *Proceedings of the human language technology conference of the NAACL, Companion Volume: Short Papers*, pages 57–60. Association for Computational Linguistics.

Jena D Hwang. 2014. Identification and representation of caused motion constructions.

Daisuke Kawahara and Martha Palmer. 2014. Single classifier approach for verb sense disambiguation based on generalized features. In *LREC*, pages 4210–4213.

Karin Kipper, Anna Korhonen, Neville Ryant, and Martha Palmer. 2006. Extending verbnet with novel verb classes. In *Proceedings of LREC*, volume 2006, page 1. Citeseer.

Karin Kipper and Martha Palmer. 2000. Representation of actions as an interlingua. In *Proceedings of NAACL-ANLP Workshop on Applied Interlinguas: practical applications of interlingual approaches to NLP,*, pages 12–17. Association for Computational Linguistics.

Beth Levin. 1993. *English Verb Classes and Alternations: A Preliminary Investigation*. University of Chicago Press.

Edward Loper, Szu-Ting Yi, and Martha Palmer. 2007. Combining lexical resources: mapping between propbank and verbnet. In *Proceedings of the 7th International Workshop on Computational Linguistics, Tilburg, the Netherlands*.

Anjali Narayan-Chen, Colin Graber, Mayukh Das, Md Rakibul Islam, Soham Dan, Sriraam Natarajan, Janardhan Rao Doppa, Julia Hockenmaier, Martha Palmer, and Dan Roth. 2017. Towards problem solving agents that communicate and learn. In *Proceedings of the First Workshop on Language Grounding for Robotics*, pages 95–103.

Tim O'Gorman, Sameer Pradhan, James Gung, and Martha Palmer. 2019. The unified propbank landscape. *Ms*.

Martha Palmer. 2009. Semlink: Linking propbank, verbnet and framenet. In *Proceedings of the generative lexicon conference*, pages 9–15. Pisa Italy.

Martha Palmer, Daniel Gildea, and Paul Kingsbury. 2005. The proposition bank: An annotated corpus of semantic roles. *Computational linguistics*, 31(1):71–106.

Martha Palmer, James Gung, Claire Bonial, Jinho Choi, Orin Hargraves, Derek Palmer, and Kevin Stowe. 2017. The Pitfalls of Shortcuts: Tales from the word sense tagging trenches. *Springer series Text, Speech and Language Technology*, Essays in Lexical Semantics and Computational Lexicography - In Honor of Adam Kilgarriff.

Matthew Peters, Mark Neumann, Mohit Iyyer, Matt Gardner, Christopher Clark, Kenton Lee, and Luke Zettlemoyer. 2018. Deep contextualized word representations. In *Proceedings of the 2018 Conference of the North American Chapter of the Association for Computational Linguistics: Human Language Technologies, Volume 1 (Long Papers)*, pages 2227–2237.

J. Pustejovsky. 1995. *The Generative Lexicon*. Bradford Book. Mit Press.

James Pustejovsky. 2013. Dynamic event structure and habitat theory. In *Proceedings of the 6th International Conference on Generative Approaches to the Lexicon (GL2013)*, pages 1–10. ACL.

James Pustejovsky and Jessica Moszkowicz. 2011. The qualitative spatial dynamics of motion. *The Journal of Spatial Cognition and Computation*.

James Pustejovsky, Martha Palmer, Annie Zaenen, and Susan Brown. 2016. Verb meaning in context: Integrating verbnet and gl predicative structures. In *Proceedings of the LREC 2016 Workshop: ISA-12, Potoroz, Slovenia*, volume 2016.

J. Allbeck N. Badler A. Joshi R. Bindiganavale, W. Schuler and M. Palmer. 2000. Dynamically, altering agent behaviors using natural language instructions. In *Proceedings of the 4th International Conference on Autonomous Agents (AGENTS)*, pages 293–300.

Karin Kipper Schuler. 2005. Verbnet: A broadcoverage, comprehensive verb lexicon.

Lei Shi and Rada Mihalcea. 2005. Putting pieces together: Combining framenet, verbnet and wordnet for robust semantic parsing. In *International conference on intelligent text processing and computational linguistics*, pages 100–111. Springer.

Annie Zaenen, Daniel G Bobrow, and Cleo Condoravdi. 2008. The encoding of lexical implications in verbnet predicates of change of locations. In *LREC*.

Semantically Constrained Multilayer Annotation:
The Case of Coreference

Jakob Prange[*] **Nathan Schneider**
Georgetown University

Omri Abend
The Hebrew University of Jerusalem

Abstract

We propose a coreference annotation scheme
as a layer on top of the Universal Conceptual Cognitive Annotation foundational layer,
treating units in predicate-argument structure
as a basis for entity and event mentions. We
argue that this allows coreference annotators
to sidestep some of the challenges faced in
other schemes, which do not enforce consistency with predicate-argument structure and
vary widely in what kinds of mentions they annotate and how. The proposed approach is examined with a pilot annotation study and compared with annotations from other schemes.

1 Introduction

Unlike some NLP tasks, coreference resolution
lacks an agreed-upon standard for annotation and
evaluation (Poesio et al., 2016). It has been approached using a multitude of different markup
schemas, and the several evaluation metrics commonly used (Pradhan et al., 2014) are controver-
sial (Moosavi and Strube, 2016). In particular,
these schemas use divergent and often (language-
specific) syntactic criteria for defining candidate
mentions in text. This includes the questions of
whether to annotate entity and/or event coreference,
whether to include singletons, and how to identify
the precise span of complex mentions. Recognition
of this limitation in the field has recently prompted
the Universal Coreference initiative,[1] which aims
to settle on a single cross-linguistically applicable
annotation standard.

We think that many issues stem from the common practice of creating mention annotations from
scratch on the raw or tokenized text, and we suggest
that they could be overcome by reusing structures
from existing semantic annotation, thereby ensuring compatibility between the layers. We advocate

for the design pattern of a **semantic foundational
layer**, which defines a basic semantic structure that
additional layers can refine or make reference to.
Some form of predicate-argument structure involving entities and propositions should serve as a natural semantic foundation for a layer that groups
coreferring entity and event mentions into clusters.

Here we argue that Universal Conceptual Cognitive Annotation (UCCA; Abend and Rappoport,
2013) is an ideal choice, as it defines a foundational
layer of predicate-argument structure whose main
design principles are cross-linguistic applicability
and fast annotatability by non-experts. To that end,
we develop and pilot a new layer for UCCA which
adds coreference information.[2] This coreference
layer is constrained by the spans already specified
in the foundational predicate-argument layer. We
compare these manual annotations to existing gold
coreference annotations in multiple frameworks,
finding a healthy level of overlap.

Our contributions are:

- A discussion of multilayer design principles
  informed by existing semantically annotated
  corpora (§2).
- A semantically-based framework for mention identification and coreference resolution
  as a layer of UCCA (§3). Reusing UCCA
  units as mentions facilitates efficient and consistent multilayer annotation. We call the
  framework **Universal Conceptual Cognitive
  Coreference** (UCoref).
- An in-depth comparison to three other coreference frameworks based on annotation guidelines (§4) and a pilot English dataset (§5).

---

[*]Contact: `jakob@cs.georgetown.edu`

[1]`https://sites.google.com/view/crac2019/`

[2]Our annotations are available under
`https://github.com/jakpra/UCoref`.

Proceedings of the First International Workshop on Designing Meaning Representations, pages 164–176
Florence, Italy, August 1st, 2019 ©2019 Association for Computational Linguistics

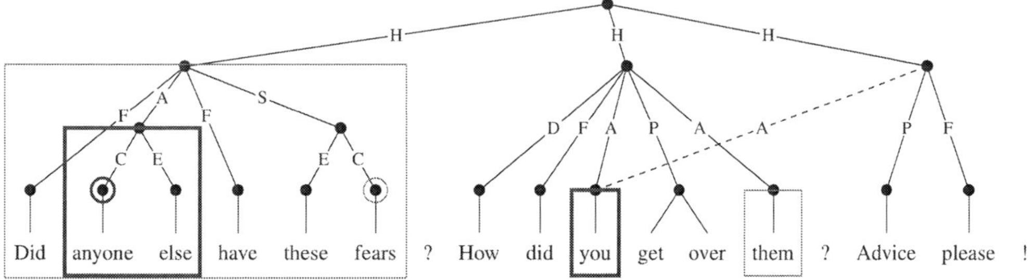

Figure 1: A foundational UCCA analysis of three consecutive sentences from the Richer Event Description corpus, with examples of coreferent units superimposed (boxes). The context is that the speaker is posting a message to a forum in which she shares her own fears and asks for advice; *you* is coreferent with *anyone else*, and *them* refers back to the whole first scene.[3] Circled nodes indicate semantic heads/minimal spans, as determined by following State (S) and Center (C) edges. In the third sentence, *Advice please!*, the addressee/adviser is a salient, but implicit Participant (A) which is expressed with a remote (dashed) edge to a prior mention. Remaining categories are abbreviated as: H – Parallel Scene, P – Process, E – Elaborator, D – Adverbial, F – Function.

2 Background and Motivation

We first consider the organization of semantic annotations in corpora, arguing that UCCA's representation of predicate-argument structure should serve as a foundation for coreference annotations.

2.1 Approaches to Semantic Multilayering

A major consideration in the design of coreference annotation schemes, as well as meaning representations generally, is what the relevant annotation targets are and whether they should be normalized across layers when the text is annotated for multiple aspects of linguistic structure. Should coreference be annotated completely independently of decisions about syntactic phrases and semantic predicate-argument structures? On the one hand, this decoupling of the annotations might absolve the coreference annotators from having to worry about other annotation conventions in the corpus. On the other hand, this is potentially a recipe for

inconsistent annotations across layers, making it more difficult to integrate information across layers for complex reasoning in natural language understanding systems. Moreover, certain details of coreference annotation may be underdetermined such that relying on other layers would save coreference annotators and guidelines-developers from having to reinvent the wheel.

We can examine existing semantic annotation schemes with regard to two closely related criteria: a) **anchoring**, i.e. the previously determined underlying structure (characters, tokens, syntax, etc.) that defines the set of possible annotation targets in a new layer; and b) **modularity**, the extent to which multiple kinds of information are expressed as separate (possibly linked) structures/layers, which may be annotated in different phases.

Massively multilayer corpora. A few corpora comprise several layers of annotation, including semantics, with an emphasis on modularity of these layers. One example is OntoNotes (Hovy et al., 2006), annotated for syntax, named entities, word senses, PropBank (Palmer et al., 2005) predicate-argument structures, and coreference. Another example is GUM (Zeldes, 2017), with layers for syntactic, coreference, discourse, and document structure. Both of these resources cover multiple genres. Different layers in these resources are anchored differently, as noted below.

Token-anchored. Many semantic annotation layers are specified in terms of character or token offsets. This is the case for UCCA's Foundational Layer (§2.2), FrameNet (Fillmore and Baker, 2009), RED (O'Gorman et al., 2016), all of the layers in GUM, and the named entity and word sense

---

[3] Following UCCA's philosophy, we interpret both *fears* and *them* mainly as evoking the emotional state of having fears (i.e., "how did you get over them" ≈ "how did you get over being afraid"). This analysis abstracts away from the more direct reading as the specific objects of fear; but either way, the proper semantic head of the first sentence has to be *fears* (not *have*), and from our flexible minimum/maximum span policy it follows that any mention coreferring with *fears* automatically corefers with the whole scene.

Further, we interpret both *anyone else* and *you* as referring to the unknown-sized set of audience members sharing the speaker's fears. Whereas *you* introduces a presupposition that this set is non-empty, this is not the case for the negative polarity item *anyone else*. Although questionable in terms of cohesion (as the presupposition created by *you* fails if the answer to the first question is 'no'), this is a typical phenomenon in conversational data and can be explained by recognizing that the second question is implicitly conditional: "**If so,** how did you get over them?"

annotations in OntoNotes. Though the guidelines may mention syntactic criteria for deciding what units to semantically annotate, the annotated data does not explicitly tie these layers to syntactic units, and to the best of our knowledge the annotator is not constrained by the syntactic annotation.

Syntax-anchored. Semantic annotations explicitly defined in terms of syntactic units include: PropBank (such as in OntoNotes); and the coreference annotations in the Prague Dependency Treebank (PDT; Nedoluzhko et al., 2016). In addition, PDT's "deep syntactic" tectogrammatical layer, which is built on the syntactic analytic layer, can be considered quasi-semantic (Böhmová et al., 2003).

Transformed syntax. In other cases, semantic label annotations enrich skeletal semantic representations that have been deterministically converted from syntactic structures. One example is Universal Decompositional Semantics (White et al., 2016), whose annotations are anchored with PredPatt, a way of converting Universal Dependencies trees (Nivre et al., 2016) to approximate predicate-argument structures.

Sentence-anchored. The Abstract Meaning Representation (AMR; Banarescu et al., 2013) is an example of a highly integrative (anti-modular) approach to sentence-level meaning, without anchoring below the sentence level. AMR annotations take the form of a single graph per sentence, capturing a variety of kinds of information, including predicate-argument structure, sentence focus, modality, lexical semantic distinctions, coreference, named entity typing, and entity linking ("Wikification"). English AMR annotators provide the full graph at once (with the exception of entity linking, done as a separate pass), and do not mark how pieces of the graph are anchored in tokens, which has spawned a line of research on various forms of token-level alignment for parsing (e.g. Flanigan et al., 2014; Pourdamghani et al., 2014; Chen and Palmer, 2017; Szubert et al., 2018; Liu et al., 2018). Chinese AMR, by contrast, is annotated in a way that aligns nodes with tokens (Li et al., 2016).

Semantics-anchored. The approach we explore here is the use of a *semantic* layer as a foundation for a different type of semantic layer. Such approaches support modularity, while still allowing annotation reuse. A recent example for this approach is multi-sentence AMR (O'Gorman et al., 2018), which links together the previously annotated per-sentence AMR graphs to indicate coreference across sentences.

2.2 UCCA's Foundational Layer

UCCA is a coarse-grained, typologically-motivated scheme for analyzing abstract semantic structures in text. It is designed to expose commonalities in semantic structure across paraphrases and translations, with a focus on predicate-argument and other semantic head-modifier relations. Formally, each text passage is annotated with a directed acyclic graph (DAG) over semantic elements called **units**. Each unit, corresponding to (anchored by) one or more tokens, is labeled with one or more semantic **categories** in relation to a parent unit.

The foundational layer[4] specifies a DAG structure organized in terms of **scenes** (events/situations mentioned in the text). This can be seen for three sentences in figure 1, where each corresponds to a Parallel Scene (denoted by the category label H) as three events are presented in sequence. A scene unit is headed by a predicate, which is either a State (S), like *these fears*, or a Process (P), like *get over*. Most scenes have at least one Participant (A), typically an entity or location—in this case, the individuals experiencing fear. Semantic refinements of manner, aspect, modality, negation, causativity, etc. are marked with the category Adverbial (D). Time (T) is used for temporal modifiers. Within a non-scene unit, the semantic head is marked Center (C), while semantic modifiers are Elaborators (E). Function (F) applies to words considered to add no semantic content relevant to the scene structure.

Some additional structural properties are worthy of note. An **unanalyzable unit** indicates that a group of tokens form a multiword expression with no internal semantic structure, like *get over* 'surmount'. A **remote edge** (reentrancy, shown as a dashed line in figure 1) makes it possible for a unit to have multiple parent units such that the structure is not a tree. This is mainly used when a Participant is shared by multiple scenes. Texts are annotated in passages generally larger than sentences, and remote edges may cross sentence boundaries—for example, when a Participant mentioned in one sentence is implicit in the next, such as *you* as the implicit advice-giver in the sentence *Advice please!*. **Implicit units** are null elements used when there is a salient piece of the meaning that is implied but not expressed overtly *anywhere* in the passage. (If

---

[4]Annotation guidelines: `https://github.com/UniversalConceptualCognitiveAnnotation/docs/blob/master/guidelines.pdf`

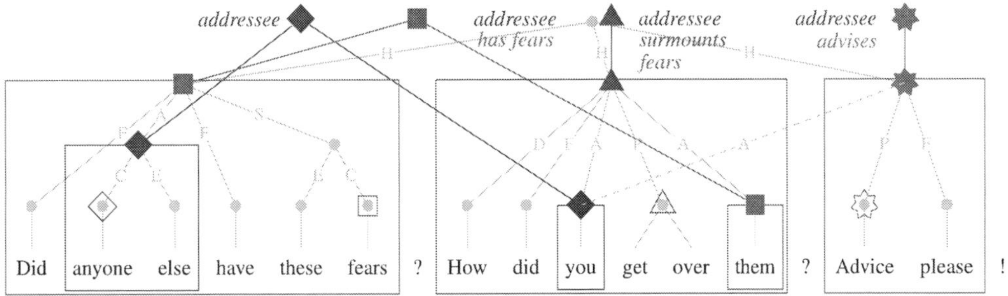

Figure 2: The reference layer UCoref on top of UCCA's foundational layer. A new "referent node" is introduced as a parent for each cluster of coreferring mentions. Colors and shapes indicate coreferring mentions. By virtue of the remote Participant edge (dashed line), the addressee referent implicitly participates in the third scene as well.

the third sentence from figure 1 was annotated in isolation, the advice-giver would be represented by an implicit unit.)

2.3 Insufficiency of the Foundational Layer

In addition to the benefits of a semantic foundational layer for coreference annotation (§2.1), we point out how adding such a layer to UCCA would rectify shortcomings of the foundational layer.

First and foremost, UCCA currently lacks any representation of "true" coreference, i.e., the phenomenon that two or more *explicit* units are mentions of the same entity. Second, though remote edges are helpful for indicating that a Participant is shared between multiple scenes, this is problematic if the referent is mentioned multiple times in the passage. Because the information that those mentions are coreferent is missing, the choice which mention to annotate with a remote edge is underdetermined. This leads to multiple conceptually equivalent choices that are formally distinct, opening the way for spurious disagreements. For example, the implicit advice-giver in figure 1 could be marked equally well with a remote edge to *anyone else* instead of *you*, resulting in a structurally diverging graph (taking the presented analysis as the reference).[5] And third, many other implicit relations relevant to coreference (e.g., implied common sense part/whole relations, via *bridging*) are not exposed in the foundational layer of UCCA. A layer that annotates identity coreference could be extended with such additional information in the future.

3 The UCoref Layer

The underlying hypothesis of this work is that the spans of words that form referring expressions, i.e., evoke or point back to entities and events in the world, are also grouped as semantic units in the foundational layer of UCCA. This assumption is motivated by the fundamental principles of UCCA as a neo-Davidsonian theory: The basic elements of a discourse are descriptions of scenes ($\approx$ events), and their basic elements are participants ($\approx$ entities). We can thus automatically identify scene and participant units as referring. With this high-precision preprocessing and a small set of simple guidelines for identifying other UCCA units as referring, the process of *mention identification* in UCoref is very efficient. Figure 2 illustrates how UCoref interacts with the foundational layer. Four referents and six mentions (two singletons) are identified based on the criteria below.

Scene and Participant units. The vast majority of referent mentions can be identified by two simple rules: 1) All **scene** units are considered mentions as they constitute descriptions of actions, movements, or states as defined in the foundational layer guidelines. 2) Similarly, all **Participant** units are considered mentions as they describe entities that are contributing to or affected by a scene/event (including locations and other scenes/events).

Special attention should be paid to relational nouns like *teacher* or *friend* that both refer to an entity and evoke a process or state in which the entity generally or habitually participates.[6] According to the UCCA guidelines, these words are analyzed internally (as both P/S and A within a nested unit over the same span), in addition to the

---

[5] While additional, more restrictive guidelines could to some extent curb such confusion (e.g., by specifying that the closest appropriate mention to the left should always be chosen as the remote target), this would require the foundational layer annotators to be confident in the notion of coreference to determine which mentions are "appropriate", eliminating the modularity and intuitiveness we desire.

[6] A teacher is a person who teaches and a friend is a person who stands in a friendship relation with another person. Cf. Newell and Cheung (2018); Meyers et al. (2004).

context-dependent incoming edge from their parent. However, the inherent scene (of teaching or friendship) is merely *evoked*, but not *referred to*, and it is usually invariant with respect to the explicit context it occurs in. Moreover, treating one span of words as two mentions would pose a significant complication. Thus, we consider these units only in their role as Participant (and not scene) mentions.

Non-scene-non-participant units. A certain subset of the remaining unit types are considered to be mention *candidates*. This subset is comprised of the categories, *Time, Elaborator, Relator, Quantity*, and *Adverbial*. We give detailed guidelines for these categories, as well as for coreference markup, in the supplementary material (appendix A).

Center units. For simplicity, a referring unit with a *single* Center usually does not require its Center to be marked separately, as a unit always corefers with its Center (see §4 and §5.1 about how this relates to the min/max span distinction).

Multi-Center units receive a different treatment: One use of multi-Center units is coordination, where each conjunct is a Center. Here we do want to mark up the conjuncts in addition to the whole coordination unit—provided the whole unit is referring by one of the other criteria—and assign them to separate coreference clusters. Another class of multi-Center units, which we call *relative partitive constructions*, is less straightforward to handle. Consider a phrase like *the top of the mountain*. The intuition given in the UCCA guidelines is that while the phrase is syntactically and, to some extent, semantically headed by *top*, it can only be fully understood in relation to *mountain*; thus, both words should be Centers. This construction is clearly less symmetric than coordination, but at this point we do not have a reliable way of formally distinguishing the two in preprocessing, purely based on the UCCA structure and categories. Thus, multi-Center units deserve a more nuanced manual UCoref analysis in future work; however, for the sake of consistency and simplicity, we treat all multi-Center units in the same way as we treat coordinations in our pilot annotation (§5).

Implicit units. Implicit units may be identified as mentions and linked to coreferring expressions just like any other unit, as long as they meet the criteria outlined above.

4 Comparison with Other Schemes

The task of coreference resolution is far from trivial and has been approached from many different angles. Below we give a detailed analysis of the theoretical differences between three particular frameworks: OntoNotes (Hovy et al., 2006), Richer Event Description (RED; O'Gorman et al., 2016), and the Georgetown University Multilayer corpus (GUM; Zeldes, 2017).

Singletons and events. RED and UCoref annotate all nominal entity, nominal event, and verbal event mentions, including singletons.[7] OntoNotes does not include singleton mentions in the coreference layer.[8] Further, only those verbal mentions that are coreferent with a nominal are included. GUM includes all nominal mentions, including singletons and nominal event mentions, and follows the OntoNotes guidelines for verbal mentions.

Syntactic vs. semantic criteria. GUM and OntoNotes, despite not being *anchored* in syntax, specify syntactic criteria for mention and coreference annotation. The criteria in RED and UCoref, on the other hand, are fundamentally semantic. Rough syntactic guidance is only given where appropriate and at no time is a decisive factor.

Minimum and maximum spans. The policy on mention spans is often one of two extremes: *minimum* spans (also called *triggers* or *nuggets*), which typically only consist of the head word or expression that sufficiently describes the type of entity or event; or *maximum* spans (also called *full mentions*), containing all arguments and modifiers. GUM and OntoNotes generally apply a maximum span policy for nominal mentions, with just a few exceptions.[9] For verbal mentions, OntoNotes chooses minimum spans, whereas GUM annotates full clauses or sentences. RED always uses minimum spans, except for time expressions, which follow the TIMEX3 standard (Pustejovsky et al., 2010). One of the main advantages of UCoref is that the preexisting predicate-argument and head-modifier structures of the foundational layer allow a flexible and reliable mapping between minimum and maximum span annotations. Addition-

---

[7]For event coreference specifically, see also EventCoref-Bank (ECB; Bejan and Harabagiu, 2010) and the TAC-KBP Event Track (Mitamura et al., 2015), which uses the ACE 2005 dataset (LDC2006T06; Doddington et al., 2004).

[8]A separate layer records all *named* entities, however, and non-coreferent ones can be considered singleton mentions.

[9]The GUM guidelines specify that clausal modifiers should not be included in a nominal mention.

ally, UCoref has 'null' spans, corresponding to implicit units in UCCA.[10]

Predication. OntoNotes does not assert a coreference relation between copular arguments.[11] RED distinguishes several relation types depending on the "predicativeness" of the expression and in particular asserts a set-membership (i.e., non-identity) relation when the second argument is indefinite. In GUM, relation types are assigned based on different criteria,[12] and, depending on the polarity and modality of the copula, its arguments may be marked as coreferring mentions, even if they are indefinite.[13] A slightly different distinction is made in UCoref, where, thanks to the foundational layer, evokers of set-membership and attributive relations are marked as stative scenes in which the modified entity participates. Definite identity is handled in the same way as in RED, as well as relational nouns except for the special case of generic mentions (appendix A.2).

Apposition. In RED and OntoNotes, punctuation is considered a strict criterion for marking appositives, while GUM relies solely on syntactic completeness. In OntoNotes and GUM, ages specified after a person's name are considered separate appositional mentions, coreferring with the name mention they modify. UCoref takes advantage of UCCA's semantic Center-Elaborator structure, abstracting away from superficial markers like punctuation which may not be available in all genres and languages (details in appendix A.2).

Prepositions. Whereas OntoNotes and GUM stick to the syntactic notion of NPs, UCoref includes prepositions and case markers within mentions. This does not have a major effect on coreference, but contributes to consistency between languages that vary in the grammaticalization of their case marking.

Coordination. Our treatment of coordinate entity mentions is adopted and expanded from the GUM guidelines, where the span containing the full coordination is only marked up if it is antecedent to a plural pronominal mention. OntoNotes does not specify how coordinations in particular should be handled; while the guidelines state that out of *head-sharing* (i.e., elliptic) mentions only the largest one should be picked, we assume that coordinations of multiple *explicitly headed* phrases are not targeted as mentions in addition to the conjuncts. The minimum span approach of RED precludes marking full coordinations in addition to conjuncts.

Summary. That OntoNotes does not annotate singleton mentions makes it the most restrictive out of the compared frameworks. Despite its emphasis on syntax, GUM is closer to our framework as it includes singletons and marks full spans for non-singleton events; the marking of bridging relations, directed coreference links, and information status present in GUM is beyond our scope here. RED is conceptually closest to UCoref in marking all entity, time, and event mentions, except for the difference in span boundaries. This can largely be resolved as we will show in §5.1.

5 Pilot Annotation

In order to evaluate the accessibility of the annotation guidelines given above and in appendix A, and facilitate empirical comparison with other schemes, we conducted a pilot annotation study. We annotated a small English dataset consisting of subsets of the OntoNotes (LDC2013T19), RED (LDC2016T23), and GUM[14] corpora with the UCCA foundational and coreference layers.[15]

The OntoNotes documents are taken from blog posts, the GUM documents are WikiHow instructional guides, and the RED documents are online forum discussions. Because all annotations were done by a single annotator each and not reviewed, our results are to be understood as a proof of concept; measuring interannotator agreement will be

---

[10]The coreference layer of the Prague Dependency Treebank (Nedoluzhko et al., 2016), quite similarly to the proposed framework, marks null-mentions arising from control verbs, reciprocals, and dual dependencies (in general, null-nodes arising from obligatory valency slot insertions into the tectogrammatical layer)—the syntactic equivalents of implicit units and remote edges in UCCA. Further, in case the mention is a root of a nontrivial subtree, it is underspecified whether the mention spans only the root, the whole subtree or some part of it.

[11]Neither do Poesio and Artstein (in the ARRAU corpus; 2008).

[12]In particular, the notion of *bridging* is interpreted differently between GUM and RED: GUM reserves it for entities that are expected (from world knowledge) to stand in some relationship (e.g., part/whole) with each other, which is reflected in a definite initial mention of the 'bridging target' (*My car is broken; it's **the motor***). RED uses it for copular predications involving relational/occupational nouns like ***John is a/the killer***, which are simple 'coref' (or 'ana'/'cata', if one mention is a pronoun) relations in GUM. We consider neither of these definitions in this work (see appendix A.2).

[13]See also Chinchor (1998).

[14]https://github.com/amir-zeldes/gum

[15]Since the RED documents are not tokenized (character spans are used for mention identification), we preprocessed them with the PTB tokenizer and the Punkt sentence splitter using Python NLTK.

	GUM	OntoNotes	RED
sentences	70	17	24
tokens	1180	303	302
↪ non-punct	1030	261	274
UCCA units	1436	336	379
↪ candidates	911	195	186

Table 1: Overview of our pilot dataset. *Candidates* refers to the UCCA units that are filtered by category for mention candidacy before manual annotation.

necessary in the future to gauge the difficulty of the task and quality of guidelines/data.

Table 1 shows the distribution of tokens and UCCA foundational units, and table 2 compares the distribution of UCoref units with the respective "native" annotation schema for each corpus. We can see that about one third of all UCCA units are identified as mentions, in all corpora. The automatic candidate filtering based on UCCA categories simplifies this process for the annotator by removing about one third to one half of units. There are similar amounts of scene and Participant units (both of which are always mentions), but it is important to note that Participant units can also refer to events. We can see this reflected by the majority of referent units being event referents. We can also see that most of the referents in GUM, RED, and UCoref are in fact singletons, and the number of non-singleton referents is quite similar between each scheme and UCoref. Most implicit units and targets of remote edges are part of a non-singleton coreference cluster, which confirms the issue of spurious ambiguity we pointed out in §2.3.

5.1 Recovering Existing Schemes

Next we examine the differences in gold annotations between our proposed schema and existing schemas and how we can (re)cover annotations in established schemas from our new schema. We can interpret this experiment as asking: If we had a perfect system for UCoref, could we use that to predict GUM/OntoNotes/RED-style coreference? And vice versa, if we had an oracle in one of those schemes, and possibly oracle UCoref mentions, how closely could we convert to UCoref?[16]

Exact mention matches. A naïve approach would be to look at the token spans covered by all mentions and reference clusters and count how often we can find an exact match between UCoref and one of the existing schemes.

---

[16]See also Zeldes and Zhang (2016), who base a full coreference resolution system on this idea.

In UCoref, we use maximum spans by default, but thanks to the nature of the UCCA foundational layer, minimum spans can easily be recovered from Centers and scene-evokers. For schemas with a *minimum span* approach, we can switch to a minimum span approach in UCoref by choosing the head unit of each maximum span unit as its representative mention. This works well between UCoref and RED as they have similar policies for determining semantic heads, which is crucial for, e.g., light verb constructions. This would be problematic, however, when comparing to a minimum span schema that uses syntactic heads. For schemas with a *non-minimum span* approach, we keep only the maximum span units from UCoref and discard any heads that have been marked up representatively for their parent (e.g., as remote targets).

Fuzzy mention matches. Because our theoretical comparison in §4 exposed systematically diverging definitions of what to include in a mention span, we also apply an evaluation that abstracts away from some of these differences. We greedily identify one-to-one alignments for maximally overlapping mentions, as measured by the Dice coefficient:

$$m_A^*, m_B^* \leftarrow \operatorname*{arg\,max}_{m_A \in (A \setminus L_A), m_B \in (B \setminus L_B)} \frac{|m_A \cap m_B|}{|m_A| + |m_B|}$$

where L_A (L_B) records the mentions from annotation A (B) aligned thus far, and stopping when this score falls below a threshold μ. μ is a hyperparameter controlling how much overlap is required: $\mu = 1$ corresponds to exact matches only, while $\mu = 0$ includes all overlapping mention pairs as candidates (we report fuzzy match results for $\mu = 0$). Once a mention is aligned it is removed from consideration for future alignments.

We align referents by the same procedure. Results are reported in table 3.

5.2 Findings

We can see in table 3 that UCoref generally covers between 60% and 80% of exact *mentions* in existing schemes ('R' columns), however, the amount of UCoref units that are present in other schemes varies greatly, between 21.3% (OntoNotes) and 79.5% (RED; 'P' columns). This is generally expected based on our theoretical analysis in §4. Fuzzy match has a great effect on the maximum span schemes in GUM and OntoNotes, resulting in up to 100% of mentions being aligned, and a lesser,

| | WikiHow | | Blog | | Forum | | | | WikiHow | | Blog | | Forum | |
	GUM	UCR	ONT	UCR	RED	UCR			GUM	UCR	ONT	UCR	RED	UCR
mentions	288	466	40	128	120	117	**referents**		155	291	20	96	82	78
↪ event	158	208	–	47	70	54	↪ event		108	180	–	43	58	47
↪ entity/A	127	215	–	66	47	58	↪ entity		47	108	–	46	21	27
↪ other	3	43	–	14	3	5	↪ time		0	3	–	7	3	4
↪ NE	–	–	10	–	–	–	↪ non-singleton		46	36	10	13	9	18
↪ IMP	–	26	–	6	–	4	↪ IMP		–	26	–	1	–	4
↪ remote	–	10	–	3	–	1	↪ remote		–	7	–	2	–	1

Table 2: Distribution of mentions and referents in the datasets. **Mentions**: Under *event*, we count UCoref (UCR) scenes, GUM mentions of the types 'event' or 'abstract', and RED EVENTs; under *entity*, we count UCR A's, GUM 'person', 'object', 'place', and 'substance' mentions, and RED ENTITYs. *NE* stands for OntoNotes (ONT) named entities and IMP and remote for implicit and remote UCR units. A coreference cluster (**referent**) is classified as an *event* referent if there is at least one event mention of that referent, as a *time* referent if there is at least one UCR T / GUM 'time' / RED TIMEX3 mention of that referent, and as an *entity* referent otherwise; we also report how many of the IMP and remote units are part of non-singleton referents.

| | mentions | | | | | | | | | referents | | | | | | | | | |
| | GUM | | | OntoNotes | | | RED | | | | GUM | | | OntoNotes | | | RED | | |
	P	R	F	P	R	F	P	R	F		P	R	F	P	R	F	P	R	F
=	41.7	60.6	49.4	21.3	67.5	32.3	79.5	77.5	78.5	=	19.3	24.4	21.6	3.1	15.2	5.2	*52.6*	*50.0*	*51.3*
										≈	31.6	40.0	35.3	9.4	45.0	15.5	*66.7*	*63.4*	*65.0*
≈	67.0	97.2	79.3	31.5	100.0	47.9	*88.9*	*86.7*	*87.8*	=	43.9	55.6	49.0	5.2	25.0	8.6	*66.7*	*63.4*	*65.0*
										≈	59.6	75.6	66.7	10.4	50.0	17.2	*80.8*	*76.8*	*78.8*

Table 3: Exact (=) and fuzzy (≈) referent matches based on exact and aligned mentions between UCoref and GUM, OntoNotes, and RED. Precision (P) and recall (R) are measured treating gold UCoref annotation as the prediction and gold annotation in each respective existing framework as the reference. Italics indicate minimum UCoref spans are used. Implicit UCoref units are excluded from this evaluation, and children of remote edges are only counted once (for their primary edge).

but still positive effect on RED.[17] We observe a similar trend for *referent* matches, which follows partly from the mismatch in mention annotation, and partly from diverging policies in marking coreference relations, as discussed above. Whether or not singleton event and/or entity referents are annotated has a major impact here. Below we give examples for sources of non-exact mention matches that can be resolved using fuzzy alignment.

GUM and OntoNotes. A phenomenon that is trivially resolvable using fuzzy alignments is punctuation, which is excluded from all UCoref units, but included in GUM and OntoNotes. Another group of mentions recovered are prepositional phrases, where UCoref includes prepositions (*to them, since the end of 2005*), and GUM and OntoNotes do not (*them, the end of 2005*). As mentioned in §4, GUM deviates from its maximum span policy for clausal modifiers of noun phrases, which are stripped off from the mention. Noun phrases modified in this way can be fuzzily aligned

with the maximum spans in UCoref, even if the modifier is very long: *people who are stuck on themselves intolerant of people different from them rude or downright arrogant* (UCoref) gets aligned with *people* (GUM).

RED. Almost 80% of both RED and UCoref mentions match exactly, but there are some cases of divergence: 1) One subset of these are time expressions like *this morning*, where, as pointed out above, RED marks maximum spans. However, in UCoref these are internally analyzable—thus their Center will be extracted for minimum spans (here, *morning*). On the other hand, idiomatic multiword expressions (MWEs) such as verb-particle constructions (e.g., *pass away* 'die') are treated as unanalyzable in UCCA, but only the syntactic head (*pass*) is included in RED. 2) Also interesting are predicative prepositions and adverbials in copular or expletive constructions: *there will be lots of good dr.s and nurses around*. Here, UCoref chooses *around* as the (stative) scene evoker (and would mark the prepositional object as a participant, if it is explicit), while RED chooses the copula *be*. 3) UCCA treats some verbs as modifiers rather than predicates themselves: e.g., *stopped* in

---

[17]Note, though, that this evaluation only shows us *if* we can find a fuzzy alignment, not whether the aligned spans are actually equivalent. As purely span-based alignment is prone to errors, a future extension to the algorithm should take information about (ideally semantic) heads into account.

i m [sic] *stopped feeling her move* and *it seemed* in *it seemed tom* [sic] *take forever*. The former, as an aspectual secondary verb, is labeled Adverbial (D); the latter, which injects the perspective of the speaker, is labeled Ground (G). Since we do not generally consider these categories referring, these are not annotated as mentions in UCoref, though they are in RED.

5.3 Discussion

For the non-minimum span schemas GUM and OntoNotes, we can use a fuzzy mention alignment based on token overlap to find many pairs which aim to capture the same mention, only under different annotation conventions. RED is most similar to UCoref in defining what counts as a mention, though our corpus analysis showed that the notion of *semantic heads* is interpreted differently for certain constructions, where UCCA is more liberal about treating verbs as modifiers rather than heads. While counting fuzzy matches allows us to recover partially overlapping spans (time expressions, verbal MWEs), other phenomena (adverbial copula constructions, secondary verbs) have inconsistent policies between the two schemes that require more elaborate methods to align. We can thus, to some extent, use UCoref to predict RED-style annotations, with the additional gain of flexible minimum/maximum spans and cross-sentence predicate-argument structure for a whole document. Furthermore, we see that UCoref subsumes all OntoNotes mentions and nearly all GUM mentions and is able to reconstruct coreference clusters in GUM with high recall.

6 Conclusion

We have defined and piloted a new, modular approach to coreference annotation based on the semantic foundational layer provided by UCCA. An oracle experiment shows high recall with respect to three existing schemes, as well as high precision with respect to the most similar of the three. We have released our annotations to fuel future investigations.

Acknowledgments

We would like to thank Amir Zeldes and two anonymous reviewers for their many helpful comments, corrections, and pointers to relevant literature. This research was supported in part by NSF award IIS-1812778 and grant 2016375 from the United States–Israel Binational Science Foundation (BSF), Jerusalem, Israel.

References

Omri Abend and Ari Rappoport. 2013. Universal Conceptual Cognitive Annotation (UCCA). In *Proc. of ACL*, pages 228–238, Sofia, Bulgaria.

Laura Banarescu, Claire Bonial, Shu Cai, Madalina Georgescu, Kira Griffitt, Ulf Hermjakob, Kevin Knight, Philipp Koehn, Martha Palmer, and Nathan Schneider. 2013. Abstract Meaning Representation for sembanking. In *Proc. of the 7th Linguistic Annotation Workshop and Interoperability with Discourse*, pages 178–186, Sofia, Bulgaria.

Cosmin Bejan and Sanda Harabagiu. 2010. Unsupervised event coreference resolution with rich linguistic features. In *Proc. of ACL*, pages 1412–1422, Uppsala, Sweden.

Alena Böhmová, Jan Hajič, Eva Hajičová, and Barbora Hladká. 2003. The Prague Dependency Treebank: A three-level annotation scenario. In Anne Abeillé, editor, *Treebanks: Building and Using Parsed Corpora*, Text, Speech and Language Technology, pages 103–127. Springer Netherlands, Dordrecht.

Wei-Te Chen and Martha Palmer. 2017. Unsupervised AMR-dependency parse alignment. In *Proc. of EACL*, pages 558–567, Valencia, Spain.

Nancy A. Chinchor. 1998. Overview of MUC-7/MET-2. In *Proc. of the Seventh Message Understanding Conference (MUC-7)*, Fairfax, Virginia.

George Doddington, Alexis Mitchell, Mark Przybocki, Lance Ramshaw, Stephanie Strassel, and Ralph Weischedel. 2004. The Automatic Content Extraction (ACE) program - Tasks, data, and evaluation. In *Proc. of LREC*, pages 837–840, Lisbon, Portugal.

Charles J. Fillmore and Collin Baker. 2009. A frames approach to semantic analysis. In Bernd Heine and Heiko Narrog, editors, *The Oxford Handbook of Linguistic Analysis*, pages 791–816. Oxford University Press, Oxford, UK.

Jeffrey Flanigan, Sam Thomson, Jaime Carbonell, Chris Dyer, and Noah A. Smith. 2014. A discriminative graph-based parser for the Abstract Meaning Representation. In *Proc. of ACL*, pages 1426–1436, Baltimore, Maryland, USA.

Eduard Hovy, Mitchell Marcus, Martha Palmer, Lance Ramshaw, and Ralph Weischedel. 2006. OntoNotes: the 90% solution. In *Proc. of HLT-NAACL*, pages 57–60, New York City, USA.

Bin Li, Yuan Wen, Lijun Bu, Weiguang Qu, and Nianwen Xue. 2016. Annotating The Little Prince with Chinese AMRs. In *Proc. of LAW X – the 10th Linguistic Annotation Workshop*, pages 7–15, Berlin, Germany.

Yijia Liu, Wanxiang Che, Bo Zheng, Bing Qin, and Ting Liu. 2018. An AMR aligner tuned by transition-based parser. In *Proc. of EMNLP*, pages 2422–2430, Brussels, Belgium.

Adam Meyers, Ruth Reeves, Catherine Macleod, Rachel Szekely, Veronika Zielinska, Brian Young, and Ralph Grishman. 2004. The NomBank project: an interim report. In *Proc. of the Frontiers in Corpus Annotation Workshop*, pages 24–31, Boston, Massachusetts, USA.

Teruko Mitamura, Zhengzhong Liu, and Eduard Hovy. 2015. Overview of TAC-KBP 2015 Event Nugget Track. In *Proc. of TAC*, Gaithersburg, Maryland, USA.

Nafise Sadat Moosavi and Michael Strube. 2016. Which coreference evaluation metric do you trust? A proposal for a link-based entity aware metric. In *Proc. of ACL*, pages 632–642, Berlin, Germany.

Anna Nedoluzhko, Michal Novák, Silvie Cinková, Marie Mikulová, and Jiří Mírovský. 2016. Coreference in Prague Czech-English Dependency Treebank. In *Proc. of LREC*, pages 169–176, Portorož, Slovenia.

Edward Newell and Jackie Chi Kit Cheung. 2018. Constructing a lexicon of relational nouns. In *Proc. of LREC*, pages 3405–3410, Miyazaki, Japan.

Joakim Nivre, Marie-Catherine de Marneffe, Filip Ginter, Yoav Goldberg, Jan Hajič, Christopher D. Manning, Ryan McDonald, Slav Petrov, Sampo Pyysalo, Natalia Silveira, Reut Tsarfaty, and Daniel Zeman. 2016. Universal Dependencies v1: a multilingual treebank collection. In *Proc. of LREC*, pages 1659–1666, Portorož, Slovenia.

Tim O'Gorman, Michael Regan, Kira Griffitt, Ulf Hermjakob, Kevin Knight, and Martha Palmer. 2018. AMR beyond the sentence: the Multi-sentence AMR corpus. In *Proc. of COLING*, pages 3693–3702, Santa Fe, New Mexico, USA.

Tim O'Gorman, Kristin Wright-Bettner, and Martha Palmer. 2016. Richer Event Description: Integrating event coreference with temporal, causal and bridging annotation. In *Proc. of the 2nd Workshop on Computing News Storylines*, pages 47–56, Austin, Texas, USA.

Martha Palmer, Daniel Gildea, and Paul Kingsbury. 2005. The Proposition Bank: An annotated corpus of semantic roles. *Computational Linguistics*, 31(1):71–106.

Massimo Poesio and Ron Artstein. 2008. Anaphoric Annotation in the ARRAU Corpus. In *Proc. of LREC*, pages 1170–1174, Marrakech, Morocco.

Massimo Poesio, Roland Stuckardt, and Yannick Versley, editors. 2016. *Anaphora Resolution: Algorithms, Resources, and Applications*. Theory and Applications of Natural Language Processing. Springer, Berlin.

Nima Pourdamghani, Yang Gao, Ulf Hermjakob, and Kevin Knight. 2014. Aligning English strings with Abstract Meaning Representation graphs. In *Proc. of EMNLP*, pages 425–429, Doha, Qatar.

Sameer Pradhan, Xiaoqiang Luo, Marta Recasens, Eduard Hovy, Vincent Ng, and Michael Strube. 2014. Scoring coreference partitions of predicted mentions: a reference implementation. In *Proc. of ACL*, pages 30–35, Baltimore, Maryland.

James Pustejovsky, Kiyong Lee, Harry Bunt, and Laurent Romary. 2010. ISO-TimeML: An international standard for semantic annotation. In *Proc. of LREC*, pages 394–397, Valletta, Malta.

Marta Recasens, Zhichao Hu, and Olivia Rhinehart. 2016. Sense anaphoric pronouns: Am I one? In *Proc. of the Workshop on Coreference Resolution Beyond OntoNotes (CORBON 2016)*, pages 1–6, San Diego, California.

Ida Szubert, Adam Lopez, and Nathan Schneider. 2018. A structured syntax-semantics interface for English-AMR alignment. In *Proc. of NAACL-HLT*, pages 1169–1180, New Orleans, Louisiana.

Aaron Steven White, Drew Reisinger, Keisuke Sakaguchi, Tim Vieira, Sheng Zhang, Rachel Rudinger, Kyle Rawlins, and Benjamin Van Durme. 2016. Universal Decompositional Semantics on Universal Dependencies. In *Proc. of EMNLP*, pages 1713–1723, Austin, Texas, USA.

Amir Zeldes. 2017. The GUM corpus: creating multilayer resources in the classroom. *Language Resources and Evaluation*, 51(3):581–612.

Amir Zeldes. 2018. A predictive model for notional anaphora in English. In *Proc. of the First Workshop on Computational Models of Reference, Anaphora and Coreference*, pages 34–43, New Orleans, Louisiana.

Amir Zeldes and Shuo Zhang. 2016. When annotation schemes change rules help: A configurable approach to coreference resolution beyond OntoNotes. In *Proc. of the Workshop on Coreference Resolution Beyond OntoNotes (CORBON 2016)*, pages 92–101, Ann Arbor, Michigan.

A Detailed Guidelines

A.1 Identifying Mentions

Non-scene-non-participant units. A certain subset of the remaining unit types are considered to be mention *candidates*. This subset is comprised of the categories, *Time*, *Elaborator*, *Relator*, *Quantity*, and *Adverbial*.

Time (T) Absolute or relative time expressions like *on May 15, 1990*, *now*, or *in the past*, which are marked Time (T) in UCCA, are considered mentions. However, frequencies and durations, which are also T units in UCCA, are discarded. In order to reliably distinguish these different kinds of time expressions from each other, they have to be identified manually.

Elaborator (E) Elaborators modifying the Center (C) of a non-scene unit are considered mentions if they themselves describe a scene or entity. This is the case, for example, with (relative) clauses and (prepositional) phrases describing the Center's relation with another entity as in

$$[\textit{ the book}_C \textit{ [about the dog}_C \textit{]}_E \textit{]},$$

as well as contingent attributive modifiers, which are stative scenes in UCCA, like *old* in

$$[\textit{ the [old}_S \textit{ (book)}_A \textit{]}_E \textit{ book}_C \textit{]}.$$

By contrast, Elaborator units that do not evoke a person, thing, abstract object, or scene are not considered referring, as in

$$[\textit{ medical}_E \textit{ school}_C \textit{]},$$

where *medical* is an inherent property and thus non-referring.

In English, this often corresponds to units whose Center is an adjective, adverb, or determiner.[18] Bear in mind, however, that these syntactic criteria are language-specific and should only be taken as rough guidance, rather than absolute rules. Thus, referring non-scene Elaborators should be identified manually. By contrast, E-scenes will be identified as mentions automatically, by the scene unit criterion.

Relator (R) Relators should be marked as mentions if and only if they constitute an anaphoric (or cataphoric) reference *in addition to* their relating function.

As an illustration what we mean by that, consider the two occurrences of **that** in the following example, which are both Relators in UCCA:

*I didn't like **that**$_1$ he said the things **that**$_2$ he said.*

Here, *that*$_2$ is an anaphoric reference to *things*, whereas *that*$_1$ is purely functional and thus should not be identified as referring. In English, this corresponds to the syntactic category of relative pronouns.

Most R units, however, are non-referring expressions like prepositions, so identification of the few referring instances of Relators has to be done manually.

Quantity (Q) Partitive constructions like *one of the 5 books* contain mentions of two distinct referents: *the 5 books* and *one of the 5 books*. According to the v2 UCCA guidelines, these expressions should be annotated as an Elaborator-Center structure with a remote edge:

$$[[\textit{ one}_Q \textit{ (books)}_C \textit{]}_C \textit{ [of}_R \textit{ the}_F \textit{ 5}_Q \textit{ books}_C \textit{]}_E \textit{]}_X$$

Such an annotation will result in correct identification of the two mentions based on the guidelines given so far (by choosing the E unit and the whole X[19] unit), without the need to identify the Quantifier (Q) unit *one*$_Q$. However, in foundational layer annotations made based on the UCCA v1 guidelines the same phrase would receive a flat structure (cf. discussion of Centers above):

$$[\textit{ one}_Q \textit{ of}_R \textit{ the}_F \textit{ 5}_Q \textit{ books}_C \textit{]}_X$$

In this case, we choose the whole X unit as a mention of the one book (respecting semantics rather than morphology), and the Q unit *5* as a mention of the five books.

Adverbial (D) While most Adverbial units (D) are by default not considered to be referring (they describe secondary relations over events), in some cases D units can be identified as mentions (also see **coordinated mentions** in appendix A.2).

One such phenomenon are prepositional phrases like *for another reason* and *in the majority of cases* are annotated as D in the corpus, as they modify scenes, not entities.

Another class of Adverbial units that may be identified as referring are the so-called secondary verbs like *help*, *want* and *offer*, which, according to the UCCA guidelines, modify scenes evoked

---

[18]According to the UCCA v1 guidelines, articles are to be annotated as Elaborators. In the v2 guidelines, the default category for articles has changed to Function.

[19]We use the placeholder X here as the actual category depends on the context (i.e., sibling and parent units) in which a unit is embedded.

by primary verbs, but do not themselves denote scenes. However, the relations described by them can sometimes be coreferring antecedents independently from the main scene:

$$\underline{[\ I_A\ lost_P\ [\ 10\ lbs\ ]_A\ .\ ]_j}$$
$$[\ I_A\ was_F\ extremely_D\ happy_S\ \underline{[\ about_R\ that_C\ ]_{Aj}}\ ]\ .$$
$$\text{vs.}$$
$$[\ She_A\ \underline{helped_{Di}}\ me_A\ lose_{Pj}\ [\ 10\ lbs\ ]_A\ .\ ]$$
$$[\ I_A\ really_D\ appreciated_P\ \underline{that_{Ai}}\ ]\ .$$

In both examples, *losing weight* is the main scene according to UCCA, however, in the second example the object of appreciation is *helping*. Thus, we do mark secondary verbs as mentions, but *only if* they are referred back to in the way demonstrated above.

A.2 Resolving Coreference

Appositives. Appositives and titles cooccurring with (named) entity mentions are annotated as Elaborators in UCCA and thus automatically included in the entity mention they modify. They should be marked as separate mentions, coreferring with the modified unit.

If a title or occupational noun occurs by itself or as a copular argument, we treat it as a relational noun as described in the next paragraph.

Extensional vs. intensional readings. A coordinated mention of a group of individuals, such as *John, Paul, and Mary* evokes a referent that is distinct from the possibly already evoked referents of *John*, *Paul*, and *Mary*, respectively.

Relational nouns (e.g., "the president [of Y]"), which are instantiated by a specific individual or a fixed-size set of individuals (e.g., "[X's] parents") at any given point in time, should usually be marked as coreferring with their instances, as inferred from context. This corresponds to an *extensional* (or set-theoretical) notion of reference: a distinct referent is identified by the individuals in which this concept manifests (extension).

Only in clearly generic statements like

The president's power is limited by the constitution.

You should always do what your parents tell you to.

should they evoke separate referents from any specific presidents or parents also mentioned in the same discourse. This corresponds to an *intensional* (or indirect) notion of reference: a distinct referent is identified by its general idea or concept (intension), rather than its instances.

Mentions of group-like entities with undetermined size, such as *the committee* or *all committee members*, should always be analyzed intensionally, evoking a referent separate from the possibly mentioned referents for the individuals comprising it.[20]

Negated scenes. Mentions of scenes are referring and should be marked as coreferring with other mentions of the same scene (same process or state and same participants), regardless of whether or not that scene really took place or is hypothetical:

I hoped $\underline{she\ liked\ the\ pizza_i}$ and was relieved when I learned $\underline{she\ did_i}$.

When both a scene and its negation are mentioned, these mentions should evoke separate referents:

I hoped $\underline{she\ liked\ the\ pizza_i}$ and was surprised when I learned $\underline{she\ didn't_j}$.

Coordinated mentions. When entities or events are described in conjunction, they evoke a separate referent for each of the conjuncts, and a third one for the set comprising them. The whole coordination can be explicitly referred to with another (pronominal) mention:

*It is likely [that [$\underline{the\ shock\ will\ dislocate}$]$_i$ **and** [$\underline{(the\ shock)\ break\ both\ your\ arms}$]$_j$]$_k$; nevertheless $\underline{this_k}$ is a small price to pay for your life.*

*I want [$\underline{Ivy_i}$ **and** $\underline{William_j}$]$_k$ on my debate team, because $\underline{[\ both\ of\ them\ ]_k}$ are great.*

However, if the mentions are presented in *dis*junction, no separate mention for the full disjunction should be marked. If an anaphoric pronoun occurs, there are several options.

For events, a secondary relation (marked D in UCCA) that holds for both conjuncts, if available, should be marked instead:

It is likely$_k$ [that [$\underline{the\ shock\ will\ dislocate}$]$_i$ or [$\underline{(the\ shock)\ break\ both\ your\ arms}$]$_j$] ; nevertheless $\underline{this_k}$ is a small price to pay for your life.

If such a unit is not available, and for entities, no coreference relation exists:

I want [$\underline{Ivy_i}$ or $\underline{William_j}$] on my debate team, because $\underline{[\ both\ of\ them\ ]_k}$ are great.

---

[20]But singular and plural mentions of the same group can corefer (Zeldes, 2018).

Remote edges. Different types of remote edges call for different coreference annotations. *Non*-head (i.e., non-Center, -State, or -Process) remote edges indicate that the same entity/scene modifies or participates in two (potentially also coreferent) unit mentions, namely its primary parent (or the primary parent of the unit it heads) and its remote parent. This corresponds to zero anaphora, or a "core" element that is implicit in one context and explicit in another. *Head* remote edges, however, merely indicate the *category* of entity/event that is shared between a full and an elliptic or anaphoric mention ("sense anaphora"; Recasens et al., 2016). E.g., *books* in "two of the 5 books" is category-shared between *5 books* and *two (books)*, which are separate non-coreferent mentions. Whether the primary and remote parent are coreferent or not is contingent on context.

Towards Universal Semantic Representation

Huaiyu Zhu
IBM Research - Almaden
650 Harry Road,
San Jose, CA 95120
huaiyu@us.ibm.com

Yunyao Li
IBM Research - Almaden
650 Harry Road,
San Jose, CA 95120
yunyaoli@us.ibm.com

Laura Chiticariu
IBM Watson
650 Harry Road,
San Jose, CA 95120
chiti@us.ibm.com

Abstract

Natural language understanding at the semantic level and independent of language variations is of great practical value. Existing approaches such as semantic role labeling (SRL) and abstract meaning representation (AMR) still have features related to the peculiarities of the particular language. In this work we describe various challenges and possible solutions in designing a semantic representation that is universal across a variety of languages.

1 Introduction

Natural languages have many syntactic variations for expressing the same meaning, not only within each language but more so across languages, making syntactical analysis cumbersome to use by downstream applications. Semantic understanding of natural language is fundamental for many applications that take natural language texts as part of their input. Semantic Role Labeling (SRL) analyzes the predicate-role structure at the shallow semantic parsing level (e.g., PropBank (Kingsbury and Palmer, 2002)). At a deeper level, Abstract Meaning Representation (AMR) provides a rooted, directional and labeled graph representing the meaning of a sentence (Banarescu et al., 2013), focusing on semantic relations between concepts such as PropBank predicate-argument structures while abstracting away from syntactic variation.

Many applications require multilingual capabilities, but SRL and AMR annotation schemes designed for individual languages have language-dependent features. For example, Hajic et al. (2014); Xue et al. (2014) observed AMRs designed for different languages have differences, some accidental but others are more fundamental. Several efforts are underway to create more cross-lingual natural language resources. Universal Dependencies (UD) is a framework for cross-linguistically consistent grammatical annotation.(De Marneffe et al., 2014). The Universal Proposition Banks project aims to annotate text in different languages with a layer of "universal" semantic role labeling annotation, by using the frame and role labels of the English Proposition Bank to label shallow semantics in sentences in new target languages(Akbik et al., 2015). Similarly, Damonte and Cohen (2018) use AMR annotations for English as a semantic representation for sentences written in other languages, utilizing an AMR parser for English and parallel corpora to learn AMR parsers for additional languages.

Despite these efforts, some remaining interlanguage variations important for practical usage are not yet captured by the efforts so far. They create obstacles to a truly cross-lingual meaning representation which would enable the downstream applications be written for one language and applicable for other languages. The purpose of this paper is two-fold. One objective is to highlight some of these remaining issues and call the attention of the community to resolving them. Another objective is to advocate a form of abstract meaning representation geared towards cross-lingual universal applicability, in the same spirit of AMR but somewhat simplified, with the following major similarities and differences

- Like AMR, it makes use of PropBank style predicate-argument structures.

- It does not have AMR style concept nodes. It does not infer relations among instances and concepts other than those expressed explicitly, nor perform co-reference resolution.

- It is geared towards cross-lingual representation of logical structures, such as conjunctions and conditionals.

- It assigns features to nodes, to promote structural simplicity and to increase extensibility.

Proceedings of the First International Workshop on Designing Meaning Representations, pages 177–181
Florence, Italy, August 1st, 2019 ©2019 Association for Computational Linguistics

We will illustrate, through several examples, the kinds of issues that arise from attempting to create a universal meaning representation, and the challenges in resolving these issues. We will describe our tentative solutions and call the attention of the community to these issues.

2 Examples of semantic variations

Across different languages, semantic structures are much more uniform than syntactic structures. However, there are still language variations in shallow semantics. In this section we look at a number of examples.

2.1 Temporal semantics

Predicates often represent actions that happen, or states or properties that exist or change, in a certain time frame. Different languages have different ways to express such temporal relations. In English, auxiliary verbs and main verbs are usually combined with morphological change to express tense and aspect. For example,

> *I am going to speak* to him. (future-simple)
> *I have spoken* to him. (present-perfect)
> *I was speaking* to him. (past-progressive)

Similar meanings are represented differently in other languages. For example, German usually does not distinguish verbs between present-perfect and the past-simple as English, even though it formally has corresponding syntactic structures. Instead the distinction is implied by temporal arguments such as a prepositional phrases. In Chinese the corresponding concepts are represented by adverbs and participles. For example,

> *I have been reading* for a week. (pres.-perf.-prog.)
> *Ich lese seit einer Woche.* (past-simple)
> 我已经读了一个星期了. (adverb-verb-participle)

A more abstract representation for tense should be able to unify all these variations. Among available linguistic theories, Reichenbach (1947)'s theory of tense covers a large proportion of these variations. It consists of three points in time: point of event (E), point of reference (R) and point of speech (S), and two ordering relations: anteriority and simultaneity among these points. In English, the relation between S and R corresponds to tense, and the relation between R and E corresponds to aspect. For example, "E–S,R" corresponds to present-perfect and "E,R–S" corresponds to past-simple. The "progressive" aspect is not represented in this framework. It can be

added as an additional property. In related work, Smith (1997) provides a richer semantics by regarding temporal aspects as relations among time intervals. TimeML (Saurı et al., 2006) defines a rich variety of time related concepts.

2.2 Expressing modality

In English, modal verbs are auxiliary verbs that express various likelihood of the main verb. These include certainty and necessity (must, shall), intention (would), ability or possibility (can, may, might), etc. Additional idiomatic expressions provide similar functionality. For example,

> *is capable of, used to, had better to, is willing to*

AMR represents syntactic modals with concepts like possible-01, likely-01, obligate-01, permit-01, recommend-01, prefer-01, etc. This English-inspired classification of modality must be extended for other languages. For example, in Chinese the modal verbs include at least the following: 能 (can, may), 会 (can, will, be able to), 要 (want, wish, intend to), 肯 (be willing to, consent), 敢 (dare), 可能 (may), 可以 (can, be allowed to), 应该 (should), 愿意 (be willing to). When combined with negation, these also include 不愿意 (be reluctant to, be unwilling to), etc. There is no compelling reason, other than English convention, that modality has special relation to modal verbs. Considerations of additional languages will likely further extend types of such meanings as well as further refine these meanings.

A cross-lingual framework must allow for all these variation, while providing basic features that allow easy categorization of them. In analogy of Reichenbach's theory of tense, we propose to categorize the modality by considering several dimensions that jointly affect the likelihood of an action:

- Probability or certainty
- Requirement or obligation
- Advisability, recommendation or suggestion
- Ability, capability or permit
- Desire or hope
- Willingness or intention

Each modality expression may have values in one or more of these dimensions.

2.3 Conditionality

The most basic language construct expressing "if A, then B" probably exists in most languages with syntactic variations. For example, in English it is more natural to say "if A, B" or "B if A". Syntactical differences aside, such structures essentially express a relation of two things, A as antecedent and B as consequent. Natural languages can also express, but often not in the same sentence, the more complete structure "if A, then B, else C", There does not appear to be a generally adopted linguistic term for the C part.

Unlike formal logic, natural language often associates additional mood, modality and temporal element with these expressions

> *X only if Y*
> *X as long as Y*
> *If it were not you, it would not have ....*
> *Had I known it, I would have ...*

In English, the subjunctive mood is often associated with conditional structures in making counterfactual assumptions. The term subjunctive corresponds to several different concepts in different languages. For example, in Spanish, the subjunctive can be used with verbs for wishes, emotions, impersonal expressions, recommendations, doubt, denial, hope and other verbs to express what is essentially modality. To accommodate such variations across different languages, one possible design is to consider the two aspects of conditionalality expressions separately. One aspect deals with the logical implication $A \rightarrow B$. The other aspect is to assign tense and modality to the conditionals. The tense can be useful for expressions like "Do A until B", and the modality assigned to the conditional can be used to express the modality associated with the conditional itself, not to the antecedent or consequent.

3 A framework for cross-lingual meaning representation

The refined meanings discussed in previous section must be expressed in a certain framework. SRL does not have sufficient abstract structures for this task. AMR is a better candidate, but we have found it lacking in two aspects. On the one hand, it has a substantial amount of extra information that is neither explicitly expressed in the sentence nor required by downstream applications. On the other hand, it still lacks sufficient structure to express the refined meanings discussed above.

We propose a meaning representation that attempts to simplify AMR while allowing easy incorporation of additional features. The proposed representation is a graph with a small number of node types, flexible features on the nodes, and labeled and directed connections among the nodes. It is not necessarily a tree.

3.1 Nodes

We consider the following types of nodes:

Predicate A predicate in the sense of PropBank

Role A core argument, such as A0, A1, etc., in the sense of PropBank.

Context A non-core argument, such as AM-TMP, AM-LOC, etc. in the sense of PropBank.

Conditional Representation of "if-then-else" structure, including variations like "unless", "as long as", "whenever".

Conjunction Representation of "and", "but", "or", etc. Linguistic conjunctions include "and", "but", "or", "nor", etc. Like AMR, it includes both conjunctions and disjunctions as well negated expressions in terms of logic.

Relational Representation of a linguistic relation among entities that is usually expressed in English with prepositions such as "in", "on", "under", or similar structures representing possessive (e.g, "A's B" vs "B of A").

3.2 Features

Each node is associated with additional features specific to the node type. For example, a Predicate node is associated with features such as the verb sense (eg."speak.01"), as well as tense, modality, polarity, etc.

3.3 Edges

The nodes are connected by edges with well defined types

- Role and Context nodes are connected to Predicate nodes with SRL labels. Context might also be connected to other nodes, such as Conditional, as discussed above.

- A Conditional node is connected to an antecedent node and a consequent node, and optionally to an "else" node.

- A Conjunction node is connected to its constituents.

- A Relation node is connected to its constituents.

3.4 Example representation

An example can illustrate various aspects of this framework. Consider the sentence

Had I studied harder last year, I would have been able to pass the exam by the end of the winter and got an A.

This sentence is constructed so that it can be used to illustrate the issues discussed in this paper.

We will express the graph by describing the nodes and their features. We use Json style notation for features as key-value pairs. Some of the values are literal values, others are references to other nodes, essentially representing the edges with labels. In this example, for the sake of exposition, we will use features that correspond more closely to conventional English linguistic features. For example, Predicates have features tense, aspect, modality and polarity.

A = Conditional {mood: conterfactural, antecedent: B, consequent C }.
B = Predicate {sense: study.01, tense: past, aspect: simple, polarity: positive, modality: normal}.
B_1 = Role {content: I, predicate: B, type: A0 }.
B_2 = Context {content: harder, predicate: B, type: AM-MNR }.
B_3 = Context {content: last year, predicate: B, type: AM-TMP }
C = Conjunction {type: and, members: [C_1, C_2] }
C_1 = Predicate {sense: pass.07, tense: past, aspect: perfect, polarity: positive, modality: ability}.
C_2 = Predicate {sense: get.01, tense: past, aspect: perfect, polarity: positive, modality: ability}.
C_{11} = Role {content: I, predicate: C_1, type: A0 }.
C_{12} = Role {content: exam, predicate: C_1, type: A1 }.
C_{13} = Context {content: by the end of the winter, predicate: C_1, type: AM-TMP }
...

Note the following points:

- The structure of this graph is simpler than AMR graph, mostly by virtue of removing the AMR concept nodes.

- For the remaining nodes the edges connecting them are similar to those in AMR graphs.

- The nodes are typed. Each type has a specific set of features.

Although we have used more traditional feature sets in this example, it is obvious that more orthogonal feature designs as discussed in the previous section can be used instead, without changing the overall structure of the graph.

3.5 Learning features from data

Using techniques similar to those used to transfer SRL and AMR from one language to another(Akbik et al., 2015; Damonte and Cohen, 2018), it is possible to transfer labeling schemes for the additional fewatures and structures discussed in this paper from one language to another. The cross-lingual transfer may also help to discover better feature sets from data. For example, by analyzing equivalent sentences in different languages, it is possible to discover additional candidates for modalilty or better classification of modality. Akbik et al. (2016) showed that it is possible to use correspondences between verb senses in two languages to discover the duplication and aliasing of verb senses. Similar techniques can be applied to verb features such as tense and modality, as well as structural featues such as conditional and relational features. It is our hope that this framework provides a sufficiently versatile scafolding for the community to work together towards a more complete cross-lingual representation of meanings.

4 Conclusions

Creating a universal semantic representation that works across a large number of languages is an important objective for the NLP community. In this paper we described our attempts towards this goal, highlighting the issues and challenges that arise from such efforts. In particular, we described specific issues related to representing tense and modality of predicates, as well issues for expressing relational structures among the entities and predicates. We also present a framework for creating an overall structure to hold the cross-lingual semantics. It is similar to AMR but with a different emphasis. Instead of identifying all the intricate relations among the constituents of a sentence as well as the concepts they correspond to, this representation is aimed at expressing the essential structures and important features of these structures in a cross-lingual fashion. As such it sacrifices certain capabilities of AMR (such as concepts and variables) while emphasizing others (such as defining the features for various node types). It is our hope that this framework can stimulate the community to make progress on the design issues for various features of these structures, and we call upon the community to work together to refine this framework.

References

Alan Akbik, Marina Danilevsky, Yunyao Li, Shivakumar Vaithyanathan, Huaiyu Zhu, et al. 2015. Generating high quality proposition banks for multilingual semantic role labeling. In *Proceedings of the 53rd Annual Meeting of the Association for Computational Linguistics and the 7th International Joint Conference on Natural Language Processing (Volume 1: Long Papers)*, volume 1, pages 397–407.

Alan Akbik, Xinyu Guan, and Yunyao Li. 2016. Multilingual aliasing for auto-generating proposition banks. In *Proceedings of COLING 2016, the 26th International Conference on Computational Linguistics: Technical Papers*, pages 3466–3474.

Laura Banarescu, Claire Bonial, Shu Cai, Madalina Georgescu, Kira Griffitt, Ulf Hermjakob, Kevin Knight, Philipp Koehn, Martha Palmer, and Nathan Schneider. 2013. Abstract meaning representation for sembanking. In *Proceedings of the 7th Linguistic Annotation Workshop and Interoperability with Discourse*, pages 178–186.

Marco Damonte and Shay B. Cohen. 2018. Cross-lingual abstract meaning representation parsing. In *Proc. 2018 NAACL-HLT*, pages 1146–1155, New Orleans, Louisiana. Association for Computational Linguistics.

Marie-Catherine De Marneffe, Timothy Dozat, Natalia Silveira, Katri Haverinen, Filip Ginter, Joakim Nivre, and Christopher D Manning. 2014. Universal Stanford dependencies: A cross-linguistic typology. In *LREC*, volume 14, pages 4585–92.

Jan Hajic, Ondrej Bojar, and Zdenka Uresova. 2014. Comparing Czech and English AMRs. In *Proceedings of Workshop on Lexical and Grammatical Resources for Language Processing*, pages 55–64.

Paul Kingsbury and Martha Palmer. 2002. From Tree-Bank to PropBank. In *LREC*, pages 1989–1993.

Hans Reichenbach. 1947. *Elements of Symbolic Logic*. Macmillan & Co, New York.

Roser Saurı, Jessica Littman, Bob Knippen, Robert Gaizauskas, Andrea Setzer, and James Pustejovsky. 2006. TimeML annotation guidelines version 1.2. 1.

C.S. Smith. 1997. The parameters of aspect.

Nianwen Xue, Ondrej Bojar, Jan Hajic, Martha Palmer, Zdenka Uresova, and Xiuhong Zhang. 2014. Not an interlingua, but close: Comparison of english amrs to chinese and czech. In *LREC*, volume 14, pages 1765–1772. Reykjavik, Iceland.

A Dependency Structure Annotation for Modality

Meagan Vigus, Jens E. L. Van Gysel, and William Croft
Department of Linguistics
University of New Mexico
{mvigus, jelvangysel, wcroft}@unm.edu

Abstract

This paper presents an annotation scheme for modality that employs a dependency structure. Events and sources (here, conceivers) are represented as nodes and epistemic strength relations characterize the edges. The epistemic strength values are largely based on Saurí and Pustejovsky's (2009) FactBank, while the dependency structure mirrors Zhang and Xue's (2018b) approach to temporal relations. Six documents containing 377 events have been annotated by two expert annotators with high levels of agreement.

1 Introduction

Representing modality is fundamental to creating a complete representation of the meaning of a text. Modality characterizes the reality status of events, i.e. whether they occur in the real world, or in any number of non-real 'worlds'.

In this paper, we develop an annotation scheme that builds on Saurí and Pustejovsky's (2009) Fact-Bank annotation scheme and Zhang and Xue's (2018b) temporal dependency structures. Although we have only applied this annotation to texts in English, we intend for it to be applicable cross-linguistically (see Van Gysel et al. 2019).

Like FactBank, we combine modality and polarity values and relate both back to a source (or, in our terms, conceiver); the modality/polarity values represent the source's perspective on an event. We propose two main innovations to FactBank's annotation scheme: the interpretation of epistemic strength values in the domains of deontic and dynamic modality, and the representation of modality in a dependency structure.

Modality is generally taken to encompass epistemic, deontic, and dynamic modality (e.g., Palmer 2001). Epistemic modality corresponds most straightforwardly to factuality in that it characterizes whether an event occurs in the real world.

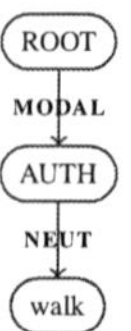

Figure 1: *Mary **might** HAVE WALKED the dog.*

We propose that epistemic modality may be interpreted in the domain of deontic modality as degree of predictability (see 3.2.2) and within the domain of dynamic modality as the strength of a generalization over instances (see 3.2.3).

The second main innovation of this paper is the representation of modal annotation as a dependency structure. The dependency structure is a directed, acyclic graph with conceivers and events as nodes and edges between the nodes labelled with epistemic strength values. A simple example of this can be seen in Figure 1; Figure 1 shows that the author has neutral epistemic stance towards the occurrence of the walking event.

This modal dependency structure is based largely on Zhang and Xue's (2018b) temporal dependency tree structure. Structuring the annotation of temporal relations as a dependency tree allows for the same values to be used for temporal relations between events, between time expressions, and between an event and a time expression. This leads to a perspicuous representation of the temporal structure of an entire document.

For modality, the dependency graph structure allows for the nesting of modal values that is necessary to represent certain types of linguistic constructions (see 3.3). The dependency structure also allows for the explicit representation of scope relations between modality and negation. Most of the time, the dependency graph for modality is also a tree: each node only has one parent. However, there are rare cases that require a single event to

Proceedings of the First International Workshop on Designing Meaning Representations, pages 182–198
Florence, Italy, August 1st, 2019 ©2019 Association for Computational Linguistics

have two parents in the graph; see 3.3.

A dependency structure for modal annotation has another advantage: it closely mirrors the mental spaces theory of modality (Fauconnier, 1994, 1997). This allows for the insights of the mental spaces theory of modality to be straightforwardly imported into our modal dependency structure (see 2.2).

The modal dependency annotation scheme was tested on six documents[1] containing 108 sentences. A total of 377 events were annotated for modality by two expert annotators. Agreement scores were relatively high and similar to those reported in Zhang and Xue (2018b).

2 Background

2.1 Related work

Modality, factuality, certainty, or veridicality of statements in text has been addressed in a variety of ways in the computational linguistics literature (see Morante and Sporleder 2012). In this section, we briefly survey some of the annotation schemes intended to capture modality and polarity distinctions in general-domain texts (see also Nissim et al. 2013; Lavid et al. 2016; Prasad et al. 2008). Although we focus on manual annotation, there have also been automatic annotations of modal information (e.g., Saurí and Pustejovsky 2012, Baker et al. 2010).

Wiebe et al. (2005) focus on the annotation of opinions, emotions, and sentiments, in addition to modality. Importantly, Wiebe et al. (2005) introduce the notion of *nested sources*, including the representation of all in-text sources as nested underneath the author. This notion has been widely adopted and we adopt it in the modal dependency structure.

Rubin et al. (2005) and Rubin (2007) annotate certainty in a corpus of news articles. They annotate four dimensions: level of certainty, perspective (i.e., source), focus (abstract vs. factual), and time reference. Level of certainty is divided into a four-way distinction (absolute, high, medium, and low), however Rubin (2007) reports low inter-annotator agreement for this four-way distinction and suggests a binary distinction may lead to higher agreement. De Marneffe et al. (2012), however, find that annotators actually

reached higher agreement scores using FactBank's three-way modality distinctions (see below) as opposed to using a smaller number of distinctions.

Matsuyoshi et al. (2010) annotate seven modal categories: source, time, conditional, primary modality, actuality, evaluation, and focus. Conditional distinguishes between propositions with conditions and those without. Primary modality distinguishes between a number of fine-grained modality categories (e.g., volition, wish, imperative). Their actuality category refers to level of certainty; evaluation refers to an entity's attitude towards an event.

Ruppenhofer and Rehbein (2012) annotate the MPQA corpus (Wiebe et al., 2005) with modality information, focusing on sense disambiguation of grammaticalized modal verbs. In addition, their annotation scheme identifies the modalized Proposition, the Source, and the Link that introduces the source. They focus on distinguishing the modality type (epistemic, deontic, etc.) as opposed to the degree of likelihood, the focus of the current paper. Ruppenhofer and Rehbein (2012) are more restricted than the current scheme in that they limit their annotations to grammaticalized modal verbs.

Rubinstein et al. (2013) report on a language-independent modal annotation that has been applied to the MPQA corpus (Wiebe et al., 2005). Rubinstein et al. (2013) identify and annotate "modal expressions" for modality type, polarity, propositional arguments, source, and a few other categories. They find that annotators are only able to reliably distinguish between rather coarse-grained modality types, essentially epistemic vs. root modality (what they call non-priority vs. priority). Similar to Ruppenhofer and Rehbein (2012), Rubinstein et al. (2013) focus on the type of modality, but do not annotate the propositional arguments with their degree of likelihood (the focus of the current scheme).

FactBank (Saurí and Pustejovsky, 2009) presents a corpus annotated with information about event factuality. They distinguish three levels of factuality: certain (CT), probable (PR), and possible (PS). These interact with a binary polarity distinction, positive (+) and negative (-).

FactBank also introduces an unspecified value (U) for both factuality and polarity. FactBank uses the unspecified values for cases where the factual status of an event is not clear. This can be because the source does not know the factual sta-

---

[1] These documents were excerpted from Strassel and Tracey (2016), Garland et al. (2012), and *The Little Prince* (de Saint-Exupéry and Woods, 1943).

tus of an event (e.g., *John does not know whether Mary came.*; Saurí and Pustejovsky 2009, 247; compare the '?' mental space relation in Fauconnier 1994, 86) or because the source does not communicate the polarity of an event (e.g., *John knows whether Mary came.*; Saurí and Pustejovsky 2009, 247; compare the '!' mental space relation in Fauconnier 1994, 86). In total, FactBank distinguishes eight factuality values: CT+, CT-, PR+, PR-, PS+, PS-, CTU, and UU.

As mentioned above, FactBank represents these values as tied to a particular perspective, or source. When a source is not explicitly mentioned in the text, the author of the text is the implied source. FactBank also allows for the nesting of sources (as in Wiebe et al. 2005); whenever a source is mentioned in the text, it is annotated as nested underneath the author.

De Marneffe et al. (2012) annotate pragmatic factuality information on top of the more lexically-based factuality information from FactBank. Similarly, this paper proposes an annotation scheme for modality based on the full context of sentences, and not the general meaning of lexical items.

2.2   Mental spaces

Mental space theory was developed by Fauconnier to solve problems of referential opacity and presupposition "projection" (Fauconnier 1994, 1997; see also McCawley 1993). These problems arise because referents and presupposed events may exist only in a non-real *mental space*. A mental space is a representation of alternative realities to the real world—more precisely, the world of the author's beliefs. Mental spaces present alternative realities as cognitive, that is, in the mind of a conceiver, rather than as metaphysical entities, as is done in possible worlds semantics. Mental spaces have entities that are counterparts to real entities (though some may not have real world counterparts), with associated properties and events that are different from those of the real world entities.

The alternative realities represented by mental spaces include both events whose factuality is less than certain, including negative events, which are typically expressed by grammatical modality and negation; and events that are believed, desired, feared, and so on by a conceiver, which are typically expressed by propositional attitude, desiderative, and other such predicates. These alternative realities give rise to the paradoxes in reference and

presupposition that interested Fauconnier. We are, however, interested in using the mental space representation to model modality, negation, and predicates that give rise to alternative realities. All such constructions are *space builders* in Fauconnier's terms.

Mental spaces can be nested within other mental spaces. For example, the space representing a person's desire to go to Florence is nested in the space representing that person's beliefs. The nested mental space structure allows one to capture scope relations between modality, propositional attitude predicates, and negation. In fact, the dependency graph structure of nested mental spaces is a more powerful representation than linear scope relations and is able to handle the sorts of semantic and pragmatic problems that Fauconnier analyzes in his work. The dependency structure of mental space relations allows us to adapt the temporal dependency annotation scheme of Zhang and Xue (2018b) to the annotation of modality and related concepts.

3   Modal dependency structure

The modal dependency structure consists of three parts: conceivers/sources, events, and the relations between them. Section 3.1 describes the types of nodes in the dependency structure and 3.2 describes the types of edges.

3.1   Nodes in the modal dependency structure

There are two distinct types of nodes in the modal dependency structure: conceivers and events. Events may have either conceivers or events as parents; conceivers only ever have other conceivers (or, ROOT) as parents. That is, conceivers are never the children of events.

3.1.1   Conceivers

The mental-level entities whose perspective on events is modeled in the text are called CONCEIVERS. Each text will automatically have at least one AUTHOR conceiver node, representing the perspective of the creator of the text. Texts with multiple creators (e.g., dialogues) will have multiple AUTHOR nodes.

When the author models the mental content of other entities, those entities are also represented as conceiver nodes in the dependency structure. Certain types of predicates inherently involve conceivers: report, knowledge, belief, opinion, doubt, perception, and inference (Saurí and Pustejovsky,

2009, 236). For example, in *Mary thinks the cat is hungry*, the author is asserting something about the content of Mary's attitudes and beliefs. Therefore, MARY is identified as a conceiver and added as a node in the graph.

In contrast to FactBank, we introduce conceiver nodes for deontic events (e.g., volition, intention). FactBank excludes them because they express an attitude that is not "epistemic in nature" (Saurí and Pustejovsky, 2009, 237). However, we take a broader view of sources as conceivers whose mental content is expressed in the text; a person's desires or intentions are based on their own set of beliefs, and not the author's beliefs (McCawley 1993, 421; Fauconnier 1994, 93). For deontic events, this allows us to annotate the strength of likelihood that the future event will occur based on the conceiver's mental attitude. Wiebe et al. (2005) also annotate sources for deontic events.

Also following Wiebe et al. (2005), we represent conceiver nodes as children of the AUTHOR node. Another conceiver's mental space is always mediated by the author's perspective. For example, in *Mary thinks the cat is hungry*, the author is attributing a belief to Mary; as readers, we don't have direct access to Mary's mental content, only to the author's perspective on Mary's beliefs. Therefore, the MARY node is represented as a child of the AUTHOR node.

There may be an indefinite number of nested conceivers. For example, *Mary said that Henry told her that John thinks the cat is hungry* has four conceivers (including the author). The JOHN conceiver node is nested underneath the HENRY node, which is in turn nested underneath the MARY node; finally, the MARY node is a child of the AUTHOR node.

Although conceivers are prototypically mental-level entities, conceiver nodes can also be used to represent the "world" in which a particular event takes place in the case of stories, drawings, movies, etc. For example, in *Aeneas flees Troy in The Aeneid*, AENEID is identified as a conceiver; all events in the story, such as *flee*, are nested underneath AENEID.

3.1.2 Events

The other type of node in the modal dependency structure represents the events themselves. We largely follow TimeML's event identification criteria (Pustejovsky et al., 2005).

The only semantic type of event which we ex-clude from our modal dependency structure are events that attribute beliefs to a conceiver (e.g., *think, believe*). These events correspond straightforwardly to the edges in the modal dependency structure (see 3.2), and therefore they are not represented as nodes. For the same reason, we also do not represent grammaticalized modal auxiliaries (e.g., *may, must*) as nodes in the dependency structure.

3.2 Edges in the modal dependency structure

As mentioned in 1, the edges in the modal dependency structure correspond to combined epistemic strength and polarity values. These characterize the type of mental space in which a particular event holds. Edges can link two events, two conceivers, or a conceiver and an event.

In a cross-linguistic study drawing on data from fifty languages, Boye (2012) finds that three levels of epistemic support are sufficient to characterize epistemic modal systems across languages. That is, languages tend to have forms that distinguish three levels of epistemic support. Boye (2012) uses the term "support" to refer both to epistemic modality proper and the combination of evidential and epistemic modality (see 3.2.1). Following Boye (2012), we label our values FULL, PARTIAL, and NEUTRAL. Since we extend our values outside of prototypical epistemic and evidential modality, we refer to these values as characterizing epistemic "strength". These three values correspond to FactBank's CERTAIN, PROBABLE, and POSSIBLE values.

Also like FactBank, we combine these values with a binary polarity distinction (POSITIVE/NEGATIVE) for a total of six values. These strength/polarity values represent the modality as scoping over negation. For less grammaticalized forms that express combinations of modality and negation, the dependency structure represents the scope relations between the two.

The combined modality-polarity values are shown in Table 1. These values characterize the likelihood that a particular event occurs (or does not occur) in the real world. The lexical item in the examples that expresses the epistemic strength of the sentence is in bold. For the POS value, the simple declarative sentence in English conveys full positive epistemic strength; this is very common cross-linguistically (Boye, 2012).

Epistemic strength is generally only used to de-

Label	Value	FactBank	Definition	Example
POS	full positive	CT+	complete certainty that event occurs	*The dog* BARKED.
PRT	partial positive	PR+	strong certainty that event occurs	*The dog* ***probably*** BARKED.
NEUT	positive neutral	PS+	neutral certainty that event does/n't occur; expressed positively	*The dog* ***might*** *have* BARKED.
NEUTNEG	negative neutral	PS-	neutral certainty that event does/n't occur; negation expressed	*The dog* ***might not*** *have* BARKED.
PRTNEG	partial negative	PR-	strong certainty that event does not occur	*The dog* ***probably didn't*** BARK.
NEG	full negative	CT-	complete certainty that event doesn't occur	*The dog* ***didn't*** BARK.

Table 1: Strength values

scribe phenomena like those in Table 1: the factuality of a single instance of a specific event in the past or present. We use the notion of epistemic strength to characterize evidential justification, deontic modality, and dynamic modality.

Although epistemic strength is interpreted slightly differently in these domains, it still refers to the likelihood of occurrence of the event in question in the real world. It is important to note that the modal dependency structure itself does not distinguish between episodic, deontic, or dynamic events. However, the modal annotation scheme may be used in conjunction with other annotations which do distinguish between these types of events (e.g., temporal or aspectual annotation).

3.2.1 Evidential justification

Following Boye (2012) and Saurí and Pustejovsky (2009), we characterize evidential justification in terms of epistemic support.

Boye (2012) finds that there is cross-linguistic evidence for lumping epistemic support and evidential justification together into the same relations. Specifically, languages may encode direct evidential justification (sensory perception) with the same forms as full epistemic support; indirect justification (hearsay, inferential) may be encoded by the same forms as partial epistemic support.

Example 1 shows how direct and indirect justification correspond to epistemic support.

(1)   a.   *I **saw** Mary* FEED *the cat.*

       b.   *Mary **must** have* FED *the cat.*

In 1a, the author has direct knowledge of the feeding event, by way of witnessing it. Therefore, *feed* would be annotated with POS strength. In 1b, however, *must* signals that the author is inferring that the feeding event occurred without direct, perceptual knowledge. Therefore, *fed* in 1b would be annotated with PRT strength.

3.2.2 Deontic modality

We analyze deontic modality (e.g., desires, intentions, demands) as a subtype of future events, since the event that is desired, demanded etc. will take place in the future if it takes place at all. We group together deontic events and simple assertion of future events as 'future-oriented' events.

In the modal dependency structure, we interpret epistemic strength within the future-oriented domain as degree of predictability, rather than degree of factuality, because future events are unverifiable at the present moment.

Example 2 shows the three degrees of epistemic strength within the future-oriented domain.

(2)   a.   *Bill **will** * DRIVE *to Pisa.*

       b.   *Bill **is planning** * TO DRIVE *to Pisa.*

       c.   *Bill **wants** * TO DRIVE *to Pisa.*

Example 2a, the plain future, represents the highest degree of predictability for future-oriented events; therefore, this corresponds to FULL strength. Intention, as in 2b, is annotated as PARTIAL strength in the future-oriented domain: once an agent forms an intention, the event is likely to occur. Desire, as in 2c, corresponds to NEUTRAL strength: one may or may not act on one's desires.

Future-oriented events can also occur in the past (i.e., the future-in-the-past), as in example 3.

(3)   a.   *Bill **would** * DRIVE *to Pisa (the next morning).*

       b.   *Bill **was planning** * TO DRIVE *to Pisa.*

       c.   *Bill **wanted** * TO DRIVE *to Pisa.*

Akin to 2, the future-in-the-past can also occur with different strengths. That is, 3a implies that the driving event happened, i.e. FULL strength.[2] Example 3b expresses past intention, which opens

---

[2]The main clause use of *would* is not the same as *would* occurring in conditional constructions (Fillmore, 1990).

up the possibility that the driving event didn't actually happen; this corresponds to PARTIAL strength. In 3c, only a past desire is expressed, without any indication whether or not the driving event actually took place; this is NEUTRAL strength.

3.2.3 Dynamic modality

Epistemic strength is generally not considered to apply to dynamic modality or generic statements because they do not refer to a specific instance of an event, but a generalization over instances.

In this paper, we tentatively propose that dynamic modality and generics can be subsumed under the same analysis as generalizations that can be mapped onto actual, episodic events.[3] The two levels of dynamic modality (possibility and necessity) combined with generics creates a three-way distinction that can be characterized in terms of strength. Dynamic possibility, as in *Owls can hunt at night*, corresponds to epistemic possibility, i.e. NEUTRAL strength. Dynamic necessity, as in *Owls must hunt at night*, corresponds to epistemic necessity, i.e. FULL strength. Generic events, as in *Owls hunt at night*, represent a generalization between "possibly" and "necessarily"; generics express that something occurs "usually" or "normally". Therefore, we analyze generics as PARTIAL strength.

The correspondence between strength values with episodic and generic events can also be thought of in these terms: a FULL strength generic can be falsified by one negative episodic event, a NEUTRAL strength generic is verified by one positive episodic event, and a PARTIAL strength generic cannot be falsified by one negative episodic event, but there must be enough relevant episodic events to infer that the event is typical or characteristic.

3.2.4 Edges between conceiver nodes

Edges between conceiver nodes are characterized by the same set of strength distinctions. That is, just as conceivers may express different strengths towards events, they also may express different strengths towards the modeling of another conceiver's mental content. This can be seen in Table 2. The epistemic strength values correspond to the relation between the AUTHOR conceiver node and the MARY conceiver node.

Value	Example
POS	*Mary knows the cat ate.*
PRT	*Mary **probably** knows the cat ate.*
NEUT	*Mary **might** know the cat ate.*
NEUTNEG	*Mary **might not** know the cat ate.*
PRTNEG	*Mary **probably doesn't** know the cat ate.*
NEG	*Mary **doesn't** know the cat ate.*

Table 2: Edges between conceiver nodes

3.2.5 Summary of edge values

Extending epistemic strength to cover evidential justification, future likelihood, and strength of generalization over instances allows us to use a single set of distinctions to characterize (and annotate) events in different modal domains.

3.3 Dependency structure

The second main innovation in this annotation scheme is the representation as a dependency structure, as opposed to assigning a single modal value to an event. The dependency structure allows us to nest modal strengths between events. This can be seen in example 4.

(4) *Mary **might need** TO CHECK the weather.*

This example contains two modal expressions: epistemic *might* and deontic *need*. That is, *might* expresses a NEUTRAL epistemic stance towards the needing event; *need* expresses a PARTIAL epistemic stance towards the checking event.

If we were to assign a single annotation value to *check*, it is not clear if this should be NEUT from *must* or PRT from *need*. The dependency structure allows us to explicitly represent this nesting of strength values. This can be seen in Figure 2. Here, *check* is represented as the child of *need*, with a PRT relation. The *need* event is represented with a NEUT relation to the AUTHOR node.

Example 5 illustrates another case where representing the nesting of modal relations between events is necessary.

(5) *I'll **probably allow** EATING in the classroom this year.*

Here, *probably* indicates PRT strength, whereas *allow* indicates NEUT strength; see Figure 3.

As mentioned in 1, there are rare cases where a single node has two parents in the dependency

---

[3] We also tentatively propose that all generics are represented with their own node in the dependency graph. That is, *Owls hunt at night* would require two nodes: one for the generic and one for *hunt*. This is necessary in order to capture situations in which epistemic modals scope over the generic, e.g. *Owls might hunt at night*. This includes dialects of English in which double modals (e.g., *might can*) occur.

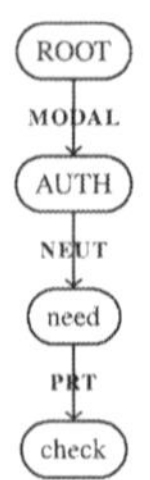

Figure 2: Strength nesting: *Mary might need to check the weather.*

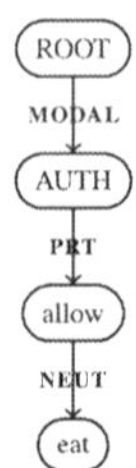

Figure 3: Strength nesting: *I'll probably allow eating in the classroom this year.*

graph. The clearest example of this is with *know*, as in 6 below.

(6) *Mary **knows** the cat* ATE *breakfast.*

The issue here is that *know* tells us something both about Mary's beliefs and the author's beliefs. That is, *know* in 6 implies that the author shares Mary's beliefs about the eating event. Thus, the eating event is represented as a child of both the AUTH node and MARY node; see Figure 4.

4   Annotation

4.1   Annotation procedure

The modal dependency structure annotation proceeds in three passes. Disagreements were resolved between each pass. In the first pass, the events that will be annotated for modality are identified. This is done based largely on TimeML's (Pustejovsky et al., 2005) event identification;

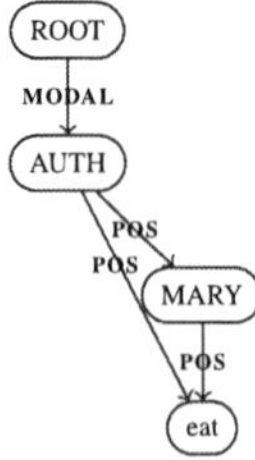

Figure 4: Multiple parents: *Mary knows the cat ate breakfast.*

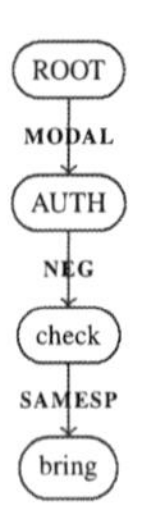

Figure 5: Same space: *Mary didn't check the weather or bring a map.*

events are identified based on semantic criteria and not morphosyntactic structure or part of speech.

The next pass involves setting up the modal 'superstructure'. This is akin to the identification of time expressions in Zhang and Xue (2018b); it builds the top of the graph, which applies to an entire document. At the top of each graph is a ROOT node. For modality, there is also always an AUTHOR conceiver node. Underneath the AUTHOR conceiver node are nodes for all of the other conceivers in the text. As mentioned in 3, the edges between conceiver nodes are distinguished by the epistemic strength relations.

The third pass involves the modal annotation. For each event identified in the first pass, annotators select a parent node (either another event or a conceiver) and the appropriate strength relation between the parent and child nodes.

In addition to the strength relations in Table 1, we introduced a Same Space (SAMESP) relation between nodes. The SAMESP annotation indicates that two events hold in the same mental space, i.e. they have the same strength relation from the same conceiver node. For example, in *Mary didn't check the weather or bring a map*, both *check* and *bring* have a NEG relation to the AUTHOR node. This would be annotated with a NEG relation between *check* and MARY and a SAMESP relation between *bring* and *check*; see Figure 5.

4.2   Current Implementation

The modal dependency structure annotation has been tested on six documents, containing 108 sentences with 377 identified events. These documents have been annotated by two expert annotators. Please refer to the supplementary material for annotated sections from these documents, including their representation as a dependency graph. In addition to the manually-created dependency graphs, the supplementary material also contains graphs generated automatically with the Abstract

Pass	Measure	News	Narr.	Forum	Total
Event ID	Precision	0.95	0.95	0.98	0.94
	Recall	0.92	0.92	0.87	0.93
	F-score	0.94	0.93	0.92	0.93
Con-ceiver	Precision	0.9	0.86	1	0.91
	Recall	0.82	0.75	0.64	0.77
	F-score	0.86	0.80	0.78	0.83
Event space	Precision	0.93	0.84	0.78	0.88
	Recall	0.93	0.83	0.78	0.88
	F-score	0.93	0.83	0.78	0.88

Table 3: IAA for modal annotations

Meaning Representation Reader (Pan et al., 2015).

The inter-annotator agreement scores for each of the three annotation passes are shown in Table 3. These agreement scores reflect only true disagreements between annotators; they disregard cases in which annotators used a different annotation to represent the same modal analysis.[4]

The annotated documents represent three different genres: news stories, narratives, and discussion forums. The first row shows precision, recall, and F-score for the first pass, event identification, in all three genres, following Zhang and Xue (2018a). The middle row shows the same measures for the second pass, the identification of the conceiver nodes in the superstructure; the bottom row shows these measures for the third pass, the mental space annotation of each event - 228 in the news genre, 85 in the narrative genre, and 64 in discussion forum texts.

Zhang and Xue (2018b) report the following F-scores (for news and narrative respectively): .94, .93 for event recognition, .97, 1 for timex recognition, and .79, .72 for event relations.

Our event identification F-scores are identical to Zhang and Xue (2018b) in the news and narrative genres. Their timex recognition corresponds to our modal superstructure (essentially conceiver recognition). Our superstructure F-scores are noticeably lower than their timex recognition F-scores. We believe this is because of the relative difficulty of identifying when an entity's mental content is modeled vs. when a linguistic expression refers to a locatable point in time. See 4.3 for a more detailed discussion.

Importantly, our event annotation F-scores are largely consistent with, if not slightly higher than

Zhang and Xue (2018b) report for their event relation scores. This suggests that annotators are able to consistently assess the epistemic strength relations and relevant conceivers in a text and uniformly model them in a dependency structure.

4.3 Modal error analysis

This section will discuss and exemplify the types of disagreements that arose between annotators for the second and third passes.

Error type	Percentage of total
Lexical item	53%
Childless conceiver	29%
Different parent	12%
Co-referential nodes	6%

Table 4: Conceiver errors

Table 4 shows the types of errors that arose in the second pass. The most common disagreement between annotators was whether a particular lexical item required the introduction of a conceiver node in the superstructure. That is, annotators disagreed about whether a particular lexical item represented the author's modeling of another entity's mental content, as in 7.

(7) *Christie is being set up on this one and* THE LEGISLATOR *called his bluff.*

The issue here is whether the idiom *call...bluff* invokes the mental content of its subject, here *the legislator*. That is, is the author simply reporting an event, or is the author ascribing mental content (e.g., the knowledge that Christie is bluffing) to *the legislator*? Like many of the disagreements based on which lexical items invoke conceivers, this seems like a case of genuine ambiguity.

The second most common type of superstructure error was whether childless conceivers were represented in the modal superstructure. Annotators differed on whether they added nodes to the superstructure for conceivers whose nodes would not have any events as children; this is shown in 8.

(8) PEOPLE *seeking bargains* lined up at a state-run food store in La Paz on Thursday...

Here, it is clear that *seek* requires modeling the mental content of another entity, *people*. However, there would be no event represented as a child of the PEOPLE conceiver node, since the object of *seek* is not an event. For subsequent annotation,

---

[4]The SAMESP label led to cases where the annotators had the same strength relation underneath the same conceiver (i.e., the same modal analysis), but one annotator notated it with SAMESP. These types of notational errors made up 34% of total errors. Therefore, we have removed the SAMESP label from the modal annotation scheme.

we have decided that conceivers should be represented in the modal superstructure, even if they won't have any events as children; this should alleviate these types of disagreements.

The different parent disagreements refer to cases where annotators identified the same entities as conceivers, but differed on whether they were children of the AUTHOR or another conceiver in the text. Finally, there was disagreement between annotators based on whether entities mentioned in the text were co-referential or not. That is, annotators agreed about when conceiver nodes were necessary, but disagreed about whether two conceiver instances referred to the same entity.

For the third pass, the modal annotation of events, Table 5 shows the types of disagreements between annotators.

Error Type	Percentage of total
Lexical item	34%
Space scope	23%
Conceiver scope	16%
Space type	14%
Miscellaneous	9%
Annotator error	4%

Table 5: Event annotation errors

The most common disagreements concern the strength of particular lexical items, as in 9.

(9) *Lerias **called for** more rescuers* TO COME *to the site...*

The issue here is the strength that *call for* implies for *to come*; annotators disagreed on whether *to come* has PRT strength or NEUT strength. The frequency of this type of disagreement can probably be diminished by training annotators with more specific guidelines for each strength relation; however, some of these types of disagreements will likely be inevitable.

Space scope disagreements refer to cases where annotators disagreed about whether a particular event belongs in the same mental space as the preceding event in the text. This is shown in 10.

(10) *In the book it said: "Boa constrictors swallow their prey whole, without chewing it. After that they are not able* TO MOVE *..."*

Both annotators agreed that *swallow* and *chewing* belong in a "usually", i.e. PRT strength, generic space. Annotators also agreed that *not able* indicated NEG strength of the *to move* event. The

disagreement is whether the PRT strength generic scopes over the *to move* event. That is, is *to move* the (direct) child of BOOK or the child of an event in the PRT generic space? Some cases like these may be resolved by more detailed guidelines on determining the scope of spaces over events.

Similarly, the scope of conceivers over events was a source of disagreement. This generally occurred with indirect speech predicates, as in 11.

(11) *Lerias called for more rescuers to come to the site to help look for bodies as heavy earth moving equipment could not* WORK *in the mud...*

Here, annotators disagreed on whether LERIAS or AUTHOR was the source for the *work* event. These errors appear to represent textual ambiguity.

Space type errors refer to cases where annotators disagreed on whether an event was in an episodic, generic, or future-oriented space. Although the modal annotation scheme does not directly distinguish these different space types, annotators' interpretation was evident in the strength relation chosen, as in example 12.

(12) *Military helicopters were able* TO REACH *the area despite heavy clouds...*

Annotators disagreed about whether this sentence represents a NEUT strength "possibility" generic, based on the use of *able*, or whether *to reach* represents full POS strength because the past tense implies that the event did occur.

5 Conclusion

A modal annotation scheme structured as a dependency graph, like the temporal annotation scheme of Zhang and Xue (2018b), captures the complexity of modal relations (mental space structure) in sentences and documents with a relatively simple annotation: each event has a single annotation of the event's modal relation to another event or a conceiver, not unlike the single annotation of an event's temporal relation to another event or a time expression. The pilot annotation indicates that this annotation scheme is relatively easy to implement, at least as much as the annotation of temporal dependency structure.

Acknowledgments

This research was supported in part by grant 1764091 by the National Science Foundation to the last author.

References

Kathryn Baker, Michael Bloodgood, Bonnie J. Dorr, Nathaniel W. Filardo, Lori Levin, and Christine Piatko. 2010. A modality lexicon and its use in automatic tagging. In *Proceedings of the Seventh conference on International Language Resources and Evaluation (LREC '10)*, pages 1402–1407, Valette, Malta. European Language Resources Association (ELRA).

Kasper Boye. 2012. *Epistemic meaning: A crosslinguistic and functional-cognitive study*, volume 43 of *Empirical Approaches to Language Typology*. De Gruyter Mouton, Berlin.

Gilles Fauconnier. 1994. *Mental spaces*, 2 edition. Cambridge University Press, Cambridge.

Gilles Fauconnier. 1997. *Mappings in thought and language*. Cambridge University Press, Cambridge.

Charles F. Fillmore. 1990. Epistemic stance and grammatical form in English conditional sentences. In *Papers from the 26th Regional Meeting of the Chicago Linguistic Society*, pages 137–62, Chicago. Chicago Linguistic Society.

Jennifer Garland, Stephanie Strassel, Safa Ismael, Zhiyi Song, and Haejoong Lee. 2012. Linguistic resources for genre-independent language technologies: user-generated content in bolt. In *Workshop Programme*, page 34.

Julia Lavid, Marta Carretero, and Juan Rafael Zamorano-Mansilla. 2016. Contrastive annotation of epistemicity in the multinot project: preliminary steps. In *Proceedings of the ISA-12, Twelfth Joint ACL-ISO Workshop on Interoperable Semantic Annotation, held in conjunction with Language Resources and Evaluation Conference*, pages 81–88.

Marie-Catherine de Marneffe, Christopher D. Manning, and Christopher Potts. 2012. Did it happen? the pragmatic complexity of veridicality assessment. *Computational Linguistics*, 38:301–333.

Suguru Matsuyoshi, Megumi Eguchi, Chitose Sao, Koji Murakami, Kentaro Inui, and Yuji Matsumoto. 2010. Annotating event mentions in text with modality, focus, and source information. In *Proceedings of the Seventh conference on International Language Resources and Evaluation (LREC '10)*, pages 1456–1463, Valette, Malta. European Language Resources Association (ELRA).

James D. McCawley. 1993. *Everything that Linguists have Always Wanted to Know about Logic* (*but were too afraid to ask)*. University of Chicago Press, Chicago.

Roser Morante and Caroline Sporleder. 2012. Modality and negation: An introduction to the special issue. *Computational Linguistics*, 38:223–260.

Malvina Nissim, Paola Pietrandrea, Andrea Sanso, and Caterina Mauri. 2013. Cross-linguistic annotation of modality: a data-driven hierarchical model. In *Proceedings of the 9th Joint ISO - ACL SIGSEM Workshop on Interoperable Semantic Annotation*, pages 7–14, Potsdam, Germany. Association for Computational Linguistics.

F. R. Palmer. 2001. *Mood and Modality*. Cambridge University Press, Cambridge.

Xiaoman Pan, Taylor Cassidy, Ulf Hermjakob, Heng Ji, and Kevin Knight. 2015. Unsupervised entity linking with abstract meaning representation. In *Proceedings of the 2015 Conference of the North American Chapter of the Association for Computational Linguistics: Human Language Technologies*, pages 1130–1139, Denver, Colorado. Association for Computational Linguistics.

Rashmi Prasad, Nikhil Dinesh, Alan Lee, Eleni Miltsakaki, Livio Robaldo, Aravind Joshi, and Bonnie Webber. 2008. The penn discourse treebank 2.0. In *Proceedings of the Sixth International Conference on Language Resources and Evaluation (LREC'08)*, Marrakech, Morocco. European Language Resources Association (ELRA).

James Pustejovsky, Robert Knippen, Jessica Littman, and Roser Saurí. 2005. Temporal and event information in natural language text. *Language Resources and Evaluation*, 39:123–164.

Victoria L. Rubin. 2007. Stating with certainty or stating with doubt: Intercoder reliability results for manual annotation of epistemically modalized statements. In *NAACL 07: Human Language Technologies 2007: The Conference of the North American Chapter of the Association for Computational Linguistics; Companion Volume, Short Papers*, pages 141–144, Morristown, NJ, USA. Association for Computational Linguistics.

Victoria L. Rubin, Elizabeth D. Liddy, and Noriko Kando. 2005. Certainty identification in texts: Categorization model and manual tagging results. In *Computing Attitude and Affect in Text: Theory and Applications*, volume 20 of *Information Retrieval Series*, pages 61–76. Springer-Verlag, New York.

Aynat Rubinstein, Hillary Harner, Elizabeth Krawczyk, Daniel Simonson, Graham Katz, and Paul Portner. 2013. Toward fine-grained annotation of modality in text. In *Proceedings of the IWCS 2013 Workshop on Annotation of Modal Meanings in Natural Language (WAMM)*, pages 38–46, Potsdam, Germany. Association for Computational Linguistics.

Josef Ruppenhofer and Ines Rehbein. 2012. Yes we can!? annotating the senses of English modal verbs. In *Proceedings of the Eighth International Conference on Language Resources and Evaluation (LREC-2012)*.

Antoine de Saint-Exupéry and Katherine Woods. 1943. *The Little Prince*. Harcourt, Brace & World, New York.

Roser Saurí and James Pustejovsky. 2009. Factbank: a corpus annotated with event factuality. *Language Resources and Evaluation*, 43:227–268.

Roser Saurí and James Pustejovsky. 2012. Are you sure that this happened? assessing the factuality degree of events in text. *Computational Linguistics*, 38:261–299.

Stephanie Strassel and Jennifer Tracey. 2016. Lorelei language packs: Data, tools, and resources for technology development in low resource languages. In *Proceedings of the Tenth International Conference on Language Resources and Evaluation (LREC 2016)*, Paris, France. European Language Resources Association (ELRA).

Jens E. L. Van Gysel, Meagan Vigus, Pavlina Kalm, Sook–kyung Lee, Michael Regan, and William Croft. 2019. Cross-lingual semantic annotation: Reconciling the language-specific and the universal. In *First Workshop on Designing Meaning Representations, Association for Computational Linguistics*. Association for Computational Linguistics.

Janyce Wiebe, Theresa Wilson, and Claire Cardie. 2005. Annotating expressions of opinions and emotions in language. *Language Resources and Evaluation*, 39:165–210.

Yuchen Zhang and Nianwen Xue. 2018a. Neural ranking models for temporal dependency structure parsing. In *Proceedings of the 2018 Conference on Empirical Methods in Natural Language Processing*, pages 3339–3349.

Yuchen Zhang and Nianwen Xue. 2018b. Structured interpretation of temporal relations. In *Proceedings of the 11th Language Resources and Evaluation Conference (LREC-2018)*, Miyazaki, Japan.

Supplementary Material

Genre: Discussion Forum

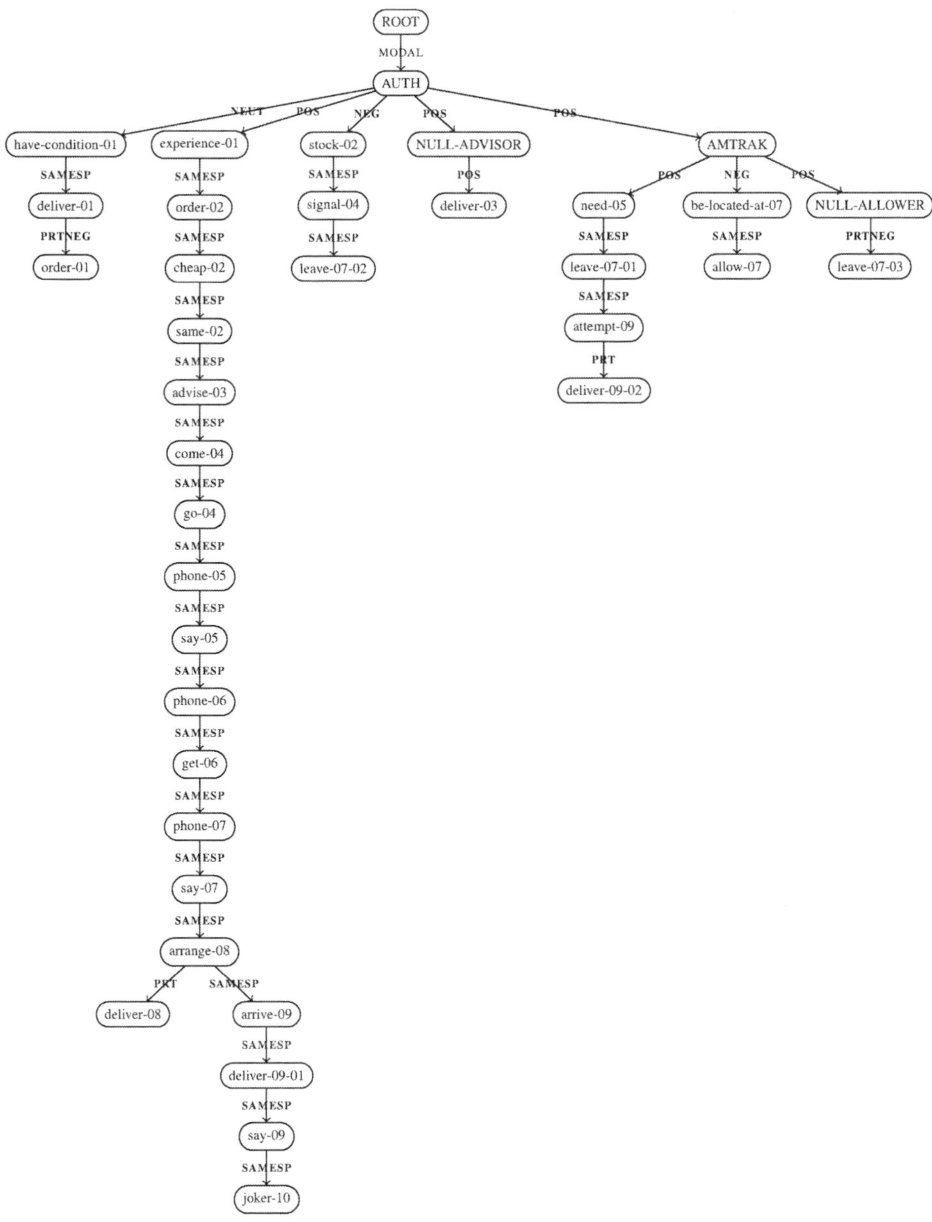

1 Don't **order** anything online if Amtrak **are delivering** it - here's my **experience**.
2 **Ordered** a 32" TV online, **cheaper** than Argos-who didn't **have** it **in stock**-but with the delivery charge the cost **was the same**.
3 **Advised** that it **would be delivered** by Amtrak on Tuesday.
4 Tuesday **came** and **went**, no **sign**.
5 **Phoned** Amtrak on Wednesday, "we **need** a consignment number".
6 **Phoned** online company and **got** it.
7 **Phoned** Amtrak "a card **was left** on Tuesday as you **weren't there**" (no it **wasn't** of course), and "we're not **allowed to leave** it with a neighbour".
8 **Arranged** for another **delivery** on Saturday.
9 **Arrived** home yesterday-it **had been delivered** next door yesterday, with a card **saying** this was their first **attempt** at **delivery**...
10 What **a bunch of jokers**.

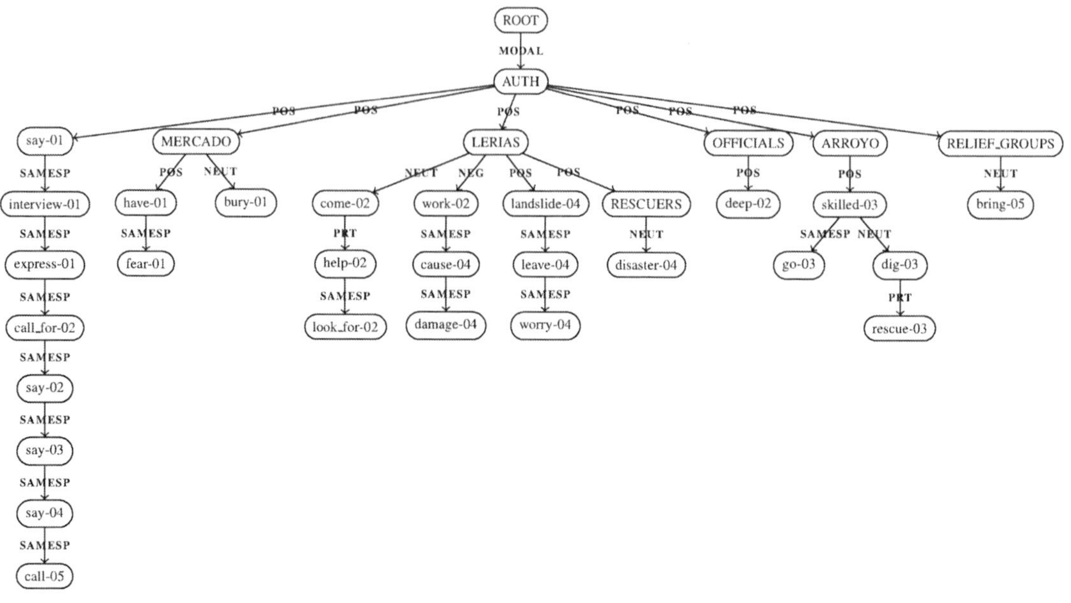

1 Leyte congressman Roger Mercado **said** in a radio **interview** that the village **had** a population of 3,000 to 4,000 and **expressed fears** that as many as 2,000 people **had been buried**.
2 Lerias **called for** more rescuers **to come** to the site **to help look for** bodies as heavy earth moving equipment **could not work** in the mud, which officials **said was** more than six metres (yards) **deep** in many areas.
3 Volunteer rescue teams from the country's mining companies, **skilled** in **digging** through the earth **to rescue** people, **were** also **going** to the area, President Arroyo **said**.
4 Lerias **said** a smaller **landslide** later in the afternoon **caused no damage** but **left** many of the rescuers **worried** about a possible new **disaster**.
5 Relief groups **called for** drinking water, food, blankets and body bags **to be brought** to the scene.

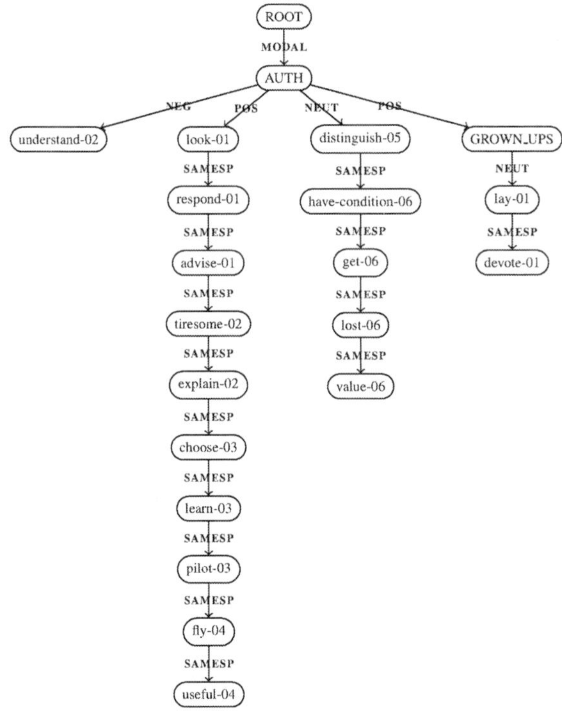

1 My Drawing Number Two **looked** like this: The grown-ups' **response**, this time, was **to advise** me **to lay** aside my drawings of boa constrictors, whether from the inside or the outside, and **devote** myself instead to geography, history, arithmetic and grammar.
2 Grown-ups **never understand** anything by themselves, and it **is tiresome** for children **to be** always and forever **explaining** things to them.
3 So then I **chose** another profession, and **learned to pilot** airplanes.
4 I **have flown** a little over all parts of the world; and it is true that geography **has been** very **useful** to me.
5 At a glance I **can distinguish** China from Arizona.
6 If one **gets lost** in the night, such knowledge **is valuable**.

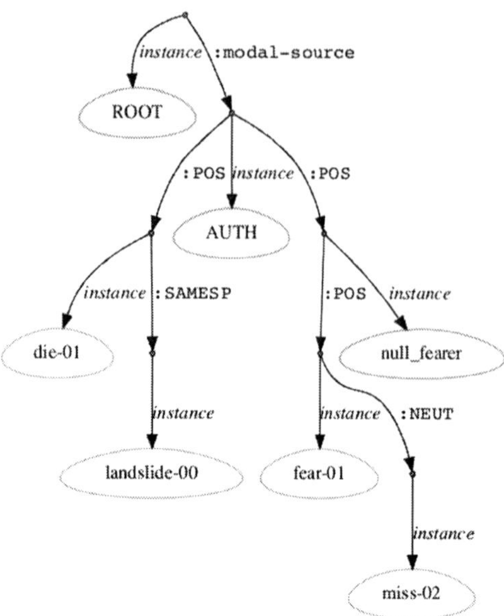

200 dead, 1,500 feared missing in Philippines landslide.

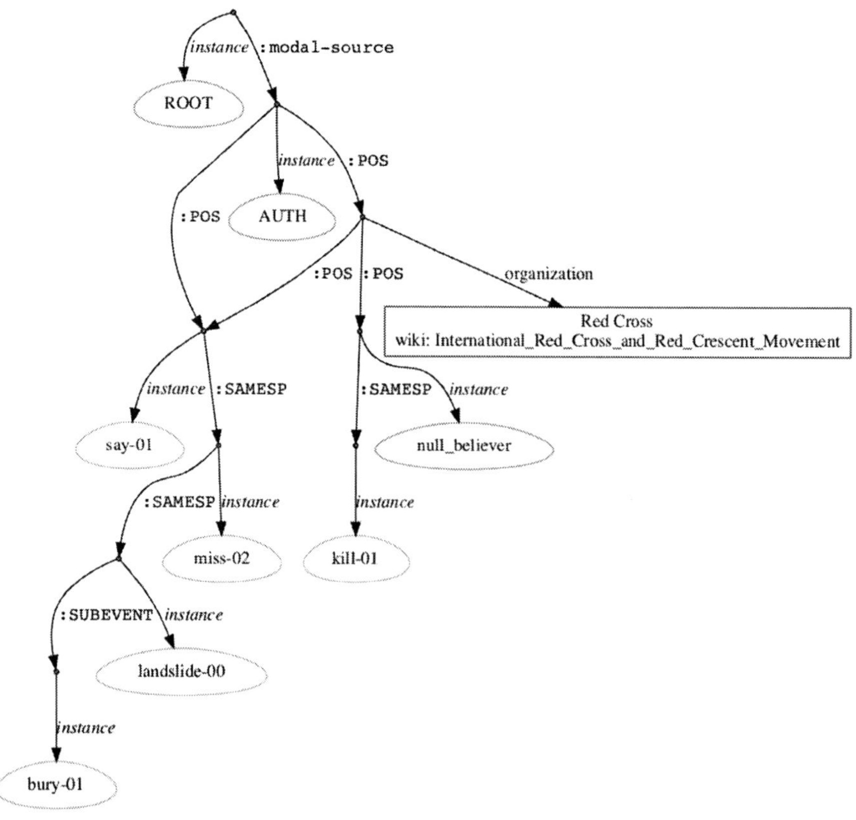

About 200 people were believed killed and 1,500 others were missing in the Central Pilippines on Friday when a landslide buried an entire village, the Red Cross said.

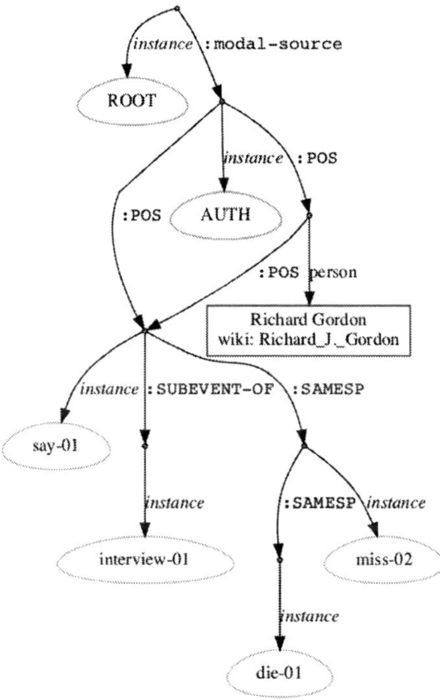

"There are about 1,500 missing, 200 dead," Richard Gordon, the head of the Philippine Red Cross, said in a radio interview.

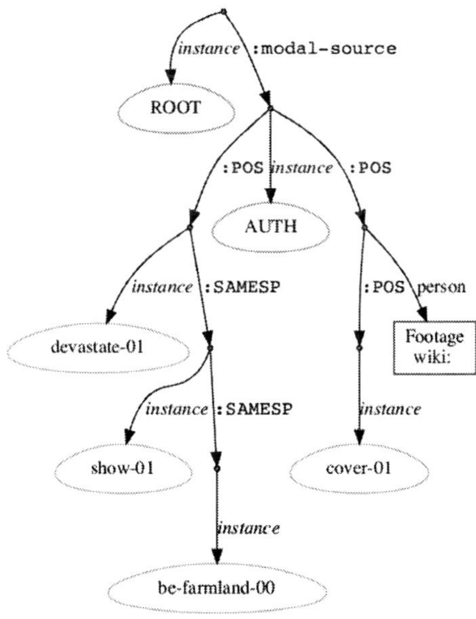

The first footage from the devastated village showed a sea of mud covering what had been lush green valley farmland.

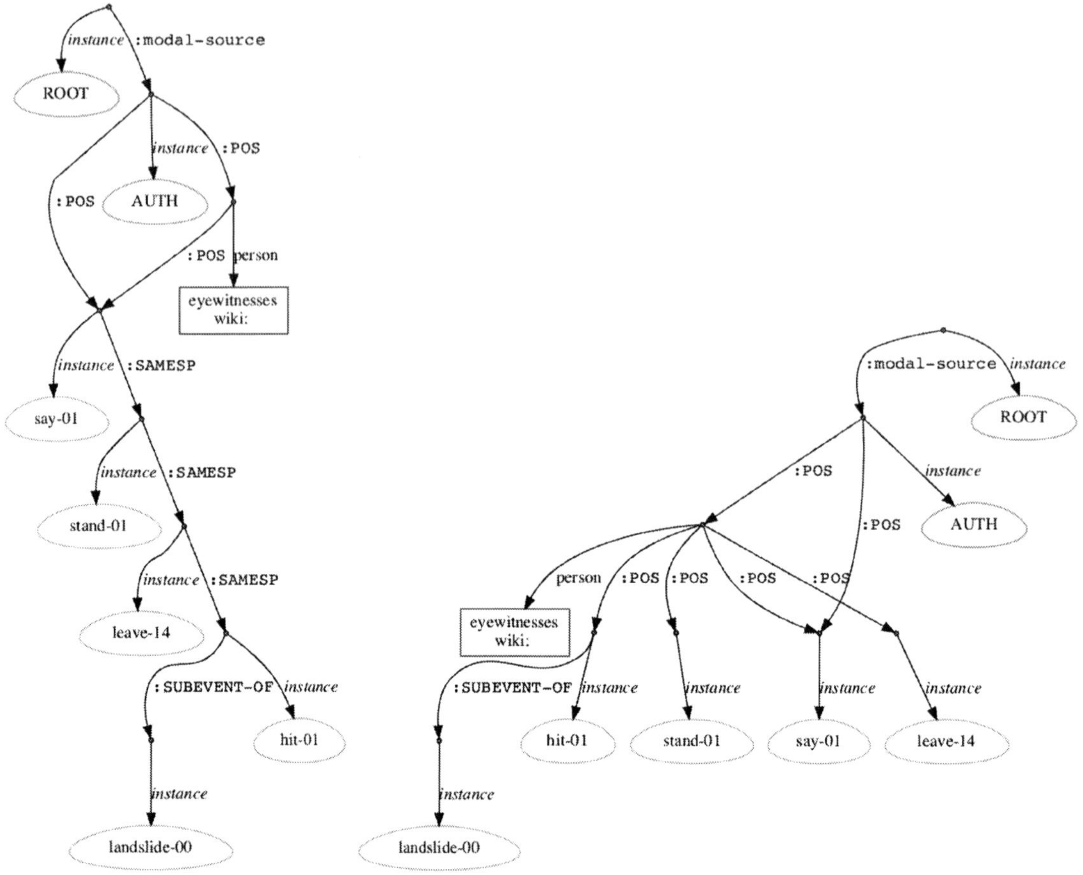

Eyewitnesses said only a few houses were left standing after the landslide hit the village of Guinsaugon in the south of the Philippine island of Leyte.

The two graphs on this page show the difference between using the SAMESP annotation (on the left) and not using SAMESP (on the right). We believe that, while SAMESP may introduce too many non-substantive errors into the annotation, it is a useful tool for visualization. This is because it visually groups together events with the same modal strength. Although we have removed the SAMESP edge label in later versions of the annotation scheme, SAMESP may be automatically re-introduced into the annotations for the purpose of visualization.

Augmenting Abstract Meaning Representation for Human-Robot Dialogue

Claire Bonial[1], Lucia Donatelli[2], Stephanie M. Lukin[1], Stephen Tratz[1],
Ron Artstein[3], David Traum[3], and Clare R. Voss[1]

[1]U.S. Army Research Laboratory, Adelphi, MD 20783
[2]Georgetown University, Washington DC 20057
[3]USC Institute for Creative Technologies, Playa Vista, CA 90094
`claire.n.bonial.civ@mail.mil`

Abstract

We detail refinements made to Abstract Meaning Representation (AMR) that make the representation more suitable for supporting a situated dialogue system, where a human remotely controls a robot for purposes of search and rescue and reconnaissance. We propose 36 augmented AMRs that capture speech acts, tense and aspect, and spatial information. This linguistic information is vital for representing important distinctions, for example whether the robot has moved, is moving, or will move. We evaluate two existing AMR parsers for their performance on dialogue data. We also outline a model for graph-to-graph conversion, in which output from AMR parsers is converted into our refined AMRs. The design scheme presented here, though task-specific, is extendable for broad coverage of speech acts using AMR in future task-independent work.

1 Introduction

We describe an augmented version of Abstract Meaning Representation (AMR) for use as a conduit for natural language understanding (NLU) in a robot dialogue system. We find that while AMR is promising for NLU, refinements are needed in order to capture information critical for live, situated communication. Specifically, we propose the addition of a set of speech acts, tense and aspect information, and parameters that help specify spatial location.

After providing background on our broader research goals and the AMR project, we motivate our choice to explore the use of AMR for NLU (sections 2, 3). We then detail our findings on gaps in the representational coverage of existing AMR for human-robot dialogue (4), and we describe our refinements (5). We next describe ongoing and future work to implement an augmented AMR-based NLU that uses existing parsers and graph-to-graph AMR conversion to replace a more

limited statistical classifier (6). We then compare to related work (7) and conclude.

2 Background: Human-Robot Dialogue

The broad goal of this research is to develop a system for conducting dialogue between a person and a remotely located robot in collaborative navigation tasks common to disaster relief and search-and-rescue scenarios. Efficient communication is essential: the robot must be able to interpret both the language used by the human and the intention behind it, as well as to carry out the instructions in these dynamic environments and coordinate with the human by providing appropriate feedback of the status of instructions at different times.

In the language of this domain, we find that people communicating with robots often employ multiple ways of saying the same thing: *Turn/rotate left, Drive/move/go forward*. However, they also employ very similar syntactic structures to say different things: *Can you take a picture?*, intended as a polite request for a picture, and *Can you speak Arabic?*, intended as a question of the robot's abilities. To get at the underlying meaning of these utterances despite surface variations and similarities, our goal is to develop semantic representations for this project. We plan to use these representations in an implemented, live system to facilitate both NLU of the robot-directed instructions as well as Natural Language Generation (NLG) of robot responses and feedback.

2.1 Human-Robot Dialogue Corpus

We collected a corpus of observed data from the target domain collected via a phased Wizard-of-Oz approach (Marge et al., 2016, 2017), in which a participant directed what they believed to be an autonomous robot to complete search and navigation tasks. In reality, the participant was speaking with two "wizard" experimenters responsible for the robot's dialogue and navigation capabili-

Proceedings of the First International Workshop on Designing Meaning Representations, pages 199–210
Florence, Italy, August 1st, 2019 ©2019 Association for Computational Linguistics

#	Left floor		Right Floor		Annotations		
	Participant	**DM → Participant**	**DM → RN**	**RN**	**TU**	**Ant**	**Rel**
1	move forward 3 feet				1		
2		ok			1	1	ack-wilco
3			move forward 3 feet		1	1	trans-r
4				done	1	3	ack-done
5		I moved forward 3 feet			1	4	trans-l

Table 1: Example of a Transaction Unit (TU) which contains an instruction initiated by the participant, its translation to a simplified form (DM to RN), and the execution of the instruction and acknowledgement of such by the RN. TU, Ant(ecedent), and Rel(ation type) are indicated in the right columns.

ties. This setup allowed for the creation of a corpus of human-robot interactions that shows how people communicate with a robot in collaborative tasks when they are unconstrained in their communication.

Dialogues in the corpus follow a set procedure: a dialogue manager wizard (DM) listens to the participant's spoken instructions and replies to the participant with feedback and clarification requests via text messages. Executable instructions are passed along by the DM to a robot navigator wizard (RN) via text messages in a separate chat stream unseen by the participant. The RN then tele-operates the robot to complete the participant's instructions. Finally, the RN provides spoken feedback to the DM of completed actions or problems that arose, which are relayed by the DM to the participant. A sample interaction can be seen in Table 1.

The corpus contains dialogues from a total of 82 participants across three separate phased data collections. The participants' speech and the RN's speech are transcribed and time-aligned with text messages generated by the DM and sent either to the participant or the RN.

2.2 Dialogue Structure Annotations

The corpus also includes annotations of several aspects of dialogue structure (Traum et al., 2018) that allow for the characterization of distinct information states (Traum and Larsson, 2003). The portion of the data that we used, constituting about 20 hours of interaction, has been annotated with this scheme, specific to multi-floor dialogue that identifies high-level aspects of initiator intent and signals relations between individual utterances pertaining to that intent.

An example annotation can be seen in Table 1. The scheme consists first of *transaction units (TU)*, which cluster utterances from multiple participants and floors into units according to the joint realization of an initiator's intent. *Relations* indicate the graph structure of utterances within the same TU, and are indicated with a *Relation type (Rel)* (e.g., "ack-done" in row 4 of Table 1, signals that an utterance acknowledges completion of a previous utterance) and an *Antecedent (Ant)* for the relation. The existing annotation scheme highlights *dialogue structure*, but does not provide a markup of the semantic content of participant instructions, which is the goal of our work.

3 Background: AMR

The AMR project (Banarescu et al., 2013) has created a manually annotated semantics bank of text drawn from a variety of genres. Each sentence is represented by a rooted directed acyclic graph in which variables (or graph nodes) are introduced for entities, events, properties, and states; leaves are labeled with concepts (e.g., (d / dog)). For ease of creation and manipulation, annotators work with the PENMAN representation of the same information (Penman Natural Language Group, 1989), as in Figure 1.

```
(w / want-01
    :ARG0 (d / dog)
    :ARG1 (p / pet-01
            :ARG0 (g / girl)
            :ARG1 d))
```

Figure 1: AMR of *The dog wants the girl to pet him.*

A goal of AMR research is to capture core facets of meaning while abstracting away from idiosyncratic syntactic structures; thus, the same underlying concept realized alternatively as a noun (*a left turn*), verb (*turn to the left*) or light verb construction (*make/do a left turn*) will all be represented by identical AMRs.

3.1 Motivation for AMR in Human-Robot Dialogue

A primary motivation for using AMR is that there are a variety of fairly robust AMR parsers we can employ for this work, enabling us to forego manual annotation of data and facilitating efficient automatic parsing in a future end-to-end system.

The structured graph representations of AMRs additionally facilitate the interpretation of novel instructions and grounding instructions with respect to the robot's current physical surroundings. This structure allows us to pinpoint those actions that are executable for the robot. This latter motivation is especially important given that the target human-robot dialogue is physically situated and therefore distinct from other dialogue systems, such as chat bots, which do not require establishing and acting upon a shared understanding of the physical environment and often do not require any intermediate semantic representation (see Section 7 for related work). AMR thus offers both efficient and accurate parsing of natural language to a structured representation, as well as ease of conversion of this broad coverage representation to the domain-specific representation discussed in this paper (see 6.2 for more on graph conversion).

The fact that AMRs abstract away from surface variation is a complementary motivation for exploring their use within an NLU component. The AMRs "tame" some of the variation of natural language, representing core concepts in the human's commands, which must ultimately be mapped into the robot's low-level mechanical operations. Therefore, the robot will only be trained to process and execute the actions corresponding to semantic elements of the representation (see Section 6).

This processing and execution can be seen with a concrete example. Throughout the corpus data, participants use the commands *Take a picture* and *Send image* (as well as other variants) with the same intention that the robot take a picture of what is in front of it and send that image to the participant's screen. While *take* is a light verb in this usage (and therefore dropped from the representation according to existing AMR guidelines), *send* maintains its semantic weight and argument structure. For the purposes of our task, we can abstract away from this variation and convert both types of utterances into `send-image` commands (see 5.2). Though future work may deem these distinctions of lexical choice and syntax meaningful, the current task generalizes them for ease of task completion.

4 Evaluating Suitability of AMR

We began our assessment of AMR for human-robot dialogue by producing a small, randomly selected sample (137 sentences) of gold standard, manual annotations (provided by one senior and two recently trained AMR annotators), based on existing guidelines.[1] We then examined how effectively these gold, guideline-based AMRs can capture the distinctions of interest for human-robot dialogue and how accurately two available AMR parsers generate those gold annotations.

Common instructions in the corpus include *Move forward 10 feet*, *Take a picture*, and *Turn right 45 degrees*. People also used landmark-based instructions such as *Move to face the yellow cone*, and *Go to the doorway to your right*, although these were less common than the metric-based instructions (Marge et al., 2017). In response to these instructions from the DM to the participant, common feedback would be indications that an instruction will be carried out (*I will move forward 10 feet*), is in progress (*Moving...*), or completed (*I moved forward 10 feet*). Given that current AMR guidelines do not make tense/aspect distinctions, these three types of feedback from the robot are represented identically under the current guidelines (see Figure 2). The distinctions between a promise to carry out an instruction in the future, a declarative statement that the instruction is being carried out, and an acknowledgment that it has been carried out are critical for conveying the robot's current status in a live system.

```
(m / move-01
    :ARG0 (i / i)
    :direction (f / forward)
    :extent (d / distance-quantity
        :quant 10
        :unit (f2 / foot)))
```

Figure 2: Identical AMR for *I will move / I am moving / I moved forward...10 feet*.

Although the imperative *Move forward 10 feet* should receive an AMR marker `:mode imperative`, our evaluation of the existing

---

[1] https://github.com/amrisi/amr-guidelines/blob/master/amr.md

parsers JAMR (Flanigan et al., 2014) and CAMR (Wang et al., 2015) showed that parser output does not include this marker as it is rare if not entirely missing from the AMR 1.0 or 2.0 training corpora (Section 6).[2] As a result, the command to move forward also received the identical above AMR (Figure 2) in parser output. While this suggests that additional training data is needed that includes imperatives, this speaks to a larger issue of AMR: the existing representation is very limited with respect to speech act information. Current AMR includes `:mode imperative` and represents questions through the presence of `amr-unknown` standing in for the concept or polarity being questioned. All unmarked cases are assumed to be assertions. We found that more fine-grained speech act information is needed for human-robot dialogue.

5 Refinements to AMR

To design a representative set of augmented AMRs that capture the breadth of information necessary for collaborative dialogue in our domain, we started by creating a histogram of existing dialogue annotation categories for the 20 hours of experimental data available (described in Section 2.2). This allowed us to see which types of dialogue utterances are most prevalent in the corpus, as well as to view the range of utterances that comprise each category. Based on this data, we designed a set of AMR "templates"—skeletal AMRs in which the top, anchor node is a fixed relation corresponding to a speech act type (e.g., `assert-02`), one of its arguments is a fixed relation corresponding to an action (e.g., `turn-01`), and arguments of these relations are filled out given the specifics of a particular utterance. These skeletal AMRs can be modified and leveraged for NLU and generation in future human-robot collaboration tasks. We note that our objective is to produce a set of refined AMRs that provide coverage for human-robot dialogue, rather than an attempt to change AMR on a general scale.

We augmented AMR with the following information: i) coarse-grained information related to the *when* (tense) and *how* (aspect) of events (5.1); ii) speech acts (5.2); and iii) basic spatial information pertinent to robot functioning (5.3).

[2] https://catalog.ldc.upenn.edu/LDC2014T12, https://catalog.ldc.upenn.edu/LDC2017T10

5.1 Tense & Aspect

AMR currently lacks information that specifies *when* an action occurs relative to speech time and whether or not this action is completed (if a past event) or able to be completed (if a future event). This information is essential for situated human-robot dialogue, where successful collaboration depends on bridging the gap between differing perceptions of the shared environment and creating common ground (Chai et al., 2014).

Our tense and aspect annotation scheme is based on Donatelli et al. (2018), who propose a four-way division of temporal annotation and three multi-valued categories for aspectual annotation that fits seamlessly into existing AMR annotation practice. We reduced the authors' proposed temporal categories to three, to capture temporal relations before, during, and after the speech time. In addition to the aspectual categories proposed by Donatelli et al. (2018), we added the category `:completable +/-` to signal whether or not a hypothetical event has an end-goal that is executable for the robot (described further in Section 5.3). Our annotation categories for tense and aspect can be seen in Table 2.

TEMPORAL ANNOTATION	ASPECTUAL ANNOTATION
`:time`	
1. `(b / before`	`:stable +/-`
`:op1 (n / now))`	`:ongoing +/-`
2. `(n / now)`	`:complete +/-`
3. `(a / after`	`:habitual +/-`
`:op1 (n / now))`	`:completable +/-`

Table 2: Three categories for temporal annotation and five categories for aspectual annotation are used to augment existing AMR for collaborative dialogue.

Notably, this annotation scheme is able to capture the distinctions missing in Figure 2. Updated AMRs for utterances that communicate information about a "move" event relative to the future, present, and past are now re-annotated as in Figure 3. Using the scheme in Table 2, our augmented AMRs allow for locating an event in time and expressing information related to the boundedness of the event, i.e. whether or not the event is a future event with a clear beginning and endpoint, a present event in progress towards an end goal, or a past event that has been completed from start to finish.

```
1. (m / move-01 :completable +
       :ARG0 (i / i)
       :direction (f / forward)
       :extent (d / distance-quantity
               :quant 10
               :unit (f2 / foot))
       :time (a / after
               :op1 (n / now)))

2. (m / move-01 :ongoing + :complete -
       :ARG0 (i / i)
       :direction (f / forward)
       :extent (d / distance-quantity
               :quant 10
               :unit (f2 / foot))
       :time (n / now))

3. (m / move-01 :ongoing - :complete +
       :ARG0 (i / i)
       :direction (f / forward)
       :extent (d / distance-quantity
               :quant 10
               :unit (f2 / foot))
       :time (b / before
               :op1 (n / now)))
```

Figure 3: Updated AMRs for (1) *I will move...*, (2) *I am moving...*, and (3) *I moved....* New temporal information is in blue; new aspectual information is purple.

5.2 Speech Acts

Annotation of speech acts allows us to capture how dialogue participants use language (its pragmatic effect) in addition to what the language means (its semantic content). The existing annotation on the corpus involves only dialogue structure (section 2.2). Our longer-term goal is to create a set of speech acts that i) cover the range of in-domain language use found in the corpus and ii) are generalizable to speech acts in other dialogue and conversational settings. To inform this work, we drew upon classical speech acts work such as Austin (1975) and Searle (1969).

To capture the range of speech acts present in the corpus, we arrived at an inventory of 36 unique speech acts specific to human-robot dialogue, inspired loosely by the dialogue move annotation of Marge et al. (2017). These 36 speech acts are classified into 5 types. In Figure 4, these are listed with the number of their subtypes in parentheses, along with a list of example subtypes for the type `command`. A full listing of subtypes and can be found in the Appendix.

To integrate speech acts into AMR design, we selected existing AMR/PropBank (Palmer et al., 2005) rolesets corresponding to each speech act (e.g., command-02, assert-02, request-01, etc.)

```
SPEECH ACT TYPES
c / command (6)  →    command:move
a / assert (9)        command:turn
r / request (4)       command:send-image
q / question (3)      command:repeat
e / express (5)       command:cancel
                      command:stop
```

Figure 4: Five proposed speech act types for human-robot dialogue are listed on the left with number of subtypes in parentheses. Examples of the range of subtypes for `:command` are given to the right.

that serve as the anchor node in our augmented AMR. One argument of each of these top-level speech act relations corresponds to the action being commanded or asserted, or in general the content of a question, command, or assertion (e.g., turn-01, move-01, picture-01, etc.). For each speech act constituting the top relation and each action constituting one argument of the speech act relation—i.e. each speech act subtype in Figure 4—there is a corresponding AMR template. All utterances of a particular speech act and action combination are mapped to one template. For example, see (1) in Figure 6 for a blank `assert:turn` template and (2) and (3) for completed AMRs using that template. Note that semantically similar utterances using different vocabulary choices (e.g., *rotate, spin*), which would have slightly distinct AMRs under existing guidelines, would all map to the same AMR template using turn-01 (see Section 6.2 for plans on how to map parser output to templates).

5.3 Spatial Information

A key component of successful human-robot collaboration is whether or not robot-directed commands are executable. In the dialogues represented in the corpus, for a command to be effectively executable by the robot, it must have a clear beginning and endpoint and comprise a basic action. For example, *Move forward* is not executable, since it lacks a clear endpoint; *Move forward two feet*, which identifies an endpoint, is executable. Additionally, a command such as *Explore this room* is currently too high-level for our robot to execute. For implementation within a robot's system, a semantic representation must include well-defined, low-level actions that can then be combined into more complex actions.

Thus, our set of AMRs make explicit any implicit spatial roles in the PropBank/AMR verb role sets (in this sense, we follow the annotation practices of O'Gorman et al. 2018 for Multi-Sentence AMR). Our AMRs also specify additional spatial parameters necessary for a command to be executable, in the form of new core and non-core roles, when these are not already present in the original relation's set of arguments. If all required roles are present and instantiated by an utterance, then our AMR is marked with `completable` +; if any required roles are missing, the AMR is marked with `completable` -. For example, see Figure 5 for a non-executable command that requires more information to be carried out.

```
(c / command-02
    :ARG0 (c2 / commander)
    :ARG1 (r / robot)
    :ARG2 (m / move-01 :completable -
        :ARG0 r
        :direction (f / forward)
        :extent (a / amr-unknown)
        :time (a2 / after
                :op1 (n / now))))
```

Figure 5: *Move forward* (non-executable) is missing spatial information to complete the action. An existing AMR concept, `a / amr-unknown`, is employed to stand in for the missing parameter.

5.4 Final AMR Templates

Our final set of AMRs needed to provide coverage for the search and navigation domain includes 36 templates (one template corresponding to each speech act and action combination), which capture i) tense and aspect information; ii) speech acts; and iii) spatial parameters required for robot execution. In addition to a command example in Figure 5, we provide an example of a blank `assert:turn` template with filled-in examples of assertions about the future and present moments in Figure 6.

Note that we do not yet know how effective these templates will be in facilitating task-oriented human-robot dialogue. Future evaluation will include examining the coverage of these templates in mapping to a robot-specific action specification as well as generating appropriate responses and feedback. Our plans for implementation for further evaluation are presented in the next section.

6 Implementation

The intent behind our exploration of AMR for human-robot dialogue is to create a representation that is useful for an eventual live implemented sys-

```
1. (a / assert-02
    :ARG0-speaker
    :ARG2-listener
    :ARG1 (t / turn-01
        :ARG1-thing turning
        :direction
        :extent
        :destination))

2. (a2 / assert-02
    :ARG0 (r2 / robot)
    :ARG1 (t / turn-01 :completable +
        :ARG1 r2
        :direction (r / right-04
            :ARG2 r2)
        :extent (a / angle-quantity
            :quant 90
            :unit (d / degree))
        :time (a2 / after
        :op1 (n / now)))
    :ARG2 (c / commander))

3. (a2 / assert-02
    :ARG0 (r2 / robot)
    :ARG1 (t / turn-01 :ongoing +
        :complete -
        :ARG1 r2
        :direction (r / right-04
            :ARG2 r2)
        :extent (a / angle-quantity
            :quant 90
            :unit (d / degree))
        :time (n / now))
    :ARG2 (c / commander))
```

Figure 6: Final AMR template of `assert:turn`. Blank template in (1), followed by a future *I will turn right 90 degrees* and a present, follow-up *turning*.

tem. To accomplish this goal we intend to i) leverage existing parsers to gain automatic AMR parses for the corpus data; ii) use graph-to-graph transformations to move from parser output to one of the 36 augmented in-domain AMRs; and iii) integrate the resulting AMRs with a language understanding component.[3] Our planned pipeline is presented in Figure 7. Ongoing work on each of these components is described in the sections to follow.

6.1 AMR Parsers

We initially developed a triple-annotated and adjudicated gold standard sample of 137 sentences from the given corpus to serve as a test set for evaluating the performance of the existing AMR parsers. Inter-annotator agreement (IAA) among the initial independent annotations obtained ade-

---

[3]Although we do plan to explore the utility of AMR for NLG, we focus first on the NLU direction of communication.

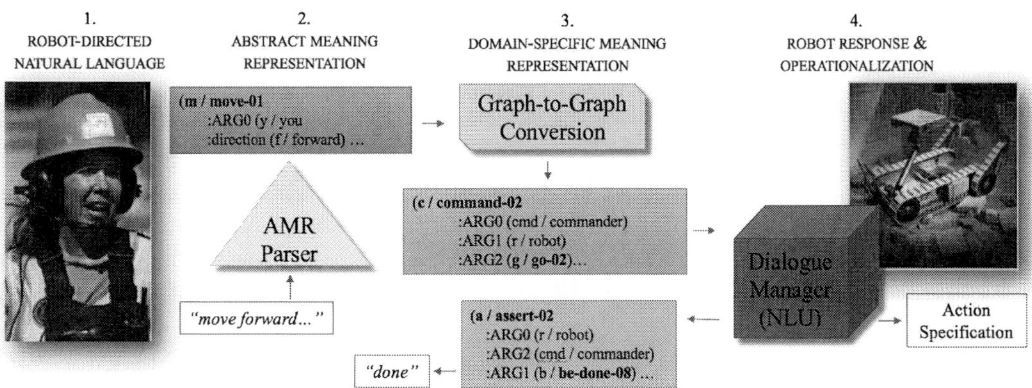

Figure 7: Planned pipeline for implementing AMRs into our human-robot dialogue system: natural language instructions are parsed using AMR parsers into existing AMR, which is then converted via graph-to-graph transformation into one of our augmented AMR templates. If all required parameters in the template are complete and the instruction executable, it will be mapped onto one of the robot's action specifications for execution. Clarifications and feedback from the robot are generated from the AMR templates.

quate scores of .82, .82, and .91 using the Smatch metric (Cai and Knight, 2013). According to AMR development group communication, 2014, IAA Smatch scores on AMRs are generally between .7 and .8, depending on the complexity of the data.

Having created a gold standard sample of our data, we ran both JAMR[4] (Flanigan et al., 2014) and CAMR[5] (Wang et al., 2015) on the same sample and obtained the Smatch scores when compared to the gold standard. We selected these two parsers to explore because JAMR was one of the first AMR parsers and uses a two-part algorithm to first identify concepts and then to build the maximum spanning connected subgraph of those concepts, adding in the relations. CAMR, in contrast, starts by obtaining the dependency tree—in this case, using the Charniak parser[6] and Stanford CoreNLP toolkit (Manning et al., 2014)—and then applies a series of transformations to the dependency tree, ultimately transforming it into an AMR graph. As seen in Table 3, CAMR performs better on both precision and recall when trained on AMR 1.0, thus obtaining the higher F-score. However, compared to their self-reported F-scores (0.58 for JAMR and 0.63 for CAMR) on other corpora, both under-perform on the human-robot dialogue data.

Given the relatively poor performance of both parsers on the human-robot dialogue data and er-

Parser	Data	Precision	Recall	F-score
CAMR	1.0	0.33	**0.51**	**0.40**
JAMR	1.0	0.27	0.44	0.33
JAMR	2.0	0.46	0.28	0.35
JAMR	2.0+D	**0.56**	0.27	0.36

Table 3: Parser performances on human-robot dialogue test set after being trained on AMR 1.0, AMR 2.0 corpus and on AMR 2.0 corpus combined with small in-domain training set of human-robot dialogue data.

ror analysis of the output, we concluded that additional in-domain training data was needed. To this end, we manually selected 504 sentences (distinct from the original 137 test set) made up of short, sequential excerpts of the corpus data representative of the variety of common exchange types that we see. These sentences were independently double-annotated (IAA 87.8%) and adjudicated to create our new small training set. We retrained JAMR in several iterations. First, we retrained JAMR on the larger AMR 2.0 corpus (which includes and expands upon the AMR 1.0 corpus), then we retrained JAMR on the AMR 2.0 corpus and our in-domain data combined. Comparative results are summarized in Table 3. We are currently exploring retraining CAMR and plan to investigate other more recent parsers, such as Lyu & Titov (2018).

Although F-score improvements are modest, they are trending upward, and qualitative analysis of the output of the system making use of in-domain training data shows notable improvements

---

[4]https://github.com/jflanigan/jamr

[5]https://github.com/c-amr/camr

[6]https://github.com/BLLIP/bllip-parser

in some of the common navigation-related language. For example, compare the output of the system trained on AMR 2.0 to the system trained on AMR 2.0 plus in-domain data for a common instruction, shown in Figure 8.

```
1. (m / move-01
      :ARG1 (f / foot
            :quant 15)
      :direction (f2 / forward))

2. (m / move-01
      :direction (f2 / forward)
      :extent (d / distance-quantity
            :quant 15
            :unit (f / foot)))
```

Figure 8: (1) Output from JAMR trained on AMR 2.0 for *move forward 15 feet*. Note that *foot* is incorrectly represented as the `ARG1` of move, or the *thing-moved*. (2) Output from JAMR trained on AMR 2.0 plus in-domain data. Note that *15 feet* is correctly treated as an extent of the movement

Despite improvements, the system trained on the small sample of in-domain data still fails to represent `:mode imperative` and also fails to include implicit subjects. Thus, we conclude that additional data more similar to the corpus is still needed, and we are currently working with other research groups to develop a larger training sample of human-agent dialogue that includes movement direction-giving. However, note that we do not yet know what downstream impact improvements in F-score will have on the final system. Since we do not plan for the robot to act upon parser output AMRs, but rather in-domain AMRs, it may be that the a graph-to-graph transformation algorithm could be robust to some noise in the parser output but still map to the correct in-domain AMR.

6.2 Graph-to-Graph Transformations

We are in the early stages of exploring graph-to-graph transformations that will allow us to move from the parser-output AMRs to our set of in-domain AMRs. Rather than train parsers to parse directly into the augmented AMRs described here, a graph-to-graph transformation allows us to maintain the parser output as a representation of the sentence meanings themselves as input, while the output captures our contextual domain-specific layer and includes speaker intent on top of the sentence meaning. To create training data for graph-to-graph transformation algorithms and to evaluate the coverage and quality of the set of in-domain

AMRs, we have begun this exploration by manually mapping a set of our gold-standard AMRs to the 36 in-domain AMR templates.[7]

Necessary transformations so far include the following: i) changing participant roles, for example *I/you* to *robot/commander*); ii) creating a merge step for all actions of similar type, for example merging movement commands of *move, go, walk, back up* into the `go-02` frame (following our `command:move` template); and iii) expanding AMR frames to include implicit roles. Next steps will include the general tasks of pairing utterances with one of the 36 speech act types, making use of linguistic cues (for example, when an utterance lacks a personal pronoun or named entity like "robot", it is likely a command), and identifying when a command is not executable and further information is necessary.

6.3 Revising, Adapting NLU Component

In previous work using the same human-robot dialogue corpus, Lukin et al. (2018) implemented a preliminary dialogue system which uses a statistical classifier for NLU (NPCEditor, Leuski and Traum, 2011). The classifier relies on language model similarity measures to associate an instruction with either a "translation" to be sent forward to the RN-Wizard or a clarification question to be returned to the participant. The system also exploits the dialogue structure annotations (section 2.2) as features. Error analysis has demonstrated that this preliminary system, by simply learning an association between an input string and a particular set of executed actions, fails to generalize to unseen, novel input instructions (e.g, *Turn left 100 degrees*, as opposed to a more typical number of degrees like 90), and is unable to interpret instructions with respect to the current physical surroundings (e.g., the destination of *Move to the door on the left* needs to be interpreted differently depending where the robot is facing).

Our proposed domain-specific AMRs from section 5 are intended as a replacement for the classifier functionality of the current preliminary dialogue system, allowing a much richer representation of the semantics of actions, including allowing previously unseen values, and compositional construction of referring expressions. A downstream dialogue manager component will be

---

[7]We plan to eventually model our graph-to-graph transformation on work by (Liu et al., 2015) for abstractive summarization with AMR, though in the opposite direction.

able to perform slot-filling dialogue (Xu and Rudnicky, 2000) including clarification of missing or vague descriptions and, if all required parameters are present, will use the domain-specific AMR for robot execution.

7   Related Work

7.1   Semantic Representation

There is a long-standing tradition of research in semantic representation within NLP, AI, as well as theoretical linguistics and philosophy (see Schubert (2015) for an overview). Thus, there are a variety of options that could be used within dialogue systems for NLU. However, for many of these representations, there are no existing automatic parsers, limiting their feasibility for larger-scale implementation. An exception is combinatory categorical grammar (CCG) (Steedman and Baldridge, 2011); CCG parsers have been incorporated in some current dialogue systems (Chai et al., 2014). Although promising, CCG parses closely mirror the input language, so systems making use of CCG parses still face the challenge of a great deal of linguistic variability that can be associated with a single intent. Universal Conceptual Cognitive Annotation (UCCA) (Abend and Rappoport, 2013), which also abstracts away from syntactic idiosyncrasies, and its corresponding parser (Hershcovich et al., 2017) merits future investigation.

7.2   NLU in Dialogue Systems

Broadly, the architecture of task-oriented spoken dialogue systems includes i) automatic speech recognition (ASR) to recognize an utterance, ii) an NLU component to identify the user's intent, and iii) a dialogue manager to interact with the user and achieve the intended task (Bangalore et al., 2006). The meaning representation within such systems has, in the past, been predefined frames for particular subtasks (e.g., flight inquiry), with slots to be filled (e.g., destination city) (Issar and Ward, 1993). In such approaches, the meaning representation was crafted for a specific application, making generalizability to new domains difficult if not impossible. Current approaches still model NLU as a combination of intent and dialogue act classification and slot tagging, but many have begun to incorporate recurrent neural networks (RNNs) and some multi-task learning for both NLU and dialogue state tracking

(Hakkani-Tür et al., 2016; Chen et al., 2016), the latter of which allows the system to take advantage of information from the discourse context to achieve improved NLU. Substantial challenges to these systems include working in domains with intents that have a large number of possible values for each slot and accommodation of out-of-vocabulary slot values (i.e. operating in a domain with a great deal of linguistic variability).

7.3   Speech Act Taxonomies for Dialogue

Speech acts have been used as part of the meaning representation of task-oriented dialogue systems since the 1970s (e.g., Bruce, 1975; Cohen and Perrault, 1979; Allen and Perrault, 1980). For a summary of some of the earlier work in this area, see Traum (1999). There have been a number of widely used speech act taxonomies, including an ISO standard (Bunt et al., 2012), however these often have to be particularized to the domain of interest to be fully useful. Our approach with speech act types and subtypes representing a kind of semantic frame is perhaps most similar to the *dialogue primitives* of Hagen and Popowich (2000). Combining these types with fully compositional AMRs will allow flexible expressiveness, inferential power and tractable connection to robot action.

8   Conclusions

This paper has proposed refinements for AMR to encode information necessary for situated human-robot dialogue. Specifically, we elaborate 36 templates specific to situated dialogue that capture i) tense and aspect information; ii) speech acts; and iii) spatial parameters for robot execution. These refinements come after evaluating the coverage of existing AMR for a corpus of human-robot dialogue elicited from tasks related to search-and-rescue and reconnaissance. We also manually annotated 641 in-domain gold standard AMRs in order to evaluate and retrain existing AMR parsers, JAMR and CAMR, for performance on dialogue data. Future work will continue to annotate situated dialogue data and assess the performance of both a graph-to-graph transformation algorithm and an existing statistical classifier for eventual, autonomous human-robot collaboration. We plan to make our AMR-annotated data publicly available; please contact the authors if you would like access to it beforehand.

Acknowledgments

We are grateful to anonymous reviewers for their feedback and to Jessica Ervin for her contributions to the early stages of this research. The second author was sponsored by the U.S. Army Research Laboratory (ARL) under the Advanced Research Technology, Inc. contract number W911QX-18-F-0096; the fifth and sixth authors were sponsored by ARL under contract number W911NF-14-D-0005.

References

Omri Abend and Ari Rappoport. 2013. Universal Conceptual Cognitive Annotation (UCCA). In *Proceedings of the 51st Annual Meeting of the Association for Computational Linguistics (Volume 1: Long Papers)*, volume 1, pages 228–238.

James F Allen and C Raymond Perrault. 1980. Analyzing intention in utterances. *Artificial Intelligence*, 15(3):143–178.

John Langshaw Austin. 1975. *How to Do Things with Words*, 2nd edition. Harvard University Press and Oxford University Press.

Laura Banarescu, Claire Bonial, Shu Cai, Madalina Georgescu, Kira Griffitt, Ulf Hermjakob, Kevin Knight, Philipp Koehn, Martha Palmer, and Nathan Schneider. 2013. Abstract Meaning Representation for sembanking. In *Proceedings of the 7th Linguistic Annotation Workshop and Interoperability with Discourse*, pages 178–186.

Srinivas Bangalore, Dilek Hakkani-Tür, and Gokhan Tur. 2006. Introduction to the special issue on spoken language understanding in conversational systems. *Speech Communication*, 48(3–4):233–238.

Bertram C. Bruce. 1975. Generation as a social action. In *Theoretical Issues in Natural Language Processing*, pages 64–67.

Harry Bunt, Jan Alexandersson, Jae-Woong Choe, Alex Chengyu Fang, Koiti Hasida, Volha Petukhova, Andrei Popescu-Belis, and David Traum. 2012. ISO 24617-2: A semantically-based standard for dialogue annotation. In *Proceedings of the Eighth International Conference on Language Resources and Evaluation (LREC'12)*, pages 430–437.

Shu Cai and Kevin Knight. 2013. Smatch: an evaluation metric for semantic feature structures. In *Proceedings of the 51st Annual Meeting of the Association for Computational Linguistics (Volume 2: Short Papers)*, volume 2, pages 748–752.

Joyce Y. Chai, Lanbo She, Rui Fang, Spencer Ottarson, Cody Littley, Changsong Liu, and Kenneth Hanson. 2014. Collaborative effort towards common ground in situated human-robot dialogue. In *Proceedings of the 2014 ACM/IEEE international conference on Human-robot interaction*, pages 33–40. ACM.

Yun-Nung Chen, Dilek Hakkani-Tür, Gokhan Tur, Jianfeng Gao, and Li Deng. 2016. End-to-end memory networks with knowledge carryover for multi-turn spoken language understanding. In *Interspeech 2016*, pages 3245–3249.

Philip R Cohen and C Raymond Perrault. 1979. Elements of a plan-based theory of speech acts. *Cognitive science*, 3(3):177–212.

Lucia Donatelli, Michael Regan, William Croft, and Nathan Schneider. 2018. Annotation of tense and aspect semantics for sentential AMR. In *Proceedings of the Joint Workshop on Linguistic Annotation, Multiword Expressions and Constructions (LAW-MWE-CxG-2018)*, pages 96–108.

Jeffrey Flanigan, Sam Thomson, Jaime Carbonell, Chris Dyer, and Noah A Smith. 2014. A discriminative graph-based parser for the Abstract Meaning Representation. In *Proceedings of the 52nd Annual Meeting of the Association for Computational Linguistics (Volume 1: Long Papers)*, pages 1426–1436.

Eli Hagen and Fred Popowich. 2000. Flexible speech act based dialogue management. In *1st SIGdial Workshop on Discourse and Dialogue*, pages 131–140.

Dilek Hakkani-Tür, Gokhan Tur, Asli Celikyilmaz, Yun-Nung Chen, Jianfeng Gao, Li Deng, and Ye-Yi Wang. 2016. Multi-domain joint semantic frame parsing using bi-directional RNN-LSTM. In *Interspeech 2016*, pages 715–719.

Daniel Hershcovich, Omri Abend, and Ari Rappoport. 2017. A transition-based directed acyclic graph parser for UCCA. In *Proceedings of the 55th Annual Meeting of the Association for Computational Linguistics (Volume 1: Long Papers)*, pages 1127–1138.

Sunil Issar and Wayne Ward. 1993. CMU's robust spoken language understanding system. In *Third European Conference on Speech Communication and Technology (Eurospeech 93)*, pages 2147–2150.

Anton Leuski and David Traum. 2011. NPCEditor: Creating virtual human dialogue using information retrieval techniques. *AI Magazine*, 32(2):42–56.

Fei Liu, Jeffrey Flanigan, Sam Thomson, Norman Sadeh, and Noah A Smith. 2015. Toward abstractive summarization using semantic representations. In *Proceedings of the 2015 Conference of the North American Chapter of the Association for Computational Linguistics: Human Language Technologies*.

Stephanie M. Lukin, Felix Gervits, Cory J. Hayes, Anton Leuski, Pooja Moolchandani, John G. Rogers, III, Carlos Sanchez Amaro, Matthew Marge,

Clare R. Voss, and David Traum. 2018. ScoutBot: A Dialogue System for Collaborative Navigation. In *Proceedings of ACL 2018, System Demonstrations*, pages 93–98, Melbourne, Australia.

Chunchuan Lyu and Ivan Titov. 2018. Amr parsing as graph prediction with latent alignment. In *Proceedings of the 56th Annual Meeting of the Association for Computational Linguistics*, pages 397–407.

Christopher Manning, Mihai Surdeanu, John Bauer, Jenny Finkel, Steven Bethard, and David McClosky. 2014. The Stanford CoreNLP natural language processing toolkit. In *Proceedings of 52nd Annual Meeting of the Association for Computational Linguistics: System Demonstrations*, pages 55–60.

Matthew Marge, Claire Bonial, Brendan Byrne, Taylor Cassidy, A. William Evans, Susan G. Hill, and Clare Voss. 2016. Applying the Wizard-of-Oz technique to multimodal human-robot dialogue. In *RO-MAN 2016: IEEE International Symposium on Robot and Human Interactive Communication*.

Matthew Marge, Claire Bonial, Ashley Foots, Cory Hayes, Cassidy Henry, Kimberly Pollard, Ron Artstein, Clare Voss, and David Traum. 2017. Exploring variation of natural human commands to a robot in a collaborative navigation task. In *Proceedings of the First Workshop on Language Grounding for Robotics*, pages 58–66.

Tim O'Gorman, Michael Regan, Kira Griffitt, Ulf Hermjakob, Kevin Knight, and Martha Palmer. 2018. AMR beyond the sentence: The multi-sentence AMR corpus. In *Proceedings of the 27th International Conference on Computational Linguistics*, pages 3693–3702.

Martha Palmer, Daniel Gildea, and Paul Kingsbury. 2005. The proposition bank: An annotated corpus of semantic roles. *Computational Linguistics*, 31(1):71–106.

Penman Natural Language Group. 1989. The Penman user guide. *Technical report, Information Sciences Institute*.

Lenhart K Schubert. 2015. Semantic representation. In *AAAI*, pages 4132–4139.

John Rogers Searle. 1969. *Speech acts: An essay in the philosophy of language*. Cambridge University Press.

Mark Steedman and Jason Baldridge. 2011. Combinatory categorial grammar. In Robert Borsley and Kersti Börjars, editors, *Non-Transformational Syntax: A Guide to Current Models*, chapter 5, pages 181–224. Wiley-Blackwell.

David Traum, Cassidy Henry, Stephanie Lukin, Ron Artstein, Felix Gervits, Kimberly Pollard, Claire Bonial, Su Lei, Clare Voss, Matthew Marge, Cory Hayes, and Susan Hill. 2018. Dialogue structure annotation for multi-floor interaction. In *Proceedings of the Eleventh International Conference on Language Resources and Evaluation (LREC 2018)*, pages 104–111, Miyazaki, Japan. European Language Resources Association (ELRA).

David R. Traum. 1999. Speech acts for dialogue agents. In Anand Rao and Michael Wooldridge, editors, *Foundations of Rational Agency*, pages 169–201. Kluwer.

David R. Traum and Staffan Larsson. 2003. The information state approach to dialogue management. In Jan van Kuppevelt and Ronnie W. Smith, editors, *Current and new directions in discourse and dialogue*, pages 325–353. Springer.

Chuan Wang, Nianwen Xue, and Sameer Pradhan. 2015. A transition-based algorithm for AMR parsing. In *Proceedings of the 2015 Conference of the North American Chapter of the Association for Computational Linguistics: Human Language Technologies*, pages 366–375.

Wei Xu and Alexander I. Rudnicky. 2000. Task-based dialog management using an agenda. In *Proceedings of the 2000 ANLP/NAACL Workshop on Conversational systems-Volume 3*, pages 42–47.

Appendix

Type	Subtype	Example
Command	Move	Move forward 5 feet
	Turn	Turn left 90 degrees
	Send-Image	Take a picture
	Repeat	Do that again
	Cancel	Cancel that
	Stop	Ok stop here
Assert	Move	I will move forward 5 feet
	Turn	I turned right 90 degrees
	Send-Image	Sent
	Do	Executing…
	Confirm	Correct
	Scene	I see two doorways ahead
	Ability	I can't manipulate objects
	Map	The table is 2 feet away
	Task	Calibration complete
Request	Wait	Please wait
	Confirm	I'll go as far as I can, ok?
	Clarify	Can you describe it another way?
	Instruct	What should we do next?
Question	Ability	Can you speak Arabic?
	Scene	Have you seen any shoes?
	Map	How far are you from wall?
Express	Greet	Hello!
	Thank	Thanks for the help!
	Good	Good job!
	Mistake	Woops!
	Sorry	Sorry!

Table 4: Listing of Speech Act Types and Subtypes (actions), with example utterances. Note that each subtype corresponds to a unique augmented AMR template. 27 subtypes are listed here; the Assert-Task subtype has several subtypes of its own, which are omitted here.

Author Index

Abend, Omri, 141, 164
Abzianidze, Lasha, 15
Artstein, Ron, 199

Başıbüyük, Kezban, 73
Blache, Philippe, 110
Bonial, Claire, 199
Bonn, Julia, 154
Bos, Johan, 15
Brown, Susan Windisch, 154

Chersoni, Emmanuele, 110
Chiticariu, Laura, 177
Choe, Hyonsu, 128
Choi, Jinho D., 82
Croft, William, 1, 100, 182
Crouch, Richard, 44

dePaiva, Valeria, 44
Donatelli, Lucia, 199
Duong, Viet, 56

Goldstein, Felicia, 82
Gung, James, 154

Hajicova, Eva, 66
Hajjar, Ihab, 82
Han, Jiyoon, 128
Huang, Chu-Ren, 110
Hwang, Jena D., 141

Kalm, Pavlina, 1, 100
Kalouli, Aikaterini-Lida, 44
Kane, Benjamin, 56
Kim, Gene, 56
Kim, Hansaem, 128

Lai, Ken, 28
Lee, Sook-kyung, 1
Lenci, Alessandro, 110
Li, Bin, 92
Li, Mengmei, 82
Li, Yunyao, 177
Lin, Zi, 34
Linh, Ha, 148
Liu, Yihuan, 92

Lukin, Stephanie M., 199

McGuire, Graeme, 56
Mendiratta, Muskaan, 56
Myers, Skatje, 136

Nguyen, Huyen, 148

Palmer, Martha, 136, 154
Park, Hyejin, 128
Petruck, Miriam R L, 121
Platonov, Georgiy, 56
Prange, Jakob, 164
Pustejovsky, James, 28, 154

Qu, Weiguang, 92

Rambelli, Giulia, 110
Rappoport, Ari, 141
Regan, Michael, 1, 100

Sackstein, Sophie, 56
Schneider, Nathan, 141, 164
Schubert, Lenhart, 56
Shalev, Adi, 141
Song, Li, 92
Srikumar, Vivek, 141

Tratz, Stephen, 199
Traum, David, 199

Van Gysel, Jens E. L., 1, 182
Vigus, Meagan, 1, 182
Voss, Clare, 199

Xue, Nianwen, 28, 34

Yan, Peiyi, 92

Zaenen, Annie, 154
Zeyrek, Deniz, 73
Zhu, Huaiyu, 177